THE AUTOBIOGRAPHY OF
FRANCIS PLACE

FRANCIS PLACE IN HIS SIXTIES

The Autobiography of
FRANCIS PLACE
(1771-1854)

EDITED WITH
AN INTRODUCTION AND NOTES BY
MARY THALE
University of Illinois, Chicago

CAMBRIDGE
AT THE UNIVERSITY PRESS
1972

CAMBRIDGE UNIVERSITY PRESS
Cambridge, New York, Melbourne, Madrid, Cape Town, Singapore, São Paulo, Delhi

Cambridge University Press
The Edinburgh Building, Cambridge CB2 8RU, UK

Published in the United States of America by Cambridge University Press, New York

www.cambridge.org
Information on this title: www.cambridge.org/9780521083997

© Cambridge University Press 1972

This publication is in copyright. Subject to statutory exception
and to the provisions of relevant collective licensing agreements,
no reproduction of any part may take place without the written
permission of Cambridge University Press.

First published 1972
This digitally printed version 2008

A catalogue record for this publication is available from the British Library

Library of Congress Catalogue Card Number: 78-174265

ISBN 978-0-521-08399-7 hardback
ISBN 978-0-521-28048-8 paperback

CONTENTS

Francis Place in his sixties	*frontispiece*
Preface	*page* vii
Editor's introduction	ix
Major events in Place's autobiography	xxxix
THE AUTOBIOGRAPHY OF FRANCIS PLACE	1
Appendix	298
Index	299

PREFACE

Since the beginning of the twentieth century, Francis Place's autobiography has been the major personal source of information about social conditions of working-class London in the late eighteenth century. Historian after historian has sat in the Manuscript Room of the British Museum, reading the neat regular handwriting in which Place recorded his memories of life among small shopkeepers, poor artisans and their children, in the crowded streets between Temple Bar and Charing Cross. Some of Place's recollections of this London have been presented to us by social historians.

From such a social history I first learned of Place's autobiography. A quotation in which Place described his schooling made me want to read the whole work from which the excerpt was taken. I soon discovered that the autobiography had never been published. After reading it in manuscript, I thought it should be made available to other readers. The autobiography is worth reading solely for its unique record of what Place called 'correctly detailed domestic history' and 'manners and morals' of the past. It is also valuable for its intentional and unintentional revelations of the character of this important and controversial figure in the Reform Movement.

In preparing this edition, I was helped by many people in many ways. To all of them I am grateful. Frank X. Thale, Janet Fendrych and George P. B. Naish assisted me in establishing the text. The attendants in the Manuscript Room and the Reading Room of the British Museum patiently and willingly located other Placean materials. H. A. V. Warner investigated copyright regulations. Edward P. Thompson made many valuable suggestions about my introduction and notes. William D. Grampp, Yohma Gray and Wren Staley read and recommended useful changes in my introduction. Most of all and longest of all, Jerome Thale helped, advising me in every detail at every stage of the editing.

I wish to thank the British Museum for permission to publish the autobiography, the National Portrait Gallery for permission to reproduce the picture of Place (most likely by Samuel Drummond in 1833), and the English Department of the University of Illinois at Chicago Circle for assuming the cost of typing and duplicating the manuscript.

London S.E.17
September 1971

MARY THALE

EDITOR'S INTRODUCTION

1

Francis Place was known to his contemporaries (and has passed into history) as 'the radical tailor of Charing Cross.' The description implies three of the roles in which he was known in his time – reformer, member of the working class, and Londoner. In the present work we see Place in a fourth role – autobiographer and historian – and one that arises out of the first three.

As a Londoner, Place ranks with Pepys and Johnson – three men who were absorbed in the activity of the city. Unlike the other two, Place had a lifelong involvement with London. He was born (in 1771) opposite the south side of Drury Lane Playhouse, and died (in 1854) in Earls Court. In between he lived in seventeen other houses in London, the most famous of which was at No. 16 Charing Cross, where he lived for thirty-two years. During his first thirty-eight years he only once went more than thirty miles from London. The only visit of friendship which ever took him away from the city for more than a night, he recalled, was to see James Mill. During his adult years in London he recorded the city as it had been in his youth and the changes he saw in the lives of working-class Londoners and the improvements in housing, streets, lighting, bridges, etc. From the time he gained leisure, Place was constantly walking through back streets, dockside areas, fairs, observing and noting the details of lower-class London. His lower-class London was a world seen from a patronizing distance by Boswell and Johnson, not seen at all by the inmates of Parson Woodforde's circle, unimaginable to Jane Austen's characters. Place's London is remarkable, and he was rare in realizing that it was worth observing and describing.

Place experienced London life with a sharp eye and a retentive memory, but he did not merely record recollections. He attempted to record and understand his youth and the London of that era in the light of later times. Fortunately he had the leisure to reflect and to study London life because, having risen from poverty to affluence, he retired from business at the age of forty-eight. The account of his economic success has many of the marks of the Horatio Alger story. Starting out poor but clever, he worked hard and prospered. He was apprenticed at fourteen to a master in the leather breeches trade. After he married at nineteen he had trouble supporting his wife; two years later, after he managed an unsuccessful strike of journeymen breeches-makers and was proscribed by all the masters, he had even more of poverty and hunger. He spent his eight

The Autobiography of Francis Place

months of unemployment reading and studying, hoping and planning. His more conservative wife hoped only that they could have journeyman's wages again. But Place aimed higher. He saw that only by becoming a master could he pull himself and his family out of poverty. His chance to make the upward leap came in 1799 when he opened a tailoring shop with his lodger, Richard Wild. For eighteen months they prospered, and Place approached the Christmas of 1800 with hopes that his aim of financial security was about to be realized. But on Christmas morning he discovered that Wild was planning to break up their partnership. Ten days later, when the partnership ended, Place and his family moved from the lodgings above the shop. By then, he had so impressed customers with his business ability that they loaned him £1,600 to start his own business. On March 8, 1801, three months after the end of his partnership, he opened a tailoring shop at No. 16 Charing Cross. He succeeded so well that in 1816 he made a net profit of £3,000. In 1817, having achieved his aim of securing a comfortable living for his family, he handed the business over to his son, Francis Place Jr. He was now a man of leisure and might have aspired to the status of a gentleman, but neither he nor his enemies ever forgot that he was that most ungentlemanly of beings, a tailor.

The retired London tailor then became a full-time reformer, an appropriate career for an intelligent, self-educated ex-working-class man who would not bow before his social betters. In the course of his long life he was active in almost every major reform movement of the first half of the nineteenth century – the repeal of the Combination Laws, the Anatomy Bill, the establishment of London University, the Reform Bill, the Penny Postage, the Chartist Movement, the Anti-Corn Law League.

His apprenticeship in political life began in 1793 with a minor reform activity, a strike of the journeymen leather breeches-makers. He took over the direction of a faltering strike and persuaded the men to take measures which enabled them to hold out much longer. Though they lost the strike, Place showed the talent on which he most prided himself – 'the power I have possessed of influencing or governing other men individually and in bodies.'[1] In the next year, when he joined the London Corresponding Society, he extended the scope of his activities in influencing men. He rapidly rose from an ordinary member to being a member of the general committee, and then the chairman of the general committee of the society, which was dedicated to annual parliaments and universal suffrage. When the government arrested two LCS members who had been sent to Birmingham, Place was dispatched to arrange bail and organize their defence. In 1798, when the government arrested the

[1] See below p. 244.

Editor's introduction

whole general committee of the LCS, Place, though no longer a member, organized a subscription of funds for the relief of their families. He managed this fund until 1799 when he and Wild opened their shop in Charing Cross.

This date marks the end of his apprenticeship in political life. For the following six years he devoted himself to his tailoring shop and to the needs of his large family (eventually, fifteen children). When he next set out to influence opinion, he was in the big league. He was a master.

This entry into the larger arena of reform came in 1807 when he successfully managed the campaign which resulted in the election to Parliament of Sir Francis Burdett. Since 1780 the Whigs and Tories had maintained a gentleman's agreement whereby they split the two seats for Westminster. Consequently, although Westminster was a borough in which every rate payer was allowed to vote, the electors were virtually disenfranchised by this Whig–Tory arrangement. Place had become friendly with some of the other electors of Westminster, mostly shopkeepers like himself or artisans; and the evening after Parliament was dissolved in April of 1807, some of these electors came to Place's library, above his shop, and decided to run two reform candidates. Place recorded in detail his version of this election. 'We were all of us,' he wrote, 'obscure persons, not one man of note among us, not one in any way known to the Electors generally, as insignificant a set of persons as could well have been collected to undertake so important a public matter as a Westminster Election, against, Wealth – and Rank and Name and Influence.'[1] In particular, they worked without the advantage of wealth, for their candidate, Sir Francis Burdett, refused to spend his time or money in this election. Place managed the campaign, plotting the strategy, keeping the records of money spent, and always staying quietly in the background. During the polling (which lasted fifteen days) he was at the committee room every morning at seven o'clock and he stayed until after midnight every night except the last. When it was evident after three days that Burdett was not winning enough votes, Place himself went out canvassing. He even agreed to a measure which offended both his thrift and his republicanism – hiring ponies and fancily dressed riders to go about advertising the candidate. On the fifteenth and last day, Burdett was 5,000 votes ahead of the second candidate, a maverick Whig. The official Whig and the official Tory candidates each had about half as many votes as Burdett. The Whig–Tory alliance for Westminster was destroyed; and for twenty years Place and the other members of the Westminster Committee determined the candidates for Westminster.

[1] Add. MS 27850, f. 67.

The Autobiography of Francis Place

For almost thirty years thereafter Place's library was a meeting place and information centre for the parliamentary reformers in London. Place seldom went to the homes of these reformers, but made himself available in his library for several hours every day and evening. After retiring from business in 1817, he spent even more time in his library on reform activities. He drafted minutes and queries to be presented in Parliament; he advised Burdett, Joseph Hume, Joseph Parkes, John Cam Hobhouse, George Grote and others.

Besides the parliamentary manoeuvring, Place had a hand in many other reform projects. He often represented groups of labourers petitioning for better working conditions. He was active in the London Lancastrian associations, which tried to provide inexpensive (a penny a week) schooling for children. He also helped found the London Mechanics' Institute (now Birkbeck College), and rejoiced at the large numbers of workers who attended lectures on astronomy and chemistry.

Early in this period of intense reform activity Place gained two close friends who influenced his notions of reform – James Mill and Jeremy Bentham. Mill and Place were frequent visitors to each other's homes and regular correspondents when Mill was away from London. Mill's son John Stuart also became a correspondent and a visitor to Place's library. Bentham and Mill invited Place to visit them at Ford Abbey, their rented summer home in Devon; there Place spent two months in 1817, studying and talking. His feeling toward Bentham was almost reverential. He was a Utilitarian of the Benthamite kind and spoke of Bentham as 'my good master,' 'my constant, excellent, venerable preceptor,' 'my twenty years friend.'

Like other disciples of Bentham, Place helped to produce a couple of the master's books (*Not Paul, but Jesus* and *Plan of Parliamentary Reform*). His reform activities were like those of the Benthamites, but, unlike some of the Benthamites who were interested primarily in such middle-class movements as the repeal of the Corn Laws, Place was especially eager 'to promote the welfare of the working people.' Place was not always clear how to do this. He once wrote, 'I was not . . . for many years sufficiently acquainted with the Principles of Political Economy to be able to judge accurately what were the true means permanently to better their condition.'[1] The Benthamites believed they knew what the true means were. One of them, although it was not as consequential as others they advocated, was the repeal of the Combination Laws which were oppressive to the working class.

The repeal of these Combination Laws in 1824 was the great achieve-

[1] Add. MS 27798, f. 5.

Editor's introduction

ment in Place's attempts 'to promote the welfare of the working people.' These laws forbade either masters or journeymen to organize in order to change the hours or wages of their work. In practice, violations by masters were ignored, but violations by workers were often severely punished. Place had felt the tyranny of these laws in the 1790s when he was an apprentice and a journeyman breeches-maker, especially when he managed the organizations of workers who had to disguise their real aims by pretending they were forming a society to benefit their sick members. Place opposed these laws not only because they humiliated workers by forcing them to subterfuge, but also because he believed they produced an atmosphere of hostility towards employers which encouraged the workers to enter into combinations. If the laws were repealed, he was convinced, combinations, or trade unions, would 'fall to pieces.' In 1814 he seriously set to work to have the Combination Laws repealed. Whenever he heard of a case involving them, he wrote to the parties and requested information; he sent articles to the newspapers; he tried to convert individual members of Parliament. Joseph Hume, a radical M.P. whom Place regarded as his protege, announced in Parliament in 1822 that he intended to introduce a bill for the repeal of the laws. Thinking Hume was premature, Place did not urge him to do more than announce his intention. At the next session of Parliament, a select committee, with Hume as chairman, was ordered to investigate the efficacy of the Combination Laws. Place interviewed all the delegates of the working people at his home and made briefs for Hume to use when examining them. Each brief contained all the questions Hume should ask a witness and the answers the witness would give. This interviewing and arranging took all Place's time for three months. In the end the committee submitted to the House resolutions urging the repeal of the Combination Laws. To Place's annoyance, Hume employed a barrister to draw up the bills from Place's manuscripts. He made a mess of the matter, and Place and Hume rewrote the bills. They passed both Houses in 1824. 'Place's achievement,' said E. P. Thompson, 'was a remarkable feat of intelligent wire-pulling and of enormously industrious and well-informed lobbying.' According to the admiring Hammonds, 'the repeal of the Combination Laws . . . is perhaps the most remarkable achievement in this period. It is certainly the greatest achievement in Place's remarkable life.'[1]

It may have been the greatest achievement in his life: it was by no means the last, for during the following twenty years he shared in several other important reforms. In the long campaign for the Reform Bill,

[1] E. P. Thompson, *The Making of the English Working Class*, 1968, p. 564; J. L. and Barbara Hammond, *The Town Labourer*, 1917, pp. 134–5.

during the 1820s and early 1830s, Place managed public meetings, advised reform members of Parliament, helped organize the Parliamentary Candidates' Society and the National Political Union, and even made contact with high-ranking military officers when the reformers envisaged revolution. This was an extreme action for Place to take because he believed in orderly reform and was averse to mobs.[1] The Reform Bill as it was passed he regarded as inadequate. Still hoping to achieve the London Corresponding Society's aims of annual parliaments and universal suffrage, Place became an active member of the Chartist movement and drafted its basic document, the 'People's Charter.' The founders of the Working Men's Association, which issued the 'People's Charter,' consulted with him and accepted his advice about the format of their meetings. In 1838, when Chartism was to be officially inaugurated in London at a large open-air meeting, the Working Men's Association asked Place to be one of its delegates. Two years later, in 1840, when the newly founded Anti-Corn Law League sent a deputation to London to organize a chapter, the deputation was told to go to Place and enlist his assistance. He at first declined, saying he wanted to stay at home, but he finally agreed to become the business manager of the London branch.

In 1841, although he had a severe cold, Place went to a meeting of the Anti-Corn Law League at Manchester because he believed he was needed to persuade a prominent Birmingham member to accept the limited goal of the League. Place succeeded, but the trip worsened his illness; he did not recover for nine months, and from then on his health was never really good. Whenever he could, he attended meetings of the Anti-Corn Law Committee until the Corn Laws were finally repealed in 1846.

During the last few years of his life – he died on January 1, 1854 – his influence was slight. He was old and ill, and some of his notions of what was conducive to the welfare of the workers had been outdated by events (for example, his Benthamite convictions that trade unions would die out if the Combination Laws were repealed and that wage strikes could not increase the workers' buying power).[2] Unwilling to be idle in his old age, he spent his days pasting into large guard books his lifetime accumulation of newspaper cuttings, most of which deal with the conditions

[1] Place has some similarity to Martin Luther King Jr, in that both reformers were regarded as dangerous radicals by people who should have been grateful that they urged reform within the system and not revolution.

[2] I have not attempted a critical examination of Place's achievement as a political reformer. This is an undertaking better left to the social and economic historians, who must disentangle the curious confluence in Place of Benthamite theory, working-class militancy, and what we would identify as middle-class self-help attitudes and belief in constitutional reform.

Editor's introduction

of the working class. We do not know how many such books he assembled, but the British Museum now has one hundred and eighty-one volumes of these newspaper cuttings.

The accumulating and assembling of these volumes of cuttings reflect several traits of Place's career as a reformer – his patience, his thoroughness, his tenacity. But especially they reflect his desire to work away without publicity or prominence for himself. Of course, he could not have played the role he did without some awareness of its becoming public. The conservative periodicals – *The Times, Frasers* – had unpleasant things to say about him; the *European Magazine* suggested that his was the real voice behind the speeches of Burdett and Hobhouse, and that he and Hume manufactured the philosophies of Bentham, Mill and Birkbeck.[1] But this publicity was unsought. Place refused to run for Parliament. His name seldom appeared in lists of persons collecting for a good cause. Indeed, in his first venture into political action, the Westminster election of 1807, one of his earliest recommendations was that the names of the committee members should not be advertised. Before Place's retirement from his shop, he was partly motivated in his desire for anonymity by business considerations; he had learned that 'gentlemen' do not wish to give their custom to a tailor who has wider interests than tailoring. But the more important reason for his staying in the background may have been his republicanism. He believed improvement came from groups of people working together for their betterment, not from an inspired leader advocating change. Though well aware of the blindness, indifference, or self-interest of most working-class people, Place remained confident of the possibility that groups of clear-sighted, disenchanted workers could improve the welfare of the working class, particularly if they followed his advice. Accordingly, his preferred mode of action was to convince the committee or the group of workers of the reasonableness of his position, and then to have them demand reform. Although, for tactical reasons, Place did not seek publicity, when he wrote his account after the event he did give his own actions a good deal of prominence and did recount matters from his own point of view. In all these accounts, however, Place showed himself working – or trying to work – within the group.

By temperament, too, Place was a committee man rather than a firebrand. The notion of a compelling leader implies a passion and emotionalism which Place found frightening in his own character. (He always regretted that he had raged against his wife during the period of unemployment in 1793.) On the other hand, committee action implies the

[1] *European Magazine*, n. s. II (1826), 227–33.

The Autobiography of Francis Place

power of reason, the rationality on which Place prided himself and which, in one form or another (e.g. education), he urged as a cure for the social ills. 'Be persuaded,' he wrote to his wife about their children, 'that whatever cannot be effected by reason, cannot be effected at all.'[1] Behind-the-scenes committee work rather than public oratory also accorded with Place's temperament in that he craved power not publicity. Publicity could come to any highwayman who ended up at Tyburn. But power, in Place's social class, required force of character. In addition to his statement that he prided himself on his power to influence bodies of men, he provided evidence in every chapter of his autobiography of his need to hold a position of power in a body of men; he recorded that he was leader of his boyhood gang, top boy at school, manager of France's tailor shop at the age of nineteen. From these positions of power, it was only a step to becoming the chairman of committees, the organizer of meetings. Very possibly, by organizing, rallying, advising the reformers in Parliament, by even writing speeches for them, Place exerted more real power to change English life than he could have exerted if, with all the liabilities of his status as a tailor, he had been in Parliament.

As a result of his preference for staying in the background and of changes in theories of reform, Place's reform activities were slipping from people's memories by the time of his death and were generally ignored for the next forty years. At the beginning of this century Place was hailed as an ultra-liberal, a precursor of the trade union movement. More recently he has been treated as an *ersatz* reformer because he rejected schemes now popular among reformers (e.g. Thomas Spence's land communism) or because he appears to have been more nearly a middle-class conservative than a working-class radical. The autobiography can support either view. It can also support a middle view of Place, showing him as a reformer trying to help the working class by bending the middle-class political structure. There is a curious parallelism between Place's view of his own character and the view of him as a reformer that emerges from his autobiography. Place strikes us as a self-made man with many of the features of the type – the sense of his own virtue that appears in his references to the improvidence of others; the sense that a man who is diligent and patient may succeed, rise, find the happiness of achievement (as opposed to the man who proposes that the structure of society needs to be changed). Place was not a conservative; he laboured to make important changes in the character of his society, with an eye always upon the condition of the working class. But like

[1] Add. MS 35143, f. 298v.

Editor's introduction

many self-made men he had a certain sense that the society which had rewarded him with wealth, power and position was not wholly bad.

Just as Place's life seemed to prove that the truly diligent could flourish if they would only work hard and be patient, so his approach to reform suggested that reforms may be made within the system, and that they must be made by patient, diligent, responsible men. It is not surprising that later ages have admired Place; he is indeed a hero of the age of reform, that is, the age which proves that reform will work and revolution is not needed.

2

Place began to record his reform activities in the second decade of the century, when he started writing histories of the elections he had helped manage and of the reform societies in which he had been active; at about the same time he also began to collect data on the social conditions of the late eighteenth century. By the time of his death he had filled about one hundred large volumes with these histories and data. Some of the volumes or portions of them have disappeared; but ninety-one of them remain. It is from this unpublished collection in the British Museum manuscript department that Place is now known as a writer.

These guard books are of much more interest than Place's published writings. The published works – one book, three or four pamphlets, and many articles – are mostly sound but uninteresting pieces of argumentation, rightly intended to be useful only at the time of composition. Perhaps a partial exception should be made of Place's book *Illustrations and Proofs of the Principle of Population* of 1822. As its title indicates, this contribution to the arguments of Malthus and Godwin was intended to be more philosophical than most of Place's publications. Ironically, Place, who no more sought publicity from his writing than from his other activities (most of his writings were unsigned), gained notoriety from the book because he outraged decency by advocating contraception. But apart from its marking Place as the first to urge publicly the use of contraceptives, the book is not of great interest.

On the other hand, many of the unpublished volumes are of great interest, because they contain unmatched records of the past. To accumulate these records Place kept copies of most of the letters he sent as well as the letters he received. With the thoroughness of a scholarly hoarder he preserved such documents as accounts of the moneys disbursed in 1798 and 1799 to the families of the state prisoners and money collected in 1828 for the subscription for Thomas Hardy, the founder of the London Corresponding Society. It is not that he valued trivia, but that, ahead of his time, he was working from the perspective of an historian who did not restrict his focus to M.P.s, generals and admirals. His history of the Westminster election of 1807 illustrates the virtues of his perspective. He started with himself and other shopkeepers meeting and discussing politics, hearing rumours of a new Whig–Tory alliance, responding to it. Then he described the rigged meetings of the electors of Westminster, leading to the unopposed nomination and election of Lord Percy. Instead of proceeding to the next dissolution of Parliament, Place described the Hogarthian scene of post-election benefactions which made him determined to oppose the Whig–Tory alliance in Westminster. 'I saw the servants of the Duke of Northumberland in their shewey dress liveries, throwing lumps of bread and cheese among the dense crowd of vagabonds they had collected together . . . these vagabonds [were] catching at these lumps, shouting swearing.' In the next paragraph he described himself and some fellow 'respectable' shopkeepers watching with disgust as the mobs broke open the butts of beer, fought for it, even scooped it up from the gutters.[1] After revealing the indignation he and others felt at this 'disgraceful scene,' he continued from his shopkeeper's viewpoint, 'I therefore suggested the propriety of looking out for a proper person to represent Westminster.' Place then recounted all the small actions of these Westminster shopkeepers – their visiting Burdett's city house and finding him gone, their travelling to his country house, his refusing to see them (because they were nobodies), their meeting at the Crown and Anchor tavern, their reacting to the poor showing of Burdett at the beginning of the polling, and so forth. In short, he showed how a series of minute events, involving insignificant people, helped create a big event.

This same thoroughness in preserving details of everyday behaviour pervades his six volumes of data on manners and morals. Place was irritated by charges that the behaviour of the working class was becoming constantly more dissolute (and by the consequent implication that more restrictive laws were in order). To counter this accusation he began to assemble data showing that the manners and morals of his countrymen had greatly improved since the previous century. (Place's optimism – his belief that the manners and morals of the working class were improving and were capable of more improvement – resembled the optimistic side of Benthamism and the views of his young followers who constituted the philosophical radicals.) Part of the data Place collected consists of charts on such matters as mortality rates and the consumption of spirits. Part consists of summaries, synopses, and quotations which

[1] Add. MS 27850, fs. 19–20.

Editor's introduction

illustrate his thesis. But part also consists of his own observations on the improvement in decorum, sanitation, cleanliness, humaneness of punishments, etc. He recorded all the obscene songs he had heard as a boy; he revisited and described changes in the tenements, taverns, tea gardens, dockside streets, and fairs that he had frequented as a young boy or as an apprentice.

The comprehensiveness of Place's historical records creates an effect of accuracy that may not be wholly warranted. Where there are records correlative to Place's narratives of elections and reform movements they do not always show Place as the central figure he makes himself out to be. And they sometimes show that Place's 'power . . . of influencing or governing other men' was seen by other reformers as cantankerous bossiness. Moreover, some of his proof of the improvement in manners and morals may be suspect. He did have a thesis and, while comparatively conscientious, he was hardly a systematic social researcher. But despite challenges to Place's larger hypotheses and to certain features of his self-portrait, his historical writings remain of immense value, because Place was of a class we now find important and yet enough apart from it to record exhaustively the details others would take for granted or dismiss as unimportant.

3

Consequently, in 1823 when Bentham and Mill urged him to write his autobiography in order to show how a man could rise to wisdom and prosperity from an unpropitious background, Place had already trained himself to recollect and record details. And he had long since appreciated the importance of writing history from the perspective of the people acting it, particularly if they were people of the lower classes.

As a result, the strongest interest of the autobiography is its portrait of a kind of life we can scarcely believe existed. The father who regularly beat his sons until the stick broke. The brother-in-law under sentence of death who was a great favourite with his gaolers. The employers (France, Allison) who made the swift descent to the workhouse or the madhouse. The 'respectable' customers of his father's public house who were reduced to selling a ward or a niece. A society of such people almost seems as if it must be a caricature. But this society was reported not by a sentimental reformer or by a horrified blue book writer but by a man for whom all this was simply a matter of fact, the way life was. A fine case in point is Place's brief, matter-of-fact narrative of his apprenticing. He told his father he did not want to become a lawyer. 'This was in the evening, and my father went immediately into his parlour and offered me

The Autobiography of Francis Place

to any one who would take me. A little man named France said he would, and I was sent the very next morning.'[1]

In the course of this almost Dickensian history, Place has told us how he became a tailor and later a respectable merchant, but he has not told us what a modern reader might most want to know – how and why he became a radical.[2] Place did not directly explain this process because he was not curious about his own character. Or rather he did not understand his character. He saw himself as a man whose character had been formed by a series of reasoned responses to situations. On the few occasions where reason could not control feeling (e.g. after the death of his wife), he believed he had displayed a flawed character. His extraordinary confidence in the reasoning power by which he educated himself, prospered in business and persuaded bodies of men to accept his thinking quite blinded him to other sides of his character. A frightening obtuseness and arrogance about himself, his father, and his children is revealed in a sentence he wrote to Mrs Grote in 1836. After she had read the first part of his autobiography, she commented that very few of the good people she knew had 'worthy' parents. Place replied: 'Worthy parents but too generally prevent the development of energy in their children and real efficient goodness is incompatible with mediocrity in this oddly constituted best of all possible worlds.'[3]

If Place's unawareness of his character prevented him from telling us directly how and why he became a radical, he did tell us indirectly. The harsh self-discipline which was necessary for survival in his London and the even tighter discipline necessary for success gave him the curb on immediate appetites, the vision of long-range goals, which are starting points for any effective constitutional reformer. More important, though, the cruelty of his father, which he could not combat, led him to transfer the notion of oppressor from father to government, which he could openly attack. Two points are suggested here. When Place showed his memoir to Mrs Grote and she made comments on it he replied at length to every comment of hers, except one. He had no amplification to make to her observation, 'What an eminent savage that was who begat you!'[4] Then, in the autobiography he specifically connected his father with the

[1] See below p. 71.
[2] It is an interesting question just what kind of radical Place was. Since the interest of the autobiography is as a revelation of character and social history rather than as a source of information about the political aspects of radicalism, I have not attempted to assess Place's radicalism. Such an assessment would have to weigh the charge that he was a government spy in the LCS.
[3] Add. MS 35144, fs. 348, 358. Not only does this passage show Place's obtuseness about self, father and children, but it also has for us alarming socio-political implications.
[4] Ibid. f. 346.

Editor's introduction

larger social order. After describing some of his father's savage ways, he added, 'These were common notions, and were carried into practice not only by the heads of families and the teachers of youth generally, but by the government itself and every man in authority under it.' A few words later, he started a new paragraph with a phrase as applicable to his father as to the government – 'Indiscriminating, sanguinary and cruel as our Statutes are . . .'[1]

After reading the account of his cruel father, of the working conditions of breeches-makers, of his management of their strike, of his tough stand against the families of the state prisoners in 1798, we see why he became pugnacious and a bit hard in pursuit of justice and of a less hard society. We see, in short, how he became a paradoxical kind of reformer, strange to us who may think of reformers as sentimental men of good will.

Little as we may have expected to find Place a tough and unsentimental reformer, even less would we have expected to discover, as we do in the autobiography, that this working-class radical possessed and extolled some of the Victorian virtues we have come to scorn or to patronize, those Samuel Smiles virtues of thrift, industry and self-reliance. But because his sense of social fact, of economic reality, was so good Place has enabled us to understand these Victorian virtues. Quite without self-pity he has made clear the terrible pressures that drove him to be so concerned with them.

But even after coming to understand the reasons for thrift and industry, we may be bothered by another Victorian virtue which often seems at worst repugnant and at best puzzling – respectability. Place has never allowed us to forget how important this virtue was to him; he stressed that he and his wife 'contrived to dress . . . respectably,' that they worked 'to keep up . . . respectable appearance.' He kept contrasting the 'loose characters' of the past with the 'highly respectable' families of the present, the 'sad miscreants' like Old Joe France with the 'well doing respectable persons' who abounded in the 1820s. If a preoccupation with respectability seems repellent to us, Place's autobiography may help us to understand how the significance of the word has changed. For us it is an external matter, the good repute which, rightly or wrongly, other people accord us. But for Place it was primarily an internal disposition, even though such externals as clothes may have helped create it. Respectability meant having a good self-image, a sense of one's self as an important being. Furthermore, we may sneer at respectability because we have always had it and have found it of little use or importance. But to Place and his associates respectability was a hard-

[1] See below p. 62.

xxi

won and perilous acquisition. All around him he saw failures, people whose ruin was tied to their loss of respectability – his fellow apprentices, the patrons of his father's public house, his own sister. In the world which he presents, every reinforcement of respectability was some insurance against destitution, the workhouse, prison, or prostitution. Respectability was almost a condition of survival. Place called attention to these alternatives of respectability or ruin when he wrote that a respectable appearance is 'a matter of the greatest importance to every working man, for so long as he is able to keep himself up in this particular, he will have resolution to struggle with . . . his adverse circumstances. No working man, journeyman tradesman is ever wholly ruined until hope has abandoned him.'[1]

4

Place's respectability and other 'Victorian' virtues are amply revealed in the autobiography, and I am not going to labour them or attempt a complete analysis of his character. But there are some aspects of his personality which either do not come out in the autobiography or do not emerge in their full force. Since they subtly modify the picture of Place in the autobiography they warrant some consideration.

The first of these traits is one we would hardly expect from our reading of the autobiography – romanticism. In the autobiography Place presented himself as a man of practical traits, a no-nonsense, sturdy Victorian pursuing success. In good measure Place created this limited picture of himself in pursuance of the goal set by Bentham and Mill, showing how he educated himself and became successful. But there is evidence that Place shared with the poets of the Romantic period a need for, and an intense response to, external nature. Just after his marriage, when he had little employment and much leisure, he used to go out into the fields all around London and deep into Surrey. Later when he was a journeyman, working long hours in the one room where he and his family lived, he often had to put down his work and run to Hampstead, Norwood or some other rural spot. Then, refreshed, he could return, as he said, 'to my vomit.'[2] Afterwards, when he had established his business securely, he delighted in making excursions to picturesque parts of the countryside. His account of his first sight of the sea is Wordsworthian in sentiment, though certainly not in style. At Christmas 1809, as he was riding

---

[1] See below p. 128. Place's insistence on respectability was shared by other reformers he knew, such as Hardy, the Grotes and the Manchester activists.
[2] *Improvement of the Working People: Drunkenness – Education*, 1834, pp. 14–15.

Editor's introduction

over a hill near Chelmsford to take an order for mourning clothes, he unexpectedly saw the sea in the distance. After describing the circumstances and the sight, Place summed up his reaction thus: 'My sensations were very remarkable. I was so extremely elated that I was scarcly conscious my own body had any gravity. It seemed as if I could leap from the chaise to the ocean. I was at the moment more exhilerated than I ever had before been or ever have been since.'[1]

Place's romantic response to nature had no tinge of religious feeling; we would not expect any after reading some of his irreligious comments in the autobiography. But perhaps these comments scattered through the autobiography fail to convey the intensity of his atheism, or infidelity. As he explained, he first doubted the Gospel account of the Virgin birth, and then doubted the whole concept of a supernatural agency. From then on he was an avowed atheist, dismissing his sister's religious practices as 'absurd' and 'fanatical,' expressing mild contempt for a former associate's attempts to convert him, and generally noting with disgust religious practices and clergymen. When he read a prison chaplain's testimony that many families were demoralized by the drunkenness of the mother, though he could not recall an exact instance, Place carefully wrote in the margin: 'This saint is as usual a Twaddler.'[2] Late in life, when he pasted into a guard book a newspaper cutting about the christening of Queen Victoria's fourth daughter, he annotated this too with a comment which sums up his feelings about religion – 'Surely the time will come when these Barbaric Ceremonies will cease.'

His atheism was more than just a matter of condemning barbarous christenings and hypocritical clergymen. It determined his choices. When he was seeking a defence attorney, his first reason for wanting Erskine was that 'he was suspected of being but a weak christian.' The same sort of motive obviously governed his choice of Steward Kyd as an attorney, for he explained that 'Mr Kyd was an infidel and a man on whom reliance could be placed.' One wonders if even Lawrence, the surgeon who operated upon Mrs Place, was not chosen in part because he was known to be a materialist. It is undoubtedly fitting that the longest obituary of Place appeared in a magazine called *The Reasoner: Gazette of Secularism* and that it lauded him for his atheism, 'a profession of opinion which Mr Place always made . . . It was known to everybody through all Mr Place's political connections, from first to last, that he was a decided materialist.' Referring to a shorter obituary, which appeared in the more prestigious *Spectator*, *The Reasoner* concluded that this tribute

[1] Add. MS 27143, f. 168.   [2] Add. MS 27830, f. 238v.

must be 'regarded as a testimony to the character, taste, integrity, and public services of an atheist.'[1]

Less explicit than his atheism is Place's egocentric insistence on the rightness of his theories. For example, once he had adopted the political goals of universal suffrage and annual parliaments, he tenaciously tried to exact written subscription to these aims from reform candidates. No arguments could convince him of the impracticability of annual parliamentary elections. This single-mindedness which contributed to his success as a reformer at the same time often made his dealings with other reformers difficult. Similarly, his relations with his first wife must have been strained by his conviction that he knew what was best. 'Suffer me to guide,' he urged, on the ground that she possessed 'that hastiness of temper, which prevents, reason and deliberation.' Place had total confidence in his own powers of reason and deliberation.

Although this egocentric atheist radical, with his insistence on reason and practicality, had some of the hardness that Dickens and others found in the nineteenth-century reformers, his philanthropy was not 'of that gunpowderous sort that the difference between it and animosity was hard to determine' (*Edwin Drood*). Place had compassion. This trait does not show up much in the autobiography; but in other writings where his concern is primarily with social conditions, he displayed a rational sympathy for groups of people who were generally disapproved of – for example, working-class drunkards. Far from condemning them for weakness of character, as many people did, Place sympathetically argued their case throughout his life – in a pamphlet, before parliamentary committees, in his unpublished writings on manners and morals (one-third of which deal with drunkenness). Those people who drink, he argued, do so because they are too ignorant to have any pleasures but the sensual ones of drinking and copulating. Yet, ignorant as they are, they know that their lives will end 'in the most abject poverty and misery,' for they have no hope of bettering their condition. What is surprising, then, is not 'that they should occasionally get drunk; [but] that it should be only occasional.'[2] The compassion he expressed for drunkards Place also extended toward another group then usually denied tolerance, the Jews. He completely lacked the anti-semitism that pervaded the nineteenth century and infected even reformers like Cobbett. Recalling his childhood, when 'it was thought good sport to maltreat a Jew,' he clearly indicated his horror at the way Jews were 'hooted, hunted, kicked, cuffed, pulled by the beard, spit up, and ... barbarously assaulted in the

[1] *The Reasoner*, xvi (1854), 209.
[2] *Improvement of the Working People*, pp. 11–12.

Editor's introduction

streets ... Dogs could not now be used in the streets, in the manner, many jews were treated.'

The cessation of such persecutions, he asserted, 'marks a considerable improvement in right habits of thinking.'[1] Place also maintained a humane attitude in the area of female chastity, where right habits of thinking were declining. In a period when there was a sharp increase in the intensity of the disapproval of unchastity (just before the period when unchaste heroines died at the end of novels), he was able to think about sex independently and originally. He recalled that in his youth the tradesmen's daughters, who were not expected to remain virgins till marriage, had made good wives. The evil, he concluded, lies not in the woman's deed but 'in the hypocrisy of men.'[2] As for prostitutes, far from condemning them as immoral women to be redeemed by preachments, he saw them as 'miserable wretches,' victims of the universal law that 'Chastity and poverty are incompatible.'[3] Place's 'law' and his unwillingness to condemn unchaste women resulted from his ability to reject conventional assumptions, to make his own analysis and distinctions. His chain of reasoning was this: Sexual intercourse is normal and appropriate; celibacy is unhealthy. Therefore people should be encouraged to marry young. Poverty and the fear of a large family often prevent early marriages. What should be repressed are poverty and fertility, not sexual instincts.

Place, as we see, could be a hard man but he could also be a compassionate one, not without a sympathetic imagination. Yet if we take the picture Place gave of himself in the autobiography and try to modify it with these and other instances of his compassion in order to produce a portrait of a not-quite-saintly reformer, untempted but sympathetic, we would be over-simplifying Place. He was much more ambivalent. His six volumes of data on the deplorable moral conditions of the eighteenth century could only have been assembled by a man who felt considerable fascination for these conditions. For example, the collection of obscene ballads which he heard in his youth, one small segment of his manners and morals series, represents great devotion. He wrote the ballads neatly, with special flourishes to the capitalized letters in the titles; he replaced inaccurate versions with correct ones when he could; and he included four pages of songs and observations recollected by one of the two friends who assisted him in compiling the songs. His ambivalence about these songs is further illustrated by his behaviour when he gave testimony before the Select Committee on Education (1835). He felt that these songs were too obscene to be read aloud to the committee members;

[1] Add. MS 27825, fs. 144–6. [2] Add. MS 27828, f. 55.
[3] Add. MS 27827, f. 193.

The Autobiography of Francis Place

but, on the other hand, he wanted to be sure they knew the songs and knew how deplorable manners used to be. He solved this desire for both concealment and exposure by giving the committee members written copies of the obscene songs.

Place's mixed feelings about the wickedness of the past are especially evident in his extensive notes on Greenwich Fair, the annual outing for working-class Londoners. Place had gone to the Fair as a child and as an apprentice. Then, about 1824, he began to go again – to see if the amusements had improved. Obviously he was delighted to be there for he kept returning year after year for the next fifteen years. But, though he clearly enjoyed it, he rejoiced that respectable people no longer let their children come. 'They have learned how to enjoy more rational amusements than could be found at Tea-gardens and Fairs, filled with all sorts of persons.'[1] The persons who then patronized the Fair engaged in more decorous amusements than those in Place's youth had done, but his description of them again reveals his pull towards the improper pleasures of his childhood. He wrote: 'All evidently enjoyed themselves and did their best to be happy, but there was little of gaity, no hilarity, no running, bawling and squalling and loud laughing as there used to be, no "Kissing in the ring" [a game he elsewhere described with mixed relish and disapprobation], no "thread my needle," no "drop handkerchief," no lively sports of any kind.'[2] These visits to Greenwich Fair resemble Gladstone's ambiguous behaviour in bringing home prostitutes so that he and Mrs Gladstone could hear their life stories. Place was not quite so wholesome and disinterested as he thought.

Analogous to his ambivalence about the deplorable morals of the past is his mixed attitude about publicity. Place did not encourage publicity by seeking a seat in Parliament, by signing all his writings, or by having his name on many published lists of committee members. Yet he spent hours and hours publicizing himself for posterity in his narratives of elections and reform movements.

In the end, he turned out to be, like most of us, a mixture of opposites. In his case it was a mixture of the respectable and radical, the rationalistic and romantic, the hard and compassionate. Like Augustine, he found the gross ways of his youth both deplorable and attractive. At the same time that he shunned publicity he was preparing to live in history. But what is finally important about Place and the story he has told us is not so much that he shared our common humanity as that he was so much more than the sum of all his contradictions. Probably every human being is more than the sum of his analysable parts; but because Place so copiously revealed the parts of his personality, we are especially aware of

[1] Add. MS 35144, f. 220.   [2] Ibid. f. 214.

Editor's introduction

the discrepancy between the picture of the man that can be made up of these jig-saw puzzle parts and the real man, whose efforts to demolish the Whig–Tory hold over Westminster, to repeal the Combination Laws, to pass the Reform Bill – in short, whose lifelong efforts 'to promote the welfare of the working class' – were major steps in the creation of a society where working-class Londoners of Walworth now describe themselves as 'the middle class.'

5

After Place's death some of his guard books were sold to his friend Joseph Parkes. Others were retained by Place's children. When Parkes' library was sold in 1868, the British Museum bought seventy volumes of the Place papers.[1] In 1897 Place's grandson, Francis C. Miers, presented to the Museum thirteen volumes of papers, including Place's autobiography and letter books.[2] In 1901 Place's biographer, Graham Wallas, presented the Museum with eight volumes of Place's memoranda and commonplace books.[3] And in 1909 the Miers family gave the Museum two volumes of letters written to Place by famous people.[4]

Place's autobiography is contained in the first three of the six volumes of manuscripts dealing with his personal life. The first thirteen chapters, which form a consecutive narrative, are in Add. MSS 35142 and 35143. The first of these volumes contains chapters one to eight, the second contains chapters nine to thirteen. This division into two volumes is Place's, for he put a separate table of contents before chapter nine. The rest of this volume (Add. MS 34143) consists of letters that Place wrote his family while he was making picturesque tours of England between 1810 and 1814 and while he was visiting Mill and Bentham in 1817. Chapter fourteen – and Place so numbered it, indicating that he intended it to be a continuation of the earlier material – comes in the middle of the third volume (Add. MS 35144), being preceded by two narratives of public events in which Place was involved and being followed by his reminiscences and observations of manners and morals of working-class people on holidays and at fairs.

Place's methodical habit of dating his narratives establishes the time when he composed the autobiography. He started the first draft in August of 1823.[5] By November he was finishing chapter three, and in December he was composing chapter four.[6] By January of 1824 he was

[1] Add. MSS 27789–27859.
[2] Add. MSS 35142–35154.
[3] Add. MSS 36623–36628.
[4] Add. MSS 37949–37950.
[5] See below p. 5 n1.
[6] pp. 67 and 94.

The Autobiography of Francis Place

up to chapter seven.[1] In June he composed the appendix to chapter ten.[2] In September he was writing the rough draft of his account of the London Corresponding Society.[3] And at some time during the year he wrote what he then intended to have as his final chapter, thirteen.[4] Not surprisingly, Place proceeded chronologically, spending a little over a year composing his autobiography.

During the next nine years he rewrote or made substantial additions to this narrative. In 1825 he rewrote part of chapter six and added the appendix on gun lock improvement to chapter thirteen.[5] In 1826 he added two long quotations to the introduction.[6] In June of 1827 he added to chapter five an extended description of one typical tradesman's family.[7] As he noted, in 1833 he rewrote the introduction.[8] In 1835 he apparently rewrote chapter thirteen, because he added that date parenthetically to a comment about the state of Charing Cross during the last twenty years; and the dated comment is part of the continuous narrative, not a later interpolation.[9] Besides making these revisions, Place made many small additions of one or two sentences. He kept adding these comments through the rest of his life; the dates on them range from 1825 all the way to 1851.

Chapter fourteen is somewhat different. Unlike the earlier chapters, the material forms neither a continuous narrative nor a chronological sequence. It consists of letters and narratives, often unrelated to each other, composed over the twenty-year period from 1825 to 1845. The first document – a letter praising Place, his reply spelling out his accomplishments, and his commentary on English society in 1825 – may well have been intended to go with the autobiography he had composed in 1823 and 1824. This document is unconnected with the following documents – copies of letters about his wife's illness and death, of letters about his courtship of his second wife, and narratives of his financial losses. These letters are dated 1827, 1828 and 1829. The narratives of his losses he composed in 1833 and 1834. But they are followed by an earlier narrative brought up to date – the history of his health, written first in 1825 and then in 1838. A still different sort of narrative follows – an account written in 1828 of a visit to Shepperton, where his father used to angle. Next, there is another account of his health, written in 1845. Finally, there is a narrative, written in 1831, of the Lord Chancellor's offer to make him an official assignee under the new Bankruptcy Act.

Place's decision to assemble these disparate documents into another chapter may have been prompted, in 1836, by Mrs Grote's enthusiasm

[1] p. 105 n2. [2] p. 166. [3] Add. MS 27808, fs. 33, 53.
[4] See below p. 226 n*. [5] pp. 97 and 230 n1. [6] p. 8 n1.
[7] p. 89 n3. [8] p. 5 n1. [9] p. 214.

Editor's introduction

for the previous chapters. On December 26, 1835 she returned the first volume (presumably chapters one to eight) with a note praising it and asking, 'Pray furnish me with more; I am ravenous.' Place complied; she rapidly read the last five chapters and on January 7, 1836 wrote, 'I hope you have got another vol: for me. Never was any novel of Sir Walter Scott's so interesting . . . I shall return this vol: on Saty. Please feed me with a fresh batch.'[1] The next day Place sent her chapter fourteen and the following note: 'My dear Mrs Grote. Your wish is accomlished, with this is Vol 3. This volume differs considerable from the two you have had.'[2] It is difficult to tell what documents then comprised the new chapter. From a later letter we know that it included the account of his financial losses. But in the letter accompanying chapter fourteen Place spoke of other documents, which Mrs Grote might see if she wished: 'From 1818 to the present time there are only detached articles. You shall see them if you wish and will tell me you do.'[3] Later in the same month, January 1836, Place had chapter fourteen back and was making additions to it. On January 26 he wrote to Mrs Grote: 'I think I sent you in the last volume a paper headed, "My own Revolution," . . . I have said that I had enough of fortune left for my own comfort, but not enough to meet occasional but unavoidable calls of my family. I have therefore put into the volume – a letter from my daughter Mary which you can read, I have also put into the volume a letter I wrote to Mill respecting my poor wife in 1827.'[4] The letter to Mill remains; the letter from his daughter has disappeared and is not listed in his table of contents for this final chapter. Place made other determinable changes to the chapter – he brought the medical history of 1825 up to date and later added a further chronicle of his state of health.

Curiously, although he often altered this material, Place never rewrote it as a continuous narrative. Perhaps he was deterred by the difficulty of compressing events of many years into one chapter, or by the lack of themes such as those which gave cohesiveness to his earlier chapters. Or, he may have found it impossible to write a narrative of his life after 1817 (his retirement year) without describing his numerous reform activities. These reform activities he had long before started to record as separate histories. Probably when he found that his account of the London Corresponding Society had become too extensive for the autobiography he decided to keep his narratives of reform activities separate from his autobiography.

6

The fact that Place had an autobiographical tale to tell was made public

[1] Add. MS 35144, fs. 347–8. [2] Ibid. f. 349. [3] Ibid. f. 354. [4] Ibid. f. 361.

The Autobiography of Francis Place

in 1835 when he testified before the Select Committee on Education. He gave the committee details of his childhood, of the kind of life he and other apprentices had led at the end of the eighteenth century. The Tory newspaper *The Times* promptly attacked these working-class reminiscences. An editorial titled 'Autobiography of Francis Place' ironically stated 'that it would be an injustice to arts and letters to allow all [Place's testimony] to remain stitched up within the forbidding blue sheets of Parliamentary collections.' After quoting several statements from Place's testimony, the writer asked, 'Was it worth incurring all the expense of a committee, of clerks . . . to have such miserable and vulgar twaddle printed?' Place's autobiographical recollections, *The Times* concluded, are 'mere trash.'[1]

In a predictable opposition to *The Times*, Place had a strong sense that his autobiography was an important historical record. He sent it not only to the Grotes for their reactions (which took the form of marvelling at his rise) but also to his devoted follower Samuel Harrison who responded with a sheaf of glosses on the manners of the past, giving further information about the dress, amusements and the schooling of Londoners as he encountered them, a decade or two after Place.

It is indeed for its record of improved manners that Place valued it (and it is this feature of the autobiography which received the most additions in later years). When Mrs Grote suggested that she might write her memoirs recording the changes in manners, Place urged her to do so and stated that autobiographies such as his or hers would do 'much good' by making 'the changes which have occurred familiar to the people.' He added that 'the errors into which they fall from want of such information are exceedingly pernicious. Well instructed in such matters a whole century of intelligence would be gained.'[2] His high opinion of such autobiographical records was expressed even more strongly in the autobiography, where he claimed that 'correctly detailed domestic history,' because 'it would enable us to make comparisons [and] shew clearly the progress of civilization' is 'the most valuable of all.'[3]

Place undoubtedly expected that his papers would be published or that he would be the subject of a biography. The autobiography was evidently intended to stand on its own, as were some of his histories of reform agitation. But about other narratives he was doubtful. On the first page of his account of the Combination Laws he stated, 'In the following papers references are made to printed papers and manuscripts contained in 5 folio and in 2 octavo Volumes. Whoever may Edit these

[1] Wednesday, Dec. 23, 1835; in Add. MS 35144, f. 326.
[2] Ibid. f. 358.   [3] See below p. 91.

Editor's introduction

Memoirs must carefully compare the M.S. with these volumes and use his own discretion as to the use he will make of their contents – either as comment notes or appendices.'[1] Still other collections of his papers he kept only in order that an editor might digest their contents. On the table of contents for his memoranda, diaries and journals of the 1820s and 1830s he put two notes, indicating this reason for preserving them. In 1838 he wrote, 'These Memorandums &c would have been put into the fire, but after consideration I thought they might be useful to any one who should Edit the Memoir, as they contain parts of political matters alluded to in other places ... They are preserved only for this purpose. When they have been used in this way they should be destroyed.'[2] Twelve years later, in 1850, when Place re-examined these documents, he added a stronger note before his diary for 1826: 'I have just now concluded looking over this Diary and request my Executors to burn it with their own hands as soon as it has been examined and such few particulars as some competent person or one of themselves may think are necessary for the elucidation of my memoir have been used.'[3]

Place was wrong in his assumption that his memoir would be edited shortly after his death, so that his executors could burn his diaries and journals. No biography of Place was published until forty-four years later, when Graham Wallas brought out his *Life of Francis Place*.[4] This biography is more favourable than Place could have anticipated. Not only did Wallas rely exclusively on Place's version of the events in which he took part but also, in the necessary process of selecting quotations, he sometimes removed evidence of warts on Place's character.

The autobiography which Place rightly valued as an example of domestic history has never before been published, though Wallas quoted portions of it detailing Place's dramatic rise in the world, and many writers on London life have quoted occasional sentences.

Place's son, Francis Place Jr evidently planned to publish it because he went through the manuscript correcting with pencil a few errors, adding a gloss or two, crossing out many passages and writing 'Delete' or 'Dele' in the margins opposite them. At least part of his editorial work was done in 1873; this date and his initials are pencilled in the margin of Add. MS 35143, f. 122.

The chief effect of the deletions intended by Francis Place Jr is to neutralize his father's atheism. Where Place spent two pages describing the reading and thinking that led him to atheism, his son scored the

[1] Add. MS 27798, f. 4.
[2] Add. MS 35146, f. 2.
[3] Ibid. f. 9.
[4] In 1898 (hereafter referred to as 'Wallas'). I am indebted to Wallas for many details in this introduction.

The Autobiography of Francis Place

whole passage for omission.[1] He also cancelled Place's explanation that he chose Erskine as a defence lawyer 'because he was suspected of being but a weak christian,' and his statement that 'Mr Kyd was an infidel.'[2] Besides these irreligious passages, the son also crossed out a few comments about people whose descendants might be living. Opposite the comment that Parke let the rooms at 16 Charing Cross 'in any way he pleased,' Place Jr pencilled in 1873 date and the comment, 'Initial must be used here some of the family still live.'[3] The same motive undoubtedly induced him to score out not only the name but also the description of the Duke of Norfolk as a man 'than whom it might upon the whole be difficult to find a greater scoundrel.'[4] Finally, in chapter fourteen, he planned to omit all the references to Place's second marriage – about ten pages of the manuscript.[5] Opposite the beginning of this massive deletion he wrote, 'So purely domestic and uninteresting out of the family that it had better be cut out.'

Several passages in the text were literally cut out, but we can guess that most of them dealt with immoral or indecorous behaviour of Place and of his father. The first of these excisions concerned what Place, in chapter three, called 'an occurrence which had considerable effect on me.' This event occurred one Thursday when the fourteen-year-old Place was left in Mr Bowis' school to hear the older girls' sums after the master had left. At this point in the text, four lines down on the page, someone cut off the rest of the sheet. On the opposite page Francis Place Jr wrote, 'The consequence was bad for both parties giving rise to much licentiousness.'[6] Later in chapter three, at the end of the section on 'Dress of Boys,' there has been an excision of all but three lines of the page. A footnote for the beginning of this excised material has been crossed out by Place, suggesting that he made this deletion. The cancelled footnote reads: 'Pages A. B. C. come in before the article on the Dress of Boys.' In the extensive table of contents that Place made later he indicated that the section before 'Dress of Boys' contained 'Specimens of Songs sung in Tradesmens Houses.' It is probable, then, that Place made this cut in order to rearrange his material and that later he or someone else removed the songs from the chapter. In chapter four, after Place described the unchaste girls he and his fellow apprentices associated with, someone cut off three-quarters of a sheet.[7] A few pages later there has been an excision of a page and a half, probably dealing with the dissolute amusements of apprentices.[8] Near the end of the chapter, a section of a page and a half was sliced off; in this deleted material, Place

[1] See below pp. 45–6.   [2] pp. 160 and 162.   [3] p. 215.
[4] p. 85.   [5] pp. 256–67.   [6] p. 56; Add. MS 35142, f. 99.
[7] See below p. 76.   [8] p. 81.

Editor's introduction

presumably explained why he left his apprenticeship several years before its expiration.[1] From the half-sentence after the excision, it appears that Place's father quarrelled with Joe France. In chapter fourteen cuts of a half-page and of two and a half pages have been made in a section describing the social discrimination Place encountered because he had been a tailor.[2] In addition to these deletions in the body of the text, there has been a total expurgation of the appendix to chapter three which contained examples of obscene songs Place had heard in his youth.[3] Place may have made some of these deletions himself, possibly members of the Miers family (Place's grandchildren) made some of them before presenting the autobiography to the British Museum. However, the comment by Francis Place Jr about licentiousness suggests that he cut off the anecdote and then provided this generalization as a substitute. If so, he may have been responsible for most of these cuts.

Why Francis Place Jr failed to publish his father's autobiography is uncertain. Why no one published it later is puzzling. Perhaps people have been discouraged by the bad reputation it has among those who have read the Place papers. In his laudatory biography of Place Graham Wallas raised no enthusiasm for it when he wrote that it was 'what might have been expected from a man whose sense of the importance of facts made him over-anxious to record every possible detail. The autobiography ... never was, and never will be, published.'[4] That judgment of 1898 was repeated in 1962 by a hostile critic of Place, W. E. S. Thomas, who said that neither the autobiography nor any of Place's other narratives was worth editing: 'his style is wooden and repetitive.'[5]

Each man's charge has some truth in it. Wallas was right that Place tried to record every detail. The inclusiveness of his literary aims sometimes leads to long stretches of tedium in his writing, as when he enumerated all the errors of fact in a letter by Lord Erskine (appendix to chapter ten). This tendency to long-windedness seemed to increase as Place grew older. For example, the second account of Place's health, written in 1845, starts with four digressive pages about a political meeting he attended.[6]

---

[1] p. 82.   [2] pp. 249 and 250.
[3] In the lengthy table of contents that he composed for his autobiography, Place itemized this material: 'Appendix to Chapter. 3. Songs. Grossness – Lewdness. Specimens of Songs sung at Tradesmen's parties. D[itt]o at Public Houses and Clubs. D[itt]o in the Public Streets and Markets. Mr Haywards remarks on these Songs and his testimony to the improvement of the public in these particulars' (Add. MS 35142, f. 4v).
[4] Wallas, p. 2.
[5] 'Francis Place and Working Class History,' *Historical Journal*, v (1962), 69.
[6] One of the worse effects of his inclusiveness is that he was so thorough in collecting materials for his history of the London Corresponding Society that he never got around to writing it. He started collecting materials for this history as early as 1798

The Autobiography of Francis Place

Place recognized in himself this inclination towards prolixity and tried to curb it. At the end of his account of the London Corresponding Society he added, 'These notes were written as part of my Memoir, but when the memoir was made up much was omitted in consequence of its being more an account of the London Corresponding Society than ... matter relating to me particularly.'[1] These notes on the LCS contain one page about the domestic affairs of Mr Allison, the tailor; this version has much more tangential detail than the finished version. In the final version Place wrote that Allison ended up in a madhouse where he died and that 'Mrs Allison kept the shop for some time after her husband's death.'[2] In the first draft Place had explained that Mrs Allison carried on the business with the foreman, that he fell in love with a girl who was being kept by Sir William Manners, and that the foreman left Mrs Allison to set up his own tailoring shop.[3] In excising these details Place was clearly trying to stop the centrifugal flow of his writing, as he was also doing when he relegated four segments of his memoir to appendices.

But this passion to record every detail, burdensome as it is in such sections as the appendix on gun lock improvement, gives the autobiography its value. From all Place's minutiae about games and gangs, his family life, the casual way his father apprenticed him to anyone in the tavern who would have the boy, the arrangement of the one room in which he and his wife and child lived and worked, the little sums they earned and spent, the acquiring and pawning of their possessions, their persuading a neighbour to undertake the 'unrespectable' action of going to and from the pawnshop, his visiting his mother after dinner, so that she would not have to spend the few extra pennies on food for him – all these details create a picture of a world as alien as the ghettos of Harlem or the *favelas* of Rio de Janeiro. Place's great virtue as an autobiographer is not so much his showing himself as an Ur-Alger hero as his showing us a society that no other writer preserved. It is a society to which his associates of the London Corresponding Society, Thomas Hardy and John Binns, paid little attention in their autobiographies. In

---

when he urged the founder, Thomas Hardy, to write an account of the Society. Place was still accumulating as late as 1837, when he zestfully described to a correspondent all the LCS materials he had amassed (Add. MS 27816, f. 305). Midway through this long period of research, Hardy wrote and asked Place if he had yet begun the history. 'Perhaps,' he suggested, 'the extensive plan you have chalked out, requiring such a mass of materials to be examined may have delayed it. Would it not be better to circumscribe your plan, and bring it within a more narrow compass, that it might be more generally read, and be much more useful, being within the reach of a numerous class to purchase, for whose use I believe you design it' (Letter of Oct. 16, 1824; ibid. f. 233).

[1] Add. MS 27808, f. 12. [2] See below p. 128. [3] Add. MS 27808, f. 2v.

Editor's introduction

contrast to Place's detailed account – about meeting his wife at a dance, courting her, quarrelling with her mother, arranging a private marriage, starting married life in a single room – Hardy's third-person account of his own marriage passes almost unnoticed. 'In the year 1781, he married the youngest daughter of Mr Priest, a carpenter and builder in Chesham, in Buckinghamshire, with whom he lived, in spite of all the tricks of fortune, in the most perfect state of connubial happiness.'[1] Place, on the other hand, by specifying the tricks of fortune and supplying the details of his married life, created a drama more believable than Hardy's generalization about 'the most perfect state of connubial happiness.'

Valuable as these details of 'domestic history' are, they do not make one of the great literary autobiographies. Place's style, as has been charged, is somewhat wooden and repetitive. His sentence structure is unimaginative; his phrasing is generally commonplace. When he is enraged, as at religion or Whiggery, there is occasionally some bite in his statements. 'Where were the shuffling Whigs then?' 'This saint was like all his crew a twaddler.' Most of the time, however, the style ranges from the unmemorable to the atrocious. An ironic attack on Place in 1826 fairly well described his style as corrected by editors and printers – 'Nothing can be more bland and inviting than the address of Mr PLACE. His sentences are keen with antithesis; and yet the language which he uses is so exquisitely classical, and so delicately chaste, that his oratory rather resembles the "soft recorders," (not of Newgate, but of Milton) than the language of an ordinary gentleman.'[2] His untreated sentences, for example those in the autobiography, are subject to these and further charges. Sometimes Place joined three or four sentences with commas; more irritatingly, he sometimes joined two sentences with a comma but capitalized the first letter of the second sentence. Occasionally, the sentences are snarled to the point of incoherence. For example, after stating that fifty pounds would have enabled him to start a business Place continued, 'But fifty pounds or any sum beyond five pounds a sum I did occasionally borrow from a member of the society named Thomas Harrison a careful honest sensible man, was all the assistance I could command, which I was willing to accept.'[3] He meant, of course, that he could not borrow fifty pounds. Further, his inclusion of unnecessary medial commas and his omission of needed ones draw attention to the generally pedestrian style of the narrative.

Admittedly, these distinctive features of Place's style do not help create a great autobiography. But they do suggest a great many things

[1] *Memoir of Thomas Hardy*, 1832, p. 9.
[2] 'Francis Place of Westminster, Esq.,' *European Magazine*, n.s. II (1826), 229.
[3] See below p. 174.

The Autobiography of Francis Place

about Place. The simple sentence structure and diction are signs of his simple social outlook – education would cure drunkenness; repeal of the Combination Laws would eliminate trade unions. The occasional snarled sentences such as the one quoted above suggest that Place's picture of himself as the rational, clear-thinking member of each social or political group was not entirely accurate, that his rational mastery of other men was achieved at the price of considerable suppression of other parts of his personality. His eccentricities in punctuation and spelling (for example, his uncertainty about the spelling of *scarcely* and *believe*) suggest all the deviations from middle-class standards that must have made Place's dealings with the better-schooled reformers more tense than he indicated. His refusal to associate with them socially may have been as much from fear of failure as from sturdy working-class independence. Those contemporary attacks on Place for not being a gentleman may sound faintly ridiculous to us; but they may have contained a truth painful to him.

7

The text of the autobiography is intended to be a faithful transcription of what Place wrote. The only significant changes are the lowering of raised letters, as in the terminal letters of *Mr* and *Jany*, and in a few instances titles of books have been italicized and final quotation marks added to reduce confusion. Some doubtful readings are placed within pointed brackets; and where Place's omission of a word or part of a word causes confusion, the missing word or letters are interpolated in square brackets.

Although most of Place's deviations from the conventions of spelling, punctuation and sentence structure are significant in the ways discussed above, others – particularly such spellings as *wa* for *was* – seem to be the accidental and non-significant mistakes of someone writing hastily. Sometimes he omitted the period when the sentence was concluded at the end of a line. Other deviations from the conventions of writing may have occurred in his transcription of those parts which he recopied. In the few pages which he preserved from his earlier draft of chapter eight, the punctuation and the use of upper and lower case letters are more conventional than in his final version. One or two of the snarls in sentence construction result from Place's revisions of his fair copy. Whenever the revision has made the sentence less clear, the previous version is also given.

Place's quotations from other writers were seldom completely accurate, although he always retained the sense of the original. His alterations of the original text have not been noted, except in a few instances where

Editor's introduction

he omitted a word or phrase which clarified the sentence. Nor have Place's changes in his own text been noted, except in the instances mentioned above and in a few sentences where the revision was intended to change the thought rather than the style. Since his marginal summaries of the paragraphs (e.g. 'Magazine,' 'Ashley removes,' 'I go with him') generally do not add to the text, they have been omitted, and the very few marginalia of significance have been put in the footnotes.

Despite the attempt to reproduce Place's text faithfully there may be some accidental changes or misreadings. I shall be grateful to any keen-eyed persons who call such slips to my attention.

(Numerals mark the editor's footnotes; other symbols mark Place's notes.)

MAJOR EVENTS IN PLACE'S AUTOBIOGRAPHY

1769 or 1770	Birth of older sister
1771 Nov. 3	Francis Place born
1773 August	Birth of younger brother
1774 March 28	Birth of Elizabeth Chadd, Place's first wife
1775 June	Birth of sister, Ann Place
1778	Place starts school
1780 June	Family move to public house in Arundel Street
1783	Place changes to school of Mr Bowis
1784	Rejects religion
1785	Father in ecclesiastical suit
1785	Place apprenticed to leather breeches-maker
1787	Brother apprenticed to lighterman
1788	Father moves to Rules of Fleet
1788–9	Older sister marries a drunkard
1789 July	Place ends apprenticeship
1790 March 17	Meets Elizabeth Chadd
1790 Spring	Father ruined by state lottery; mother becomes washerwoman
1791 March 17	Place marries Elizabeth Chadd
1792	Birth of first daughter
1793 Spring	Death of daughter and of father
1793 Spring	Strike of breeches-makers
1793 June–	Place without work for 8 months; reads Hume, Locke, Adam Smith, Godwin's *Inquiry Concerning Political Justice*
1793 end	Younger sister marries a thief
1794 April	Birth of second daughter; Place reads Paine's *Age of Reason*
1794 May 12	Thomas Hardy, founder of London Corresponding Society, and others seized on charges of high treason
1794 June	Place joins London Corresponding Society
1795 Sept.	Elected chairman of general committee of LCS
1796 Jan.	Birth of third daughter
1797	Birth of Louisa Simeon Chatterley, Place's second wife
1797 June	Place ceases paying dues in LCS
1797 July– 1798 April	Reads Helvetius, Rousseau, Voltaire
1798 April– 1799 April	Manages fund for families of detained political prisoners
1798 June	Birth of oldest son
1799 April 8	Moves to No. 29 Charing Cross and starts shop with Richard Wild
1799 May 8	Brother-in-law sentenced to death for highway robbery
1800 Dec. 25	Place learns Wild's plan to oust him from the shop
1801 Jan. 2	Ends partnership with Wild; moves out of house at Charing Cross

The Autobiography of Francis Place

1801 April 8	Moves to No. 16 Charing Cross and opens shop
1807 May	Manages Westminster election of Sir Francis Burdett
1817	Retires from business
1827 Oct. 19	Death of Mrs Place
1830 Feb. 13	Marries Mrs Chatterley
1833 Feb.–March	Learns of loss of fortune; moves to No. 21 Brompton Square
1851	Separates from second wife
1854 Jan. 1	Dies

THE AUTOBIOGRAPHY OF
FRANCIS PLACE

CONTENTS OF THE AUTOBIOGRAPHY

Introduction. Inducement to the Author to commence writing his own Memoirs. Self written Biography. Its value and claim to credence – Bentham. Its abuse and worthlessness – *Quarterly Review*. Objections anticipated and examined ... *page* 5

1   Lineage. Father's early history. Traits of character. Mother's early history. Traits of character ... 17

2   From the marriage of my father and mother to the time when he took a public house in Arundel Street in the Strand ... 22

3   Sec. 1 – From the time when my father became a publican to the time of my being bound apprentice ... 34
    Sec. 2 – School Teaching. Moral Discipline ... 40
    Sec. 3 – Dress of Boys ... 62
    Sec. 4 – Twelfth Day ... 64
    Sec. 5 – Guy Fawkes ... 65
    Sec. 6 – Bullock Hunting in the Streets ... 68

4   My Apprenticeship ... 71

5   Family history ... 83
    Sec. 1 – From the time when I was apprenticed to the time when my father sold the house in Arundel Street ... 83
    Sec. 2 – Sketches of characters – persons who frequented my father's house ... 85
    Sec. 3 – Sketch of another class of Tradesmen ... 89

6   Family history. To my Marriage – in March 1791 ... 92

7   From my marriage in 1791 to my being again employed by Mr Allison after a strike for wages in 1793 ... 104

8   From my being employed by Mr Allison to My being employed by Mrs Barnes. London Corresponding Society. Family history ... 123

9   From my removal to Fisher Street, in 1795 to my removal to Holborn, in 1796. London Corresponding Society ... 136

10   My residence at Ashley's. He goes to France. I remove to another house. ... 153
    Appendix to Chap. 10 – *Age of Reason*. Case of Thomas Williams. Conduct of Mr Erskine ... 159

11   From my removal from Ashley's in Sep. 1797 to my removal to Charing Cross in April 1799. Partnership with Richard Wild. Character and Influence of the London Corresponding Society ... 173

The Autobiography of Francis Place

12	From my removal to Charing Cross on the 8 April, 1799 – to my return to Charing Cross on the 8 April, 1801. Partnership with Richard Wild. Its termination. I remove from Charing Cross – Return to it again.	201
13	From my return to Charing Cross in 1801 to the year 1816. Business. Family	213
	Appendix to Chap. 13 – (i) The Street Charing Cross	227
	Appendix to Chap. 13 – (ii) Gun Lock Improvement 1804–1807	230
	Appendix to Chap. 13 – (iii) John King	236
14	1. Campbell's Letter to Brough[a]m, recommending an University, 1825. His praise of me. My attainments. My acquaintances. How estimated	240
	2. Letters to James Mill. Ill health of my Wife, Augst. Death, Octr. 1827	251
	3. Letters to Mr John Miers my son in Law and his Wife my daughter at Rio de Janeiro, 1828, 1829. My state and Prospects	255
	4. My own Revolution, lose nearly 2/3rds of my Income, 1833	270
	5. Let the House at Charing Cross to my Son Francis and remove to Brompton	273
	6. Early Recollections. Childhood. Manhood. State of health	275
	7. Visit to Shepperton, the place my father used to Visit as an Angler	278
	8. State of health continued	280
	9. Official Assignee. Lord Broughams Proposal. – Nov. 1831	288

Note: Place composed separate chapter summaries for most chapters of the manuscript. The present list is an editorial compilation from these half-title pages which Place inserted before each chapter.

INTRODUCTION[1]

Whether the following narrative may or may not be of any Importance must be left to the decision of others. It has been began in consequence of the repeatedly expressed wishes of several of my friends who have been more or less acquainted with me for years; and particularly by two among my most esteemed friends Mr Jeremy Bentham and Mr James Mill. Many circumstances of our lives have occasionally been subjects of conversation, and many have been the importunities of these especial friends that I would write out at length my own account of myself. Thus urged I have commenced and it is my present intention to continue, thus; write some portion every day, and devote as much time as I can spare to it every day for the purpose of enabling me to write correctly. Benjamin Franklin says, "I have come to the resolution to proceed in that work." (his own memoirs) "tomorrow and to continue it daily 'till finished" My Old friend Thomas Holcroft also put off the writing of his memoirs 'till tomorrow, unfortunately tomorrow never came to either Franklin or Holcroft, and the world has been deprived of much valuable information and some amusement.

I intend, not, to wait 'till tomorrow but to go on steadily, to give the best account I can of my parentage, for ancestors so far as my knowledge extends I have none. To relate many particulars of my early life, and especially those which appear to me to have influenced me in after life; I shall put down from memory such circumstances as may appear to me worth notice and shall carefully inquire respecting them of every person I can discover who may be able to give me correct information, to remove doubts or supply facts. This portion of my work will have especial reference to my youthful days, since from the time I became a man, the incidents of my life are too strongly marked to admit of much mistake, and the means of verification and correction can be much more easily

[1] In the upper right-hand corner of this page (numbered f. 23 in Place's original manuscript) Place put the following note, obviously not intended for publication: 'Written in August. 1823. Re-written in August. 1833. The first MS – being only a rough draft.'
    Two folios previously, Place had pasted an unidentified newspaper clipping of about eight hundred words, titled 'Trusting to Ourselves.' It starts, 'There is a duty of an important nature which we have to perform towards society; and that is, we must trust to ourselves. We have each been endowed with reason to guide us, and hands to work; why, then, unless prostrated with bodily disease, or some other infirmity, should we think of leaning upon others for support or assistance?' The article ends with the recommendation to let a person 'begin at the bottom, and he will be all the better fitted for his place when he reaches it, by having fought his way up through the lower stages.'

The Autobiography of Francis Place

made[.] I shall carefully avail myself of all the living information I can procure, and shall be able to be precise in many dates from written and printed papers.

Whether my story in *all* its particulars be one which ought to be plainly told, or whether some parts be improper to be laid before the public I leave to my sucessors to determine, You (, some of my most intimate and well informed friends have said,) "you seem to have been brought up in a school whence no good could seem to have resulted, no good predicated, No benevolent feelings could have been expected, No wisdom, no virtue, no large views of any subject no advancement of understanding, none in life, seem to follow from such a condition as yours, and we should very much like to see, as it appears to be your duty to let us see in writing, all the incidents relating to yourself as they occurred from your earliest infancy to the present time, that we and others may know how it happened that you succeeded in the many ways you have succeeded; how you obtained the command you have of yourself and hence the command you have over so many others in such varied circumstances as we have witnessed. The causes of these effects if fairly and honestly and fully stated will be both amusing and instructive." Such are the arguments my most esteemed friends have used, and these with my own have induced me to commence this work, which I trust I shall carry on with equal diligence and honesty until I have fully and faithfully written all that seems to me to deserve even such notice as my own egotism may induce me to think will be read without the merited reproof of trifling with the readers time, or wearing out his patience.

My friend James Mill is no flatterer, For the correctness of this assertion I can safely appeal to all who know him; wrote thus to my second daughter in october 1817. She had been on a visit to me at Ford Abbey in Devonshire then rented by Mr Bentham; where I had been two months, and where Mr Mill and his family resided during the summer and autumnal months. My daughter was governess to a young lady the daughter of Mr Greatheed of Langford Lodge about half way between Southampton and Salisbury. A correspondence had taken place between her and Mr Mill, and in a letter from Mr Mill to her on several subjects and especially in reply to some questions respecting intellectual attainments, Mr Mill says, "there is however the less for me or for any one to do, in the way of instruction, that you have had an instructor of no ordinary excellence, I mean your father, who is one of the most extraordinary men I have ever known. When I think of the unfavourable circumstances in which for the first twenty or rather thirty years of his life he was placed for acquiring knowledge or any good habits whatever, and now find his mind stored with knowledge to an extent few possess,

Introduction

full of acuteness ingenuity and force, a good husband a good father, a good friend, a good patriot, benefitting hundreds, and exerting himself to benefit all, I cannot easily tell you how much I admire him, and how happy I account you in being his daughter."

If this be correct, if indeed it be correct to a very limited extent, I ought to have no hesitation in complying with the desires of my friends and telling the true story of myself.

To the charge which will be made against me of Egotism, I at once, and before hand plead guilty. No man ever wrote about himself without being an egotist, in the common acceptation of the word. I am indeed no enemy to egotism in any man in whom it does not amount to insolence, when it is not obtrusive, annoying or mischievous. No man ever wrote about himself who did not think well of himself, and that too whether or not the actions he narrated were such as a good man ought to be pleased with, or such as are frivolous or contemptible or wicked. Be they either good or wicked,[1] still the writer however erroneously must have a good opinion of himself, must applaud his own conduct, must be pleased with his own notion of his own wisdom or cunning and must suppose that other men will be disposed to judge as favourably him, upon the whole nearly as favourably as he has judged himself. It would however be a prodigy were any man to lay himself fully open in all respects, and no good could arise from such an exposure if truly and fully made, even by the most virtuous man that ever lived. Such an account would be about equally, monotonous tiresome and loathsome, of this any man who has acquired the faculty of tracing back his own thoughts and impartially reviewing them may convince himself, a daily reckoning for one week, accurately kept and made up, could scarcely be comtemplated with *pleasure*[*] by any man. If it be admitted that a man really understands the motives which govern him; which very few men do, it may still be reasonably doubted that he has examined himself so closely and so carefully as to be able to make a full statement of his own thoughts and actions correctly, add to which that this kind of knowledge comes to no man early in life. None need therefore be surprised at the errors which even the most honest and best qualified to judge of themselves are sure to commit when writing their own memoirs. This is not said by way of apology for any thing this memoir may contain. It is simply a statement of the circumstances in which they who write about themselves are

---

[1] Place wrote the word 'evil' over this word.

[*] I doubt much, and that too, after much pains taking as well in observing myself and others, and comparing my own with the experience of some clever men, that any man is *conscious* of all he thinks at any interval after he has been thinking, and scarcly any one who is conscious of his own thoughts in the order in which they occur. That is, has the power of recognizing them to their full extent.

The Autobiography of Francis Place

placed, and no one who chuses to write his own memoirs has or can have any claim for indulgence, should he at any time put his M.S.S. in the form of a book before the public – He knows the conditions under which his book must appear and as he is not obliged to make the book but may abstain from it if he pleases, he can have no reasonable ground of complaint, if men as wise or wiser than himself condemn it, or treat both the book and the author with contumely.

In many instances I shall insert the names and other designations of persons alluded to, that whoever may have the care of this M.S. may see the situation and rank in life of these persons, and may thus be the better able to make accurate comparisons with persons of the same description at the time when it may be published In some cases as using names might be mischievous, and disagreeable to the descendants of some of the persons named, so the witholding of the names may be advisable, the editor stating in notes why he has witheld the names.*

[1]Two writers have recently characterized Self written Biography one favourably the other unfavourably, one has treated the subject philosophically and generally, the other practically, popularly and sarcastically.

The first is Jeremy Bentham, in his work entitled – *Not Paul but Jesus.* s. 8. p 110.[2] The section is headed thus.

"Self Written Biography.

Its superior value and claim to credence.

On the occasion of this portion of history, it seems particularly material to bring to view an observation, which on the occasion of every[3] portion of history, it will, it is believed be of no small use to have in remembrance.

---

* It is said and I believe truly that in the life of Gibbon – (Lord Sheffield told it to Mr Wakefield) and also in the memoirs of others as well women as men, letters have been witheld and passages omitted which would not only have strongly marked the character of the party but also that of the times. This is a fraud which ought to be discountenanced as much as possible, the reader has a false impression put upon him, which nothing can justify. The letters suppressed in the life of Gibbon relate to his infidelity, which is notwithstanding darkly hinted at in some places and made manifest in others. In the life and correspondance of more than one lady similar frauds have been committed because the manners of what is called good society, would be shocked by the *disclosures*, which would mark the spirit of the age the more clearly.

1 Before this sentence Place parenthetically added: '28 November. 1826[.] The following passages have been interpolated'

2 1823. Place had a hand in the production of this book (Wallas, p. 84n).
   This quotation, like the others in the autobiography, contains errors, most of them minor changes in punctuation and capitalization. These errors are noted only if they distort the meaning of the original work.

3 Place originally wrote in the word 'any.'

Introduction

In comparison with self written Biography, scarcly does any other Biography deserve the name.

Faint, indeterminate, uninstructive, deceptive, is the information furnished by any other hand, of whatsoever concerns the state of the mental frame, in comparison with what is furnished by a mans own. – Even of those particulars which make against himself, – even of those motives and intentions which he would most anxiously conceal, – more clear and correct, as far as it goes, if not more complete, – is the information given by him, than that which is commonly offered even by an impartial hand. By a mans own hand not unfrequently is information afforded, of a sort which makes against itself himself, and which would not,[1] have been afforded by any other hand, though ever so hostile. He states the self condemnatory mental facts, the blindness of self partiality concealing from his eyes the condemnatory inference, or even if his eyes be open, he lays himself under the imputation: of bartering merit in this or that inferior shape, for the merit of candour, or the hope of augmenting the probative force of his own self serving evidence, in favour of every other merit for which it is his ambition to gain credence."

N.B. This is the whole section.

The second is a writer in the *Quarterly Review.* vol 35 published on the 28 Dec. 1826 in page 148 commences an article on Autobiography. Ten works are named in the title of the article, and a severe censure is passed on most of them provoked by the disclosures of some of them of the private conduct of families to which the writers have been admitted, It observes that,

"the only legitimate object of the private autobiographer is to give the public the cream of his personal experience, and a fair enough test by which to try the merits of any work of this class is afforded, if we extract from it, in the form of simple propositions the moral and intellectual lessons it contains, and compare their importance, when thus distinctly presented to the minds eye, with the quality of the matter[2] from which they have been sifted. The tree is known by its fruit. (p. 157.)

"Few good men[3] – none of the very highest order, have chosen to paint themselves otherwise than indirectly, and through the shadows of imaginary forms, the secret workings of their own minds, nor is it likely that genius will ever be found altogether divested of this proud modesty, unless in the melancholy case of its being tinged as in Rousseau with insanity. There was therefore little danger of our having too much autobiography, as long as no book had much chance of popularity which was not written with some considerable portion of talent, or at least by a person of some considerable celebrity in one way or another. But the circle of readers has widened strangely in these times, and while an overwhelming preponderance among them[4] tempts one class of

---

[1] The original text of Bentham reads, 'which would not, because it could not, have been afforded . . .'
[2] The original reads, 'quantity of matter.'
[3] Original: 'Few great men.'
[4] Original: 'preponderance of vulgarity among them.'

writers to the use of materials which, in older times they would have held themselves far above, a still more disgusting effect is, that it emboldens beings who, at any period, would have been mean and base in all their objects and desires to demand with hardihood the attention and the sympathy of mankind, for thoughts and deeds,[1] in any other period than the present, must have been as obscure as dirty. The mania for this garbage of Confessions and Recollections, and Reminiscenses, and Aniliana, is indeed a vile symptom. It seems as if the ear of the grand impersonation the reading public,[2] had become as filthily prurient as that of an eves dropping laquey.

"If this voluntary degradation be persisted in, the effects of it will, ere long be visible elsewhere than in literature. An universal spirit of suspicion will overspread the intercourse of society, and no class of persons will suffer more that [i.e. than] that which found easy access in former days to circles much above their station, in virtue of their beleif[3] that their garrulity was not at the least the veil of a calculating curiosity, and that however poor their wit might be, they were capable of receiving kindness and condescension, without any notions of turning a penny by the systematic record of privacies too generously exposed."

They who treacherously note and publish the conversations of private life, the facts and circumstances which they themselves have noticed or have taken on trust from the relations of others. They who thus purposely to increase the desire for slander which always depraves those who receive gratification from such anecdotes and narratives as cannot fail to cause uneasiness, mortification and unhappiness in families deserve even something more than the censure of the reviewer. He has however exceeded this just condemnation, he has exhibited his own ill humour, and want of the philosophy he condemns in others, as is but too common in even the best informed and best disposed of the practised reviewers. He is an exclusive, and an advocate for exclusives. Some few persons have betrayed the hospitable, or friendly, or patronizing notice of others, and he would therefore have *all* who are rich and proud become more misanthropic than *some* of them are. His purpose is the exclusion of all but equals in wealth, rank, and circumstance, from all association with those who possess these requisites of power. If men, and especially they who deserve the reputation of being literary men, were as independent in disposition as they ought to be there could be no such exclusions as he recommends, If men who have particular acquirements, had the independence which all admire and few possess, they would neither wish to have, nor would they accept invitations which necessarily fail to put them on an equality with those who receive them as humble friends. They who become associates as humble friends, to whom an

[1] Original: 'for thoughts and deeds, that . . .'
[2] Original: 'the ear of that grand impersonation, "the Reading Public."'
[3] Original: 'of the general belief.'

Introduction

invitation is a favour, and a degradation, have little cause of complaint of any treatment which may result from their meanness, but they who make a bad use of what they receive and consider a favour, and then betray the small portion of confidence reposed in them, deserve something more of castigation than the censure of the reviewer.

It is hardly necessary except to prevent disappointment to say, that he who expects to receive gratification from any thing in these memoirs approximating to the conduct which has been reprobated will not be gratified with any such details. The principal source of attraction is therefore cut off, and all such persons may close the volume here.

OBJECTIONS ANTICIPATED AND EXAMINED[1]

Should these memoirs be published, many will object to parts of them, and that too on various grounds. Some will think that I ought to have concealed the frailties and vices of my father. Some that I ought to have suppressed many particulars relating to myself and especially those of my youth. Others will condemn my speculative opinions, and some will be offended at my political opinions. To these I reply in anticipation, that if there be really any use in writing these memoirs, if the knowledge they may perchance convey of the change of manners and the increase of intellect be worth knowing, they can alone be made so by telling the truth however agreeable or disagreeable it may be. I have risen by my own efforts to a comparative state of affluence and importance, have obtained, and secured the respect and confidence of a considerable number of persons of whom any one may justly be proud, have among my friends some of the best and wisest men in the world, and could if I chose increase the number, among men of rank, literature and science to a great extent. This I do not however think advisable, as it would compel me to incur expenses incompatible with my habits and inimical to the welfare of my large family. I should also lose more information in the time it would destroy, than I should gain in other ways. I may say that I have attained my present position *solely*, by my own exertions, excepting the wholesome operation of one mans intellect upon another mans intellect. My boyhood was like that of most boys in my rank of life, very different indeed from what it is now among boys of the same class, but from the moment I resolved to be married and that it will be seen was at a very early age, I left off every thing which could in any way tend to impede my future progress in the world, or was in any way calculated to bring deserved reproach upon me or was likely to compel

[1] This section is dated 'Nov. 8. 1823.'

The Autobiography of Francis Place

me on a close review of my conduct to reproach myself with injustice towards any one, or with having on any occasion acted meanly.

In my dealings when in business I never practiced the usual and allowed *tricks* of a tradesman to gain money. Had I pursued the same route, and adopted the same means which most tradesmen do, and made money the sole object of my desires, I might have obtained to a very considerable portion of wealth, but then I should have been a mere lover of money for its own sake, a mean contemptible sot or curmudgeon, should in all probability have had a hateful family, narrow minded, pitiful and worthless, as even now[1] but too many of those who are very much improved as compared with what they would have been some forty years ago were. These results I foresaw, long before I possessed the means of getting into business on my own account, and my resolution was taken to avoid as much as possible, every thing, the tendency of which was at all likely to debase me, or to disqualify me for the acquirements and enjoyments I contemplated. I expected to succeed in money making and was desirous to possess all the advantages which the accumulation of money puts a man into a condition to command. As it is I have reason to be satisfied, with myself, my excellent wife, and all those of my children who have grown up; they are well informed, honest, candid and industrious. If then such desirable results can be made to flow from such sources as I shall open to view, the example can scarcely fail of being useful it will prove how from very inauspicious beginnings, by a little honesty, a little practical good sense, a due portion of self respect, and continued exertion a great deal of what is most desirable may be accomplished. How could I set forth this example if I were to suppress the adverse circumstances which in my case, as in that of others appear to forbid any such progress being made, how hold out the example to others and encourage them steadily to pursue the right course, but by stating facts, these facts being such as but few youths of the present day of the same class as myself have to contend with to the same extent, yet such as are to a considerable extent applicable to those who are a grade below them. How but for the relation of adverse circumstances and their influence on my early life could I satisfy those who may be in a condition to profit by my example that the course before them is much less difficult than mine was, and consequently that in no case ought any one to despair of being able to improve his condition. How could I shew this but by relating the whole circumstances of my youth, how take from them all excuse for not doing well, by shewing how it is possible to do well under almost any circumstances, and thus leave them to shame if

[1] Marginal note: '1823.'

Introduction

they neglect to exert themselves to the utmost unweariedly. Besides these there are other weighty objections to concealment. I have an antipathy to all biography whether from a mans own pen or from that of any one else in which his real or supposed merits are alone set forth, while his frailties and evil propensities are omitted or set forth in such a way as scarcly to be discerned, or so qualified as almost, if indeed they have not the actual appearance of merits. All such Biography has the two bad qualities of fraud and evil example, they hold out as patterns for imitation; much which the reader whom they ought to benefit, is conscious cannot apply to him and can therefore have no influence on him as good examples.

In writing Biography the whole truth should be told, in relation to a mans actions. If it be not advisable to do this nothing should be written. I feel no pleasure in relating many things which I do not consider myself at liberty to suppress. Whatever had any influence on my character, so far as I can trace it, whatever tended to direct me in one channel rather than in another, ought to be noticed and will be noticed.

With respect to my opinions on speculative subjects, wise men will acknowledge, that they are not matters of choice and consequently neither deserving of praise nor censure, and that such as mine are, could not be formed without much enquiry, much discussion and much serious thinking, much indeed of pains taking in many ways, much as men in all such cases as mine would reluctantly adopt as opinions at variance with those entertained by the generality as it appeared to me of deep thinking men. If my opinions on speculative subjects should cause others to think on such subjects and to enquire more particularly than they would otherwise have done, they cannot but be useful, whatever may be the conclusion any such thinker may arrive at, since to think and to enquire, to obtain the strength and expansion of intellect necessary for comparing, analysing and deciding on such questions is undoubtedly attaining the means of being highly useful not only to individuals but to the whole human race.

My political opinions were and are as comprehensive as the views I have been able to take could make them. They never were narrow views, never those of party, always intended to benefit mankind, and they will I have no doubt have justice done to them. I am contented that they should be decided on by experience hereafter.

But says some body, why talk thus, why give yourself this egotistical importance? Really I want no more importance in this, or in any other respect than I merit, and I know that hitherto I have possessed quite as much, if not indeed more importance than I have merited. I am not one of those who think that men obtain less consideration than they are honestly intitled to receive. I am satisfied that almost every man who has any really good parts about him, any qualities which are deserving the respect and esteem of other men almost always obtains esteem and is treated with consideration as far as he is known either personally or by reputation much above his actual merits.

These are all the explanations which to me seem necessary to be made, and it is better they should be made by me now, than that they should be left to be made by my friends here after, who would probably make them in the way of apology, whilst to me, no apology seems to be at all necessary.

The circumstances which it will be seen I have mentioned relative to the ignorance, the immorality, the grossness, the obscenity the drunkenness, the dirtiness, and depravity of the middling and even of a large portion of the better sort of tradesmen, the artizans, and the journeymen tradesmen of London in the days of my youth, may excite a suspicion that the picture I have drawn is a caricature, the parts of which are out of keeping and have no symmetry as a whole. It may be objected, that if the people really were as dissolute as I have described them, that I am bound to ascertan the causes which have produced the changes. This is a matter of great importance. It has not been wholly neglected, many are the publications which contain accounts of proceedings of individuals and societies the objects of which were improvement in right thinking and better habits of acting among the middle and working classes. I have collected many particulars which I intend to place under the heads of Manners and Morals as evidence of the former and present state of the people and proofs that I have not exaggerated the facts.*
Some of the good producing causes are a better regulated Police, and a better description of Police Magistrates. The extension of the Cotton Manufacture which has done all but wonders in respect to the cleanliness and healthiness of women. The rapid increase of wealth and its more

---

* They will come under the following sub-heads. viz
  1. Places of Public Entertainment and Amusement
  2. Grossness
  3. Songs
  4. Drunkenness
  5. Sports and Pastimes – Holidays – Fairs
  6. Crimes and Punishments
  7. Police – Trading Justices
  8. Cleanliness – Dirtiness – Persons, Houses
  9. Decency, Indecency
  10. Dress
  11. Books – School Books – Childrens Books – Obscene Books
  12.
  13.
  14.

Introduction

general diffusion, subsequent to the Revolutionary War with the North American Colonies and their wonderful and perpetual increasing prosperity. The French Revolution which broke up many old absurd notions, and tended greatly to dissipate the pernicious reverence for men of title and estate without regard to personal knowledge or personal worth. The stimulus it gave to serious thoughts on Government, and the desire for information in every possible direction. The promotion of Political Societies, which gave rise to reading clubs, the independent notions these encouraged, and the consequent reformation of manners. The introduction of sunday schools, and the invaluable mode of teaching employed by Joseph Lancaster, exquisitely adapted for the actually poor. The introduction and establishment of schools on the plan of Dr Bell, and the miscalled National Schools, little as they teach.[1] The desire which the general movement produced in all below the very rich to give their children a much better education than they had themselves received, and the consequent elevation all these matters have produced on the manners and morals of the whole community.

Examples will be adduced to prove that the classes of persons more particularly noticed were as I have represented them. Many are the elderly men, and some few women with whom I have of late compared notes who confirm my account in every particular in respect to the state of society, so far as they were acquainted with it at the time I was a youth. If it be objected that my account extends to the Metropolis only and that the people in other places are not changed, but are just what they were half a century ago, as some have contended, I shall reply that I am not aware of many existing documents to which reference can be made to prove the contrary still the field is not wholly barren and it will be found upon enquiry that the people of the Metropolis have not as indeed it was impossible they should be the only portion of the community who have made advances in knowledge and moral conduct.

The manners of the people, have seldom been attended to by writers of any repute, excepting now and then on extraordinary occasions and those generally when they were mischievously disposed, and when something to their discredit could be alleged against them. What is known of them can be gleaned only from a few passing incidents. But I have no

---

[1] Lancaster and Andrew Bell had devised methods of teaching by which large numbers of children could be taught cheaply, the older ones monitoring and drilling the younger ones, all of them in a single large room with a teacher overseeing the group. The lessons were based on items familiar to poor children: an elementary lesson dealt with a spade, its use, its parts, the materials from which the parts are made, the sources of these materials. Place was an early supporter of Lancaster and belonged to Lancastrian associations organized to spread this mode of teaching. The 'National Schools' were Lancastrian off-shoots controlled by the established church; they gave much attention to teaching the bible.

The Autobiography of Francis Place

doubt at all, that in manners, morals, dress, information there have been as many improvements in the country as there have been in London.

There is now 1823 in the employment of my son, a very respectable man as his foreman who has been well known to me for upwards of 30 years, and was for several years employed as my foreman.* Upwards of 40 years ago he came from Chester towards London with what clothes he had except those he wore at his back in a bundle as was the custom with tradesmen "on the tramp" seeking work. In many places he was set upon by men, women and children and hooted through their villages merely because he was a stranger. At one place in Cheshire and at two other places in Lancashire he was pelted with stones, and called an "outcomeling." Similar cases have been related to me by other men when travelling seeking work. Mr Moritz† in his travels through several parts of England in 1782. relates some curious facts which when now compared with the conduct of those then barbarous people, shew an immense improvement.

I can remember the time when to be able to read and to indulge in reading, would if known to a master tradesman, have been so serious an objection to a journeyman, that he would scarcely have expected to obtain employment. It was a serious objection to me, that I knew too much, and had I continued in the condition of a journeyman I should have felt the inconvenience very seriously.

Mr Adams the father of my eldest daughters husband came to London when a very young man to work as a journeyman currier he was respectably dressed and this prevented him obtaining employment One Wycott, then the principal currier in London, told him to "go and get rid of his mothers wool and then perhaps he might employ him," meaning his decent cloaths, Mr Adams says that at the time to which he alludes and for many years afterwards a journeyman currier was never expected to be seen, but in his working jacket.

Mr Adams has long been a principal master currier in London.

* Mr William Keasbury [Kingsbury].
† *Travels chiefly on foot through several parts of England in 1782, described in a letters to a friend.* by Charles P. Moritz.
Translated from the German by a Lady 1795 – 12 mo 3/6
Reprinted in Pinkerton's *Collection of Voyages and Travels* [vol. II, 1808]. See *Quarterly Review*, vol. xv [1816], pp. 542–4.

CHAPTER 1[1]

Lineage

I have no Lineage that I can trace beyond a generation or two. I have heard my Mother say that my Paternal grandfather was a native of Bury St Edmonds where he married. I have heard her say also that my father was born in Shoreditch, whence his father and mother returned to Bury while he was an infant. My grandfather was I conclude a labouring man and died, as I suppose whilst my father was a child.

I have heard my father say, he was born in 1717 and was bound apprentice to a Baker at Bury when about twelve years of age. How he had been occupied 'till he was bound apprentice I never heard, he seems as far as school teaching went to have been wholly neglected, which was not at that time a reproach to any body under the degree of a gentleman. He could sign his name, but could not write a letter of business, and never, I conclude, had read a book of any kind during his life.

His mother whom I have heard him describe as an old woman living in a cottage, or some such dwelling and alone; died as I conjecture when he was about thirty years of age. He had one brother who was older than himself, of whose history all I ever heard was, that he served as a common sailor on board a man of war, that he came home from sea on one occasion before I was born and in a drunken frolic with my father, broke in the windows of the bar of a public house somewhere about Drury Lane, with a cudgel, and then ran off to sea again leaving my father to pay for the damage he had done.

This story was told by my father about the year 1786 when a person came to his house in Arundel Street in the Strand, and told him, that his brother was then living in Long Island in North America, that he had a family of children and had amassed a considerable sum of money.

That he had settled in this Island soon after the peace of 1763 and dealt largely in Cattle during the American War of Independence. This is all I ever heard, either before or since of this relative. On one occasion I heard my father say that all his relatives, save one, were beggars, meaning poor people, and that one, kept an Inn I suppose at or near Bury St. Edmonds, that he died possessed of some property, but had cut him off with a shilling. The person alluded was his uncle but whether by his fathers or his mothers side I know not. It does not seem likely that my father could have had any legal claim on his uncle, but it is not unlikely

[1] This chapter is dated 'August 11, 1823.'

The Autobiography of Francis Place

that both the uncle and the nephew entertained the notion as absurd as common noticed by Blackstone (Book II. Ch. 32).

The notion as it seems to have prevailed to a great extent at the time alluded to, was, that the nearest relatives had a claim from consanguinity, of which they could only be deprived by having a small sum bequeathed to them, whence arose the custom of leaving the supposed claimant a shilling, usually expressed by the words, "cutting him off with a shilling."*

On the Maternal side I am almost equally ignorant respecting my ancestors. My mothers grandfather was, she said, a Sawyer, as was her father. It was much more common in their time, than it is now for a sawyer to be an *undertaker*, that is to undertake at a certain price a quantity of work and then to hire men to help him to perform his contract. Such a person was my great grandfather. At the time of his death he kept a public house at some spot near Hyde park corner, at that time at some distance from London. He was it seems set upon by robbers in the fields between Chelsea and the place of his residence, known 'till lately by the name of "Bloody Bridge Fields," and the "Five Fields,"[1] he was dreadfully beaten and cut with a hanger or cutlass. He made shift however to crawl to his own door where he died of his wounds. He was

---

* 'The Romans were also wont to set aside testaments as being *inofficiosa*, deficient in natural duty, if they disinherited or totally passed by (without assigning a true and sufficient reason) *any* of the children of the testator. But if, the child had any legacy, though ever so small, it was a proof that the testator had not lost his memory or his reason which otherwise the law presumed; but was then supposed to have acted thus from some substantial cause. Hence probably has arisen that groundless vulgar error, of the necessity of leaving the heir a shilling or some other express legacy in order to disinherit him effectually.' [William Blackstone, *Commentaries on the Laws of England*, ed. Edward Christian, 12th edn, 1793–5, II, 502–3.]

On this passage Professor Christian observes. 'This I concieve, seldom proceeds from ignorance, but in general is the last effusion of an unforgiving spirit, desirous of leaving an insult upon record, after it has ceased to produce either injury or disappointment.'

That this is so, now there can be no doubt, but it was not so when Blackstone wrote, or at the time when my fathers uncle died, and I can remember when I was a boy its being talked of as law. My father might have supposed, and so might his uncle that it was the law and the uncles conduct might be the result of the notion especially if he had no children of his own, that it was necessary to exclude his nephews by 'cutting them off with a shilling.'

[1] These five fields on which Eaton and Belgrave Squares are now built were until the beginning of this century [the nineteenth] as much frequented by footpads as Hounslow Heath by Highwaymen. I well recollect when scarcely 4 yrs old in 1787 my father being robbed and nearly murdered in these fields . . . this place was so notorious though so near London that few persons ventured to pass through alone, my father was in haste but was called fool hardy for venturing [Samuel Harrison's comment on the manuscript of this memoir, which Place sent him; in Add. MS 35144, f. 405].

1 Lineage

according to my mothers account an old man at the time he was murdered. His son, I never heard of any other child of his, my mothers father lived at Chelsea. This is all I ever heard of him. I can remember his coming to my fathers house in Ship and Anchor Court near Temple Bar, to nurse the children on washing days, he was a very old man and wore a red coat. This was previous to the year 1781, what he then was, or when he died I never heard. Of my mothers mother I do not recollect having heard a word, except that she lived with her husband at Chelsea as did my mother also until her marriage with my father.

MY FATHERS EARLY HISTORY – TRAITS OF CHARACTER

Of my fathers early history I know very little, I have already noticed his being put apprentice to a Baker at Bury St. Edmonds at an early age. I never heard him mention his father, or any other person having any care of him, whence I conclude that he was probably apprenticed by the parish.[1]

Of his ever having been apprenticed at all, I never should have heard but for an anecdote I have heard my mother relate of him, which caused him to run away from his master and come to London. The anecdote is as follows. One day his master who was a sad brute was abusing him and his fellow apprentice as they were cutting up wood for the oven. The place in which they cut the wood was a yard and close by them was a well, the master by the sound of his own voice, by the words he used and by the behaviour of the apprentices became furious and taking the weights with which he weighed the bread threw them at the boys, who picked them up and cast them into the well. Doubly enraged at this, the master took up a billet of wood and threw it at them, it struck my father and hurt him, and he on the impulse of the moment swung the hatchet he had in his hand at his master and cut him across the buttocks. He fled immediately and came on foot to London, another lad probably his fellow apprentice came along with him. They arrived in London all but pennyless and got a cheap bed in Petticoat Lane Whitechapel in which they were so annoyed by vermin that they could not sleep, worn out with travelling and want of rest, in a strange and miserable place unknown and knowing nobody they prowled about in a state of despair. Accident brought my father in contact with the Huntsman of Earl Corn-

[1] Up to the mid-nineteenth century each parish had to provide poor relief for those born in the parish. A common means of disposing of foundlings, illegitimate children, and the children of those on parish relief – Simon Place belonged to this latter group – was to apprentice the child to any master who would have him or even to force a master to take a child as apprentice (M. Dorothy George, *London Life in the Eighteenth Century*, 1965, Ch. 5, 'Parish Children and Poor Apprentices').

The Autobiography of Francis Place

wallis who knew him, and to whom he related his tale, the man found him employment about the stables and Kennels and here he remained two years,[1] and then returned to his business as a journeyman baker. Of his course of life until he married my mother I never heard a syllable excepting an incident which transpired in consequence of some proceedings against him in the Ecclesiastical Court which in his old age greatly contributed to his ruin, as will be related in its proper place.

My father was a very bony muscular man about five feet six or seven inches in height dark complexion and very strong for his height. I have heard my mother say that he has carried two sacks of flour on his back at the same time.[2] He was an elderly man from the earliest recollection I have of him, so he appeared to me, troubled with severe fits of Gout, yet when free from the disorder robust and active. He was a resolute daring straight forward sort of a man, governed almost wholly by his passions and animal sensations both of which were very strong, he was careless of reputation excepting in some particulars in which he seems to have thought he excelled. These were few, mostly relating to sturdiness and dissoluteness. Drinking, Whoring, Gaming, Fishing and Fighting, he was well acquainted with the principal boxers of his day; Slack and Broughton were his companions.[3] Some of these desires and propensities never left him, though most of them became all but extinct with old age. He was always ready in certain cases to advise and to assist others, all who knew him placed the utmost reliance on his word, and as the habits of all ranks then as compared with the habits of each class of men now, were exceedingly dissolute, his conduct was not then obnoxious to the censure of others as such conduct would be now. With all his follies and vices he was much respected. Simon Place was the man to be depended upon in all emergencies good or bad and he was just as likely to enter into a mans concerns on the wrong as on the right side and to work through them with equal perseverance and vigour. It was enough for him that he was asked to assist any one who was in difficulty, or who could not help himself. From these causes according to the common acceptation of the term he had abundance of friends.

[1] Probably at one of the two seats of Earl Cornwallis in Suffolk: Broome, or Culford Hall, near Bury St Edmonds. [2] Marginal note: '5. cwt.'
[3] Jack Broughton (1704–89) was boxing champion of England for ten or fifteen years before 1750, when he lost the title to Jack Slack, a dirty and dishonest fighter. In addition to these men, Simon Place knew other fighters, for his son recorded: 'Mendoza [Daniel Mendoza, boxing champion] mentions the great favour in which Boxing and Boxers was held at this time 1785 and for some years afterwards – and he names some of the eminent Boxers – the persons of most of whom I knew. They were – J. Ward – W. Ward – Humphreys Jackson – still alive. Johnson, Perrins – Big Ben – Hooper the Tinman – Wood – and George the Brewer. Harry Lee – Jim and Tom Belcher. Nov. 9 – 1832' (Add. MS 36625, f. 21v).

1 Lineage

MY MOTHERS EARLY HISTORY — TRAITS OF CHARACTER

All I know on the subject of my mothers early history has been related. She was a handsome woman about 5 feet 3 or 4 inches high, rather dark complexioned, straight, well made, her face was oval and her features regular. I thought her very handsome and I have heard persons who had known her for many years speak of her as a remarkably handsome woman. She was one of the best women that ever existed. Clean, neat, kind cheerful, good tempered, warm hearted and always ready to do services to every body, whom it seemed to be possible for her to serve. She was much respected by all who knew her, and greatly beloved by those who knew her best.

At what period my father and mother were married or under what circumstances they became acquainted, I am utterly ignorant. I have often heard her say that "her first Hannah was born on the same day as the Prince of Wales, that is on the 12 August 1762 and that my father was thirteen years older than she was. If he was born in 1717 he must have been 45 years of age or thereabouts and she about 33 years of age at the time this child was born. This was not I think her first child. I think I have heard her say she was 25 years of age at the time of her marriage. If she were married at 25 years of age my father must have been about 38 years of age at the time, which was about the years 1755–6

My mothers maiden name was Gray she had a brother who was employed as superintendant at some Salt works at Northwich in Cheshire, he was married and had a family. She had a sister also married to a Mr Pearson who was Clerk or Sexton to the Parish of St Bride in Fleet Street, they had three sons, one of whom went out young to the Island of Antigua where he has ever since resided as manager or in some such office on the estates of the Codrington family, what became of the others I know not.

CHAPTER 2

From the marriage of my father and mother to the time when he took a public house in Arundel Street in the Strand

Father a Journeyman and Master Baker, Ruined by gaming. Leaves my mother in distress. Becomes a Marshalsea Court Office, Keeps a Lock-up House, Practices – Act to prevent vexatious arrests. His business falls off. Takes a public house.

My father at the time of his marriage was I conclude a Journeyman Baker. The earliest account I can remember to have heard of him, was, that he was a Journeyman Baker and worked at Clapham, whence he came home to my mother every saturday night, at her lodgings in the Borough of Southwark, bringing with him a loaf and a parish pudding.* After this he became a master Baker, I believe in the Borough, and had a flourishing business, but his propensity for drinking and gaming ruined him. At one sitting he lost every thing he had in the world, even the furniture of his house and the good will of his business, having done this and executed the requisite assignments of his property, he took himself off without the knowledge of my mother and she was turned into the Street; she took a lodging and maintained herself by needlework, to which she had applied herself during the time my father worked as a journeyman. For several months my mother heard nothing of my father but was at length informed by letter that he had resided for some time at Plymouth, was ill of a fever and not expected to recover. She raised all the money she could and set out for Plymouth. Travelling at that time was a slow process if compared with its present rate by means of Stage Coaches, and before she could reach Plymouth he was convalescent, they staid here some time and then set out for London, and travelled on foot a considerable part of the way. I have heard my mother give an account of their crossing Salisbury Plain a distance of 21 miles on a day in which it rained from morning till night. There was at that time no house on the plain nor any sort of shelter.

On their arrival in London they took lodgings in the Borough again, probably as being better known there than any where else and more likely to procure employment and credit than in a strange place. Here my

---

* a parish pudding is a compound of materials taken from every body's dish and baked in the oven.

2   Parents' married life to June 1780

father had a relapse of his complaint and was a long time before he perfectly recovered. I have heard my mother talk of the extreme distress which this relapse occasioned, and of an incident which greatly assisted to improve their circumstances. As soon as my father was able to walk he went to see some acquaintance of his on the Middlesex side of the river, for the purpose of procuring employment when he should be able to undertake it. On one of these excursions he remained till it was dark and going along some part of St Georges Fields he fell into one of the ditches of which there were then many, & into which the tide flowed. It was a wide deep ditch and close to a bridge or archway under which he swam. An alarm was given and he was with difficulty extricated from his perilous situation, the arch being too small for him to turn in. He was taken to a public house, whence some humane man carried him home in a coach, this person became his friend and rendered him great assistance I never heard his name. He soon recovered his health and worked at his business. Where he lived or what sort of life he led for a long time after this I know not. The next account of his proceedings, is a relation of my mothers; I have heard her tell the tale with much grief as well she might. My Father was settled again in a well accustomed Bakers Shop in Windmill Street in the Parish of St James Westminster and had saved £800 in money This he lost by gaming; and as he had done before, he went on Gambling till he was obliged to sell the Lease and Good will of his house and business, and became destitute. Again he deserted my mother leaving her with a child and some furniture. She was once more brought to great distress. Whither he went, or what he did for a year I never heard, and it is probable he never informed my mother of his exploits whilst absent. I once heard him say that he walked from Belfast to Dublin without spending a shilling for food or lodging, the people all along the road readily supplying him with both. From Dublin he came to Bristol. Here he sold his silver knee buckles, and at Bath his silver shoe buckles and came back to my mother just as if he had returned from a walk, but of course pennyless. Here is another blank in his history which continued to the time of my birth which happened on the third of November 1771 at a house in Vinegar Yard Brydges Street,[1] which forms a broad space and is part of Russell Court.[2] The house in which I was born is opposite the south side of Drury Lane Play House and is numbered [space left for no.].[3] The back of the House forms part of the inclosure of the Burial Ground of St Mary Le Strand. My father must have lived in this house sometime as my elder sister who is nearly two years older than I am was born in it.

[1] Now Catherine Street.   [2] Now part of Tavistock Street.
[3] Place did not insert the number.

The Autobiography of Francis Place

Of the period to which the forgoing narrative relates I have heard my mother speak in great anguish of my fathers conduct as well in relation to her as to his own affairs. He seems to have observed no bounds, but to have indulged his propensities to the utmost whilst his conduct towards her was generally morose and sometimes barbarous.

That such a man should have been able to make his way in the world seems strange, that he should have brought himself to ruin and his family to the most perfect state of Distress and yet have recovered again and again appears to us sober people of the present day almost incredible. But such men as he was, were by no means uncommon in his time. I have related two occasions in which his propensity for gaming produced his ruin, but I am almost certain there were three such occasions. That he did recover again and again is certain, and this proves, that in some respects his knowledge was considerable, that he possessed much resolution and unextinguishable confidence in his own powers and resources, but at the same time a want of sufficient judgment to determine him to continue in the right course. When he took the house in Russell Court he must have been as he was to the latter end of the year 1780 a Marshalsea Court, or Palace Court Officer.* The house was what was called a "lock-up house," or a "spunging house," it was a private house and had Iron bars to most of the windows to prevent the escape of persons whom he was employed to arrest and detain or who were brought to his house by other officers for safe custody.[1]

* Marshalsea Court or Palace Court see papers – Title Marshalsea Court [Add. MS 35147].
    Marshalsea Court. No business has been done in this Court for a great number of years, but it is regularly opened and adjourned with the Palace Court. A suit in this court must be between persons who are of the Kings Household.
    Palace Court. This is a court of the Record, held every friday in Scotland Yard. The Judges, Counsel, Attorneys and Officers are the same as in the Marshalsea Court.   *Poor Mans Almanack.* 1832.

[1] When a person was arrested for debt, if he seemed to have any means he was taken to a spunging house rather than to Marshalsea, the debtors' prison. At the spunging house he was charged exorbitant prices for everything. If he demanded to be transferred to the more squalid living conditions at Marshalsea, he was charged a fee for the transfer, and another for admission to prison (Sir Walter Besant, *London in the Eighteenth Century*, 1903, pp. 574–5).
    As early as 1775 Jonas Hanway complained about the extortions practised at spunging houses: 'Under the authority of the sheriff's office, many a prisoner taken into custody, is conveyed to a *spunging-house*; not originally intended to suck up the blood of the unhappy; though by a horrible abuse of mercy, the prisoner is even robbed by extortion, and the temptation afforded of purchasing humane treatment, by plunging so much deeper in debt. Of this I have lately seen an instance, in the person of a young woman, whose health could not bear a pint of ale, charged with eight shillings a day in strong liquor: – So much was actually charged to her, and she was *detained* till the spunging house bill, amounting, *in three days time,* to half as much as the debt, was also paid!' (*The Defects of Police*, 1775, p. xiv). These

2 Parents' married life to June 1780

From the time my father became a Marshalsea Court Officer he seems to have been somewhat less irregular in his conduct and more attentive to his family. Soon after I was born my father removed to a house in Ship and Anchor Court in the Strand (now Picket Street) near Temple Bar. In this house in the month of August 1773 my brother named George was born and in June 1775 Ann my youngest sister and the last child my mother had was born. The Court in which the house was situate had, and has, a narrow entrance like a door way between two houses now numbered [space left for no.] and [space left for no.] it was a square area of which the backs of two houses in the Strand formed the southern side, a high wall the eastern side, the northern side was a public House called the Ship and Anchor, and on the western side was the house kept by my father. It was a good but not a large house, having windows next the court only The windows of the Kitchen, the Parlour and the first floor were secured with strong Iron bars and on the stair-case leading from the street door to the first floor was a strong door. This door as well as the street door was secured by a large lock and a peculiar sort of massive key as security against the escape of prisoners. The house was light and particularly neat and clean,

[Here Place added a lengthy footnote:
REMINESCENCAS [sic]
September. 5. 1840. Went this morning to the house in Ship and Anchor Court. On the parlour window of the house formerly kept by my father was a bill, "a first second and third floor to be let unfurnished". Saw a dirty Ruffianly looking man in the Parlour in which there wa[s] an old Mangle and great appearance of miserable poverty.

I soon got into conversation with the man. I told him that the house was formerly kept by my father that I lived in it when quite a child, that a sister and brother of mine were both born in it and that we removed from it in 1780. This made us friendly which at first the man did not seem disposed to be. He remarked that this was sixty years ago and that I therefore must have been quite a child at the time. I said I very was very nearly nine years of age at which or rather at my being 69 years of age he wondered and this made us entirely friends. He said I could not know much about a house I had left so long and so young unless I had been in it many times since. I said I had never been in it since I left it but was certain I could describe the whole of it accurately. I described the Kitchen the Parlour the staircase with a well by the side of it next the wall, the shape of the room on the first and second floor and the two Garretts – Aye said the man it is so but you have made one mistake there is only one garret. Then said I it has been made into one since my time, they were then distinct and used as bed rooms, the stair went up to the door of one

---

extortions continued into the nineteenth century; Thackeray describes one of these spunging-houses in chapter 53 of *Vanity Fair*.

room and there were steps on one side, the left hand side to the other room. No said he there is only one door and there could never have been any steps on the left hand side. I asked leave to go up the staircase and up I went. I found the house exactly as I had described it. at the top of the garrett stairs were the marks where the 3 steps had formerly been and there was the door fastened up permanently. On coming down again, I saw a woman who owned the Mangle. She said *she* had kept the house 18 years but had never noticed that the garretts had been two nor that there were any marks of steps which had been taken away. But it had before her time been a printing office and most likely the whole had been made into one room by the Printers.

Every part of the house was precisely what I expected it was, but the rooms were very much smalled than I expected to find them, and the whole house was in a sad state of dilapidation.

Went into the Tobacconists shop at the corner of the Court. No. [space left for no.] still kept by a Mr Skinner. Asked a respectable man behind the counter, if he could tell me how long the family had lived in that house, he motioned me towards a small desk, I went to it, sitting at it was a rather small elderly looking very respectable man he had heard my question, he looked cautiously and I said to him I was acquainted with the family upwards of 60 years ago when I was a child and played with the children in a room at the top of the old gable ended house long since pulled down. The room we played in was called "Pidgeons room".

Right said he you are quite correct the children used to play in Pidgeons room

I. Pray sir is your name Skinner.

He. Yes.

I. Mr William Skinner.

He. No my brother William who was the eldest died about 18 years ago.

I. Remember him very well his younger brother, whom I conclude you are, and his sister.

He looked at me very attentively and said are you Mr Place.

I. Yes

He. Well I thought so. I can well remember playing with your family it must have been your brother and sisters. I remember seeing your father several times after he left the neighbourhood. I thought you must be his son.

This seemed very strange to me and I asked him what had led him to the conclusion.

He said the conversation we had had, he had seen my father not long before he died and the character of the family was strongly marked in me.

We were now friends again from old associations he said he was 66 years of age. The family had lived in the old and in the new house nearly if not fully 90 years and he was only one of the second generation, his father having commenced the business about 90 years ago.]

It [the house] was one of the best if not indeed the very best of the sort, and was therefore seldom without an inmate or two of the most respectable or wealthier class of prisoners, if the word wealthy can be

2 Parents' married life to June 1780

applied to persons confined for sums seldom amounting to fifty pounds, they were however such as could best afford to pay for comfortable accomodation, and were willing to pay, in preference to being lodged in the Marshalsea Court Prison.

I have a distinct recollection of a custom which at that time prevailed of the bailiff taking the word of his prisoner or a bond as it was called of the prisoner, or of the prisoner and a friend to appear at the house on a certain day or to pay the debt and costs on or before the day named, and this was often acceeded to by the creditor as the likeliest means of procuring payment, it was generally however without the consent or knowledge of the creditor, for the sake of the fees as they were called. A warrant or capias was often transferred from one Bailiff to another, when one had less confidence or was less able to take the risk of an escape than another, Certain it is that by means of these accomodations my father notwithstanding he was an extravagant man accumulated money. It was the custom at this time as it had long been for almost every man who had the means to spend his evenings at some public house or tavern, or other place of public entertainment. Almost every public house had a parlour, as some still have, for the better sort of customers. In this room which was often large and well lighted with tallow candles the company drank and smoked and spent their evenings – many constantly supped in these rooms either alone or in parties of from two to as many as a table would hold which was generally six, in some places eight. There were several houses of this sort near Temple Bar, two of which were famous in their time, namely, the Cock in Fleet Street, and the Three Herrings in Bell Yard Temple Bar. The latter named house had a large detached room in which was nightly assembled the House of Lords. It was frequented principally by the more dissolute sort of barristers, attorneys, and tradesmen of what were then called the better sort, nobody however who wore a decent coat was excluded. The regular frequenters were the Lords, they who had not undergone the ceremony of taking a seat were the strangers whom it was pretended were admitted from courtesy. The Lords took on solemn occasions their seats according to rank, each bearing a title as nearly as was possible from the place he came from. My father being a Norfolk man was Duke of Norfolk and Earl Marshall which gave him precedence as the first peer next to the Kings family and intitled him to take the chair in the absence of the Lord Chancellor who was always a barrister. In this room he spent most of his evenings and some of his nights. The conduct of all who frequented these places was more or less dissolute the largest number by far were what would now be called extremely dissolute in almost every respect. My father, at this time, kept a horse and chaise in which he not only went about his particular

The Autobiography of Francis Place

business, but in which he used also to visit more than one woman who lived at a distance from London, sometimes staying out all night, without at all intimating any such intention to my mother. He used to go occasionally to Shepperton for two or three days or a week at a time angling at which he was expert, on some of these expeditions he used to take me with him in his chaise.[1]

When quite a child I was put to nurse or rather under the care of a respectable labourer and his wife who had a cottage at Wimbledon, this was I believe after I had recovered from a fever, and is the only case I can remember of any indication of my ever having been ill, excepting the usual complaints of children, and afterwards, of occasional headaches. I have an indistinct recollection of the place, and a clear recollection of some circumstances whilst I was there and these are among the earliest of my recollections I have of being in existence. My Father who generally did his business for himself and left nothing undone in any matter which he once took in hand used to walk to Wimbledon to see how I was treated and that he might not be deceived by false appearances, he used to make his appearance when my nurse was just rising in the morning or at her dinner time or on a very rainy day. It was never known when he would come, and this uncertainty he looked upon as the surest guarantee for my being well attended to. This must have been before he kept a horse and chaise as I often heard of his walking but never of his riding to Wimbledon

It was his [custom], as it was that of a vast many others who were housekeepers, well doing persons, and persons in business who ought from the quantity of business they did; to save money; to go to some public garden on a sunday afternoon, to drink tea smoke and indulge themselves with liquor, My fathers principal place of visit was Bagnigge Wells, then standing in the fields. To this and other places in fine weather he generally took my mother and all the children.[2] Of these places of

[1] Place's father went often enough to Shepperton and spent enough money to be remembered there fifty years later (cf. chapter 14 no. 7). These angling expeditions, the horse and chaise, the gold-trimmed coat, the nightly attendance at the 'House of Lords,' the intimacy with Sir John Fielding suggest that the Places lived on an affluent scale in the 1770s.

[2] Bagnigge Wells, located at what is now the west side of King's Cross Road, contained Nell Gwyn's house and gardens, through which ran the River Fleet, its banks decorated with willows, elder bushes, docks and rustic bushes. Other attractions were the arbors surrounding the gardens, a cottage with a grotto, a bowling green and a skittle alley (Warwick Wroth, *The London Pleasure Gardens of the Eighteenth Century*, 1896, pp. 56ff). Samuel Harrison added to Place's memoir:
'From 1790 to 1800 I can recollect well the concourse of men women & children on Sunday evenings at Bagnigge wells – White Conduit house – the Boot & Bowling green – Copenhagen house & Hornsey Wood house – many others in the outskirts – At the two former I well remember the difficulty in finding seats & waiters to bring

2 Parents' married life to June 1780

amusement and dissipation I shall speak hereafter. Another of my fathers customary amusements was to take some of the children and when he had no person in custody or some one who staid voluntarily (which was no uncommon circumstance) to take all the children and my mother on an excursion to the Cock on Clapham Common, or to Hornsey Wood, or to Wimbleton common or to a Public House at Winchmore Hill.[1] The smaller children were dragged along in a childs chaise. A bottle of wine was always put into the seat of the chaise as was also a convex glass now in my possession with which to light his pipe, sometimes provision for the day was also taken. These journeys were to me excessively fatiguing, as every one who was able was compelled to share the labour of dragging the chaise. Yet I was always fond of these excursions. Another of my fathers customs was to walk the elder children as far as he judged their strength would enable them to go, and he often pushed these trials to the utmost. My feet have been sadly blistered in these walks, and I have been so exhausted as scarcly to be able to reach home, yet I never dared to complain, any symptom of uneasiness even was sure to bring down punishment. My mother was made uneasy and sometimes unhappy at seeing us thus worn out with fatigue, but she never ventured to speak to my father on this any more than on many other parts of his conduct, scarcly indeed did she venture to allude to them in any way, all such observations and remarks were by him treated as offences, which he resented and punished to the utmost extent of his power by all sorts of annoyances and by absenting himself from home for two or three days and nights.

At the age of four years I was sent to school to an old woman in Bell

---

the tea cups & hot water – extra gates were opened on Sundays & often Struggling to get in like the theatre – 2 & 3 Shillings or more were spent by each party & not only on Sundays but other evenings when the organ and singing attracted – from what I recollect of the class of persons frequenting these places, I should say that scarcely an individual of the same class but would consider himself degraded at this time in finding himself in any similar places (if any such existed) to say nothing of the females of his family – At the same time I believe nothing immoral or improper was to be found at these tea gardens – the Dog & Duck – Belvidere & many others were I believe very bad but they were known to be so . . .' (Add. MS 35144, f. 418).

[1] In his six-volume collection of observations and information about manners and morals, Place included two copies of a newspaper article (which he dated July 1810) on Hornsey Wood. Place underlined that portion stating that this was the first public house in metropolitan London, or perhaps in England, for tea-drinking. On the same page, Place pasted another unidentified newspaper cutting, this one repeating statistics about the frequenters of tea-gardens in 1789. Of the 200,000 persons thought to frequent tea houses on a Sunday, the writer of 1789 'calculates the returning situation of these persons as follows: – Sober, 50,000; in high glee, 90,000; drunkish, 30,000; dead drunk, 5,000; – Total, 200,000' (Add. MS 27832, f. 255).

The Autobiography of Francis Place

Yard Temple Bar and with her I remained until I was sent to another school in Wine Office Court Fleet Street when I was about seven years of age. At this old womans school it can scarcly be said that I learned any thing, all I knew, when I left it, was how to read in Dilworths Spelling Book and that too badly.

In 1779 was passed the Act 19 Geo III cap 70 intiluted "An act for extending the provisions of an act made in the twelfth year of King George the first, intiluted an Act to prevent frivolous and vexatious arrests and for other purposes."

The Preamble recites the act 12. Geo. I. cap 29. S. 1.* "No person shall be held to special bail (detained in custody) upon any process issuing out of any superior court when the cause of action shall not amount to the sum of Ten Pounds and upwards nor out of any inferior court where the cause of action shall not amount to the sum of forty shillings or upwards," and then it goes on thus. "And whereas the power of arrest and imprisonment on mesne process issuing out of such inferior court, where the cause of action does not amount to ten pounds, is found by experience to be attended with much oppression to great numbers of his majesty's subjects; for remedy whereof – it is enacted from and after the first day of July 1779 no person shall be arrested or held to special bail upon any

* But while in other countries imprisonment for debt was only tolerated as a remedy against other process, not only did the law of England provide no such preliminary proceedings to its exercise, but in discontinuing its ancient habit of requiring on the part of the plaintiff pledges to prosecute, it abandoned all security for the justness of a demand, and even down to the first year of the reign of Geo I. a party might at the caprice of a solitary creditor be immured within the walls of a Gaol, 'for any sum of money however trifling, or to any amount however considerable', and that too without even the caution of an oath, and with no other solemnity than the payment of the fees incidental to the issuing of a process The 12 Geo I. cap 29 first injoined an affidavit before the warrant of arrest could be obtained, and restricted the application of that warrant to cases in which the cause of action amounted in the superior courts to 10£ and upwards and in the inferior courts to forty shillings and upwards, and substituted serviceable process only, for all sums below these amounts. That statute being only temporary in its operation, a subsequent act was passed to give it perpetuity. Other enactments affixed the same restrictions upon the proceedings of inferior courts, as were by the former part of that act enjoined on the superior courts, and the 51 Geo III cap 124. extended the restriction to 15£ with an exception in favour of bills of Exchange and promissory notes which were still left under the operation of the former statute – since extended to 20£ *West Review* Vol 9. p. 55. 1828

So biggotted were our legislators to their heriditary panacea that it was not until the year 1759 that the stat Geo II. which originated in the house of Lords called the Lords act, first provided a formal means of escape from that savage maxim of the common law tha[t] a debtor once taken in execution was to be kept "*in salva et arcta custodia* until the satisfaction of his debt.["] *Tidd's Practice.* c. VIII. p. 106 [This note of Place's, including the citations to other works, is taken almost word for word from a review of four books on debtors' laws, a review which appeared in the issue of *Westminster Review* cited by Place.]

2   Parents' married life to June 1780

process issuing out of any inferior court where the cause of action shall not amount to ten Pounds and upwards." This act in one stroke abolished three fourths of the business of a bailiff of the Marshalsea Court. By Stat 21 Jac. 1. c. 23. any suit may be removed from the Marshalsea Court if the Plaintiff by his declaration claimed Five Pounds and upwards. The Marshalsea Court whilst it had the power of arresting the person for forty shillings had a large quantity of business. Arrest was a summary process and however vexatious and expensive in proportion to the sum claimed, the process was, to the person arrested; the plaintiff was generally certain that he should be paid when the debt was under Five Pounds. In fact he never failed to recover when the person arrested had the means of paying the debt and satisfying the exorbitant demands of the bailiff who had him in custody. This was also the case very frequently when the sum did not exceed Ten Pounds, for by the connivance of the bailiff whose interest it was to keep the person arrested out of prison, a man who had not the ready means of payment was allowed to remain in his business until he could muster as much money as was sufficient to pay the debt and satisfy the bailiff for his indulgence. Often too the bailiff was the means of making an arrangement between the debtor and his creditor by compounding the debt, or by a more extensive arrangement between the debtor and all his creditors, this was frequently done by an agreement to pay the debts or a composition for the debts, and a cognovit was signed by the debtor. In many cases the bailiff contrived to have the creditor as well as the debtor for his clients and obtained money on both sides. In these arrangements the attornies of the Court also took part, under the pretense of favouring those who employed them and saving costs, whilst in fact both Plaintiff and Defendant were plundered. By these means the greatest possible sum was obtained from those who sued and those who were sued. Litigation was encouraged for even the smallest sums, and revenge indulged to a very great extent, any man to whom another was indebted in the sum of 40 shillings had the power of annoyance in his hands. He could have him arrested taken to a "spunging house" and kept there until the office was searched to ascertain whether or not there were more writs against, him. A man might therefore be locked up for a whole day though he was ready to pay the debt and costs. If arrested in the afternoon when the office was closed he was kept till noon on the following day, and if he were arrested on the saturday afternoon he might be detained till monday at noon. This was a source of great emolument to the bailiffs who captured a man who could not be absent from his business, and perhaps known to be in custody, in these cases money was paid for the caption and for a sham bail bond, and a complimentary fee to the bailiff for not locking him up. Such fees, as they were called, were taken from the plaintiff to lock a man up and from the debtor for leaving him at large. Debts between five and ten pounds were also compromised in various ways and their removal from the jurisdiction of the court prevented but in all cases the parties were plundered to the greatest extent which could be calculated upon with safety to the Bailiffs and Attorneys.

A person was appointed by the Court to go round to the lock-up houses every other day, to see that persons in custody were not detained more than forty eight hours before they were transferred to the Prison of the Court. Every thing was exceedingly corrupt in the practice of the Court and the object in sending the man round was to prevent the Court and its officers being cheated by the bailiffs of the fees they pocketed on the admission and discharge of a prisoner. In these fees the Knight Marshall, his Deputy the Prothonotary the Gaoler and his Clerk all shared. These fees amounted to a large sum and could only be demanded of those who had entered the prison walls. Hence arose further means of extortion Persons in custody at the Lock up houses were told that they must be taken to prison and this was confirmed by the inspector at his visits. A new bargain was therefore made for the accomodation of the captive who was robbed of such a sum as satisfied the cupidity of the parties concerned. The means of extortion were endless so long as any thing could be got from the debtor who unless he was bailed, or paid the debt and costs, or compromised with his creditors, was seldom allowed to go to Gaol until he had parted with his last shilling. As long indeed as a person in custody had money it was in many cases useless for him to satisfy his detaining creditor in the expectation that he would be released, the Bailiff and the Attorneys instigating his creditors one by one to issue fresh processes as fast as that for which he was in custody was paid. The act put an end to these enormous and scandalous frauds, for when no person could be arrested for less than ten pounds few comparatively would sue in the Marshalsea Court, since every person sued could remove the action into a superior Court and compel the plaintiff to begin *de novo* very few would commence an action which they had any reason to fear would be so removed. Thus was the business of the Marshalsea Court destroyed to a very great extent and more particularly that part of it which related to the Bailiffs whose emoluments arose principally from captions and the consequence to which they led.

Thus circumstanced my father continued his business for about a year from the passing of the act, when he sold his office for what it would fetch, and bought the lease and good-will of a public house in Arundel Street in the Strand.

Of the Marshalsea Court, its Gaol and the manner in which it was

2 Parents' married life to June 1780

conducted, a number of facts and some rather curious circumstances are related in the Appendix.[1]

[1] Apparently Place never composed this appendix. Another volume of the Place papers contains an extensive collection of extracts from books about Marshalsea (Add. MS 35147, fs. 92–197), part of which is headed 'Appendix – NB. These appendices need revising and Arranging' (f. 138). The material following this note was copied out between August and October 1823, when Place was writing the early chapters of the autobiography. Presumably this was the rough matter of the intended appendix.

CHAPTER 3

SEC. 1   FROM THE TIME MY FATHER BECAME A PUBLICAN TO MY BEING BOUND APPRENTICE

My father commenced business as a publican, in a house in Arundel Street in the Strand known by the sign of the Kings Arms; in the year 1780 at midsummer. This circumstance was impressed in my memory by two incidents. The first was the apprehension my father had that his house would be burned by *the* Rioters as Lord George Gordons Mob were called. They Burnt Newgate the Kings Bench – the Fleet – Prisons – several Roman Catholic Chapels and some private houses, and his fear arose from his keeping a lock up house.[1] This was early in the month of June and I remember seeing men go from house to house in Wine Office Court each having an iron bar in his hand, a rail torn from an area, and demanding money. The other is illustrative of my fathers character. I, my sister, who was older than myself and my brother who was younger were sent as usual on a sunday morning to church, but instead of going to church we went to see the ruins of the places burned by the rioters, and whilst we were peeping through the hoard which inclosed the ruins of the Fleet Prison, I felt a ropes end at my back, my father was there. It was his custom to carry in one of his coat pockets a piece of rope nearly as large as a mans little finger turned up at each end and spliced into itself, the sailors called it "a coste,"[2] Beating and that too in excess was with him the all in all in the way of teaching, "a word and a blow but the blow always first." I received a severe beating and can well remember running up stairs in the house in Arundel Street, not daring to come down to dinner nor to shew myself for the rest of the day.

The house my father had taken was a house of rendezvous for sailors. At the time of which I am speaking it was customary for Government to permit the opening of a number of public houses as recieving houses for soldiers and sailors, a press gang made head quarters for the one sort of

[1] The Gordon Riots, the most ferocious riots London has ever experienced, lasted from June 2 to 8, 1780. A crowd of perhaps 100,000 assembled at the instigation of Gordon, president of the Protestant Association, to petition against Parliament's supposed leniency towards Roman Catholicism. The crowd soon became a mob, and besides looting and burning Roman Catholic chapels and private homes they attacked prisons (where some of their number had been locked up). It was 'one of the most dreadful spectacles this country ever beheld . . . every thing served to impress the mind with ideas of universal anarchy and approaching desolation' (*Annual Register*, pp. 261–2).

[2] A colt, 'a short piece of rope with a large knot at one end, kept in the pocket for starting skulkers' (Smyth's *The Sailor's Word Book*, 1897).

3.1 Father a publican (1780) to my apprenticeship (1785)

house, a serjeant and a number of crimps associated at the other sort of house. In these houses the basest of villainies were practiced. In most such houses there was a strong room in which men who had been impressed or crimped were locked up until they could be removed to the Tender off the Tower or to the Savoy Prison.[1]

When a man was pressed very little ceremony was used towards him and very little more if he entered or was decoyed into the house, he was delivered to the press gang put into a boat rowed by six of the press gang and put into the hold of the tender.*[2] They who were crimped were taken before a Justice of the peace, a trading justice and sworn in whether they consented or not.[3] Men who had been pressed or crimped were usually handcuffed like felons and in this condition were marched through the streets, amongst a people who sang *Britons never will be slaves*. Of these trading Justices Sir John Fielding, with whom my father was on terms of intimacy, speaks thus. "A Stranger in London will be liable, if he be in the streets by night, to the insolence of a set of abusive fellows who will provoke his resentment with injurious language and afterwards conduct him before the Magistrate, not hesitating even at wilful perjury, to make a prey of him. These miscreants are in general the bullies of loose women in the neighbourhood. And there have been even sufficient reason for suspecting that the Magistrates themselves have been guilty of injustice to extort money."[4]

> Fieldings [*A Brief*] *description of the Cities of London and Westminster* 1776. p. xxx.

In the debate in the House of Commons on the motion on calling out the military in consequence of a public meeting of the electors of Westminster. Mr Burke asked, "how dared such reptiles, as Middlesex Justices attempt to call out a body of armed men upon a peaceful meeting so respectable.["] He said the justices of Middlesex were gener-

---

[1] As Place indicated here, pressing and crimping were almost identical. His distinction – pressing for the navy and crimping for the army – is unusual.

* An old frigate lying off the Tower.

[2] Pressing for the navy – that is, forcible enrollment of unwilling recruits – had such a long tradition that it was regarded as part of common law (Blackstone, book I, c. 13). As Place indicated, the victim went from freedom to the receiving house, where his captors detained him until they were ready to take him to the tender. There he was confined until transferred to a warship.

[3] For the army, the houses of rendezvous and the connivance of the trading justice were necessitated by the statute 8 Geo. III. c. 7, s. 70, which specified that the 'inlisted' soldier must be brought before the nearest justice, within four days but no sooner than twenty-four hours after his 'inlistment,' to have the magistrate certify that the enlistment was voluntary (*The Justice of the Peace and Parish Officer*, ed. Richard Burn, 11th edn, 1770, IV, 184–5).

[4] Like all of Place's quotations, this one contains some minor omissions and inaccuracies in punctuation and capitalization.

The Autobiography of Francis Place

ally the scum of the earth, carpenters, brick-makers and shoe-makers, some of whom were notoriously men of such infamous characters, that they were unworthy of any employ whatever, and others so ignorant that they could scarcly write their names.

Mr Rigby defended the Middlesex Magistrates, he said that the office was a very troublesome one, that no person of distinction or family, would undertake it and therefore it was right to *give douceurs* to those who would.

Parliamentary History Vol XXI. [1814,] p. 592. May 8. 1780.

The conduct of the trading Justices was such as the people of the present day can form no accurate conception of, and between them, the Crimps and the Press Gangs iniquity to a monstrous extent and in a vast variety of ways was practised.[1] There was one among these Justices who made himself conspicuous for his rogueries, his name was Hyde, he had been a journeyman carpenter, then a thief taker, and then a Justice of the Peace. His shop was in Litchfield street near Newport Market. It was called a "rotation office"[2] and so notorious and so infamous was his conduct that a song was made on it and sung about the streets. The whole of this is a proof of the very low state of the morals and manners of the time.*

---

[1] This corrupt body of magistrates who traded justice for money developed by default in London, particularly in Westminster. Few reputable citizens wanted the office of justice of the peace, for the work was time-consuming, difficult and underpaid. The eighteenth-century magistrate was a combination police officer and judge: he issued warrants for arrest, questioned prisoners, heard cases – and was in danger of catching typhus from gaol prisoners. But, since the magistrate could keep the money he obtained from fees and fines, a good living could be made by an unscrupulous justice. So good was the living that most magistrates bought their jobs and then promoted business (Patrick Pringle, *Hue and Cry*, 1955, Ch. 3, 'Law and Disorder'). In Westminster alone there were over a hundred justices of the peace (Patrick Colquhoun, *A Treatise on the Police of the Metropolis*, 1800, p. 416). Samuel Harrison described one of the venal magistrates from this number: 'From 1791 to 1795 one of these trading Justices lived & kept an office in Hyde Street. Bloomsbury – he was a little meagre old man & called Polly Walker – his office was opposite the day School to which I went during those years – & was well known for cheap warrants & summonses – all the Irish in St Giles resorted here for Justice & whilst the principals disputed before his Worship – the mob of followers fought it out in the Street – Assault Warrants were issued to any who would pay & generally cross warrants – one to each party – the office was crowded all day as well as the avenues – the fights in the Street causing great increase of business – ' (Add. MS 35144, f. 417).

[2] Rotation office, a public office (precursor of the police office) where the duties were shared by at least two magistrates sitting in turn. According to George, *London Life in the Eighteenth Century* (p. 21), the rotation offices were established to curb the activities of the trading justices. If so, Place was wrong in saying that the office of a trading justice was called a rotation office.

* These facts should be remembered by the reader when he comes to read many particulars in other parts of these memoirs which are so greatly at variance with

3.1 Father a publican (1780) to my apprenticeship (1785)

The press gang which frequented the Kings Arms, had as a resident there, a sturdy good looking ruffianly fellow of a sailor named Jack Fletcher, who lodged in the house. A flag staff was erected in front of the house next Arundel Street, the foot of the staff stood on the leads above the Parlour windows and the top reached nearly or quite as high as the parapet wall of the house. To this flag staff which was lashed to the garret windows was attached a large Union Jack, the common sign of a house of rendezvous. When my father was about to take possession of the house he requested the gang to quit it, and told Jack Fletcher to strike his flag and give up the room he occupied, but Jack refused either to remove or to strike his flag. My father then complained to the Admiralty but no attention was paid to his complaint, he then applied to the Magistrates whom he found disposed to take part with Jack Fletcher against him. Seeing no chance of redress in these ways he watched his opportunity till he saw Jack in the street. He called to him from one of the garrett windows, and on Jack looking up he let go the lashings and down went the flag and staff across the street. Jack was now refused admittance up stairs, and on his attempting to force his way up he was thrust into the street. How the matter was settled I know not, but Jack and my father became friends, though he was not permitted to lodge in the house, and the Press Gang was removed to the Watermans Arms in the same Street.

My father had accumulated some money and was in good credit. He paid for the lease, good will, and fixtures, and he put the house in good condition, made everything new in the Tap Room, and refitted the parlour. This was a square room, the door was in the middle of one of the sides and the fire-place in the middle of another side. The benches were affixed to the sides They were covered with leather and stuffed, there were as many mahogany tables as were necessary in front of the benches. A grate of a particular construction was made and the jambs of the chimney were cut away that the heat from the fire might not be obstructed. In cold weather the room was thoroughly heated and no one was permitted to stand before the fire, or in the vacant space in the middle of the room, by this arrangement the company sat face to face and each one could see every other one. It was a very superior public house parlour for the time when it was thus fitted up. This parlour was filled every evening with the neighbours many of whom supped in it. My father attended to this room himself, his seat which was directly opposite the door was always reserved for him.

---

present customs and manners as almost to seem incredible and which could not have existed in any but the very low moral state of society here alluded to.

The Autobiography of Francis Place

Besides this parlour there was a club room over it on the first floor and a second club room on the same floor. In the largest of the two rooms was held a punch club on every monday evening and another on every friday evening. They commenced at eight o clock and terminated when all the members were drunk which usually happened from twelve o clock at night to two in the morning. The members of these clubs paid a shilling on each club night whether present or absent. There were about thirty members in each of these clubs, some persons belonged to both clubs, and as my father was a famous maker of punch, some of the members came from a considerable distance. There were also two lottery clubs one on the tuesday the other on the saturday evening, each member of these clubs paid a sum weekly towards purchasing lottery tickets and shares and sixpence for liquor, which was always spent by those who attended the Club meetings. There was also in the smaller club room a company of cutter lads but these were soon dismissed, they assembled on wednesday evenings and sunday mornings, and occasionally at other times from a fortnight before Easter to the beginning of october, which was the rowing reason.[1]

When my father commenced public house keeping it was the custom for Brewers to bring the beer in barrels of thirty six gallons and start the beer into butts in the publicans cellar. A very large strong tub capable of holding about six barrels was placed at the opening of the cellar, strong peices of wood with brass rollers in them were fixed across the top of the tub on which two barrels at a time could be placed, each barrel when thus placed had the bung taken out and was then turned round so that the bung hole was underneath and the beer ran out into the large tub whence it was pumped or was allowed to run through a leather hose into the butts, publicans used to have as many butts as their cellars would hold. My fathers cellars occupied the whole of the basement and there was also a large vault along one front of the house and half of another of the three fronts and in this vault the butts stood up on their ends close together, the intention was to have as large a stock as possible that the beer might acquire age before it was drawn. Besides these cellars the brewers used to hire cellars in various parts of the town, which were appropriated to particular publicans but the Brewers always kept the keys. My father said that they used to cheat the publicans by sending them new beer and supplying others with the old beer which they ought to have had. He therefore bargained with the brewers to have

[1] Cutter lads were clubs of apprentices who raced their rowing boats on the Thames. A few years later Place became a member of a cutter club. From his description of the behaviour of these groups of apprentices, it is not surprising that Simon Place ousted them from his public house.

3.1 Father a publican (1780) to my apprenticeship (1785)

the keys of two very large cellars at as convenient distances as they could be procured, and he gave a bond with securities for the beer started into these cellars, my father on account of the quantity of beer he had in these cellars and the long time he kept it paid the rent of the cellars which was unusual. My father made it a rule never to draw any beer which had not been in one of his cellars at least twelve months, and the strongest sort called "Brown Stout" was never drawn until it had been at the least twenty months in his cellar, some of the beer was more than two years old before it was drawn, and the stout was frequently three years old. The beer was as usual paid for as it was drawn monthly. There are no publicans store cellars now the beer is kept by the brewers in large vats and butts and served to the publican as he needs it, having perhaps a months supply at a time.

The reputation of my fathers stout was so great that it was sent for from considerable distances.

It must be evident, that in a low rented house, with the business which has been described my father could not fail to make money, his modes of wasting it however prevented him saving any considerable sum, and a circumstance to be mentioned presently occasioned his ruin.

The Kitchen in Ship and Anchor Court was always used to dine in, as was the Tap Room in Arundel Street Against a post in the Kitchen, in Ship and Anchor Court, which seperated the windows hung a clock, and at twelve to a minute the dinner was on a large oak table beneath the Clock. The table had a flap on the front which when raised made it semi-circular. At the front of this table sat my father with a carving knife made purposely for him, he dextrously carved the meat, cutting off as much as he thought would be eaten, my mother served it round, and fifteen minutes by the clock was allowed for eating, and then the table was cleared. The servant maid, the only servant kept, sat at the table with the family. Afterwards when he kept a public house the time of dining was limited to ten minutes, the hour of dining a quarter past one, this time was selected as most convenient on account of a number of working men who dined at twelve o clock and remained till one, and as few persons who were not working men dined, till two o clock, there was an interval when very little business was done. There were three large tables in the taproom with high partitions between them so as to make each of them to some extent private. The family always dined in the centre box. Before we sat down to dinner a number of Pots and Pints of Beer and quarterns and glasses of Gin were placed in view of the table, they who came for liquor took what they wanted, if ready drawn, if however they wanted any thing which was not ready; they were either obliged to wait, or go without it, for during the ten minutes no one was permitted to leave the dinner table on any account whatever, and both the servant maids and the pot boy always sat at the table and dined with the family. There was seldom more than a single joint and vegetables excepting on sundays when there was either a large pie or a pudding. The dinner was always hot, what was left being sold to working men who dined or supped in the room. Short as was the time allowed for eating every one contrived to eat enough, and though my father chose to dine in the tap-room, nothing was so offensive to him as any one looking at him or at the table, and when any one did so he would shew his resentment by a burst of passion vented in sufficiently offensive language.

SEC. 2 SCHOOL TEACHING. MORAL DISCIPLINE[1]

Soon after my fathers removal to Arundel Street my two sisters were sent to school at what was called a very respectable day school in the same street, here almost every thing was professed to be taught. It was the best of the sort in the neighbourhood. My sisters were here taught various kinds of needle work and the rudiments of the french language. The eldest was a clever girl and made what was then called great progress – and this made my mother who was by no means a good judge of her attainments very proud of her. My brother was after some time sent to the school in Wine Office Court with me, about a mile from our house. The school was kept by a tall stout well looking man named Jones, proverbially, "savage Jones" this name he got from the boys of his own school and from those of two other schools in the neighbourhood in consequence of the frequent punishments he inflicted on the boys and the delight he seemed to take in punishing them.

There were about 120 boys in this school. There were two very large rooms each occupying the whole size of the house excepting the narrow staircases, one on the first and the other on the second floor both of which were used as school rooms. The doors to these rooms were in the middle and opened immediately on to the staircases, from the doors to the opposite sides of the rooms were passages formed by the ends of the desks and forms which were perpendicular to the passages. The master sat at a desk at the right of the room the usher at the left hand, and thus they had a perfect view of the whole of the boys. In this school the boys were taught to read and write and some to cipher as it was called. The spelling book was Dilworths, the reading book the Bible. The only book

[1] In Place's list of contents for this chapter the two sections, 'School Teaching' and 'Discipline' are numbered separately, making seven sections in all. In the text of the manuscript he combined them into a single section but did not renumber the later sections, as has been done here.

3.2 School teaching, moral discipline

I ever saw in the school for teaching Arithmetic was Dilworths School Masters Assistant. School hours were from 9 to 12 and from 2 to 5. The mode of teaching was this. Each of the boys had a column or half of a column of spelling to learn by heart every morning He also wrote a copy every morning. In the afternoon he read in the Bible and did a sum, on Thursdays and Saturdays he was catechised, that is he was examined in the Church of England Catechism, for which an hour was allotted from 12 'till 1 and the afternoons were holidays. The master on one side of the school room and the usher on the other side called six boys in rotation out of the forms, who passed the master or usher and stood in a row at the end, of the desk, the boy nearest to the master read his lesson or spelled his column or shewed his sum and was dismissed to his seat, if any one failed he was obliged to go out and stand at a short distance from the master holding out first one hand and then the other to receive on each a stroke with a stout cane, the strokes were from two to twelve in extreme cases fourteen have been given. This punishment was very severe, and was more or less so as the master was in a good or a bad humour. A few strokes would swell the hands considerably and when intended would bruise the hands sadly. If a boy endeavoured to evade the blow or shrunk from it, he was sure to have a rap on the under side to make him hold his hand fair, and such was the dexterity of the master that he could spread the blows all over the hand, and when he meant to be more severe than usual he would make the end of the cane reach to the wrist. The usher was not allowed to beat the boys, but was obliged to send them to the master with a mark on their book or slate denoting the number of blows the boy was to have. In the lower room there were two ushers, they had the care of the smaller boys and treated and taught them or neglected them as they pleased. If any person made complaint of the treatment of their boy or boys, the answer was, that the rules of the school could not be broken. If any one complained of any thing which occurred in the court after the boys left the school, the reply was, the master had nothing to do with the boys out of school. It must be evident that as far as school learning went, very little could be obtained at this school, yet being sent to this school had considerable influence on my after life. I was in this school from the time I was between seven and eight until I was nearly twelve years of age and was well drilled in several respects. To avoid punishment it was necessary to be punctual in attending at nine and at two o clock, no excuse was permitted and unless a boy brought a note accounting for his absence whether of a day an hour or even five minutes he was sure to be beaten on the hands. There was constant emulation among the boys to shew how they could bear punishment. I never failed to be ready with my lesson never was behind my time and never should have been beaten at all if I had not chosen to provoke the master to beat me, yet I was frequently beaten. Challenges were given and accepted to shew how well a large number of strokes on the hand could be taken without wincing, and to bring this to trial a noise was intentionally made by the boys whose emulation it was to shew their courage and this was continued until they were called out and punished. Another of these circumstances was occasioned by the big boys encouraging the smaller boys to fight and making up boxing matches between them, sometimes a fight was got up between boys of unequal sizes when the smaller boy was a sturdy pugnacious fellow. I was one of those who had gained the favour of the bigger boys, and could at length beat any boy of my own size and some who were much larger, there was something of science in these fights, the big boys teaching the small boys and attending them as seconds in all regular fights. In another court called Kings Head Court at the top of Wine Office Court was a sort of finishing day school, where latin was pretended to be taught, as well as bookkeeping and Navigation The boys in this school were stout lads, and matches used to be made for two of the small boys in our school to fight one of the large boys in the other school. In these battles I was generally one of the combatants and was almost always victorious.

At a short distance was another large school exactly such an one as ours kept by a Mr Bird, and between the two war was almost constantly waged, sometimes school fought school sometimes half a dozen or more from each side had regular sets to in the presence of both schools. The whole affair was systematically conducted – a large place called Gough Square was the arena and each school took its station across the space leaving an open area in the middle between them, victory was sometimes in favour of one side sometimes on the other side. Neither school ever obtained preeminence for more than a week or two.

There is nothing like these schools now, they abounded at the time I am speaking of and the conduct of all was alike. From this school I and my brother were removed to another school of a similar sort; a small school in Windsor court near the New Church in the Strand. It never contained more than forty boys seldom so many. The school room was on the third floor and at one corner of it was a smaller room for girls. In this school there was a slight approximation to a better system than in that before described. There was a head boy and a weekly monitor, each of the boys in the first form being monitors in turn. The head boy heard all the boys on his side of the school and on the cross bench read, each once every other day, spell on the other days, and he had to examine their sums every day. If he thought proper he sent the boy he had heard to the

3.2 School teaching, moral discipline

master and if the master found him deficient he punished him. The Monitor had reference to the head boy as the head boy had to the master, thus every boy in the first class was examined twice and every boy in the second class three times before he was punished. The system was a mild one, the punishments were a double task, remaining in the school room for an hour, or for the whole of the dinner time, or a few slaps on the hand were given with a leather strop. The master, a Mr Bowis was a good man, greatly beloved by his pupils. This school had a remarkably bad effect upon my brother. As I was head boy my brother who was a perverse fellow was under my charge and because I was placed over him he resolved to do as little as possible and to give as much trouble as possible. Punishment was useless he would not learn, and as far as he could he prevented others from learning. As no other means than punishment were used towards perverse boys, and as he rather courted than avoided punishment, to shew to the other boys what he considered an example of fortitude, and to annoy and plague me, he was at length permitted to take his own course and his progress was very slow. The perverse habit he had acquired was confirmed and remained with him through life, and was the principal cause of his want of success in any one of his several undertakings.

As the time approached when I was to be put out in the world, Mr Bowis was directed to have me taught Ingrossing and German Text, both of which I learned in a very short time, as any boy may easily do. I was to be pushed on in arithmetic that I might get through the Rule of three,[1] I had however without my father knowing any thing of the matter gone through all the rules in common arithmetic and vulgar fractions, had he known it, it would not have made any difference, he would have supposed that they preceeded the rule of three. Yet ignorant as he was of arithmetic; he had a method of his own by which he could calculate values by his head more rapidly and quite as correctly as I could do by my arithmetical process.[2]

Mr Bowis must have been an ordinary man in respect to learning – he was not learned in any thing, but at the time I was under his care he

[1] Engrossing is the style of clear handscript used in such legal documents as contracts and deeds; German text is the elaborate black lettering used in wills and in the opening phrases of other legal documents. The rule of three is the method of determining a fourth number from three given numbers, the first of which is in the same proportion to the second as the third is to the fourth.

'The instruction my father gave to my schoolmaster was, that when I got to the end of the Rule of Three, I was to be taken away, as that was he thought a competent education for his class of persons' (Place's testimony before the Select Committee on Education, *Parliamentary Report . . . on Education*, 1835, p. 69).

[2] Place added this paragraph, on the verso of the preceding page, after he had written the final draft of his memoir.

seemed to me, to be a prodigiously learned man and a very wise one. He took pains with his scholars and taught them as well as he was able. He gave them good advice, pointed out to them the probable situations they would fill when men and did all he could by advice and by quoting examples to induce them to be industrious, humane careful and respectable. To the advice he gave me, and the care in other respects which he took of me I can trace the germs of many right notions, and much of the faculty which served me well when I became a man, namely, the talent of distinguishing, of seperating matters and drawing conclusions. This dexterity and power of reasoning kept me from more extensive evils in my youth, than those I fell into, and prevented many evil consequences which others who were not so well taught in these particulars could not avoid. They kept me from being entangled in much mischief and furnished me with the means of procuring much of the happiness I have enjoyed, and notwithstanding the adverse circumstances in which for many years I was placed, I am of opinion, that greater happiness has upon the whole been enjoyed by but very few men.

It was a custom with my schoolmaster to give out a text of scripture every thursday and to preach a short moral sermon from it. On the saturday he read a chapter from the New Testament and made a comment on it. Before he commenced reading he called upon the boys for their remarks on his discourse of the preceeding thursday and his reading and comment on the preceeding saturday, his purpose was to induce them to observe to think and to reason. The boys who made the best observations were rewarded by some token of respect and occasionally by a small present. I was distinguished among the boys for my observations and became a great favorite with my master.

His discources were adapted to the capacities of the boys and though like all other efforts they failed to produce all the good he wished they were highly useful. They were intended to produce such notions as should tend to make the boys honest independent, patient and intrepid. I used to think highly of them at the time as I did at particular times after I left school and I never wholly either forgot or neglected them. On some occasions they were of all but infinite service to me, as well in preventing evil, as in fortifying me in a variety of ways, and encouraging me to perseverance under unfavourable circumstances. It is to these lectures that I attribute to a considerable extent the disposition I have always had of never abandoning any thing under any circumstances, the attainment of which was worth the trouble of attaining, and of persevering on some occasions when the object to be obtained was not worth the trouble as an exercise, of perseverance. Another habit which I persuade myself I have adopted to a considerable extent I can also trace to my good

3.2 School teaching, moral discipline

masters useful instructions, namely, that of going in the straightest and shortest way to my object, without suffering myself to be drawn aside by minor objects.

Since I left school I have often suspected that my master, was by no means a religious man, I do not think he was devoid of religion, but that he had never been able to make up his mind on the truth or falshood of the Christian Religion, and that his theological teaching was more matter of duty than of inclination. Had he been religious he would not have seperated morals from religion as he always did, and certainly would never have taught them seperately as was his constant practice, He always represented religion as matter of faith, morality as matter of duty. It[1] was his practice to go regularly through the Gospels and then to begin them again. When I was about thirteen years of age he had gone through them and recommenced with the first chapter of Matthew in which is one of the accounts of the miraculous conception, and on this he commented as usual. I was at that time pretty well acquainted with what relates to the union of the sexes. Conversation on these matters was much less reserved than it is now, books relating to the subject were much more within the reach of boys and girls than they are now, and I had little to learn on any part of the subject. From having read the Bible and Testament myself as a school exercise day by day from the first time I learned to read and from hearing the boys read these books daily I was well acquainted with them and could correct a boy if he made a mistake in most cases without reference to the book, and could repeat considerable portions of the Gospels, by rote. This my master knew, and when called upon to give my exposition of the first chapter of Matthew, I had no remark to make he was confounded. I have never forgotten the embarrasment and uneasiness I endured and exhibited. Though I had learned portions of the Gospels by rote I had never thought of examining the subject in any particular. I had read a book at that time openly sold, on every stall, called Aristotles Master Piece,[2] it was a thick 18 mo, with a number of badly drawn cuts in it explanatory of the mystery of generation. This I contrived to borrow and compared parts of it with the accounts of the Miraculous Conception in Matthew and Luke, and the result was that spite of every effort I could make I could not believe the

---

[1] In the manuscript the material from this point to the end of the paragraph was pencilled through and marked 'delete' by Place's son.

[2] *Aristotle's Compleat Master Piece; in Three Parts; Displaying the Secrets of Nature in the Generation of Man*, a combination sex guide and obstetrical manual, had gone through thirty registered editions by the 1780s. Place seems to have been familiar with the unofficial cheap reprints. These were still being issued as late as the 1850s. Even later Leopold Bloom, in *Ulysses*, looked at a copy on a bookstall. The work was familiar to him, because he had previously brought home a copy for his wife.

story. I could not play the hypocrite, my master had taught me the value of truth, and to respect myself, and I could not, at least to him, make up a false statement: I doubted and was dumb. My master had preached a sermon on faith in which he said, no one was or could be a judge of his own faith, and that he might have the least when he thought he had the most. This had made a remarkable impression on me. It caused me to suspect that I was very deficient in faith and the consequence was a persuasion that I should be damned for want of faith, and as my master explained that faith came of grace, and grace was a gift, I understood that every one who was endowed with grace knew it, and as I was conscious I had no such gift I thought my case was hopeless, and this at particular moments made me uneasy. I neither concealed my doubts nor my fears but communicated them freely to several persons, no one however said any thing which appeared to me calculated to remove my doubts I read Bunyans Pilgrims progress and parts of some other equally absurd books, but all would not do, reason was too strong for superstition and at length the fiend was completely vanquished.

It is probable that I was led to these inquiries, or induced rather to persevere in them by a circumstance which was of great consequence to me not only at the time when it occurred but through my whole life. When I was about eleven years of age my father and mother were one day disputing with a Mr Sutton, a clever man but like all who used my fathers house one who dissipated his income in Clubs and drinking parties, were disputing, as is too frequently the case with most people, from want of knowledge and and want of practice in observing and marking distinctions, thus disputing to no purpose, or quarrelling or coming to erroneous conclusions which are always in some way more or less mischievous. The dispute alluded to was likely to produce a quarrel each being obstinate each mistaken, neither seeing the real merits of the case, when I interfered and pointing out a distinction which had been passed over put an end to the dispute. Mr Sutton praised my sagacity to an extent which greatly excited my vanity, and made an impression on me which has never been effaced. The true art of teaching to a very great extent depends on discovering and judiciously applying the means to create motives. This done to a considerable extent on any subject with any person at any age cannot fail to produce desirable results.[1]

It was the custom of my master to invite some of the oldest of the boys to visit him for an hour or two on half holidays, these were Thursdays and Saturdays. On these occasions he always took the boys into his study a small room on the second floor, he used to shew the boys his

[1] This paragraph also was added after Place had made the fair copy of his memoir.

3.2 School teaching, moral discipline

books and encourage them to read and ask questions, his collection of books was small and they were mostly old books in bad condition. I remember his shewing me a book on Anatomy, which stron[g]ly excited me, and made me desirous of information on the subject, which he, as far as he understood it was willing to impart, I conclude however that he knew very little about it. My desire for information was however too strong to be turned aside and often have I been sent away from a book stall when the owner became offended at my standing reading which I used to do until I was turned away, as often as I found a surgical book, I used to borrow books from a man who kept a small shop in Maiden Lane Covent Garden leaving a small sum as a deposit and paying a trifle for reading them, having one only at a time.

Excepting an old bible there was not a book in my fathers house belonging to him, and from him I never received any encouragement to read. All the money I got at home was a halfpenny on the thursday and another on the Saturday from my mother. I however found means of obtaining money. On one occasion I raked the kennel[1] of a street at the back of my fathers house (Water Street) which led down to the Thames. The old Iron I found enabled me to purchase the materials for a paper kite, it was a large one taller than myself and had upon it a multitude of stars and turkscaps[2] in gaudy colours a pair of glass eyes and fine fringed tassels. The great difficulty was, how to procure the necessary quantity of twine to send it up to a great height which in regard to the kite was the height of my ambition. I chopped wood after school hours, and on thursday and saturday afternoons for a man who kept a Chandlers shop and as I was dextrous he gave me three halfpence an hour, thus I amassed half a crown the largest sum I had ever possessed with this I bought twine, sent up the kite in the long fields and sold it on the spot twine and all for half a guinea. From this time I never wanted money. I made models of boats and rigged them Moulds for Cocks and Dumps*

---

[1] Kennel, a gutter.   [2] Reddish or purplish lilies.

* Cocks and Dumps are now out of fashion with boys, and I will therefore say a few words respecting them. They were cast in moulds made either of Fire Stone or Chalk. I soon found that a small quantity of pewter melted with the lead made the cocks much more tough, and consequently much better to be shied at as they did not bend like those made wholly of lead, and were not so easily knocked over. These Cocks as they were called were figures of Cocks, or Dogs or Horses or Trees &c stainding perpendicularly on a horizontal base which in a fair cock extented equally before and behind to a distance somewhat less than the height of the cock and were at least as wide as the cock – I contrived to have but a small horizontal projection in front, and a large projection behind which prevented the cock being easily knocked over, and by projecting the figure over the sides of the base the cock would not lie down sideways, by this contrivance I for some time won all the cocks and dumps of the boys, 'till they cried me down and then I turned merchant and sold them. Shying at Cocks was conducted thus. Each of two boys put a cock upon the

The Autobiography of Francis Place

and sold them. I excelled in all boyish games, won from the boys all their marbles, cocks and dumps and every thing else they had to lose until no one would play with me. I became more than was usually expert at these things by practice alone, I was about twelve years of age when a new source whence to obtain money presented itself. I had learned to scate and was desirous to have a good pair of scates of my own, but this was an affair not to be accomplished in a day. I however found means to purchase a pair of the best kind. The place now called Newcastle Street in the Strand was thickly covered with old wooden houses, there was then no thorough fare from the Strand to Stanhope street, though there was a way through an Inn, and the houses to the southward of Holywell street came nearly to the back of the New Church there being a rather broad passage paved with flag stones between them. A fire happened on this spot and burnt nearly thirty houses. Owing to some particular cause and contrary to the common practice, the ruins were not dug out by the Fire Insurance Offices, and a large quantity of iron and lead remained in them. A hoard was put up and in this state they were left for a long time. To these ruins an entrance was soon made at one corner between two posts through which a stout boy could squeeze himself, and they became the resort of as perfectly accomplished a gang of young rascals and thieves from Drury Lane as ever existed. These boys or some of them were constantly digging in the ruins and selling whatever they could find which any one would buy. I and some other boys my schoolfellows got into the ruins, and seeing what the other boys were at, we began to dig also, this brought on quarrelling. The Drury Lane blackguards endeavured to intimidate us by bad language and menaces, and thus to drive us away, this conduct had a partial effect and we went into the ruins but seldom, one day however after some quarrelling the leading boy struck me, this produced a set to and I beat him, but as there was some foul play I *licked* two others of them one after the other. This satisfied us that neither dirt, nor rags, nor ferocious countenances, nor bad language were proofs of either dexterity, courage or bottom.[1] We therefore resolved to have a general fight with them and

---

ground and having settled who should have the first shy the game commenced, by throwing a piece of lead or a smooth stone at the cock, he who upset the Cock won it. Another mode was shying at a cock for dumps, one or more dumps [lead counters] were staked for a shy. If the shyer did not knock the cock over he lost his dump or dumps, when he did knock it over he won it. Dumps were also used to play at pitch in the hole with. They were about the size of a farthing, and were usually sold at the rate of eight for a halfpenny. I made a mould in which I could cast eleven at a time and these I sold for a halfpenny. I therefore did a good business. Dumps were used for all sorts of Gambling for which halfpence were used.

[1] Stamina. 'Among bruisers [bottom] is used to express a hardy fellow who will bear

3.2 School teaching, moral discipline

if we were successful to expel them from the ruins as often as we were there. They on their parts seemed to have contemplated subduing us and expelling us at all times. The matter was soon brought to issue I beat my man, two or three others of us beat their men but as they were more numerous than we were they fell upon us and compelled us to retreat. Being thus expelled it was agreed that every boy in the school who was big enough to shew fight should go to the ruins on the next half holiday when each should single out a boy as his opponent and fight it out fairly. This was carried into effect and several of us got to fighting without much ceremony. It seemed certain that we should be the victors, and this led on their part to an offer of terms which were agreed to. Lines of demarcation were drawn and peace was made. As they could dig at all times, and we only at intervals a large portion of the ground was allotted to them a small one for us, neither party was to infringe upon the territory of the other, the terms were strictly observed and we became friends, within the hoard, and out of sight and hearing of all but ourselves we went on in an amicable way, digging and selling the iron and lead we obtained at the same shops. I soon procured money to buy scates, and more indeed than I had any immediate occasion for, and this was the case with some others of us. The possession of so much money led to gambling. Pitch in the hole and tossing up were the principal games. Dextrous as I was amongst my equals I was no match for the Drury Lane gentlemen and they therefore won my money, this was felt as impugning my talent which I could not bear, so I went to work in a business like way rehearsing the matter by myself and in a little time became so expert that I could pitch eight or ten halfpence into a hole not much larger than a halfpenny without spilling one of them. It was now my turn to win and winning led to quarrelling, and sometimes to blows, but as I could win all their money and beat any one of them they refused to gamble with me at pitch in the hole, but tossing up continued, at this we were about equal, each of us winning or loosing occasionally. Pitch in the hole was played thus – a round hole was carefully made in hard ground with a knife the sides of the hole were perpendicular, and the diameter as small as would take in a halfpenny and leave room for the introduction of one finger to get the money out from the bottom, the depth was that of ten or twelve halfpence two three or four played at it. From a certain distance each player pitched two or three halfpence one by one and in rotation, towards the hole and he who had two halfpence nearest to the hole or one in the hole and the next nearest had the first

---

a good beating' (Francis Grose, *A Classical Dictionary of the Vulgar Tongue*, 3rd edn, 1796).

go with all the halfpence, and in like manner was followed by the rest. If both halfpence were in the hole from two boys, or the distance from the edge of the hole was equal, it was a tye and they who tyed pitched again for precedence. The go with all the halfpence was from half the distance of the place whence the halfpence were pitched singly, it was done thus, all the halfpence were carefully placed one upon another, and if any one was bent, it was changed for one that was flat. They were balanced on the two fore fingers of the right hand and steadied by the ball of the thum, they were then pitched steadily at the hole, for the purpose of falling into it perpendicularly and it was in this I excelled. (The game is usually played by boys who are not desperate gamblers as we were with leaden dumps or buttons, and by what is called pitch and phil, the dumps or buttons scattered round the hole being philled, that is jerked by the edge of the thumb in a particular manner towards the hole that which is the furthest off being philled first, when if it is not philled into the hole the next boy proceeds in the same way with the dumps or buttons which remain.)[1]

Tossing up is performed in several ways but the game as we played it was the most desperate it was thus, each boy pitched a certain number of halfpence at a bit of stick set up as a mark and he who came nearest as in pitching at the hole had the first go. When the game was played fairly the money was picked up by the boy who had the first go and placed in one of his hands heads or tails upwards as the pieces lay on the ground, his hands were then placed one over the other and the money fairly shaken it was then thrown up and all that were heads on the ground belonged to the boy who had the go, the remainder were treated in the same way by the next boy, and so on until all came up heads, but with us as with men who gambled in the same way, the halfpence were skilfully turned heads upwards as they were picked up and care was taken that none of them should be turned between the hands in shaking them, a peculiar twist of the wrist of the right hand sent them up into the air every one of them spinning round, and by these means two thirds of them at the least would come up heads or tails as was intended when placed in the hand. At this game we were pretty much on a par, and altho I was generally a winner the winnings were not large, and sometimes I was the loser.

My father had a particular wish that I should never fight with other boys, he thought that fighting with boys would surely lead to the acquaintance with professed boxing men, pugilism being then at its height, but he never took any notice of black eyes or bruises; if however he caught me fighting he would beat me unmercifully.

[1] In the margin next to this parenthetical sentence Place wrote: 'This is to be placed as a note.'

3.2 School teaching, moral discipline

The boys who were my schoolfellows were all of them children of persons above the class of Journeymen, most of them were sons of tradesmen in respectable situations, of such persons as at present would no more expect or in any way permit such conduct as I have described, or such associations to be formed as I have mentioned than a gentlemen would in respect to his sons. It will be concluded that the manners of such boys as my associates and schoolfellows, were coarse and vulgar in their manners, that from digging in the ruins of a fire their cloaths were at times very dirty, yet no particular notice excepting a short scolding or a clout on the head was taken, except when a boy was unusually dirty and then he was chastised, by what was called a good thumping. The truth is, that the same class of persons in the present day are so far advanced in all that is decent, comfortable and respectable, as scarcely to be concieved but by those who are old enough and observing enough to mark the contrast. I have frequently and very lately conversed with elderly people, now most respectably circumstanced, and having genteel families, whose improvement has been so gradual and long, that they themselves were scarcly conscious of it, and when I have led them back to the state of morals and the common conduct of those of their own rank in their boyish days, they have invariably ejaculated their surprise at the very great changes which have taken place without their having particularly noticed them as they went on and as they had not before been recalled to their recollection.

[The observation of improvements in the working class was one of Place's principal avocations. In other volumes of his unpublished writings he noted some of the conditions of this period which he found changed: 'Obscene Prints were sold at all the principal Print Shops and at most others. At Roach's – in Russell Court where Play books and school books and stationary were sold, Mrs Roach used to open a portfolio to any boy and to any maid servant, who came to buy a penny or other book or a sheet of paper, the Portfolio contained a multitude of obscene prints – some coloured some, not, and asked them if they wanted some pretty pictures, and she encouraged them to look at them. And this was done by many others. This was common to other shops' (Add. MS 36625, f. 8).

'The increased cleanliness of the people is particularly striking [ca. 1824] and this is of itself a conclusive proof of their improvement. since I can remember, the wives and daughters of Journeymen tradesmen and shopkeepers, either wore leather stays or what were called full boned stays, and these latter sort were worn by women of all ranks. These were never washed, altho worn day by day for years. The wives and grown daughters of tradesmen and gentlemen even wore petticoats of camblet, lined with dyed lined, stuffed with wool or horsehair and quilted these were also worn day by day until they were rotten, and never were washed. A great change was produced by improvements in the manufacture of cotton goods' (Add. MS 27827, fs. 50–1).

The Autobiography of Francis Place

'Formerly the women young and old were seen emptying their pails or pans, at the doors, or washing on stools in the street, in the summertime without gowns on their back or handkerchiefs on their necks, their leather stays half laced and as black as the door posts, their black coarse worsted stockings and striped linsey woolsey petticoats "standing alone with dirt"'(Add. MS 27827, f. 52).

'The children of tradesmen and other persons keeping good houses in the Strand for instance and the streets North and South of the Strand, were all of them when I was a boy infected with vermin that is had lice in their hair, they used to be combed once a week with a small tooth comb, on to the bellows or into a sheet of paper in the lap of the mother, or some female of the family a great number, the larger number by far of the youth of both sexes had vermin in their hair, and many grown people were not free from them' (Add. MS 27828, f. 122).

'I did not see one child [in 1824] with a scald head nor one with bandy legs called cheese cutters. That is with the shin bone bowed out. The number of children who had "cheese cutters" was formerly so great that if an estimate were now made of the number it would not be credited' (Add. MS 27828, f. 125).]

I excelled all my compatriots in every kind of game practised in London, in all kinds of sports and exercises, swimming excepted. Almost every boy who was eleven years of age and some who were younger could swim. I could not, and this annoyed me much especially as I sometimes saw boys not older than myself swim across the Thames at Milbank, at about half-tide. There was then no house from the end of Mill Bank Row for nearly a mile excepting Hodges's Distillery an old barn of a place* a public house or two and a cake shop where Vaxhall Bridge has since been built. There was no wall next the river but some boards only here and there and a row of large willow trees. All along on the mud or shingle lay timbers belonging to different merchants, they were not then sawn up ready for use as they are now very generally, but were sold as logs and sawn up by the purchasers as is sometimes the case still. On these logs hundreds of boys used to dress and undress for the purpose of bathing. One fine afternoon I had been uselessly tring to swim, and had squatted down on the end of a piece of timber which was very long and ran a good way into the river, the boys were running about upon the logs and that on which I was squatted that the sun might dry me was like all the others in continued motion, so that I was not alarmed at any one coming behind me; in this position I was looking at a boy swimming in the middle of the river when I was pushed by a man from the log into the river, he had taken it for granted that I could swim, but the boys who knew I could not shouted vehemently as they expected I

* At the side of the sewer where the Gas works now are. 1834.

3.2 School teaching, moral discipline

should be drowned, the tide was running hard at nearly half ebb and carried me rapidly down the river, I felt no fear however but struck out and swam ashore, and of course could always swim afterwards. In a little time I was able to swim across the river at nearly low water from the place where the steps of the Penitentiary are now placed to Randalls Mill on the opposite side, but I never could attain eminence as a swimmer. Learning to swim at this time was soon afterwards the means of saving my life.

Several lightermen used my fathers house and I occasionally went down the river with some one of them in a barge to fetch a load of coals from the ships in the Pool, I could help to pull an oar in a barge and could row well in a boat. I was therefore sometimes allowed to take a lightermans skiff and either alone or with other boys amuse myself with rowing. Going one day along the barges to the skiff which was lying outside, I missed my distance in jumping from one Barge to another and fell in between two of them. It was high water. I rose again immediately but it was under the flat bottom of a barge. I can even now remember well the horror I felt on finding myself under the Barge. I made all the exertion in my power to extricate myself but felt I was drowning, a last desperate effort was made and with it I lost all recollection. People say that drowning is an easy death, and so it is in respect to the short time it occupies, but the distressing effect is indescribable. It comes the nearest to a very bad fit of night mare, and any one who has had a fit of this kind of the worst species must be convinced that if it could be continued for even a few minutes it would terminate in death. Had I not previously learned to swim I must have been drowned, simply from want of presence of mind which the knowledge of my own powers gave me, and which enabled me to make a last effort. This effort it seems carried me from under the barge, and as I was again sinking a lighterman who with others had ran to the spot pulled me up with a boat hook. I was carried ashore and laid on the stone steps of Arundel Stairs, where I soon came to myself. The watermen to whom I was well known did what they thought was necessary to recover me, and as some of them knew as well as I did that if I went home with wet cloaths I should have a most unmerciful beating from my father, for having been on the barges, and in the water, they furnished me with covering, whilst my clothes were taken to a public house called the watermans arms to be dried. I suffered no other inconvenience from the ducking than the distension occasioned by the muddy water and this went off in a few hours.

In a court at the back of my fathers house called Greyhound Court lived a Mr Cuthbertson a celebrated Mathimatical Instrument maker, he was very clever in his business and might had he been a careful man been eminent, but he was a sot, one of those who diligently attended his business during the day and got drunk or muddled at night, he was a member of all the clubs held at my fathers house. He was a short fat slovenly man, and his wife was like him in many respects. He employed two or three men and an apprentice, and sometimes worked himself. I had the run of his workshop a large light garrett sometimes there were four or five men at work. In this place I learned to turn and to file, and here I obtained much information on the construction and use of many instruments.

At a carpenters shop belonging to a Mr Taylor I learned the use of the saw, the plane and the Chissel and got some insight respecting carpentry and joinery.

I made many models of sailing boats and some of larger vessels. I made for my own use a small lathe of Buck wood with a brass mandril, in which I turned the dead eyes and sheaves of the blocks for the rigging of the models, I sold these models according to their size and the more or less perfect manner in which they were rigged, from a few shillings to a guinea each.

I bought some books and at the time I was put out as an apprentice before I was fourteen years of age I had a pretty large chest full.

Either the present Mr Flaxman or his father kept a shop in the Strand a few doors eastward of Somerset House and sold small figures which he exposed in his shop windows Some of his workmen frequented my fathers house and dined in a large box which had a small fire place in it, though it was part of the taproom in which in cold weather there was always a good fire. These men used to bring prepared clay with them and with bits of stick model one anothers heads, generally carricaturing some feature, they also modelled my father and mother and some other persons, from observing their method I too took to modelling from these small heads which they gave to me and for which I gained applause. My collection of heads was a very curious one and I have frequently regretted that I did not preserve it. My principal performance was a model I made of the cat, and the praise this procured for me puffed up my vanity greatly. I have sometimes been surprised at the many things I pursued as well as at those I accomplished whilst I was a school boy; but when I have reflected, that I had nearly the whole of every sunday to myself. Half a holiday every thursday and saturday. occasional holidays on some saints days – and annaversaries – ten whole days at Easter, and seventeen at Christmas and at Whitsuntide and every evening after five o clock, and never had any sort of employment assigned me I have ceased to be surprised, as the leisure hours were a third of all the time I was not in bed.

3.2 School teaching, moral discipline

[One occupation of this leisure, watching the charlatan Dr Bossy, Place recalled with horror: 'I can remember Dr Bossy, he was a short fat man, wore a cocked hat a long shirted waistcoat. Breeches and stockings and silver Shoe Buckles' (Add. MS 27828, f. 257).

'I remember Dr Bossy on his stage on Tower Hill.

'I remember his also in Covent Garden, without any stage on the ground, a space being made for him by baskets placed round it. I saw him, clean and dress sore legs, and sores on other parts, hear complaints and prescribe remedies – I remember a girl dreadfully afflicted with scrofula, he passed a silver probe in at the lower side of her jaw up her cheek, and notwithstanding I have attended the dissections of the human body, seen sores dressed and operations performed tranquilly enough I cannot write this without the sensation, of "ones flesh crawling." It made such an impression on me who was then a boy, that for years afterwards I was not devoid of apprehension that I should be afflicted with the Kings Evil' (Add. MS 27832, f. 207).

Another leisure occupation was playing 'Drop the Handerchief': 'I remember the time when "drop handkerchief["] was common at all merry makings round London and have joined in the game many times on a sunday afternoon. Any one who pleased was admitted into the ring, which consisted of a male and female alternately holding hands round, when the girl dropped the handerchief she started off in the direction she thought most likely to enable her to avoid being caught unless she wished it, and few wished it at the first run as by avoiding being caught, the girl was sure to be again selected by the next boy, since not to have a run after the girl who had beaten the first boy would have been a want of pluck, when the handkerchief was dropped, the lad at whose back it fell was usual held by the girls on each side of him as long as they could hold him, this checked him for a moment or two and another or two were lost in picking up the handkerchief so that the girl had fairly the start of him and by running round some trees or groups of people not unfrequently regained the ring without being caught, in which case she was applauded as well by the by standers as by the ring, the lad was laughed at and joked at, and was pretty sure not to have another challenge, except perhaps from mere pity, the girl went round the ring again, and was almost sure to be caught the second time as she never had time enough to recover from the exertions she had made.

'This game differed but little from kiss in the ring as played at that time, except that in kiss in the ring the girls alternately run after the boys and as the boys made no real efforts to evade them much of the interest of "drop the handkerchief" was lost to the spectators but this was perhaps made up to those in the ring by the mock marriage of the parties, while in "drop the handkerchief," the matter ended by the lad kissing the girl in the centre of the ring.

'It was remarkable enough that people who dressed decently and were in decent circumstances would not only permit their daughters to join in these amusements but would stand and look on, and evince as much gratification as other spectators' (Add. MS 27832, fs. 228–9).]

An occurrence which had considerable effect on me at the time and no small share of influence on my manners conduct and character must not be omitted here.

At Mr Bowis's school as I have before mentioned there was a garrett in which girls were taught; to reach it the girls had to pass through the boys room. This of itself is characteristic of the times. No decent tradesman would now send his daughters to any such school, and especially to a man who was a batcheler, who had only one woman servant and no female attendant for the Girls. So little were such matters as these attended to that Mr Bowis had at least a dozen girls in his school.

It was my business as head boy, to examine the sums on the Girls slates in their room, on the Thursdays and Saturdays. On these days the school business closed as usual at twelve o clock, after which on the saturday the master read the Collect Epistle and Gospel for the next day and heard the boys say the catechism. On the Thursdays he pronounced his moral discourse and when these were ended the school was dismissed, but as I had to examine the Girls sums I was always detained some time longer. The smallest girls were always despatched first and when they had passed the Master were sent away. The Master however seldom remained until the whole of the Girls were passed the business being left to me.[1]

The education I have described was the education which at this time the children of common London Tradesmen received Generally, it seldom exceeded Reading Writing and common Arithmetic, badly taught, to this must however be added the Lords Prayer and the Catechism by rote every thing else was omitted

There were however some good schools in London where a better education might be obtained. To these the children of those who were above the common run and were comparatively a small number were sent. The rudiments of Latin – Geometry &c and what was called Navigation to fit boys for the sea were the amount professed to be inculcated.

The children of the richer and prouder class immediately above these tradesmen, those who instead of frequenting the Public House Parlours assembled at Coffee Houses and Taverns were sent to boarding schools, some of which taught a little more than the common day schools, but it was a mark of distinction and encouraged pride by inducing the boy to consider himself a gentleman.

Then indeed as now a superior education could be procured but it could only be done at very considerable expense, and very few of the

---

[1] At this point in the manuscript someone cut off the rest of the page (about twenty-four lines of writing) and possibly subsequent pages. When Francis Place Jr was reviewing the manuscript he added the following note about the censored anecdote: 'The Consequence was bad for both parties giving rise to much licentiousness.'

3.2 School teaching, moral discipline

parents thought it worth the expense. Half a guinea a quarter was considered a large sum and was complained of as too much.[1]

In every respect even when compared with present manners and modes of thinking and teaching of the commonest master tradesmen respecting the education of their children was very bad indeed and none among them reasoned as many now do of the moral consideration likely to be promoted by a system of sound information to be obtained at school.

The manners of the heads of families were coarse and vulgar and frequently indecent to an extent scarcely to be credited their language was inaccurate and mean, their habits in respect to cleanliness very inferior to what they are now, and their sense of delicacy remarkably gross, as a reference to the songs sung in their domestic parties will shew. Their children were permitted to run about their filthy streets, to hear all sorts of bad language and to mix with whomsoever they pleased. Pilfering and Thieving especiall[y] were not then as now almost wholly confined to the very lowest of the people, but were practiced by tradesmens sons, by youths and young men who would now no more commit such act than would the sons of a well bred gentlemen,[2] thieving had not as yet [become] a trade to be followed by those who lived by it as it has now become. The change in this particular is complete and when I look back and reflect on the conduct of such persons as those to whom I have alluded. I, even I, am much surprised at the change, the more so when I reflect on the circumstances which came to my own knowledge, and those which since I commenced my enquiries have been related to me and yet more even when I compare all the circumstances of the times, that people so far removed from any thing approaching towards want as very considerable numbers must have should have been so depraved as they were does even yet surprise me.

Want of chastity in girls was common. The songs which were ordinarily sung by their relatives and by young men and women and the lewd plays and interludes they occasionally saw were all calculated to produce mischief in this direction. The whole of this is materially changed, the songs have all dissappeared and are altogether unknown to young girls.

Some of these songs sung by the respectable tradesmen who spent their evenings in my fathers parlour, were very gross, yet I have known the parlour door thrown wide open, that whoever was in the bar and the Tap room might hear every word. They were sung with considerable

---

[1] Twelve years later Samuel Harrison found the day schools unchanged. He calculated the fees thus: 'the quarterly charge was 10/6 to 15/ each & unless at least 100 boys could be got, after paying one usher not more than £200 a year was left to the master whilst the number prevented proper attention to any' (Add. MS 35144, f. 413).   [2] Changed from 'the well bred gentlemen.'

The Autobiography of Francis Place

humour by men who were much excited; every one within hearing was silently listening, and at the conclusion of the song expressed their delight by clapping their hands and rapping the tables.

[Place intended to include, in an appendix to this chapter, a collection of these gross songs. In an extended table of contents of his personal writings he indicated that songs in this appendix would be grouped into those sung (*a*) at tradesmen's parties, (*b*) at public houses and clubs, and (*c*) in the public streets and markets (Add. MS 35142, f. 4*v*). There is no such appendix, but in his collection of documents on manners and morals, he recorded about thirty of these songs. (Interestingly, as many deal with glorification of criminals as with explicit sexuality.) Place preceded the collection with a statement of his familiarity with them: 'The following songs and specimens of songs, are all of them from ballads, bawld about the streets, and hung against the walls. It will seem incredible that such songs should be allowed but it was so. There is not one of them. that I have not myself heard sung in the streets, as well as at Chair Clubs, Cock & Hen Clubs & Free & Easy's. Every one of them were recollected by Mr Tijou and most of them by Mr Hayward' (Add. MS 27825, f. 144). When Place testified before the Select Committee on Education he alluded to these songs: 'I remember, when a boy of 10 years of age, being at a party of 20, entertained at a respectable tradesman's, who kept a good house in the Strand, where songs were sung which cannot now be more than generally described from their nastiness, such as no meeting of journeymen in London would allow to be sung in the presence of their families' (*Parliamentary Report . . . on Education*, 1835, p. 69).

A song recollected (in part) by Place, Hayward and Tijou is 'A Hole to put poor Robin in':

> One night as I came from the play
> I met a fair maid by the way
> She had rosy cheeks and a dimpled chin
> And a hole to put poor Robin in
>
> A bed and blanket I have got
> A dish a Kettle and a pot
> Besides a charming pretty thing
> A hole to put poor Robin in.

Place recalled a snatch of another popular song, which 'was a description of a married man who had a lecherous wife, it described his being a pale fellow reduced by her to a skeleton. I can only remember the last two lines.

> 'And for which I am sure she'l go to Hell
> For she makes me fuck her in church time.'

I remember these words in consequence of the shout which was always set up as the song closed with them.'

Place claimed that he had 'long since forgotten the Words' of 'Morgan Rattler,' one of the most famous songs of the era. His friend Richard Hayward supplied one verse:

3.2 School teaching, moral discipline

> First he niggled her, then he tiggled her
> Then with his two balls he began for to batter her
> At every thrust, I thought she'd have burst
> With the terrible size of his Morgan Rattler
> (Add. MS 27825, fs. 151, 147v, 165).]

The persons who frequented my fathers parlour were principally neighbours, and others who came from a short distance, and were all of them men who had the means of living genteely and saving money had they been so disposed.

My father was a very good swimmer yet from some to me unaccountable cause he would neither permit me nor my brother to attempt learning it, and if he happened to hear that either of us had been in the water he was sure to give us a beating, as he would for several other things which were either not faults, or such small faults as should not have been taken notice of, unless for admonition or advice which he never on any occasion used. Advice was wholly out of the question and the only admonition he used was a threat accompanied by an oath or an imprecation or both. He never spoke to any of his children in the way of conversation, the boys never ventured to ask him a question, since the only answer which could be anticipated was a blow. If he were coming along a passage or any narrow place such as a door way and was met by either me or my brother he always made a blow at us with his fist, for coming in his way, if we attempted to retreat he would make us come forward and as certainly as we came forward he would knock us down. If we happened to offend him in the morning we were sure if he knew it to have no victuals that day, to no meal did we dare come nor even into the house, we used therefore to absent ourselves from home 'till 9 o clock at night our usual bed time then open the street door which was opposite the stairs and run up to bed. We were however seldom without victuals as my mother usually contrived to let us have some, or I who usually had money bought some, but this was not the case with my brother who never did any thing by which he could obtain money except digging in the ruins. When we were in bed, my father used to send the servant for our shoes and stockings, and if they were wet he would come up stairs with a stick, generally the first he could lay his hands on no matter to whom it belonged and with this he belaboured us until he broke it. I scarcly ever recollect his ceasing to strike until the stick was broken. On one occasion I and my brother wandered into Spa Fields, called also, the pipe fields, from the great number of wooden pipes in some places six or seven in a row which conveyed the water from the New River head to various parts of London some of these pipes were always leaky and the water from them flowed away in shallow ditches In these ditches the boys

The Autobiography of Francis Place

used to fish for prickle-backs the [space left for word][1] called by the boys "little bats" towards the evening we were amusing ourselves catching these fishes when some bigger boys came and annoyed us, at length one of them took my brothers hat and set it afloat on the water. I was afraid it would fill and perhaps sink, so I ran into the water up to my knees and landed on the other side of the ditch and was followed by my brother. I was much distressed at the circumstance as I knew the consequence and there was no time to dry our shoes and stockings, we had, had, no victuals all that day, fear caused us to delay and made it late before we reached home, a crime in itself quite sufficient to ensure our chastisement. When we reached home we watched an opportunity when some one opened the door and with our shoes in our hands passed so quietly up stairs that we thought we were not observed, presently however we heard the maid coming upstairs for our shoes and stockings, No one can concieve our sorrow, or the misery of being in such a situation who has not himself been similarly circumstanced, the maid a strong sturdy wench, a kind hearted good tempered simple creature was exceedingly affected at our condition as was our mother with our having suffered all day and her apprehension which on such occasions she always entertained that one of us would be killed, an apprehension which on this occasion was very near being realized. No sooner were the shoes and stockings exhibited which they very reluctantly were, than my father as usual seized a stick and proceeded to the garett in which we lay, the maid who had more than her usual fears, had locked the room door and had hidden the key, vainly hoping that the door being locked he would desist from his purpose. The moment he found the door locked he set his foot against it and burst it open. With a resolution which no one hitherto had dared to shew, the maid followed him upstairs, and entered the room at his back, he was in a furious passion and setting the candle he had in his hand upon the floor he fell to beating at us with his utmost force. My brother on hearing him come upstairs had got out of bed and crawled under the bedstead, and I rolled myself up in the bed cloaths, covering every part of me and getting as far as possible from the side next the door. To get away from the maid who was crying and bawling with all her might my father went round the foot of the bed to the opposite side, but the maid seized hold of the tail of his coat and pulled as hard as she could, he being on one side and she on the other side of the bedstead, in this state he could not strike with effect for a moment the scuffle was between my father and the maid, in her hurry she knocked the candle over and put it out, and I almost suffocated uncovered my head, at the

[1] Place evidently intended to add a word identifying prickle-backs, small three-spined fish.

3.2 School teaching, moral discipline

instant my father struck a tremendous blow at the maid across the bed, it missed her, but fell full upon my forehead, and broke the stick. Having broken the stick he retreated. How the matter ended below stairs I know not, but it is probable that he took no further notice of it. It was supposed that he had broken the stick against the bedstead and that we had escaped the intended beating. This to my poor mother and the good servant was compensation for any thing, and every thing else that could happen at the time, they knew that if he once vented his passion he would not take any more notice of the matter. We knew well enough that if any circumstance occurred to prevent him coming upstairs at the moment, we should not be molested the next day, he had been prevented from coming up on one or two occasions by being obliged to make punch for and to attend to his customers and a quarter of an hours detention was sufficient to save us. I was stunned by the blow and when I recovered I found my brother dreadfully alarmed, he supposing I was dead. I suffered greatly from the blow, but neither I nor any one else ventured to take the least notice of it, or of the bruise which was visible for a long time.

It is remarkable that on no occasion, in none of his violent gust of passion did my father ever strike either of my sisters.

The preceding narrative contains an exact account of nearly the whole of the education I received, as well the education of circumstances as that at school up to the time I was nearly fourteen years of age.

How much I owed to my good master Mr Bowis for his moral instruction, for the confidence he taught me to repose in myself and especially in whatever I believed to be true; for the notions of perseverance he caused me to imbibe, of perseverance under difficulties and a reliance on honest industry it is impossible for me to determine, but I regard his instructions as laying the foundation of much of the happiness and prosperity I have enjoyed My temperament was sanguine, my temper violent and impetuous, his good instructions enabled me to regulate both to a considerable extent as I grew up, and made me *comparatively* chaste amidst scenes of excessive debauchery and among remarkably dissolute associates, prevented me from committing myself in any way so as not to be able to retreat. Which under many trying circumstances kept me honest, prevented me from committing acts of violence, and under the most pressing of circumstances and the lowest state of poverty saved me from either recklessness or despair.

It must not be concluded that my father had any intention to injure his family or in any way to annoy them, except to promote as he thought their good. He wished, and intended that his children, should be honest, sober, industrious and in every sense of the word respectable and he does

The Autobiography of Francis Place

not seem ever to have doubted that they would be so. The modes he adopted for producing these desirable ends were such as he expected would produce them; he wished to do his duty towards his children and he thought he did do his duty. He had no notion of producing effects by advice, his passions were strong, and too little under control to permit him to produce effects by examples. In his opinion coercion was the only way to eradicate faults, and by its terror to prevent their recurrence. These were common notions, and were carried into practice not only by the heads of families and the teachers of youth generally, but by the government itself and every man in authority under it, in the treatment of prisoners and the drilling of soldiers who were publicly beaten by the drill serjeants with a cane.

Indiscriminating, sanguinary and cruel as our Statutes are, they as well as all the other practices alluded to, were much more so fifty years ago,[1] and they were administered in a much more unfeeling and barbarous manner. The manners of all were much more gross then than now, what would now be thought intolerable cruelty towards inferiors was then practiced as mere matter of course. What would now be thought gross and brutal was then as little repugnant to common notions, to good sense and good teaching, as the more mild and efficacious modes now in use are thought to be by the present generation, however much room their still is for amendment

SEC. 3 DRESS OF BOYS

The dress of boys of my class, generally consisted of a cloth coat without any collar to it and with wide skirts, it was single breasted, that is it had only one row of buttons in the front, a waistcoat of the same material and a pair of sheep-skin breeches, sometimes of a yellow, sometimes of a leaden colour, with four buttons at the knees, but neither buckles nor strings – sometimes the breeches were of cloth the same as the coat and waistcoat, worstead stockings, sometimes white cotton stockings, shoes with buckles, and a cocked hat, or rather a hat looped up on three sides which made it an equilateral triangle. Round hats were coming into fashion, and when I was quite a child I wore one, with a gold band and tassel. My father said none but thieves and persons who were ashamed to shew their faces wore them, tho' he had for many years in rainy weather worn a large round hat covered with fine canvas and painted by himself. Umbrellas were not at that time generally used and he scorned the effeminacy.[2] I used to convert my hat into what was then called a

[1] Marginal note: '1833.'
[2] So did hackney coachmen, who regarded umbrellas as trade rivals. 'I can re-

3.3 Dress of boys

knucklers cock; (knuckler was the slang used for a pick pocket,) This was done by looping up the sides in the manner some of the Clergy and the Judges weare theirs. It is now called a shovel hat.

There was then no taste displayed in the dress of boys, no attention to their convenience in this respect, and the ugly dress of an ill dressed man was common to them. Monmouth Street Seven dials was the Mart for clothes and some large shops contained little besides boys cloaths. An immense quantity of business in new and old cloaths of all sorts was carried on in this street.* To these shops the sons of a vast number of tradesmen and others were taken to be fitted with cloaths, and especially in the week before Easter Sunday when the children of all who could afford to do so were furnished with new cloaths. In this particular the custom has completely changed.

Boys up to fifteen or sixteen years of age and many 'till eighteen or twenty years of age wore their hair long and curled on their shoulders, this was the general custom, but they who aimed at being thought knowing had fashions of their own, they especially who wished to be thought *Kiddies* had the hair on the sides of their faces rolled upon peices of window lead about four inches long, they usually had three and sometimes four of these leads one above another the lowest receding the most. Neither pantaloons nor trousers had then come into fashion, every one wore breeches stockings and shoes, some had strings to their breeches knees, but knee buckles were generally worn, as were shoe buckles on long quartered shoes, the buckles were very large and nearly touched the ground on either side. A bunch of st[r]ings at the knees and about a dozen of buttons close together with white cotton or silk stocking shewed a lad who was especially knowing. The stockings were usually white with broad stripes. Afterwards patent stockings became the fashion these were woven the length way and had a bright red or blue stripe, made very narrow – and put at from a quarter of an inch to two inches apart. Lads dressed in this manner would now appear particularly grotesque.[1]

---

member,' Place reminisced, 'the hackney coachmen lashing the peoples umbrellas with their whips as they drove along' (Add. MS 27827, f. 167).

* The custom being worn out the business of Monmuth Street has for many years been changed and is and has long been one of the meanest and poorest streets of its width and length in London.

[1] The rest of the page (about twenty-five lines) has been cut off. Opposite the beginning of the excised material Place added a note which he later crossed out: 'Pages A. B. C. should come in before the article on the *Dress of Boys*.' Pages A, B and C may have contained obscene songs. In his extensive table of contents Place indicated that this portion of chapter three dealt with 'Grossness of Parents,' followed by 'Specimens of Songs sung in Tradesmens Houses,' followed by 'Dress of Boys.'

The Autobiography of Francis Place

SEC. 4   TWELFTH DAY[1]

One great fete day with boys was Twelfthday. On this day they used to divert themselves and others with a most mischievous practice, now discontinued, of nailing peoples cloaths to Pastry Cooks Shops. Different groups of boys attended at different shops at which they performed their audacious tricks. The gang to which I belonged and of which I was sometime the leader, took our station at a shop in the Strand and there did all the mischief we could. In the earlier part of the day, it was holiday time, the boys rambled about the town to look at the twelft cakes and see which of the shops was the best, or finest set out, and at noon or a little earlier took their stations for the purpose of "nailing people." At this time shop fronts were very clumsy things, and had about them a great deal of wood work the shutters of most of them when up stood in large wooden grooves, and these grooves were well calculated for the mischievous purposes of the boys. Each boy had a hammer and a quantity of short clout nails, about three fourths of an inch long with broad flat heads, most of the boys used to practice driving of nails for some days previous to twelfth day and thus they became expert, a tap fixed the nail and a blow drove it home. Scarcely any one could stop to see what was in the shop without being nailed, the tails of mens coats and the gowns and petticoats of women were generally so firmly nailed that to get loose without tearing their clothes was impossible and the quicker this was done the less was the damage. Sometimes a womans gown and the tail of a mans coat were nailed with the same nail. It frequently happened when a person was nailed that he or she turned round either to extricate himself or herself or to attack the boys and were instantly nailed on the other side also. The noisy mirth these pranks occasioned was not confined to the boys who did the mischief, but was partaken of by grown persons, who ought to have known better; not by any means by the lowest of the people, but by those who were well dressed. These persons used to give the boys money to buy nails, and have been nailed themselves while in the act of giving the money. The rage of some who were nailed was exceedingly ludicrous, while the exultation of the boys and the bystanders was in proportion to the vexation it caused the sufferers to exhibit. When any one who was nailed on one side was nailed on the other side whilst scolding exultation was at the highest pitch. The shop which I and my gang attended was one door from the corner of Norfolk Street in the Strand the foot pavement was then very narrow, and a large wooden post stood at the corner of the street. This post served the boys

[1] This section is dated '1824.'

3.4 Twelfth Day

to dodge round when they were pursued, they were never caught by the angry person, for besides the advantage the post afforded, they were protected by the lookers-on who permitted the boy who was pursued to pass between them but obstructed the pursuer. A pursuit was indeed a high point in the joke, the boys shouted and hooted and the grown people laughed at and gibed the sufferer, no pursuit was therefore long continued, the sufferer being desirous to get away from his tormentors as fast as he could. A tall gent[l]emanly man being much annoyed at what he saw going on began to lecture the crowd on the impropriety of their conduct; at as he supposed a sufficient distance from the shop to escape being nailed, found all on a sudden that one of the tails of his coat was nailed to the post; this put him in a rage, and whilst stooping on one side to extricate his coat he was nailed on the other side the persons to whom he had addressed himself encouraged the boys who drove several nails home in each skirt of his coat and made him fast to the post, the state in which the gentleman found himself and that of the spectators may be concieved but cannot be described by me, notwithstanding I have even now a very vivid idea of the whole scene. He was glad to escape from the Post and the noisy joyous mob leaving portions of his coat behind him. This shameful practice has I believe wholly ceased, the boys contenting themselves with occasionally pinning the cloaths of two people together.*

In[1] the second number of the, "Everyday Book," by Mr William Hone, published today,[2] is a humourous wood cut of the front of a Pastry Cooks shop on Cornhill, the corner of Gracechurch Street, Mr Hone says, "on twelfth *night* the boys *assemble* at the pastry cooks shops, and nail the skirts of peoples coat to the shop.["] This is I think an error. It is just possible, but very improbable Mr Hone has used the present tense instead of the past tense. Mr Hone says a constable is employed by the shopkeepers, this is correct in respect to some of the principal shops, and were boys to nail peoples cloaths to the shop as they used to do, they would be seized and sent to the watch-house.

No constables were employed by pastry cooks on twefth day when I was a boy, and there were no Street Keepers.

SEC. 5 GUY FAWKES[3]

The fifth of November was a great festival among boys. It was a holiday

---
* 1834. The New Police and the alteration in the mode of fitting up shop fronts have completely put an end to the practice.
[1] This paragraph is dated 'Jany. 8. 1825.'
[2] William Hone, *Every-day Book*, 1825, vol. I, cols. 47–50.
[3] This section is dated 'November. 1823.'

at all schools, and very many masters permitted their apprentices to play the blackguard on this day. Numerous gangs were formed. Every Gang either had a Guy, or calculated on stealing one, "smugging a Guy" as it was called. In the evening bonfires were made in many parts of the town, over each of which Guy was hanged upon a gibbet, round which a considerable mob assembled firing off crackers and serpents and other fireworks. The three principal fires near Temple Bar were those of the Butchers in Clare Market, the Glass blowers in White Fryers and ours in Norfolk Street in the Strand, where it is crossed by Howard Street. For two or three months previous to the fifth of November preparations were made for the bon-fire, every piece of wood that could be obtained, by almost any means was laid by for the fire. I had a depot in my fathers cellar, in a place where ashes were thrown, other boys also had depots and a large quantity was always collected. The Guy was made up of old cloaths stuffed with hay and straw, the head was usually an old barbers block with a mask for a face, it was seated on an old chair through which two poles passed, like the poles of a sedan chair, and was carried in the same manner by two boys. A number of boys went in front, another party behind and two or three on each side, they were all armed with bludgeons. The strongest or most valiant of the boys carried the begging box in the front and led the way. The box hung from his neck and was also fastened round his body to prevent its being smugged – (stolen), as the boys passed along they begged money. The whole gang chanted continually.

> Pray remember the fifth of November,
> Gunpowder Treason and Plot.
> I know no reason, why Gunpowder treason
> Should ever be forgot.
> A stick and a stake, for King Georges sake
> A stick and a stump for old Olivers rump
> > So pray remember the bonfire.

At the end of this doggrel a loud shout was made and then the lines were repeated.

The only Gang whom our gang feared was that composed of the Clare Market Butchers boys, who were older and sturdier than we were. When attacked by other Gangs who came to "smug our Guy" we always stood our ground and never lost the Guy, but whenever the butchers were announced our party immediately sent of[f] the Guy if that was practicable, whilst the principal party remained to shew fight, and thus gain time to save the Guy. After getting as much of a drubbing as we were disposed to take, we also retreated. Once or twice we lost the Guy, the loss was however soon repaired as we always had another ready, but a

3.5 Guy Fawkes

very inferior one to the real Guy, as without a Guy our begging must have ceased. All the money collected was equally divided at the close of the day, when all concerned made a muster of combustibles, a gibbet was erected and Guy was hanged, a portion of the combustibles was placed under the gibbet and set fire to. A great many peopled were always assembled, some bringing materials for the fire An oilman in the Strand always gave us a pitch barrel. All the money collected by the boys for some time previous to the fire as well as the money begged was expended in fireworks, many of the grown people fired pistols and some of them guns. Very few tradesmen seem to have considered it any disgrace to them or their sons that they should go with a Guy and beg money. The number of Bonfires in London was very great, and the sum wasted in fireworks and combustibles was considerable. These practices have descended to some very few of the very meanest of the people and are all but extinguished. At the time spoken of, fireworks were sold at many oil shops and at most chandlers shops, there was no impediment to their sale, none to the begging, the bonfires or the letting off of fireworks. Many respectable persons countenanced the proceedings and contributed to them. I made serpents as they were called of a superior quality and sold them for about three times as much as they cost me, they were longer burning out than common ones, and made a louder report at the conclusion. A notice from the Police Offices has of late years been annually printed posted and advertised, warning persons neither to sell fireworks, nor to use them under the penalties of an Act of Parliament and persons have been convicted of and punished for offences under the act.

This day, November 7. 1823 the following account appeared in the newspapers

THAMES POLICE, Nov. 7th. 1823

GUY FAUX. – This office yesterday morning was crowded to excess by young men, many of whom described themselves as merchants' clerks, and sons of respectable tradesmen, who on Wednesday evening were amusing themselves upon Tower Hill, with letting off fire works, contrary to public notice, and the Act of Parliament, which is imperative, and renders the party offending liable to a penalty of 20s., and in default, to go to the House of Correction for a time not exceeding one month.

The Officers belonging to this establishment were on Wednesday night particularly vigilant, having taken no less than sixty persons into custody, and conveyed them to Aldgate Watch-house, where they relieved them for the night (except some few) who had the opportunity to procure bail for their appearance at this Office.

The cases came before Capt. RICHBELL, the Presiding Magistrate, who observed, the Act of Parliament could not be evaded, and convicted the whole,

The Autobiography of Francis Place

agreeably to the statute, in 20s. each, which was immediately paid, the parties appearing most anxious to return to their various occupations; and as the Act provides that in each case there shall be two witnesses to prove the fact, the penalties go to the Officers.

There were no Bon-fires, as in the time of my boyhood I heard there was one in 1822 in Bethnal Green but I could not discover one in 1823, alhoug I went through all the meaner streets from Charing Cross though Spitalfields to Bethnal Green after 7 p.m.

Mr Hone's account[1] is somewhat incorrect, but he wrote it in a state of necessity and haste, and to produce effect, for the purpose of selling his book.

His account of the fire at the end of Great Queen Street is exaggerated. Carts did not come all day long, nor any carts at all since I can remember and I am ten years older than Mr Hone, and I never even heard of any bonfire in this place, it is however probable that there was an annual Bonfire there but not such an one as he describes.

Excepting the substitution of the present for the past tense, the two last paragraphs are correctly written.

Three or four years ago several men hired a cart, to represent Guy Fawkes going to the Gallows, one of them was dressed as Guy in a ridiculous manner, and rode with his back to the horse, another had a surplice or something to represent a surplice and sat before him with a book in his hand pretending to preach and pray to him as the cart moved through the street; others drove the cart and begged money. The year following several such carts appeared in the streets, but the parties were taken before the Justices at the Police offices, and their processions were put an end to at once.

This day[2] I went about to several parts of the town where I thought it was most likely there would by Guy's if there were any. I did not see one, I saw some boys with dolls in their hands begging money for "poor Guy" They were very poor boys. I did not hear of one bonfire In the outskirts of London there are still Guys carried about.[3]

SEC. 6 BULLOCK HUNTING

A common amusement with boys and youths was Bullock Hunting. At this I was also a leader of boys of my age, though a follower of those who

---

[1] In the manuscript, this paragraph is preceded by a lengthy cutting from William Hone's *Every-Day Book* for Nov. 5, 1825 (vol. I, cols. 1429–33). This cutting describes and illustrates the way boys celebrated Guy Fawkes day in Hone's youth.

The date of Hone's article indicates that Place added the following paragraphs in 1825.

[2] This paragraph is dated '5 Nov. 1828.'   [3] Marginal note: '1839.'

3.6 Bullock hunting in the streets

made the game. On mondays and fridays, the market days at Smithfield for cattle, a number of men and boys used to assemble at the ends of the streets leading into the market and when a drove of bullocks came along, they fixed their attention on a light long horned one, these being the most skittish and the best runners, they then divided themselves into two parties, one on each side of the drove watching an opportunity to seperate the bullock from the drove.

I have seen as many as a dozen butchers and drovers in charge of a large drove when some of the bullocks have been a little wild, half of them going before the drove and half behind, this was sure to attract the attention of the bullock hunters and no sooner had such a drove left the market than a scene of noise and confusion scarcely to be equalled commenced. Every bullock hunter man and boy had a drovers stick, this was a ground ash plant from about three to four feet long with the root shaped into a knob at one end and a nail filed to a point at the other end, with these in their hands, menacing the drovers and frightening the bullocks they accompanied the drove, hallowing, and whistling through their fingers, two of which were put into the mouth to turn down the end of the tongue when by blowing hard a peculiar shrill and very lound note was produced, this is still practised by some of the drovers and butchers boys. As soon as a favourable opportunity occured, which was generally where two streets crossed, some of the bullock hunters ran up to the drovers both before and behind the cattle and flourissing their sticks made a shew of fighting and sometime actually produced a fight. At the same moment others of the bullock hunters dashed in amongs the beasts and endeavoured by noise and blows to start the bullock which had been noticed, in which they generally succeeded, but if another ran from the herd and seemed game he was pursued by the whole body. From the moment a bullock started it was utterly useless to attempt to recover him. The noise and the blows soon forced him to his utmost speed which was kept up either till he was blown when he would stop and very often turn round on his pursuers, this was fine fun the beast partially exhausted was easily avoided, and he was teased and tormented until he became perfectly furious, the sport was then at its height, as there was the more danger, the beast sometimes pursuing his tormentors and they in turn pursuing him; when he turned on his pursuers the greatest merit consisted in avoiding him as he ran furiously along and getting behind him in doing which great risks were taken yet I never saw any one hurt, they who were now behind him worried him to the utmost, but so furious and so quick did the bullock sometimes become that every one was obliged to keep at a respectful distance from him, and it was only now and then, that any one could get a blow at him, any one who succeeded

The Autobiography of Francis Place

in this was highly applauded. The hunt continued from one to several hours, when the poor beast still furious but exhausted was compelled to stand still, making only occasional darts at his enemies which were easily avoided. In this state a couple of halters were thrown over his horns and he was pulled and driven to some slauter house. If however he was in a state of fury which made this either too dangerous or impossible he was hamstrung on one of his hinder legs – and being fastened by his horns to the tail of a Coal waggon was dragged to the slaughter house. I have more than once seen the sport suddenly ended by a daring drover, thus, the man would get in the front of the beast and let him run at him dextriously avoiding him he swang his long heavy stick above his own head and struck the animal as he passed just above the hoof on the right or left hind leg with such force as to lame him, this he repeated on the other leg and the beast being thus maimed and unable to run any longer was taken away by those to whom he belonged. Some of the butchers boys who were sent to take care of the cattle usually ran after the bullock and as far as they dared assisted to hunt him instead of taking care of him. I used to be exceedingly delighted with this sport which I could only pursue on holidays. I never saw any one of the bullock hunters receive any injury from the bullock – I have seen other people knocked down by the animals and one or two tossed. Many were however injured and now and then one was killed.

This hunting of bullocks used to collect the greatest of blackguards, thieves and miscreants of all kinds together. Its cruelty was atrocious, it led to every species of vice and crime, and proves how very low were peoples notions of morality, and how barbarous their dispositions since they could permit such a vile and mischievous pastime to be pursued without interruption for a long series of years.[1]

N.B. This was near its Conclusion as a practice before I came into it.

---

[1] Place, and others, felt that bullock hunting epitomized the vile manners of the previous century. James Sayer, a Bow Street Officer, testified about the evils of bullock hunting when he appeared before a parliamentary committee investigating the police of the metropolis. Next to his printed testimony, Place added marginally, 'NB I requested Mr Grey Bennet to push the enquiries . . . respecting Tea Gardens and Bullock hunting to the extent in order to obtain as much evidence as possible of the state of manners, within their memory. I gave him a paper as a guide, but the enquiry was very carelessly performed' (Add. MS 27826, f. 190).

CHAPTER 4

My Apprenticeship

Masters family – The neighbourhood – Companions – Reminiscences of an Old Cockney – Companions. Clubs, cutter, chair, cock and Hen. Master removes to Lambeth – Companions – Holidays. Easter, Whitsuntide, Tea &c Gardens, – Leave my Master, and become a Journeyman.

I was to have been kept at school until I was fourteen years of age and then to be put apprentice, to a conveyancer as I have before observed,[1] but some months before I had attained my fourteenth year, my father mentioned the matter, and I preremptorily refused to be "made a lawyer." I had for a long period resolved not to go to the conveyancer, I know not why, but I had an antipathy to Law and Lawyers, and was resolved not to be made one even if my refusal should as I expected it would cause my being sent to sea. Contrary to my expectation my father instead of being offended, asked me what I should like to be, and I replied any thing if it were a Trade. This was in the evening, and my father went immediately into his parlour and offered me to any one who would take me. A little man named France said he would, and I was sent the very next morning on liking for a month to learn the art and mystery of Leather Breeches making.

Mr. France was a thin spare man about five feet two inches in height, he had done what was called a good business, and might have saved money, but to do so was not then the rule but the exception among common tradesmen. He had been three times married. Who or what his first wife was, I never heard. His second wife was a small delicate genteel woman somewhat hunched in the back, she brought him, as I understood between one and two thousand pounds. His third wife who became my mistress was a large big boned vulgar woman the widow of a bargeman at Queenhithe she also brought him some five hundred pounds. By his first wife he had two sons and three daughters. At the time I was sent to him, his eldest daughter was and had been for several years a common prostitute. His youngest daughter who was about seventeen years of age had genteel lodgings where she was visited by gentlemen, and the second daughter who was a fine handsome woman was kept by a captain of an East India Ship, in whose absence she used to amuse herself as such women generally do. Neither the eldest nor the youngest of the women ever came to his house, but the other used occasionally to visit him, and

[1] Place had not mentioned this before.

The Autobiography of Francis Place

when she came to spend the evening, her father muddled himself at home instead of doing so at the public house. His eldest son was a first rate genteel pickpocket, working at his trade of Leather Breeches making as a blind, he was a gay good looking fellow. He never came to the house, but he sometimes though seldom saw his father. His other son had been a thief; was obliged to abscond, and at length to avoid punishment inlisted into a West India Regiment and went abroad where he died a short time after I was put apprentice.

By his second wife he had two girls, wretched looking little children, probably made so by the bad usage of their mother in law. His wife my mistress used to get half tipsy every night before she went to bed. Such was "Old Joe France" and his family. Were I to relate many of the occurrences which came to my knowledge or were witnessed by me, they would be believed by those only who can appreciate correctly the probable events which must happen in such a family. Yet "Old Joe France" was by no means a subject for abhorrence either with the company he kept or to his neighbours; hitherto he had paid his way, was supposed to be worth money, was good natured, simple and obliging. He was however a sad miscreant. His history was well known to my father and his company, yet neither he, nor any one of them made any objection to my being bound apprentice to him for seven years.

At the end of three weeks I was bound apprentice and my father gave his parlour guests a feast on the occasion.[1]

I had for a long time entertained a notion that it was a much greater state of slavery to be compelled to go to school at nine o clock in the morning and remain till twelve, to go again at two, and remain 'till five, having two half holidays in each week, whole holidays at least a dozen times in the year, besides the four usual vacations; than it would be to be compelled to work for at the least twelve consecutive hours six days in the week, with only three holidays at Easter Whitsuntide and Christmas, and this notion was entertained by me as long as I was an apprentice, Strange as this may seem it is by no means uncommon; I have known many boys who thought as I did on this subject.

Bell Yard Temple Bar, was as perfect a sample of second rate tradesmens families as any place could be, and contained like all such places, at that time, much that was low vulgar and dissolute. It was inhabited by many men whose businesses were such as would have enabled them to bring their families up respectably and to put them out in the world with fair prospects of success, yet scarcly any one did half as much as he might have done in this way, and nearly all did the contrary. Bell Yard

[1] Place's father probably paid France an apprenticeship fee of £10 or £15 (George, *London Life in the Eighteenth Century*, p. 165).

4 My apprenticeship (1785–July 1789)

now contains many well doing respectable persons in much the same rank as when I lived there, but of characters as different as can well be concived, some of these are the descendants of families, who lived in the same houses at the time. I am speaking of, one of the boys having perhaps been steady or having given up his evil courses established himself in his fathers business. I could name four such, men of property and character with respectably educated families. The same may be said of Fleet Street and the Strand and indeed of every part of the Metropolis. In my time, most of the youths were loose characters. Some families in the neighbourhood were even more disreputable than that of "Old Joe France". Want of Chastity in the girls was common, and was scarcely matter of reproach if in other respects they, as was generally the case, were decent in their general conduct.

It must not be concluded either from what has been or will be related that many families were not highly respectable in every sense of the word, but the number of such families was small indeed in comparison with families now living in the same places and in similar circumstances. Scarcely can any lads the son of such persons now be found who are either thieves or low blackguards or who follow any of the despicable pursuits so common when I was an apprentice. Want of chastity in the daughters of such persons as I am speaking of is as rare as it was common. In nothing has the change for the better been greater than in the moral conduct and the increase of knowledge defective as it still is amongst this class of persons.

I lived with my master nearly three years in Bell Yard and nearly two years at Lambeth altogether somewhat more than four years and a half and was a journeyman on my own hands when not more than eighteen years of age. During the whole of my apprenticeship I was under no control so long as the work expected of me was done, I might go whenever I pleased and do as I liked and this was the case with many other apprentices.

The class to which I belonged was by no means the lowest The boys with whom I associated would not keep company with Journeymen excepting in their workshops,[1] nor with other lads whose fathers were not housekeepers. After I had been apprenticed sometime my master took another boy as a turnover from a man in the same business, he was a good sort of a lad and by no means so disreputable in his practices as I and my companions were, he was the son of a labouring man and had been apprenticed by the parish of Barking in Essex.[2] It is true he could

---

[1] Obviously to Place and his companions the journeyman, by not being a master, was a kind of failure. He was a piece-work employee, expected to labour thirteen hours a day to earn a meagre living. His chances of becoming a master were slight.

[2] By an Act of 1691, anyone who had served forty days as an apprentice in a parish was considered to have settled there, and hence could become a financial liability

The Autobiography of Francis Place

not have kept company with us, since he had no money, but if he had had ever so much he would have been as he was excluded from our society. Of my associates I shall speak presently.

My master at the time I was apprenticed had nearly outlived his customers, and as the business was to a great extent one of fashion, and was undergoing great changes which he could not adopt, so he could procure no new customers. He employed but one journeyman regularly and occasionally another. He was a remarkably good judge of his business in all its details as it had been carried on to a very recent period, and was a man well calculated to make his apprentices good workmen. He used to purchase the Leather in an unfinished state and finish it at home. In this finishing, called paring and grounding, I soon became expert. This sort of labour is severe, yet I was soon able to do a days work like a man, and was paid for all I did beyond the quantity expected from a boy at half the rate of a mans wages. I soon became a very good judge of the quality and value of deer and sheep skins, and as trade fell off it became necessary for my master to make " Rag fair breeches," that is breeches for sale to clothes shops These breeches were made from skins, which were damaged either by sea water or by worms, and it required considerable judgment to purchase – prepare – and make the leather into breeches, I always went with my master to purchase the leather, and assisted him in turning it to the best account, This was afterwards of use to me when in great need of assistance. All the work I did was reckoned at the wages of a journeyman, and a certain portion above that of a boy was paid to me, this put about six shillings a week in my pocket. My mother gave me a shilling a week and sometimes an odd shilling. My eldest sister who did pretty much as she pleased at home gave me money also, so that from these sources I obtained about eight shillings a week and sometimes more. I became a great man for my age and associated with from fifteen to twenty youths who were also apprentices mostly living in Fleet Street all turbulent unruly fellows, scarcly under any sort of control.[1] Some of them were sons of persons in easy circumstances who foolishly gave them a great deal too much money, and these lads were the most dissolute and least honest of us all. All of them were older than

---

to that parish; as a result the custom arose of each parish apprenticing its poor children in another parish (George, op. cit. pp. 221–2).

[1] 'Yes, I was a Fleet-street apprentice... There were 21 apprentices who formed one gang, and these youths used to go to Temple-bar in the evening, set up a shouting, and clear the pavement between that and Fleet-market of all the persons there. The boys all knew boxing; and if anybody resisted, one or two would fall upon him, and thrash him on the spot; nobody interfered; there was no police, or any mode of interfering with these boys' (Place's testimony before the Select Committee on Education, *Parliamentary Report ... on Education*, 1835, p. 68).

4 My apprenticeship (1785–July 1789)

I was and most of them were "fine men" to some of the prostitutes who walked Fleet Street, spending their money with them in debauchery and occasionally receiving money from them.[1] It may seem strange but it is true, that on no occasion did I ever hear one of these women* urge any one of these youths to bring her more money than he seemed willing to part from, and what they gave was generally spent, the women were generally as willing as the lads to spend money when they were *flush*. With these youths and these women I SOMETIMES spent the evening eating and drinking at a public house generally in a room to which none but such as ourselves were admitted and to which few but such as ourselves would desire to be admitted. I always paid my share, and never suffered any one to treat me. I never had any connection or acquaintance in the day time with any one of these women; and never had any serious quarrel with any one of my companions male or female. Most of these youths and such as they were, in all parts of the town, came to ruin. I have just now. 5 Decr 1823 been conversing with one *such person*. He is a common place sort of man who has been many years in business, is rich and has a most respectable and well educated family, quite different in all respects from his fathers family who was a tradesman in rather a large line of business, but fell to decay in his old age and died in poverty. On reading some of the pr[e]ceeding sheets, and notes for those which are to follow, his exclamations were vehement and amusing. "God bless my soul! – why yes! – that's true! – Ah! – Ah!! I had forgotten that![''] and then he related a number of similar cases and circumstances, which he said "were nearly as fresh to him as they were forty years ago". He could see all these things just as they had occurred, they were["] as fresh as they were forty years ago." His old associations being recalled, the whole train of his former ideas were revived notwithstanding they had laid dormant for many years, and the tricks, and customs, and associates – as well as the language and songs of his youth were vividly before him, he could have talked for hours of these matters but as they differed in no particular from my own they need not be stated. He was from a different neighbourhood in "Cockney shire" where of course the same manners prevailed and the same line of conduct was pursued.

Besides the connection with the Fleet Street women each of my companions, had a sweetheart who was the daughter of some tradesman, some of these girls were handsome, well dressed and in their general conduct respectable. With these girls I and my companions were as familiar as we could be, each with his own sweetheart. These girls how-

---

[1] Marginal note: 'Associates – Apprentices and Prostitutes.'
* 1839. There were certainly ten such women then who walked Fleet Street to one who walks it now.

The Autobiography of Francis Place

ever turned out much better than the boys – in as much as in other respects they were not like them dissolute. I could name several of them now living long since married to young men who were as well acquainted with them before marriage as afterwards, and I never knew any one of them who made a bad wife. I have for many years past particularly noticed four of these women, all still living all having families as truly respectable as are the grown up sons and daughters of tradesmen in good circumstances. These cases must be very numerous. Others were married to persons in business one to a young man of property who went to the East Indies* with his wife – another the sheweyest and handsomest of them all married an attorney in Lincolns Inn, a man in very good practice.† These are all, as well the women as their husbands, dead and have left no children behind them. Others settled in various ways and dropped out of my remembrance and notice after I had left the neighbourhood.[1]

Like most of my companions I was a member of a cutter club, smoked my pipe, sang my song and rowed in the eight oared boat. The cutter lads were a sad set of blackguards, greatly below the boat companies now,[2] though to a very considerable extent they are still composed of the same class of persons, fewer of them however being boys. Our club was no better than many others, most of the members either robbed their masters or other persons to supply means for their extravagance. The Cockswain of our boat was a small little fellow he was a printer and his fellow apprentice who was tall and strong rowed the stroke oar. Many a night and all night long at the close of the month have I worked with them at the Press to enable them to do a large quantity of Magazine work for which they were paid in addition to their weekly allowance.[3] They were both of them out-door apprentices and received weekly wages.[4]

The Cockswain was some years afterwards transported for a robbery –

---

* This was a Miss Brown the daughter of a hair dresser and wig maker, she was my sweetheart and I was very fond of her.
† She was a Miss Pitt the daughter of a fashionable ladies shoe maker.
[1] Francis Place Jr marked this paragraph and its two footnotes to be deleted. After he had drawn the marginal line to indicate deletion, someone cut off the three-fourths of a page following this paragraph.
[2] Marginal note: '1824.'
[3] 'I can recollect the time when on every Press there was a Rum Bottle, when a press-man was, as Mr Hone says, "degraded and sottish," they were as drunken as dirty and as ragged as any set of workmen whatever' (Add. MS 27827, f. 78). Place was glossing an account of printing offices in Hone's *Every-Day Book* for August 25, 1825 (vol. I, cols. 1133–5).
[4] An outdoor apprentice did not live at the place where he worked; his weekly wage – a substitute for the regular apprentice's food and lodging – was often regarded suspiciously by journeymen, who saw it as a substandard salary which endangered their standard of wages.

4 My apprenticeship (1785–July 1789)

and the strokes-man was hanged for a murder he did not commit. An attempt was made to set up an *alibi*, but it was said it could not be proved where he was, he being at the time committing a burglary with some of his associates.

I was an occasional frequenter of Chair, and Cock-and Hen Clubs, there were many of these "along shore," that is in the streets and courts in the Strand and Fleet Street near the river. I think there were not less than fifteen such between Black Friars Bridge and Scotland yard. There was a famous Cock-and Hen Club at a public house in the Savoy at which some of our boats company made a conspicuous figure. This club was held in a large long room the table being laid nearly the whole length of it. *Upon* one end of the table was a chair filled by a youth, *upon* the other end another chair filled by a Girl. The amusements were drinking – smoking – swearing – and singing flash songs. The chairs were taken at 8 p.m, and the boys and girls paired of by degress 'till by 12 o clock none remained.*

[Elsewhere Place gave some other details about his amusements at this period:

'When I was a youth, Palm Sunday morning was a grand holiday, a gay jubilee. Thousands of young persons used "to go a Palming," some in couples, girls and boys, some in parties. I have been Palming many times. We used to set out at daybreak and walk five – six – seven – miles into the country. Dulwich and the valleys among the Surrey Hills, as were indeed all places within the distance named where "Palm" abounded. All the public Houses and small Inns, round London sold "Rum and Milk," and notices thereof was stuck outside their doors and in their windows, thus – "The noted Rum and Milk house" – Rum and Milk sold here" Good accomodation &c &c. Every one who went out drank "rum and milk" on that morning, and a small quantity of warm milk with rum in it would muddle the head, and a second or third does would produce intoxication. Taken early and fasting vast numbers of what are now called, as indeed they were then, respectable lads and lasses, got fuddled. As drunkenness was all but infinitely more common then than now, a large number of more elderly persons went out under the pretense of "palming" actually to get drunk.

'The sons and daughters of multitudes of tradesmen and others were then under comparatively little restraint, and the boys used to knock at the doors of the parents to get the girls to go with them, as had been previously agreed, and out they went' (Add. MS 35144, fs. 175, 176).

'When I was an apprentice I went frequently among these girls [prostitutes along St Catherine's Lane] that is I went with other lads through the same places I went to see to day [Sept. 3, 1824], and at that time spent many evenings at the dirty public houses frequented by them. At that time, they

* I never in even a single instance went home with any one of these Girls, never had the least acquaintance with any of them, and never would appear to know or to speak to any one of them out of the Club room.

wore long quartered shoes and large buckles, most of them had clean stockings and shoes, because it was to them the fashion to be flashy about the heels, but many had ragged dirty shoes and stockings and some no stockings at all, all now wore stays, many of that time wore no stays, their gowns were low round the neck and open in the front, those who wore handkerchiefs had them always open in front to expose their breasts this was a fashion which the best dressed among them followed, but numbers wore no handkerchiefs at all in warm weather, and the breasts of many hung down in a most disgusting manner, their hair among the generality was straight and "hung in rat tails" over their eyes, and was filled with lice, at least was inhabited by considerable colonies of these insects. Drunkenness was common to them all and at all times when the means of drunkenness could be found. Fighting among themselves as well as with the men was common and black eyes might be seen on a great many' (Add. MS 27828, f. 119).]

When I first became an apprentice I was required to be home by 10 o clock at night, this was soon extended to eleven, but after some time, I was left to do as I liked. My master had in fact no control over me neither did he care much about me, or what became of me so that I did the work he required. His business declined gradually and I was the principal person, no one being employed but the two apprentices, aided by himself he old as he was working at his needle some hours almost every day. Without me he could not have found means to support his family and he dared not therefore risk the doing any thing which might induce me to leave him, as I should certainly have done, had any attempt to restrain me been made. He had once made a foolish attempt to coerce me, but as the consequence was a chalenge to fight me fairly he never again made any attempt of the kind. The only restraint I felt was the dislike I had that my course of life should be made known to my father, and the unhappiness I knew it would occasion my mother, I was however pretty certain that my master would not venture to tell them any thing about it, as he knew my father would attribute the evil doings to his want of due care, and that the consequence would be that I should leave him. The Chair clubs were common all over London and I have seen master tradesmen smoking their pipes in the same room with their own apprentices.*

Before I had served three years of my apprenticeship my masters ruin was complete, he was as much in debt as he could be, and had no business except making of Rag-fair breeches. He could do little for him-

---

* There are still in some parts of the town Cock and Hen Clubs, but these are in the lowest and most disreputable neighbourhoods, and are attended by none but disreputable people mostly young thieves.
   There are also some chair clubs attended almost wholly by Labouring men. They are very different from those of former times, there is but little drunkenness and the songs they sing – do not very often go beyond an equivoke.

4 My apprenticeship (1785–July 1789)

self, and had now no means of supporting his family but what arose from the exertions of his two apprentices. His second daughter who had occasionally assisted him was no longer in a situation to do much for him, and his eldest son whom I believe contributed to his support had been convicted of a robbery and at the expense of three hundred pounds had procured his pardon on condition of transporting himself for life. He went, as I was informed to Flanders with several hundreds of pounds in his pocket the produce of his robberies and I never more heard of him. In this state and at as I suppose Sixty five years of age my master was compelled to leave a house in which he had resided some thirty years, by removing his furniture clandestinely. One afternoon he requested me particularly to be home by eleven o clock at night as he should need my assistance in a particular affair. I guessed what it was and was home soon after ten o clock. He then told me he was under the necessity of removing his furniture to a house he had taken at Lambeth and that he wanted my assistance with others to get the goods out of the house (technically called shooting the moon), many small things had been removed, in a quiet manner so as not to excite suspicion, I and my fellow apprentice slept in the shop My master and mistress in the front garrett and the two poor children in the back garett. We all lived together in the shop the parlour and the front kitchen. The first and second floors and the back-kitchen were let to a very decent family the father of which was a hackney writer, that is a man who engrossed deeds &c for a law stationer, he had two sons, whom he was bringing up to his business and one other child a daughter. The removal began at twelve o clock the lower part of the house was soon cleared and the cart moved off with the goods. Now came the difficulty, the lodgers slept on the second floor and how to remove the goods from the garrett, without alarming them seemed to require a good deal of dexterity the bedsteads had been carefully taken down in the evening and tied up the bedding had been secretly removed bit by bit, and the children had been sent away instead of being sent to bed. The beds and bedsteads and a chest of drawers with some other things remained, some of these things were got out but the drawers the beds and the bedsteads remained, on attempting to remove these the lodgers were alarmed and Mr Adair came out of his bed room to ascertain the cause of the noise we were making. I had my masters bed on my shoulders and was above him on the stairs. I told him at once what we were doing and begged of him not to interrupt us, but he put himself into a furious passion and came running up stairs towards me, when I threw the bed upon him and knocked him down, his head fell upon the floor against the wainscot and he was stunned, my mistress went to assist him but by the time he had recovered and was able again to interfere, nearly every thing was got out of the house and I was gone. I was blamed in no measured terms, but after a parley it was agreed that we should all come again the next night and remove his goods, in the mean time the shop was to be opened as usual, but early in the morning some other arrangement was made and Mr Adair remained in quiet possession of the house.

The house to which we removed was a small one in Lambeth Marsh, on the south side of the road called the Lower Marsh. It was the sixteenth house from the Westminster Bridge Road, it was a neat house with a large garden, beyond this house there were five or six others and beyond these Market Gardeners grounds On the other side of the way the houses some of which were very old were continued much further, but beyond these there was nothing but gardeners grounds and open meadows to the road which led from Black Friars Bridge to the Obelisk in Saint Georges Fields. This road or lane before the building of Westminster Bridge was the only way from the Horse-ferry at Lambeth Palace to the Borough, there was then no other horse or Carriage way excepting one close to the river. I have heard my father say that he has shot snipes in the marshes. Even at the time when I went to live at Lambeth there was no carriage way to Great Surrey Street but along the lane which came out into that road much further from Blackfriars Bridge than the street since built called Charlotte Street, and the only foot way was through a gardeners ground, called "Curtis's halfpenny hatch."* A town has since been built on the Garden Grounds and meadows and the lane called the Marsh has been made into a street.

A short time after our removal my master surrendered himself in an action and became a prisoner within the walls of the Kings Bench. The Rag-fair breeches trade was rapidly declining in consequence of the increase of the cotton manufacture, corduroys and velvateens were now worn by working men instead of leather. The consequence to us was that at the end of twelve months we could not make journeymens wages from the sale of Rag-fair breeches and our earnings could no longer maintain the family. Had it not been for the thorough knowledge of this kind of business and my energetic mode of conducting it sometimes employing a man to assist us and now and then two, the family must have been starved, as it was they were subjected to great privations occasionally.

The life I led was in nearly every respect the same as that I had led in

* 1841. The whole of the ground at that time fields – from nearly the river side to the obelisk in St Georges fields has been built up and forms a very considerable town of Itself Waterloo Bridge stands where there was a ferry and the Victoria Theatre stand where was a field. Lambeth Marsh, then a lane through the meadows is now a street through the new town.

4 My apprenticeship (1785–July 1789)

Fleet Street with a little more diversity of entertainment, and with companions not quite so dissolute as those I had left, and those with whom I still associated as a member of the cutter club during [the text at this point does not continue.][1]

The SURRY JUSTICES on Saturday, put a stop to all Music in the Apollo Gardens, Temple of Flora, &c. &c. these places not being licenced for that kind of entertainment. The lower class of people may indeed *tipple* their senses away without offending the law; but they shall not have their minds *harmonized* by a concord of *musical sounds*. Nay, to such a rigorous Interdiction is this Magistratical decree to be carried, that an order is to be served on the *Gatekeepers* of each *turnpike*, forbidding them under pain of incurring the displeasure of the Bench at Union Hall, not to admit either *Barrel Organ*, *Hurdy Gurdy*, *Violin*, or *French Horn*, or the man that whistles so many tunes with his lips, and all ballad singers without exception, from passing through on any account whatsoever, into the county of Surry.   Mar. 29. 1790.[2]

From the heedless mode of education and the want of correct notions of propriety in their relatives, want of chastity in girls of the class of which I am speaking [was] common, but it was not by any means considered so disreputable in master tradesmens families as it is now in Journeymen mechanics families. A tradesmans daughter who should now misconduct herself in the way mentioned would be abandoned by her companions, and probably by her parents, she would indeed be so debauched in mind before such a circumstance could take place, that it is almost certain she would be prepared to quit her home without any thought of returning to it, and consequently her ruin would be complete,

---

[1] Someone cut out a page and a half of text at this point. The missing page was to have a footnote which read, '* This was so before I left Bell Yard.' As a substitute for the missing page the censor pasted a small newspaper cutting in the centre of a sheet.

[2] The date is in Place's handwriting. The source of the newspaper cutting has not been identified.
   Place frequently spoke of these tea-gardens he visited as an apprentice. 'I can remember the Dog and Duck in St George's Fields, the White Conduit House, the Temple of Flora, the Temple of Apollo, the Blue Lion, the Bull in the Pond, and other such houses ... When I was an apprentice and went to those places, they were in a state utterly indescribable now for the public sight' (Place's testimony to the Select Committee on the Inquiry into Drunkenness, *Parliamentary Report ... on Drunkenness*, 1834, pp. 176–7). 'I have seen two or three horses at the door of the Dog and Duck in St George's Fields on a summer evening, and people waiting to see the Highwaymen mount' (Add. MS 27826, f. 189). 'The Dog and Duck ... I have been there when almost a mere boy, and seen the flashy women come out to take leave of the thieves at dusk, and wish them success ... In Grays Inn-lane was the Blue Lion, commonly called the Blue Cat; I have seen the landlord of this place come into the long room with a lump of silver in his hand which he had melted for the thieves, and pay them for it' (Place's testimony before the Select Committee on Education, *Parliamentary Report ... on Education*, 1835, p. 70).

but it was not so formerly being unchaste did not necessarily imply that the girl was an abandoned person as she would be now and it was not therefore then as now an insurmountable obstacle to her being comfortably settled in the world.

The progress made in refinement of manners and morals seems to have gone on simultaneously with the improvements in Arts Manufactures and Commerce. The impulse was given about sixty years ago, it moved slowly at first but has been constantly increasing its velocity. Some say we have refined away all our simplicity and have become artificial, hypocritical, and upon the whole worse than we were half a century ago. This is a common belief, but it is a false one, we are a much better people now than we were then, better instructed, more sincere and kind hearted, less gross and brutal, and have fewer of the concomitant vices of a less civilized state.

[Preceding part of text missing][1] my master abused and threatened him, and this led to the giving up of my indentures, in the month of July 1789, at which time I was seventeen years and eight months old.

We had been for some time making breeches for workhouse boys as journeywork for a contractor for which my master received only eight pence a pair, even this sort of work was now at an end and my master and his family were reduced to the lowest state of poverty. He his wife and the two unfortunate children lingered on for another year when they all went into the workhouse where the old people shortly afterwards died. What became of the poor children I never heard.

[1] At this point in the manuscript someone cut off the bottom of one page and the top of the next. What remains suggests that Place's father quarrelled with France.

CHAPTER 5

Family History

SEC. 1 FROM THE TIME I WAS APPRENTICED TO THE TIME WHEN MY FATHER DISPOSED OF HIS PUBLIC HOUSE. BROTHERS CONDUCT – ECCLESIASTICAL SUIT – CONDUCT OF THE DUKE OF NORFOLK – FATHER RUINED – REMOVES

In giving an account of myself I have somewhat overrun the order of time, but my being bound apprentice and my leaving my master were epochs and I thought it best to continue the narrative through the time between them without interruption. I shall now return to the first of these periods and relate some particulars respecting my father and the other members of the family.

My brother who was twenty one months younger than I was continud at school after I was bound apprentice until he was nearly fourteen years of age, when it came to his turn to be put out apprentice. My father wished him to go to some trade which he obstinately resolved not to do, nothing in the way of trade would do for him, he was resolved to be a lighterman. He had never shewn any desire to excel in any thing, he never was expert at any game, would never learn to swim, he could neither run, nor jump, nor sing, nor whistle, he was not dull but perverse and fond of annoying every one as much as he could. His leisure had been spent on the river, in rowing a boat or a barge generally alone, sometimes with a lighterman, he was a remarkably stout strong boy like his father in form and became more and more so as he grew up. He had made all the watermen and all the lightermen in the neighbourhood his friends, he would work for either hardly and freely. To prevent his becoming a lighterman, my father persuaded some of the lightermen to discontinue countenancing him, and to drive him off the barges as often as they could, and he furnished two or three of them with ropes ends – "cootes"[1] with which to beat him and drive him ashore. This did not at all dismay him he was not to be intimidated, and when struck instead of running away he would stand still, this produced just what he had anticipated, they ceased attempting to drive him away, and some still allowed him to go with them. On one occasion a barge was to be taken from the wharf at high water at five o clock in the morning it was towards the close of the autumn, the barge was to be taken to the Pool for coals and he resolved to go in her. He therefore got up at four o clock, and

[1] Colts. See above, p. 34 n2.

The Autobiography of Francis Place

went on board the barge. In every coal barge there are two places one in the head called the fore sheets, and one in the stern called the stern sheets the lighterman usually stands in the fore sheets to row and guide the barge, in each of these sheets is a flap on hinges which turns up, the space under these flaps is large enough to hold three or four men, My brother got under the stern sheets and when the barge was fairly out in the stream he pushed up the flap and made his appearance on the sheets, to the no small amazement of the lighterman. My brother soon made himself known and was allowed to pull an oar. When he came home in the afternoon it was concluded that neither persuasion nor force would be of any use and a Mr Woodward of Hungerford engaged either to sicken him of the business or to take him apprentice. Woodward agreed to take him at Christmas and to go down with him in a barge as soon as there should be ice floating in the river, and this was done accordingly, Early one morning he was told he must go down in a barge to Rotherhithe for a load of coals and at day break they started. Woodward was well fed and well cloathed, my brother was ill clothed and had nothing to eat, the barge drifted slowly and was loaded at the ships side, & the[1] loaded barge was drifted up again and my brother who was starved with hunger and pinched with cold came home in a most miserable plight; for some time he could do nothing but cry. My mother was greatly afflicted she nursed him and advised him not to think of being a lighterman. His promise was easily obtained and there seemed to be no chance of his becoming a lighterman, but when the next morning arrived and he was neither cold nor hungry, he marched himself off to Mr Woodward and was soon afterwards bound apprentice to him. He served his time regularly giving no offence to any body and embarking in no irregularities, beyond such as his fraternity called fun. From the day his apprenticeship expired, he never set his foot in a barge, nor scarcly ever, even if he did once, rowed in a boat during his life. When he was twenty two years of age he married a young woman with whom he obtained about five hundred pounds in money, tried his hand at several kinds of business but suceeded in none; at length he bought two coaches and some horses and commenced Hackney Coach Master driving one of his own coaches, he lived a very irregular life and died when he was thirty six years of age leaving a widow but no children.

He was a man possessed of great muscular powers for his height five feet five inches, when about twenty one years of age he trotted with a sack of flour from St Clements Church round the New Church in the Strand and back again, in less time than he could get over the ground unincumbered.

[1] Place wrote originally 'a loaded barge.'

5.1 Family history (1785–1789)

During the time he was a hackney coachman, he interfered in some meetings of the trade, for whom, or rather for him, I wrote some papers and resolutions, for which the Coachmasters presented him with a silver pint pot with an inscription; now in my possession.

About the time when I was bound apprentice my father and the Parish in which he lived got into a suit in the Ecclesiastical Court. I am not sure that I ever heard the case correctly but I understand it to be this. A woman came to the overseers and claimed parish aid as the wife of my father, in consequence, as she said, of a fleet marriage some forty years previously.[1] The Parish Officers not wishing to make the matter public advised my father to make a small weekly allowance for the woman, this he preremptorily refused to do, saying she was no wife of his, nor ever had been, and he would have nothing to do with her. Enquiries were made, altercations ensued and an action was commenced in the ecclesiastical court, it continued a long time, I suppose for three years and terminated at last by my father being excommunicated; under which interdict he remained to the day of his death. I remember being desired by him to go to the church to hear him excommunicated. I understood that a large sum of money was expended by the parish and that it had cost him several hundreds of pounds to defend himself.[2] If this account be as I think from what I heard it is, correct, he saved the payment of four and sixpence a week at the cost of a thousand pounds. A supper was given by him to commemorate the result.

SEC. 2   SKETCHES OF CHARACTERS – PERSONS WHO
FREQUENTED MY FATHERS HOUSE

The Duke of Norfolk than whom it might upon the whole be difficult to find a greater scoundrel[3] used sometimes to look in at my father's house, sometimes he used to send for my father to the Crown and Anchor Tavern and there they used to get drunk together. My fathers house as well as the Tavern was on the Dukes estate which comprised all the houses from Milford Lane on the east to strand Lane on the west, and from the Strand to the river. My fathers lease had nearly expired and the Duke promised him a renewal, but at the end of a year and after

---

[1] Prior to the Marriage Act of 1753, a valid marriage could be performed by a clergyman in orders, without registration of the marriage. In the vicinity of the Fleet large numbers of clergymen (many of them debtors) performed marriages for any couple who paid the fee.

[2] It was public outcry over the costs, the delay and the prolixity of the ecclesiastical courts that led, in 1857, to bills restricting their powers (F. A. Inderwick, *The King's Peace*, 1895, p. 219).

[3] Place's son drew a line through this description and marked 'Dele' in the margin

repeated promises had been made, a lease was clandestinely granted to a man named Thomas who kept another public house of less business near the bottom of the street called the Watermans Arms. It seems that this Thomas had been a Roman Catholic, and had lately become very religious, he attended the same chapel as did a Mr Seymour the Dukes Steward and Agent and from him Thomas obtained the lease, this was out of all regular course of proceedings, and could not have been anticipated, the tenant in possession always having the opportunity to take a new lease if he chose. It was I believe my fathers intention to have taken a new lease which would have cost him from £200 to £300 and have sold it, after some time, with the good will for £1000 which they were probably worth. His want of provident care, and his law expenses, had brought him into debt to several persons and he calculated on the new lease as the means of payment and by the surplus which would remain of trying some other mode of obtaining a living. The conduct of the Duke and his agent ruined him at once. Unable to go on, he procured a friendly action to be brought against him and went to the Fleet Prison, and after some time he took the rules and became a lodger at a public house in Fleet Lane called the Elephant and Castle.[1] The lease of his house had about two years to run and he threatened to shut it up until the expiration of the lease, thus destroying the trade and increasing the dilapidation of the premises. This alarmed Thomas who though a poor man offered to purchase the fixtures and good will, the value of the latter being very small as it was only the two years yet unexpired of the lease which could be sold. After some parlying it was agreed that the fixtures should be valued, as well as all the fittings and that Thomas should have the house if in addition to the purchase of the fixtures and fittings he would give more for the goodwill than any one else would. A day for the sale was appointed and an attorney, a friend of my father, undertook to manage the business and do the best he could. I was directed to attend and help the attorney, to receive the money and pay the debts of my father of which I had a list, but I was at any rate to secure two hundred pounds for him whether the debts were or were not paid in full. A release had been prepared and after I had put by the two hundred pounds, the remainder of the money was to be tendered to the creditors *pro rata* on their signing the release. The attorney was slow, "too wise by half," and was doing the business badly. I therefore interfered and superseded him. I attended the brokers, talked with the creditors and abused

[1] Rules: the area in the vicinity of the prison, where certain types of prisoners, particularly debtors, might live rather than in the prison. The fee for living in the rules was £10 for the first £100 of debt and £4 for each further £100. The debtor could not leave the district, except on Sunday when no one might be arrested for debt, but he could live there as long as he wished, unmolested by creditors.

5.2 Persons who frequented my father's house

Thomas who was present. When the goods fixtures and fittings had all been valued I had to dispute respecting good will. I demanded a large sum, and said that unless it was given I would sell everything there was upon the premises pay the money among the creditors and shut up the house, all the creditors supported me, not one of them was unfriendly or harsh, and some persons who came in, who were not creditors were not sparing of their invectives against the Duke his agent and Thomas. Thomas who knew my fathers obstinacy of disposition seeing I was in earnest gave a much larger sum for the good will than was expected and the bargain was closed by the payment of the money. I paid all the creditors who were present and left with the attorney a sum of money to discharge some small debts, and carried to my father three hundred and forty pounds. He was greatly pleased, and surprised, he gave me half a crown and told me never to be without a shilling in my pocket, This was the first money he had ever given me and it was the last. I was at this time nearly seventeen years of age. Thomas removed to the house and remained there many years. I believe he died there.

The following sketch of some of the persons who frequented my fathers parlour will exhibit a faint picture of the manners of the times amongst the class to whom it relates.

Nearly all the persons who were constant attendants at my fathers house died poor; most of them in wretched poverty.

I have already related the leading particulars of the catastrophe of my master and his family and shall now do the same very concisely with those of others, his associates, and my fathers very good friends.

Mr. Woollams. was a Hair dresser and wig maker in Arundel Street – His business was extensive and lucrative, he might have lived respectably and saved money, he like many others spent his time and wasted his money in public houses, outlived his business, died very poor and left his family in great distress.

Skillem a Tailor with a very good business ended in the same way, but left no family.

Robinson a Glazier and Painter in rather a large way of business, went on the same way and came to the same end leaving his family in distress.

Wood a carpenter – just like Robinson and ending like him.

Duke a Tailor his course of life was the same, his business decayed, and being nearly ruined he sold his niece whome he had brought up, to a rich man who came from the East Indies and lodged in his house, he contrived to live upon them for some time. His niece was a pretty modest girl, who pined herself to death and Duke became destitute. Soon after this his wife died and he became a beggar about the streets. He died in the workhouse.

The Autobiography of Francis Place

Bury he was a gentlemanly sort of man, and held some place in one of the government offices, he kept a shop in the Strand between Arundel and Norfolk Streets which was attended by a very respectable looking woman with whom he lived, it was a bed fringe &c shop and is still open in the same line of business – he when his circumstances declined sold his protage's daughter as Duke had sold his niece, before she was fifteen years of age. She had a child before she was sixteen and at seventeen was married to a young man who went to the West Indies leaving his wife at home, he gained some money came home and died, she lived on the money as long as she could and then became a common prostitute in the Strand, Bury died poor, and miserable in the extreme.

Bayley a Leather Stainer and Dresser he had a business which enabled him "to live sumptuously every day", but his extravance caused an expenditure beyond his income. He like the rest outlived his business died in poverty and left his family in great distress.

Seldon. He was a silk mercer in Holy-well Street, at that time occupied by more mercers than any other street in London, some of the shopkeepers were also manufacturers and did large strokes of very profitable business. Seldon spent all the money his business produced him, and died, leaving two boys who were my schoolfellows – when one was 12 the other 14 years of age, and one girl who was perhaps 15 years of age. The widow carried on the business as well as she could for some time, and endeavoured to make her fortune by insuring in the State Lottery; this soon led to her total ruin she took to drinking and died. The children were brought up in idleness as were most of those who aped gentility, and when poverty came on, they were unable to earn their living, and but ill disposed to make any effort in the right way. The boys contrived to live as they could not very honestly. One of them after leading a dissolute life died when he was about twenty three years of age in an hospital. The other was so reduced that at last he became waterman to the coach stand at St Clements Church Yard and used to water the horses; about the time of his brothers death he was found dead in the dust hole of the White Lion in Wych Street, suffocated with Gin. Ann Seldon the sister a stout handsome girl after flourishing about the streets with the boys for some time, went upon the town, a common prostitute, she soon came to an end and the family, like many others was extinct.

These are fair samples not only of the neighbourhood of St Clements Church, but of all such neighbourhoods. Many more could be given but they would be mere repetitions, I have a list of no less than twenty seven such, all of whom frequented my fathers house. Every one of the persons mentioned or alluded to, might have lived genteely, have brought up their families respectably and placed them out in the world comfortably, but

5.2 Persons who frequented my father's house

it was not the custom at that time to do so, and the result was inevitable ruin.

Others there were in abundance who were not placd in such good circumstances and they fell of without notice being taken of them.

The way of life described is not even yet wholly abandoned a *few* still follow the same course and arrive at the same end.

On[1] my having read some portion of the preceding narrative to Mr Fenn Bookseller at Charing Cross he related circumstances respecting some families in the Strand and in its neighbourhood which were similar to those I have related. He says that for one careful attentive discreet men some thirty years ago there are forty now. Several whom he named were reducd from a state of prosperity to abject poverty and some of them died in the workhouse, yet there was considerable alteration for the better at the time he alluded to, but the old sots were not then all worn out.

Query[2] – has not the change in manners and morals done much towards the great increase which has since taken place in the population.

SEC. 3[3]   SKETCH OF ANOTHER CLASS OF TRADESMEN

There was another class of tradesmen, or rather there were tradesmen whose trades could not be ruined as the trades of those were who have been mentioned. One as a sample shall be described, simply and truly without exaggeration.

I had written the following account with the names of all the parties, but as there are descendants of the family living, highly respectable and worthy people I have re-written the account suppressing all the names.

It must not be concluded that every family in the class was in all respects like this, but a vast many were so in some respects, and exceeding it in others equally disreputable. It would be difficult now to find one such family in a long street, and impossible to find one which like this and many others, at the time of which I am writing were like it, careless of censure taking no pains towards concealment, and not losing caste by the circumstances being known. It will serve as a strong contrast to the manners and habits – and morals of the class to which it relates when applied to men of the same class at the present period

A. —— was a tradesman in a large way of business in the Strand, he was a tall strong good looking man, his wife was a middle sized handsome woman. He was a man strongly imbued with the prevailing habits and vices of his time. He was a litogious man, always at law, it was said of

---

[1] This paragraph is dated '14 Augst 1828.'
[2] The query is dated '1841.'   [3] This section is dated 'June – 1827.'

him that in all his transactions of trade he paid thirty shillings in the pound as he seldom paid any one until he was sued for the money. He was as extravagant as such men commonly were, and all his pursuits of a pleasurable kind were gross, but the large profits of his extensive business carried him throgh, and when a very old man he retired with a competency kept a saddle horse and lived until he was Ninety two years of age.

He had two sons and three daughters, both his sons are living and so are two of his daughters.[1]

The eldest son was a fine manly figure a sturdy bullying sort of a fellow, he had been on board a man of war as a midshipman.

The other son was a tall well formed gentlemanly fellow

The three daughters were very fine women.

The eldest son with the aid of his father and mother carried off an idiot sort of a girl from a boarding school and married her, she had some money and a fortune something above a thousand pounds a year she was an orphan and a ward of Chancery, the matter was long before the court but it ended as it does in most such cases, the principal being settled on the children the parties being allowed the annual income. They never had a child.

He brought his wife home where she had several times visited as the friend of the youngest sister who was placed at the same school with her as a decoy; and here she lived with the whole of the family sons and daughters. The husband had another woman who was called Miss Louise and she too lived in the family as a visitor and with her the husband usually slept. The poor ideot wife, never suspected, or never gave herself the trouble to enquire about the matter. Her husband gave himself no concern about her, and so long as she was dressed in fine cloaths and treated as a child she was contented. The husband has for a great many years past lived on her income as a private gentleman.

The youngest of the two sons who was the best person in the family married the daughter of a man of property who had successfully conducted some very large undertakings and on his daughter being married he took her husband into his concerns as a partner. He was somewhat ostentatious, not a well informed man, but he was industrious and well adapted for business. He the husband has long lived as a gentleman keeping a carriage and a good house at a short distance from London, he has several children all well educated all well-doing.

The youngest daughter was married at an early age to a man in a large wholesale business he went on prosperously and was esteemed wealthy. they had no children, she died some ten years after her marriage and he

[1] Marginal note: '1826.'

5.3 Sketch of another class of Tradesmen

after her death contrived to destroy his property and became a bankrupt. He did not long survive his bankruptcy.

The next youngest of the daughters who was as chaste as Miss Louise, and the generality of her female friends, married a tradesman in a good way of business, he was a frequenter of my fathers house, like others he fell to decay, and became a publican himself in a low neighbourhood, he carried on his business to a small extent in his public house, he did not live long however after he became a publican His forman who had been his wife's lover now lived with her openly and carried on the public house concern. She had some money so they were married and took a house in a leading street at the west end of the town made a good shew of trade did a considerable quantity of business and saved money; in a few years he too died leaving her a widow with a valuable business and a good deal of money, she continued the business for some time aided by her only son a young man by her first husband, she has for several years past lived privately on the money saved and her son is well provided for in business.

The eldest daughter was a fine clever woman, with the coarse features of a man, and the conduct of a man, she was very active and of much importance to her father in his business, to which she attended in an extraordinary and unusual way, like a man – and thus in great measure supplied his neglect. She had several lovers, but at length when circumstances made it prudent she married her fathers foreman a conceited ignorant fellow whom she managed as she pleased. They went into business carried it on for many years successfully living in an extravagant stile but within their income. He died leaving two sons and one daughter, all of whom were ill educated but are married well doing well and bringing their children up well.

This outline could be filled up with many curious incidents, but enough has been done to mark the distinction between former and present times which is the object aimed at.

I am not aware of any book which contains descriptive accounts of any class of people which will enable any one to judge accurately of the manners of our ancestors; strong features are occasionally shewn, from which we may calculate some of the great changes and infer the moral condition of the people, but we have very little of correctly detailed domestic history, the most valuable of all as it would enable us to make comparisons shew clearly the progress of civilization, and make people more disposed than they are to proceed in the right way by convincing them that instead of mankind growing worse and worse they grow better and better and that the wisdom of our ancestors may be too highly prized.

CHAPTER 6

Family History. To my marriage – in March 1791

Mothers troubles – my employment – with my sisters husband – with Mr Allison – with Mr Pike – his business, conduct, sister – my discharge. Sad state of my father and mother, – His improvidence, poverty Mothers admirable conduct – My courtship – employed by Mr Lingham.

Unwilling to interrupt the narrative of my Apprenticeship I have again departed from the Chronological order I wished to observe. I shall now therefore return to the period when I let my fathers house in Arundel Street in the Strand.

My mother and my two sisters removed to my fathers lodgings in Fleet Lane on the morning of the day on which the public house was let, taking with them the necessary furniture &c for the rooms they were to occupy.

My eldest sister had for some time been courted by a young man who was apprenticed as a Cook to Mr Simpkin who kept the Crown and Anchor Tavern, (he was a very respectable young man;) who had still a few months to serve when we left Arundel Street at the expiration of which they were to be married. My sister went out to service as a sort of own maid and companion to a lady with whom she lived in a very comfortable manner. She left her service when the time came for her to be married. From some cause of which I never learned the particulars, a delay took place, and my sister took charge of the bar, of the public house in which my father lived whilst the Lanlady was confined in childbed, here she became acquainted with a young man named James Pain, a Chair carver, and after a time married him, as she herself said to spite her former lover with whom she had quarrelled and whom, she unreasonably and unjustly rejected. All her friends wished her to marry as was at first intended, but neither the entreaties of the young man who claimed her promise, nor the persuasions of her mother, nor the advice of her friends could make any impression on her, she was obdurate.

The young man who had courted my sister whose name was Ward, sought and obtained a situation as cook in a gentlemans family near Liverpool and I never again heard of him. Ben Ward was a great favorite with all the family, he was a sensible respectable young man, and had money enough by him to have established himself comfortably in business.

My sisters marriage was the first of a new series of heavy perplexities

6 Family history to my marriage (March 1791)

and misfortunes which fell successively on my mother and at length, if they did not break her heart, were the cause of a miserable existence for some time and of her death sooner than it would otherwise have happened.

Pain was a journeyman, a good workman and remarkably swift, he could easily earn full four pounds a week all the year round, and never need have wanted work, chairs, and other small articles of furniture which were to be carved were sent to his own workshop, and he always had much more than he could do. He was an ignorant bestted fellow, who would work hard and drink hard, he had never saved a single shilling, and was scarcly decent in his appearance. He was however accepted among us after his marriage, and hopes were entertained that being married he migh leave off drinking and become a steady man. This might have happened if his wife had been attached to him, one who would have humoured him a little and taken pains with him, but my sister was not in a condition either to respect him or to take any pains to make him better than he was. She despised him and took care that he should have continual proofs of it. He therefore sought for consolation in drinking and she in methodism. She went to chapel, prayed, and sung hymns at home, and was as absurd as he was, she held some office in the religious community to which she belonged, and used to attend meetings when she ought to have been at home.

She was a good looking, smart tolerably clever young woman. My mother had taken a great deal of care of her and my youngest sister, and they were well instructed in every thing likely to be useful to them in the rank of life she expected to see them placed in, in which however she was deceived as to each of them.

At the end of twelve months from her marriage my sister had a child which was christened *Mercy*, this circumstance kept her for some time from her ridiculous fanatical associates, and as she could no longer do as she pleased she became careless of herself, more than ever negligent of her house slovenly and dirty. She seemed to have no care for herself or for any one else, and matters went on in a very bad way.

When I left my apprenticeship I could not find immediate employment as a journeyman, and my sister and her husband proposed that I should contract to serve them for three years and be taught the art of carving. I was to recieve weekly wages and to maintain myself. The amount of wages was to be settled at the expiration of three weeks trial of what I could do. At the end of the first week I earned eighteen shillings, at the end of the second week twenty five shillings, and at the end of the third week thirty two shillings. It seemed quite clear to me that in a short time I should be able to earn three pounds a week. I therefore

The Autobiography of Francis Place

proposed that Pain should allow me a guinea a week for the first year, twenty six shillings the second year, and thirty two shillings the third year. He however would give me no more than eighteen shillings a week for the whole period, this I refused and we parted.

I procured employment at a Mr Allison's in the Strand, for whom I made two pairs of leather breeches and had a third pair in hand. I wanted money and therefore asked to be paid for what I had done, this was readily offered, but at a price below the regular wages. I was young and Allison attempted to take an unfair advantage of me. I demurred and was told I might help myself how I could. This was on the first day of Bartholomew fair, and the breeches I had in hand were to have been finished the next morning for a customer who was going into the country, but at noon several of my Lambeth associates called upon me, I left my work went with them to Lambeth got some of the girls to join us and went to the fair. We kept it up as late as we dared to keep the girls out, saw them home returned to the fair and staid till day light. Some went to their work and I went to bed. In the afternoon I went to my work. Allison was in a rage and threatened me with all sorts of prosecutions and punishments. I laughed at him, finished my job receved my wages and was discharged. I called on him the next day and told him that if he would employ me at the regular wages I would be punctual and never again disappoint him for a single hour, he would not employ me, but we parted apparently good friends.

Allison was afterwards a bitter enemy of mine and did me serious injury, which he afterwards compensated by doing me great service.

I now got a job where I could, first at one place and then at another, and after a time settled employment with a Mr Pike a breeches maker in Fleet Street near Temple Bar. Pike was married to a very good looking woman by whom he had two children, he had been foreman to Mr Lingham in the Strand and had commenced business on his own account about three years before I went to work for him. His wifes brother whose name was Piercey was his managing man and foreman to the tailors whom he employed. Pike had a capital business, and with due attention he might have accumulated a very large sum of money, he however was a gay fellow kept a blood horse and high company. He soon found that I was qualified for the business of his shop into which I was taken as a runner at twenty shillings a week.

My complexion was dark my hair very black and my beard thick I was rather thin but muscular was five feet six inches high and had altogether the appearance of being several years older than I was. I was punctual in my attendance and assiduous in my business. I waited on the customers gave directions to the men and assisted Pike as paster, that is, I pasted as

6 Family history to my marriage (March 1791)

is necessary, the edges of the doe skin breeches, (which Pike cut, out,) and brought them into shape, by means of broad strips of sheep or lambskin, To be a good paister was next to cutting out the most particular part of the business and one in which but few excelled I had had the best possible practice was expert and knew how to make the most of the leather. My master was pleased with me and I liked him. He used to be from home for two or three days together and then as I was not expected to cut out, that part of the trade was neglected and the men stood still from want of the work being got ready. On one occasion when several customers had been disappointed and he had been from home during a week I suggested to Mr Piercy the propriety of my venturing to cut out two or three pairs of breeches, and with his consent I did so.[1] Mr Pike was soon satisfied that I was much more clever at this part of the business than he was, and I was preferred to the place of foreman at a guinea and a half a week. I conducted my department with the utmost exactness and the greatest care, and the whole business was now carried on with regularity. Could this have continued it seems probable that Pike might have done well notwithstanding his mode of life, as we had nearly forty men at work and the profit was enormous. I kept company with such of my old Fleet Street associates as still remained and with others who supplied the places of those who had disappeared from various causes some of which were any thing but reputable. These I, should, I have no doubt, have given up after a time as I was placed in a responsible situation and felt it as such. I no longer went to Cock and Hen Clubs, neither was I a cutter lad, but our evenings were in other respects spent much in the usual way.

There were two or three amongst us who could play on the violin and these amateur performers were connected with several hops, and among them was a large and well celebrated one in Kings-Gate Street Holborn the admission to which was two-pence – a "two-penny hop." Here we sometimes staid till we were shut out either of our lodgings or our masters houses the night was then finished at some blackguard public house and I used to go to my work without having been in bed at all. Sometimes we went along the streets with our fiddlers playing in front of us to the back settlements in the "holy land" – that is to some of the narrow streets or rather lanes in St Giles's, and there in public houses which never were closed, we used to fiddle drink and dance 'till morning. I was not much of a drinker, I abhorred being drunk.

My continuing to be shut out at nights was of short duration, an intrigue with my masters sister gave me a home at all hours of the night. She slept in the parlour and used to let me in after the family had gone to

[1] Marginal note: 'Cutter as well as trotter.'

The Autobiography of Francis Place

bed. This continued till the month of April 1790. It happened that on the seventeenth of March in that year Miss Pike took me with her to a sort of dance at a pastry-cooks next door. The master of this house was named Hummerston, he was one of my fathers friends as a Mr Stiles to whom he served his time as an apprentice and whom he succeeded had also been, he (Hummerston) was from home with his wife from fear of the bailiffs and his business was conducted by an elderly man and woman who had formerly been servants to Mr Styles, and it was they who gave the dance. The young woman who served in the shop was an acquaintance of Miss Pike's she was all but sixteen years of age, full grown straight upon her legs and five feet five inches high. I thought her a very fine and handsome person. I danced with her, and fell desperately in love with her. I therefore made it my business to see her again and again. I made enquiries about her and resolved to court her, at first I hardly knew on what terms, but in a little time for a wife. I now dropped all my old acquaintance excepting Miss Pike whom as I was foreman to her brother and much in the same house I could not do, strong as my desire was to get free from her. I had saved no money, but I now ceased to spend more than would suffice for a bare existence, and if I had continued as Pike's foreman I should have saved nearly a pound a week. It happened that my new sweetheart was about to leave her place as she could not obtain payment of the wages due to her. When that circumstance took place I went home with her to her mothers, introduced myself and asked her if she would have me for a son in law, she said jokingly yes, but I chose to take it seriously and talked of it accordingly. After this Miss Pike and I did not go on quite so well together as we had been accustomed to do, and some suspicion of our intimacy being entertained by Mrs Pike we were soon detected, and Mr Pike was made acquainted with our proceedings. Pike did not like to part with me, neither did he like that I should marry his sister, the doing of which however seemed to them to be the only alternative. At length it was settled without at all consulting me that we should be married. she was several years older than I was, had as I knew had an intrigue or two before I was acquainted with her and was as intimate as she could be with Mr. Piercey. It was settled that he should break the matter to me, and he being ignorant that I knew any thing about his intimacy with Miss Pike proceeded to make the proposition, as if he and the rest of the family were about to make a great condescension and do me a great favour. I heard him out and then told him all I knew, and especially his own intrigue with Miss Pike. This caused additional embarrassment, the result of which was, that Mr Pike was persuaded to discharge me. Miss Pike died in childbed about a year afterwards, the father of the child it was said was Mr Piercey.

6   Family history to my marriage (March 1791)

Mr Pike was a very good sort of weak man. He was tall and good looking, and had a gentlemanly air with him, he was good tempered and kind to all about him. In a few years after I left him he was completely ruined and reduced to great distress. From this state he partially recovered, and when in 1812 I was serving as a Jury Man in the Sessions House at the Old Bailey I found him keeping a public house in the Old Bailey. Here his wife died and here he was again ruined. These circumstances preyed upon him and one morning he was found drowned in the water but, into which he had plunged head foremost.

Piercey who had been instrumental in his ruin in Fleet Street is now 1825 a vagabond about the streets begging for food, a ragged miserable wretch.

I must now again turn back to the time when I let my fathers house and took him the money. He was then upwards of seventy years of age, and altho he was dreadfully afflicted with gout about twice in the year, was at other times a strong man. He used to rise at four o clock on a summers morning walk to Black Friars Bridge and smoke a pipe on one of the benches, and occasionally he would walk steadily and firmly to considerable distances and home again. My mother was sadly afraid that all the money he had would be consumed and that they would be left pennyless. He had paid all the money he owed which could not be paid when I let the house or which being lent to him by particular persons no demand had been made for payment and it is therefore probable that all the money he really possessed did not exceed two hundred and fifty pound – perhaps it was not so much. My mother therefore urged him to let her take a shop and deal in any thing she could, she was clever and active, at about fifty seven years of age, and doubted not that she should be able to maintain the family, which if she could have done she would have been cheerful and if her domestic misfortunes had not been so severe she would have been happy. She was at this time notwithstanding all her troubles cheerful and lively beyond almost any person of her age and was much beloved particularly by all the young people who knew her. My father constantly put her off and in this way things went on until about the time that I left Mr. Pike. My father was at this time confined with a fit of the Gout and could not move himself nor use his hands at all The drawing of the State Lottery was nearly ended and as he could not get to his bureau to look at some lottery tickets and shares he had purchased, his impatience to know his luck increased daily and could be no longer staid. He therefore requested me to open his bureau and look at a particular draw which he pointed out, a secret drawer of which neither I nor my mother had any previous knowledge. (I have the bureau now) Here I found the tickets and some numbers on paper, I took the

The Autobiography of Francis Place

numbers of the tickets and on going to the offices at which they had been purchased found they had been drawn blanks.[1] My father heard the news without emotion, but my mother was sadly afflicted, with apprehensions which were soon confirmed All the money he had excepting a very few pounds was gone, there had been two lotteries since he had received the money and there were in the Bureau tickets as well for the former as the present lottery which had been drawn blanks, some had been drawn small prizes and the money laid out again in other shares which had been drawn blanks. He had expended all his money excepting as much as he thought would last till his tickets were drawn prizes.

There remained of the family my father my mother and my youngest sister, these were to be clothed fed and lodged and washed for. My brother who was still an apprentice, was also to be provided for in cloaths and washing.

No human being can concieve the distress of my poor mother, plunged as she and the rest of the family were all at once into what for a moment seemed irremediable poverty and misery. She had never been used to hard work of any kind, for notwithstanding she was laborious and industrious to the greatest possible extent still she had not been used to the mere drudgery of household work to any considerable extent, but she was a woman who on important occasions could decide at once and act on her decision. She soon recovered from her sorrow to a considerable extent and made up her mind to her circumstances. Without saying a word to my father lest he should oppose some obstacle to her intention she went into the neighbourhood she had left, told her tale to some of the housekeepers, and shewed the necessity there was for her doing something by which to procure the means of maintaining her family, and requested them to give her their cloaths to wash which they did not usually wash at home, they all instantly complied with her request and

[1] 'At some of the [Lottery] Offices,' Place noted, 'the people used to assemble in the evenings in hundreds and contend for admission, by quarrelling and fighting. I have waited for two hours before I could get in on one or two occasions when sent to ascertain if certain numbers were drawn.' At this time in all of England there were fifty-one lottery offices where tickets were sold for the State Lottery, the drawing of which lasted forty days. However, the lottery was so popular, particularly among the poor, that many tickets were sold illegally. Besides the money spent on the lottery ticket itself, more money was often spent insuring a number which had not yet been drawn. Place recalled a fraud in this insurance: 'I remember a man who was connected with a gang whose pride and business it was to cheat the Lottery Office Keeper, he was the man who had the care of the ring of bells at St Clements Church and used to let me up to help ring occasionally. This man used to put back the clock three, four, or five minutes; his confederates learned the winning numbers of the day at Guildhall, where the drawing took place, they then went to the Lottery Offices and insured the winning numbers before the clock signalled the deadline for insuring' (Add. MS 27825, fs. 269, 271).

6   Family history to my marriage (March 1791)

regretting her condition gave her their cloaths to wash and thus when nearly sixty years of age she became a washer-woman. It happened soon afterwards that several families returned from the East Indies and came to lodge in Arundel Street, they brought with them great quantities of linen which my mother had to wash. Not at all ashamed of honestly earning her living as she considered it her duty to her family to do she used to bring home large bundles of cloaths upon her head and take them back again in the same way. Often did she labour till twelve o clock at night, and rise again at four in the morning to pursue her occupation.

After my discharge from Pike's I could obtain no employment at my business for several weeks; but I got employment of another kind. A Gentleman in Arundel Street had a model of a frigate about two feet long, it had been a beautiful thing planked with mahogany and put together with brass pins as bolts, the hull was damaged and the rigging broken I undertood to put it into condition, I therefore took the vessel to my sweethearts mother's and worked at it with great diligence, and as this kept me away from my fathers lodgings, he and my mother began to suspect that I was employing myself in some improper way, and my brother having told them that he had seen me with a tall well dressed girl, they began to fear that I had attached myself to some loose woman. My brother was therefore set to watch me and having traced me to the house of my sweethearts mother in Wilderness Lane White Friers he reported accordingly. Upon this my father went to the place and enquired respecting the character of the parties, they were represented as respectable, and my mother then spoke to me on the subject. I explained the whole affair to her and told her I intended to be married as soon as I could obtain permanent employment. and that with her leave I would bring the *Lady* as my brother called her to see her and my father, if he would permit me. My mother said I might do as I pleased but she thought my father would affront her. It had been his custom to turn out of the room any one who called to see any of us, or even himself and this was done in the most morose and offensive way possible. He was now however considerably subdued, he could not bear to be maintained by any but his own exertions these were at an end, and he had no choice. He had all his life long been obstinate and obdurate, beyond almost any other man, and now began to feel the consequences, he would reproach himself with his former conduct, lament his follies, condemn his absurdities, and grieve over my mother, and the state to which he had brought her in the most affecting manner. This conduct of his used to produce great sorrow in her, and increase her affection for him now that he was in circumstances of so helpless a nature, yet she shook off her sorrow so long as she found business to do and strength to do it, her pride was to

The Autobiography of Francis Place

make him as comfortable as she could, and she indulged in sorrow only when his fits of despondency were strong upon him. But when business was bad and her strength began to fail, her sorrow was great indeed. She did all she could to hide it from him that his unhappiness might not be increased. It cannot be said that he was ever again cheerful, though at times he was placid resolute and manly, and when with other people preserved the appearance of having undergone little or no change. He who had never before shewn any of the usual attentions to his wife was now attentive and kind in an extraordinary manner, and officious to help or oblige or comfort her.

I introduced the Lady, when to our astonishment he rose from his seat and gave it to her, and ever afterwards treated her with more consideration and respect than he had ever done any other person.

A great affection grew up between my intended wife and my mother which continued as long as my mother lived.

I worked at the frigate with great care and assiduity for a month and was paid for it at quite as high a rate as I should have been for leather breeches making.

The education of my intended wife, I mean the school education was very narrow reading and writing and common sewing constituted the whole. Other useful education she obtained by seeing what others did and from such instructions as they could give her. At twelve years of age she was taken by a very good woman who was housekeeper to Mr Styles a pastry cook near Temple Bar, he was a batchler at nearly seventy years of age and almost continually afflicted with the gout, and needed someone to wait upon him, in this capacity she remained until Mr Styles died and the business went into the hands of Mr Hummerston who as has been noticed was formerly his apprentice and had for several years kept a shop of the same kind in Fleet Street within two doors of Chancery Lane. She now occasionally served in the shop the care of which had devolved upon the housekeeper. Her wages were not more than sufficient to provide her with a good stock of cloaths and as she expended her money in the purchase of clothes she had no money by her. She had been taught to be industrious was remarkably neat in her person, and beyond all comparison with others steady in her conduct.

Having introduced her to my father and mother and they being pleased with her. I laid before her my whole scheme of life, and proposed that we should be married as soon as I was in a condition to earn as much money as would enable us to live. I had no doubt that I should improve my condition in life; but I saw clearly that it would be a very hard struggle through many difficulties. I was not quite nineteen years of age yet I had thorugh knowledge of my business, and the experience I had

6 Family history to my marriage (*March 1791*)

gained at Mr Pikes satisfied me that I should not fail in any thing I could find an opportunity to undertake. I had managed fifteen men, and with one man to assist me in pasting had kept them at work for several weeks and after that had managed ten men, waited on customers and collected debts. I had nothing to learn and needed only practice to make me as complete in every part as any one in the trade I had compared myself with every one in the trade with whom I had come in contact and was fully persuaded that upon the whole I was better qualified for business than any one of them. This I stated to my intended wife. I said I had no doubt that I should in time find means to get into business for myself, though I could not see how this was to be done, and that once in business success was pretty certain. That as I had no one[1] able to give me a shilling or even to lend me one, it would be necessary, for us to struggle with adversity if it came and to bear up against it, that I was aware of the poverty which awaited us if at any time I should be out of employment but that if she were willing to take her chance with me we should some day be well off in the world. I do not know that I ever obtained a positive consent in words but we seemed to understand one another just as well as any words could have made us. She went to service and I obtained work at Mr Linghams in the Strand. I soon came to understand that my employment would be for as long a time as I chose to remain at it. Lingham seldom discharged a man who was a competent workman, but some discharged him. His business was conducted in a very irregular manner. So much was it neglected that even when trade was unusually brisk the work was not prepared for the men several days in succession, the customers were disappointed and the men mulcted in their earnings, all they did being paid for as piece work. Lingham therefore alway had more men in his employment than his business required, and it frequently happened that after having been kept without work for two or three days, a pair of Leather breeches would be given between two of us, in the afternoon of one day to be made by noon of the next day. A pair of breeches was reckoned as the work of two days, and consequently they who had work given them were sometimes obliged to work all night. An ordinarily good workman if he worked twelve hours a day and had work for six days in a week could earn a guinea clear of all expenses, but in the way the business was conducted no one could on an average earn more than fourteen shillings a week clear, after paying from his wages for the thread and silk he used, this answered very well for those journeymen, who had customers of their own, or procured work from other masters, which they did at their lodgings, but was just the contrary for me who had no other means of

[1] Place wrote the word 'relative' over this word.

obtaining a shilling. As my intended wife had a good stock of cloaths and I hoped that I should be able by working hard to increase my very scanty quantity, I thought we could go on well in this respect. I had now no acquaintance with any one out of my own and my wifes family. I ate bread and bread only for my breakfast and drank nothing. I dined at a public house in the Strand near Somerset house at which there was a daily ordinary for the clerks in the Government Offices. The cold meat which was left was cut up the next day and sold to such persons as came to dine from it. The dinner cost, meat fourpence bread one halfpenny a pint of porter seven farthings, altogether sixpence farthing The quantity of meat thus furnished was enough for a hearty mans dinner. I never drank the whole of the beer, half a pint was as much as I needed, and I seldom drank much more the remainder I either gave away or left on the table, the whole expense of my food did not cost more if so much as a shilling a day. I was however able to pay for my washing and lodging and to save a trifle, not by any means enough to enable me to purchase many cloaths, but I bought as many as I could. Had my work been supplied to me regularly as it ought to have been, I should soon have been able to make a respectable appearance which as it was I could not do, to any thing like the extent I wished.

My intended wife, had obtained a place in a tradesman's family in Fleet Street, there were two other servants kept and she was therefore able once or twice a week to get out for an hours and I saw her at her mothers. Her mother who had hitherto encouraged my visits, was now persuaded by one of her sisters and other gossipping women that she was sacrificing her daughter by letting her marry me. They had some reason on their side – our ages, my business which they truly said was a bad one for a journeyman, who would not be able to maintain a wife. They had been told that my temper was bad, and they were sure I should use her daughter ill. It was true that we were too young – true that my business was a bad one – true that my temper was by no means good, and the inference therefrom was fair. My wife's mother was incapable of reasoning the matter with me and she therefore sought a quarrel, told me that I should not have her daughter and forbid me the house – I told her I would have her daughter in spite of her, and would come to the house whenever I pleased, and I did so for a short time.

The place in which my intended was, did not in any respect suit her, and she soon became uncomfortable in every way, her fellow servants had their sweethearts in the house unbeknown to their master and mistress and there was a brute of a fellow a porter in the house who used to annoy her, very much being backed in his bad behaviour by her fellow servants, of these things she complained to her mother who advised her

6   Family history to my marriage (*March 1791*)

to leave her place and come home and she did so. Her mother now threatened all manner of things unless she gave up her acquaintance with me. Her relatives did all they could to persuade her to conform to her mothers wishes, but she resolutely refused compliance. This irritated her mother beyond endurance, and one evening after a disagreeable altercation, she seized the poker and threatened to knock me down. These circumstaces precipitated our marriage. Her mother had a sister named Jackson the eldest of her family, and by far the most sensible and considerate of them all, she was a widow and very poor indeed. She interfered, first to advise us to give up our intentions, and finding this advice not taken nor likely to be taken she permitted us to meet at her room near St Clements Church. She gave us the best possible advice in every respect and endeavoured to reconcile her sister to circumstances which she was convinced were unavoidable but in this she failed. To put an end to this uncomfortable state, and to relieve my intended wife from the harsh conduct of her mother I put up the banns of marriage at Lambeth Church without the mothers knowledge

CHAPTER 7

From my Marriage in 1791 — to 1793

My marriage. Wifes Parentage – Our mode of living – our earnings – Books, reading – Mother greatly distressed – Strike for Wages – I manager for the Trade – Proscribed by the Masters – and reduced to extreme poverty – Reading Learning – Again employed Expectations – Religion. Father dies – Youngest sister Marries – Mothers afflictions.

The marriage day was fixed, but it was agreed that my intended wife's mother should not be made acquanted with our intentions. Mrs Jackson had however told her all about us, under a promise that she would not interfere with our being married. Pain my sisters husband was to give me my wife and no one else was to be present at the ceremony. I left my work at the proper time and met Pain and my sweetheart in St Georges Fields, whence we proceeded to Lambath Church. My wife was to have returned to her mothers as if nothing had occurred. I was to go to my work, in the evening we were to meet at Pain's, my sister was to have told my wife's mother, what had occurred, we were then to sup at Pains, her mother with us if she chose, and then go to our lodgings.

After the ceremony I saw my wife home and instead of going to my work I went with Pain to my mothers, we had been there a very short time when my wife came in, and said her mother was acquainted with our marriage, that she had seen us married but would not come to Pain's or have any thing to do with us. She went it seems to the Church and told the clerk that her daughter who was only 17 was coming to be married without her consent, he replied that she might stop the ceremony if she pleased, but she said she would not as she was certain we should get married somewhere else, she was then let into a pew and saw us married.

Pain insisted that we should go home and dine with him to which we consented and I for the first and last time neglected Mr Linghams business. In the evening we all went to a ready furnished room which I had taken at a Coal shed at the Back of St Clements Church for which we were to pay three shillings and sixpence a week and here on the 17 March 1791. commenced my married life, which has continued for nearly thirty three years. I was at the time Nineteen years and three months old, my wife was Seventeen within eleven days. She was not a mere girl either in appearance or understanding she was tall well grown and womanish in her appearance steady and orderly in her conduct of a remarkably good temper and of quiety manners. Altogether she was as

7   1791–1793

well qualified for a working mans wife as most young women several years older than she was, usually are.

MY WIFE'S PARENTAGE

My wife's Father was a farmer's servant, her mother was also a servant. Her father was one of several children who became tall, well grown good looking honest men. He died when my wife was about fifteen years of age. I never saw him, but I afterwards knew three of his brothers who were just such men as I have described.

He had a sister a tall good looking woman with whom I was acquainted, she was married to a publican who kept a road side house on the Edgware Road.

My wifes mother was also one of several children, I knew one of her brothers and three of her sisters. They are now all dead; my wife's mother is the only one of the family who remains. My wife's father and mother are descended from families of working people long resident between Kilburne and Pinner in Middlesex, where a multitude of their relatives still reside

My wifes father whose name was Chadd came to London soon after she was born and worked as a Coal Porter at White Friers where being exposed to all weathers and to the bad example of his fellow labourers, he acquired the habit of drinking and was hurried to an early grave.

My wife's mother was married in her twentieth year and my wife was born on the 28 March 1774 at Childs Hill near Hampstead. When her father died he left her mother in possession, as a tenant at will of a small house in Wilderness Lane White Friars, the House was meanly furnished, and mostly let out to Lodgers, this with taking in of washing enabled her to maintain herself and her younger daughter, and to save some money. She as well as her sisters was a strong women,[1] and all of them excepting Mrs Jackson were pretty well off in the world, each being married to a man in a small way of business, each keeping a house and being what is called a little before the world. Mrs Jackson was the oldest of the family and a widow, she was a very good sort of woman but wretchedly poor.

I[2] earned quite as much, if not more, than any man who was employed by Mr Lingham, yet my net weekly earnings did not exceed fourteen shillings. My wife used to go, two and sometimes three days in the week to help my mother to wash and iron, this she did without direct pay, my

---
[1] Changed from 'were tall strong women.'
[2] This paragraph is preceded by the date 'Jan. 1824.'

mother was indeed too poor to be able to pay her, she would willingly enough have deprived herself of necessaries to have found means to pay, if we would have permitted her; But we both commiserated her greatly, and would take nothing from her, but my wife's board, and an occasional present of small value, which we could not refuse. What we really recieved could not exceed three shillings a week in value, and this made our income seventeen shillings a week. From this we had to pay, for lodging three shillings and sixpence a week, and on an average one shilling and sixpence a week for coals and candles, thus we had only twelve shillings a week for food and cloaths and other necessaries. Nothing could be saved from this small sum. We however contrived to dress ourselves respectably and were comfortable with each other. As our poverty would not permit us to give any thing away, we kept ourselves very much to ourselves had scarcely any acquaintance and visited nobody excepting our parents, and my eldest sister, but as she was falling off sadly, and her husband was seldom sober we saw them only occasionally. One of my old Fleet Street associates[1] who had become a saint and married his masters only child, whom he was as well acquainted with before as after marriage, used to call on me for the purpose of converting me to the only true faith, as he called the particular sort of methodism to which he had become a convert and a teacher, he was a tall big boned pale faced fellow, a capital figure for a field preacher, he was however an honest hearted man and the only one besides myself of all the twenty one Fleet Street apprentices who made his way in the world, respectably.

We soon acquired the character of being proud and above our equals, this was the certain consequence of our having no acquaintance with any one and being better dressed than most who were similarly circumstancd, and were contemptuously called *the* Lady and Gentleman.

In order to increase my income and to fill up the leisure time Mr Lingham forced on me, I endeavourd to form a breeches club, and after some time succeeded. It was held at a public house in Bell Yard Temple Barr and consisted of about twenty working men, some were watermen some lightermen, mostly sad blackguards. The plan of the Club was this. A list of prices of various kinds of breeches was agreed upon and each member of the club, at his entrance named the kind he intended to have. The club met once a week and was to continue a certain number of weeks, each member was therefore to pay such a sum weekly, as would amount to the price set on the article he was to have, within the time limited for the duration of the club. The money paid on every club night was deposited with the Landlord and when it amounted to as much as would pay for a pair of breeches, lots were drawn, he who gained the prize

[1] He is identified in the margin as Jack Charrington.

7 1791–1793

ordered a pair of breeches and when he received them the Landlord paid me for them. the man who received them giving security to continue his weekly payments. The members were not mutual guarantees for each other but as is usual in such clubs I took the risk of failure. Besides his weekly subscription each member of the club paid fourpence on the club night every week for "the good of the house." It seldom happened that half the members attended, sometimes not so many as one fourth, but they who did attend drank to the amount of the money, paid as well by those who were present as by those who were absent.

I had never before attemptd to make breeches of any material but leather, but this was not known to the members of the club. I however made the, best possible articles, and did the parties more than bare justice. I was obliged to charge very low prices and was therefore not likely to gain much by the club. It happened however that I was persuaded to let some of the members be security for other members and when they who were thus mutual securities were provided they ceased to attend the club and never paid any more money. The sum I thus lost was about equal to my profit including journeymens wages. I thus lost all my time but gained *experience*, in my new trade, which was afterwards eminently useful to me. Whilst this club was going on and before I saw what the result would be, I had with the assistance of my sisters husband formed another such club near the City Road Finsbury. This turned out very little better, and I therefore formed no more such clubs.

The house in which we lived was very old and lofty and the street which was called the back of Saint Clements was very narrow, it was a continuance of Butcher Row to Wych Street, our Landlord kept a Coal-shed, i.e sold coals in the shop, the house was very dark and dirty. The houses in Butcher Row and the Back of St Clements with the narrow courts which opened into these places, were formed by houses built with timber, lath and plaister; many of them had overhanging fronts each of the three or four stories projecting beyond the story underneath, many of the windows were casements as all of them had been, and like all such places, they were dirty, and filled with rats mice and bugs. Butcher row was what its name imports, and was a sort of Market. All these places have been pulled down and Pickett Street has been built on the ground on which some of them stood, and the main Street the Strand, which was in one part little better than a lane has been widened.

[Elsewhere Place recalled this neighbourhood: 'The place called the back of St Clements Butcher Row was formed by a wedge shaped mass of wooded houses the open pointing to Temple bar. Butcher Row was a narrow lane, and the part leading to Wych Streets called the back of St Clements was so narrow that two carts could not pass. The houses were mostly, nearly all indeed built with wood, each story as it ascended projecting over that below it. The whole was dark and dirty and the butchers shops and killing places made it, what would not be thought a perfect nuisance' (Add. MS 35147, f. 258).

Place kept returning to the subject of these loathsome eighteenth-century courts: 'The entrance to several of the courts was by a narrow passage, from three to four feet wide, a sort of door way entrance, through the house which blocked up the Court, some of these courts were so narrow in parts that the Mopsticks the poor inhabitants rigged, out from their windows to dry their clothes, met in the middle of the space between the houses – These courts were all paved with flat stones, and were of course only passable by foot passengers' (Add. MS 35147, f. 258).

'In a few years from this time [1826] it will scarcly be believed that an immense number of houses were built in narrow courts, and close lanes, each house being at the least three stories and many of them four stories above the ground floor. That in these courts and lanes the dirt and filth used to accumulate in heaps and was but seldom removed. That many of these tall houses had two three and sometimes four rooms on a floor and that from the Garretts to the cellars a family lived or starved in each room. Circulation of air was out of the question, the putrid effluvia was always stagnant in those places, and had not London been in other respects a healthy place the plague must still have continued among us' (Add. MS 35147, f. 230).

Place approved of the small new houses for poor people, because 'the privies are not within the houses, one privy common to a number of families in a large or lofty house was a great inconvenience and a horrid nuisance, there was always a reservoir of putrid matter in the lower part of the house. In a large proportion of such places as I have been speaking of but few houses were drained from the basement' (Add. MS 35147, f. 233).]

After a residence of about three months we removed to a neater and lighter room in a recently built house of two stories in Star Court, (part of this Court still remains,) the entrance is from Pickett Street. The man who kept the house was a journiman Baker, his wife a civil cleanly woman was a laundress. i-e she had the care of three or four sets of Chambers in the Temple. The great irregularity with which I was supplied with work by Lingham left considerable portions of unoccupied time on my hands, which I had not hitherto since my marriage been able to fill up to any useful purpose. In fine weather I used frequently to saunter into the fields and in these excursions I explored all the roads, lanes and paths within five or six miles of London, and to a greater distance in the County of Surrey.

On these excursions I very seldom had a companion. I usually bought a twopenny loaf and ate it outside some road or lane side public house, drinking half a pint of beer which cost a penny, and this was my dinner.

I might have dined at my mothers with my wife she would have gone without for my accomodation, had I been so cruel as to have eaten at her expense. She was not annoyed on my account, since she knew not how

7 1791–1793

I fared. About 8 o clock at night I fetched my wife home but when I had work to do she came home alone. She usually bought a German "savelor"[1] a sort of sausage of a celebrated German Pork Butcher for three halfpence for my supper and this was all the animal food I ate for very many days and weeks.

It may be supposed that I led a miserable life but I did not I was very far indeed from being miserable at this time when my wife came home at night, we had always something to talk about, we were pleased to see each other, our reliance on each other was great indeed, we were poor, but we were young, active cheerful, and although my wife at times doubted that we should get on in the world, I had no such misgivings.

My landladys husband was at home only about two hours in the evening and when the weather was wet, and cold I used to sit in her room and thus saved the expense of firing.*

My Landlady furnished me with occupation, she brought home books from the chambers she had the care of, and exchanged them for others as often as I wished. My good schoolmaster had implanted in me a love for reading, and a desire for information which was by no means wholly neglected even whilst I was an apprentice, I always found some time for reading, and I almost always found the means to procure books, useful books, not Novels. My reading was of course devoid of method, and very desultory. I had read in English the only language in which I could read, the histories of Greece and Rome, and some translated works of Greek and Roman writers. Hume Smollett, Fieldings novels and Robertsons works, some of Humes Essays, some Translations from french writers, and much on geography – some books on Anatomy and Surgery, some relating to Science and the Arts, and many Magazines. I had worked all the Problems in the Introduction to Guthries Geography, and had made some small progress in Geometry. I now read Blackstone, Hale's Common Law, several other Law Books, and much Biography. This course of reading was continued for several years until the death of my landlady, she was a very good sort of woman and was a friend of ours as long as she lived, her husband was a plodding stupid sort of a fellow whom we seldom saw and with whom there was no particular intimacy.

[1] Saveloy.
* A curious dissertation might be written on the way in which poor honest respectable persons spend the small sums which come to their hands. On many occasions I have had my attention drawn to the notions entertained by gentlemen and Ladies with whom I have become acquainted respecting the value and the expenditure of small sums by poor people, and have had great difficulty to make them obtain even a glimpse of a poor persons notions on the same subject. Few indeed among the rich can comprehend why a poor person should "look at both sides of a penny before he or she spends it" or the calulations that are made respecting how many things must not be had, how many had, for the sixpence, before it is parted with.

The Autobiography of Francis Place

During our residence in Star Court, the Leather Breeches trade had declined considerably and there was not nearly enough employment for the journeymen. Gentlemen rode in Corduroy and Cassimere Breeches, and leather was no longer commonly worn by any class of persons. Lingham had for some years been a maker of stuff breeches and it is probable that his doing so had tended to change the fashion, His leather trade had dropped off a good deal lately; but his stuff trade had increased. He however discharged none of his leather breeches makers, and as work was not to be had elsewhere they staid with him and shared the work amongst them the leather breeches trade was now conducted by him with less and less regularity, and my earnings were reduced considerably. My mothers washing had also from various causes fallen off. She was scarcely able to procure as much as would furnish a scanty maintenance for herself my father and my youngest sister, who was now absolutely necessary to her to assist her in various matters, to sew and look to domestic concerns and attend upon my father, whose fits of gout were more and more frequent and of longer duration, so much so, as to leave but short intervals of convalescence. My Brother was still an apprentice and must be found in clothes and washing

My wife continued to go to my mother at one o clock in the day and work for her in the afternoon, she did not go 'till after dinner time, which was twelve o clock, because we knew that my mother could not afford to dine her, though had she gone my mother would have starved herself to do it.

We were now reduced to great distress, frequently to great suffering. On one occasion I had done work for which I was to receive seven shillings, but Lingham was as irregular in his payments to his journeymen as he was in every other respect. We had been without money for a week, and payment of the seven shillings could not be obtained, it was in the depth of winter and we had neither food nor fire. In this state we remained so long that my wife was exhausted and was compelled to go to bed. This was too much to be endured, so I went to Linghams and demanded payment, fully expecting that I should be discharged in consequence of the demand. It happened however as was frequently the case that a pair of leather breeches were to be made in a great hurry, and as was not frequently the case they had been cut out and were ready for the workman, without any one being at the shop to take them. I was paid the seven shillings had the work given to me with directions to find a fellow workman to make half the breeches; it was usual to make breeches in halves; My cupidity could not resist the temptation to cheat a fellow workman, so instead of losing time in going to find one I took the breeches home, set to work and altho' making the breeches was as before related two days work, I never left the job until I had finished it and

7 1791–1793

had earned another sum of seven shillings. This was the only instance in which I ever committed an actual fraud.

I now saw plainly that if I continued to make leather breeches I should be kept in wretched poverty, my wife was far gone with child, and no chance remained of any provision being made for its birth by leather breeches making, and I therefore endeavoured to procure employment at stuff breeches making. Lingham employed tailors, but other breeches makers whose business were less than his were taking to stuff breeches making and as the work was occasional, they gave it to such of the leather breeches makers as thought themselves competent. After a short time, during which I had made application for employment at every breeches makers in London, I obtained an occasional job from a Mr Bristow in Piccadilly, and also from a Mr Weld in the same Street, still I could not obtain from Lingham Bristow and Weld as much work as I was desirous of doing, but I earned about a guinea a week and this enabled us to live in comfort. After some time I obtained further employment from Mr Allison for whom I had formerly worked and was now able to earn about twenty six shillings a week with a prospect of not again wanting employment. My Landlord wanted the room I lived in for a relative who was coming from the country, and we therefore took a larger and more commodious room in Little Shire Lane, and here soon after our removal my wife was brought to bed of her first child which we named Ann.

Mr Allison could not cut out stuff breeches so well as was requisite for some of his customers and he and I made a bargain, that I should cut out and make some particular kinds of breeches and any waistcoats for which he might take orders. I had never before cut out a waistcoat except two or three for myself but I thought I could manage the matter better than many did and so it proved. I had now more work than I could do, so I gave up Lingham. and Weld. My wife could assist me in this kind of work and whatever time she could spare from her child and her other domestic concerns she employed in working with me

I worked incessantly, and soon saved money enough to buy some good cloaths and a bedstead, a table three or four chairs and some bedding, with these and a few utensils we took an unfurnished back room up two pairs of stairs at a chandlers shop in Wych Street, and began to congratulate ourselves on the improvement of our circumstances and the prospect before us. We paid four shillings a week for the room we quitted and two shillings for that we removed to. This was a savings of some importance to us. We had plenty of work, the child required less attention and my wife had therefore more time to assist me, thus circumstanced we made sure of saving money rapidly.

The Autobiography of Francis Place

Some time before I was married I became a member of the Breeches Makers Benefit Society, for the support of the members when sick, and to bury them when dead. I paid my subscription regularly, but I never attended at the public house at which the club was held excepting on the evenings when the Stewards were chosen. The club though actually a benefit club, was intended for the purpose of supporting the members in a strike for wages.[1] It had now in the Spring of 1793 about £250 in its chest which was deemed sufficient a strike was agreed upon and the men left their work. It was a badly paid badly conducted trade, a good workman who was constantly employed might earn a guinea a week, but scarcly any one was fully employed; it required from an hour to an hour and a half when two were employed to cut out and get ready a pair of Leather Breeches, and as no one master had an arrangement so complete as to have work always ready, and as the whole was picework, the masters were regardless of the loss and inconvenience the men suffered, the men in the best shops could not therefore earn more than eighteen shillings a week, and in all the others much less; they had therefore resolved to strike for wages which would put them as to earnings on a level with other trades. So many of them had become makers of stuff breeches, that notwithstanding, the trade of Leather Breeches making

[1] A mass of Combination Acts (at least forty by the end of the eighteenth century) forbade either employees or masters to combine in order to set working conditions. The determination of wages and hours was considered the business of Parliament. In the tailoring trade an Act of 1721 set these conditions (see Sidney and Beatrice Webb, *The History of Trade Unionism*, 1920, pp. 24, 68; J. L. and Barbara Hammond, *The Town Labourer*, Ch. 7). A modification of the Act in 1768 remained in effect until 1825 when the combination laws were repealed, largely through the exertions of Place. By the Act of 1721 (7 Geo. I st. 1 c. 13) journeymen tailors in London and Westminster were expected to work from 6.00 a.m. to 8.00 p.m. (with an hour off for dinner) at a wage ceiling of 2s. per day from March 25th to June 20th, and 1/8d. per day the rest of the year. The Act of 1768 (8 Geo. III c. 17) lessened the working day by one hour (6.00 a.m. to 7.00 p.m.) and raised the wage ceiling to 2/7½d. per day (except during a period of general mourning). This Act also provided that any master who gave higher wages or any journeyman who received them would be liable to a sentence of hard labour for not less than 14 days nor more than two months (*Select Documents Illustrating the History of Trade Unionism*: I *The Tailoring Trade*, ed. F. W. Galton, 1896, pp. 17–18 and 60–3).

Long after the repeal of these laws Place remembered them bitterly: 'Everything on the part of the workmen was done by stealth before the repeal of the Combination Laws, and in contravention to the laws, which were unjust and exceedingly severe; workmen could not meet openly to adjust any matter relating to their business. If a few met and wished to come to an understanding with the masters they were prosecuted, not always under the Combination Laws, but at common law, and very severe sentences were passed upon them. The men had to a very great extent oaths of secrecy, all their discussions were secret, and this course of conduct demoralized them very much; it was a great impediment to their improvement, and did no good to the masters' (Place's testimony before the Select Committee on Education, *Parliamentary Report . . . on Education*, 1835, p. 74).

7 1791–1793

had declined, the proportion of hands to employment was less than formerly and trade was brisk, the leaders therefore calculated, as they thought securely on obtaining the advance they demanded, they did not forsee that the masters would represent the strike as unreasonable and persuade their customers to wear stuff breeches, at least for a time, and that they could get this sort of work done by tailors. As I had not been at the club house for more than three months, and had now no acquaintance with any one in the trade, I was neither aware of the intention to strike, nor of the strike when it took place. The first I heard of it was from Mr Bristow. On taking some work home one evening; he instead of giving me more as I expected gave me my discharge. I asked the reason, he would assign none, and I reproached him with acting unjustly, and in a way, I should not have done towards him, he then alluded to the strike to which he supposed I was a party. I assured him that I had never heard of any intention amongst the men to strike, and had no knowledge whatever on the subject, but that which he had imparted. He was a kind and reasonable man. He told me he was satisfied, I had not and would not deceive him, he was he said sorry to discharge me, but that at a meeting of the masters it had been agreed that every leather breeches maker who was employed to make stuff breeches should be at once discharged to prevent them assisting those who had struck. Allison discharged me next day. Thus at once were our hopes destroyed and our views obscured. No chance of employment remained, so I went to the Club house, and here I was informed that every man out of employment was to be paid seven shillings a week from the fund. I found that the number of men was at least equal to the number of pounds the club had in its possession, and consequently provision only for three weeks. In the evening when the men were assembled. I stood up upon one of the tables and addressed them. I pointed out the inadequacy of the sum they had collected, the privations they would probably have to endure. I proposed that as many as were willing should receive one weeks pay in advance and a certificate provided each of them would go on the tramp and engage not to return to London for a month. It was well known that a man who brought a certificate to any Leather breeches makers shop in the country would be sure of a days keep a nights lodging and a shilling to start again with the next morning, and in some of the larger towns a breakfast and half a crown in money to help him along. Many therefore were willing to leave London on the terms proposed, the proposition was adopted, and arrangements made to carry it into effect the next morning. I then proposed, that instead of giving each man seven shillings for his weeks subsistence, they should make up "Rag Fair" Breeches[1] and let

[1] See above p. 74.

as many as would take them, have two pairs a week at four shillings a pair journeymans wages, that this was a shilling a week more than was proposed to be given, and as the loss on each pair would not be more than two shillings and sixpence the fund would last more than twice as long as it would if seven shillings were given to each for doing nothing, that besides this there was another advantage, namely that every man who could procure any sort of employment could not make and would not perhaps be desirous to make two pairs of Rag fair breeches a week, and if there were men who having other employment were mean enough to take money from the fund, this would put an end to any such practice. This proposition was highly applauded and instantly adopted. A committee of three of which I was one was appointed to make the necessary arrangements and to report on the next evening. I then proposed that a very convenient shop under the Piazza in Covent Garden which I had been to look at should be taken in which the trade should be carried on. This proposition was referred to the committee who were empowered to take the shop if they approved of it. I then proposed to them to prepare an address setting forth the reasons for the strike, that it should be printed and circulated. This was also agreed to, and referred to the committee. A report on all these matters was made by me on the next evening, and as my knowledge of Rag fair breeches making was well known and duly appreciated, I was unanimously elected sole manager of the whole concern, and the Stewards of the club were directed to furnish the money necessary for the purpose. My pay was to be twelve shillings a week that I would arrange the whole business in a plain manner & conduct it and those whom I might find it necessary to employ under me in the business should have nine shillings a week each.

The business was immediately commenced, and was so managed that legal proceedings could not be taken against us, for a combination. Things went on thus till the close of the month of May when the money was all expended, and the men were compelled to return to their employment without any advance of wages. The masters in their turn punished the men as much as they could, and as the whole number of masters was small, and the whole number of men few it was by no means difficult for the combined masters to effect their purpose. All who had been in any way active in the strike were not to be employed so long as any other man was unemployed, I and another young man named James Ellis were never again to be employed in any way whatever, by any master breeches maker. I thought it next to impossible that so kind a man as Mr Bristow was* could have agreed to exclude me personally so I

* Mr Bristows father kept the shop for many years and was at his death succeeded by his son. He was a very good looking, good natured, civil well meaning man, but a

7 1791–1793

went to him and asked for employment, he told me he had none for me, and that no one else in the trade had any either for me or for James Ellis. I asked him if it was true that the masters had as was reported entered into a bond not to employ me, he said it was not true, but that each had pledged himself to all, never to give either me or Ellis any sort of employment. I then went to Allison who told me the same story. A dreadful state of poverty followed. During the strike which continued three months we expended what little we had saved.

Soon after the commencement of the Strike our child was taken with the small pox and died During the childs illness we of course lived and slept in the same room, it was a small one, and it may easily be supposed that our condition was one of extreme chagrin. To my wife it was one of great suffering. Persons who have never been in such circumstances, can form but faint ideas of the misery even the best and most frugal of workmen sometimes endure.

During the next eight months I could obtain no sort of employment either in my own trade or in any other way. At the commencement of this state of things I contrived so to conduct myself as to keep away every one who was likely to visit us, and no one excepting my brother ever called upon us, and thus none knew how poor we really were. We visited no where except now and then our parents. Pain and his wife lived in perpetual broils and had quarrelled with us, so we were left alone which in our circumstances was what we most desired. We made many efforts to procure some sort of employment, but were wholly unsuccessful, we suffered every kind of privation consequent on want of employment, and food and fire. This is the only period of my life on which I look back with shame. The tricks and pranks of my boyhood were common and were not thought disgraceful, no one would have abandoned me for what every one did and was expected to do, though the knowledge of it might have distressed my mother. My temper was bad, and instead of doing every thing in my power to sooth and comfort and support my wife in her miserable condition, instead of doing her homage for the exemplary manner in which she bore her sufferings, instead of meeting as I ought on all occasions to have done her good temper and affection, I used at times to give way to passion and increase her and my own misery. The folly and absurdity of giving way to bad temper was always apparent to me, and I never attempted either to palliate or excuse it to myself, I was indeed ashamed of it, and set about to rectify

---

very weak one. He afterwards came to ruin, I know not from what cause. He became so utterly helpless and his misery seemed so perfect that I pitied him most sincerely. I always respected him, and as by this time my circumstances were much improved I occasionally gave him some money.

it, and this I soon did to a considerable extent. It is but too common for a man and his wife whose circumstances compel them to be almost constantly together in the same room to live in great discomfort. Our disagreements were not however frequent and when they did occur the fault was always on my side. Nothing conduces so much to the degradation of a man and woman in the opinion of each other, and of themselves in all respects; but most especially of the woman; than her having to eat and drink and cook and wash and iron and transact all her domestic concerns in the room in which her husband works, and in which they sleep. In some cases men and women are so ignorant and brutal, that this mode of life is of no moment to them; but to those who have every so small a share of information and consequently of refinement it is a terrible grievance and produces sad consequences.

It is utterly impossible for any one to tell how much we suffered during the six months which followed final conclusion of the strike without my having been in any way accessory to it, or having afterwards done any thing which merited punishment. Had it been in the power of the men to have compelled the masters to raise their wages, they would have been justified in compelling them, the law was against them, and no amicable intercourse could be had with the masters, any combination to settle the matter by conference would have been prosecuted. and no way was left but to strike. The law was wholly on the side of the masters, they could keep a man in constant work, and enable him to earn as much, and live as well as journeymen in many other common trades lived, but they could limit his earnings to almost any amount, and from their bad arrangements he was always kept far below his compeers, excepting some two months in the year when trade was so brisk that hands could not be found to do it and during this short period he was fully employed. The strike failed, but its object was soon afterwards accomplished. Early in the next spring but one the masters fearing another, tho' a partial strike of those whose circumstances had made them almost reckless, gave the advance required, and reformed their mode of doing business altogether. They who had the most of the leather breeches trade had not taken to make stuff breeches and they saw that unless their businesses were carried on with more regularity and less disappointment to their customers it would become extinct, they therefore made better arrangements and thus the men who were employed were better paid and much more constantly employed, whilst many took to stuff breeches making and the whole of the Journeymen were bettered. I had a good deal to do in these arrangements, for the men, but for which I received neither recompense nor thanks, after the advance was obtained

Our sufferings were great indeed. As long as we had any thing which

7 1791–1793

could be pawned we did not suffer much from actual hunger, but after every thing had been pawned, but "what we stood upright in," we suffered much from actual hunger.[1] My wife was a fine handsome young woman and I was most affectionately and sincerely attached to her, notwithstanding the ebullitions of temper I have noticed, and when I sometimes looked at her, in her comfortless, forlorn and all but ragged condition, I could hardly endure our wretched state, and know not what mischief or crimes it might have driven me to commit, had not the instructions of my good schoolmaster and my previous reading enabled me to form something like correct notions, and to hold to them.

After about two months privation I became somewhat more reconciled to my condition hopeless as it at times seemed, and at length I obtained such a perfect command of myself that excepting commiseration for my wife, and actual hunger I suffered but little, and bore my lot without much repining. I made up my mind to endure whatever I should be compelled to suffer, and resolved to take advantage of every thing which might occur to work myself into a condition to become a master myself. I never afterwards swerved in the least from this resolution.

Soon after we had become lodgers in the house we lived in, it was let to a new tenant, a little drunken fellow an engraver named Lymans, my wife used to pay his wife the weekly rent of two shillings as long as we had the means of raising the money. My wife had never been at a Pawnbrokers and could not go. I would not go myself, hunger at last induced her to request the wife of an old man a carpenter who lived in one of the garrets to pawn something for her. This she did, and continued to do as long as there was any thing which could be pawned. This woman was about fifty years of age, she was very poor, of quiet manners, and to us, and far as we could learn, very honest. It is probable that when she was no longer employed to pawn things for us, she concluded we had nothing more to pawn, and communicated her suspicions to my landlords wife, who as well as her husband offered my wife credit for every thing they sold, and the wife almost forced, bread, coals soap and candles on her, and at the end of our probation nothwithstanding we were only half fed on bread and water with an occasional red herring we were six pounds in debt to our landlord.

I never saw my landlord until nearly the end of our state of suffering. The way I came to see him was this. He came home one evening drunk, and demanded money from his wife to go to the public house again, his

[1] When the members of the parliamentary committee on mendacity claimed that a journeyman can always get work, Place told them, 'A man cannot always get employment, I could not do and I have been starved in the town from want of employment' (Letter to James Mill, July 20, 1815; Add. MS 35152, f. 141v).

The Autobiography of Francis Place

wife would not let him have any, and to prevent his going out again had locked the street-door, and hid the key. A quarrel ensued at the door which was at the foot of the stairs. He made a great noise attempted to break open the door and beat his wife. The riot alarmed the whole house but as it happened I was the only man in it. I went down stairs and found him swearing and beating like a madman, first at the door and then at his wife, so without any ceremony or speaking a word I seized him by the collar with one hand and the waist of his breeches with the other hand, whipped him up, carried him to his parlour and seated him in a chair. His astonishment seemed to sober him somewhat, and he sat like a fool unable to speak. I gave him a few words of caution and advice and left him. We now feared, that he would not only refuse to give us any more credit, but that he would seize our goods for the rent which was due to him. The next morning however he way laid me, made an apology for his conduct, thanked me for my interference and offered me every assistance in his power. He afterwards as might be anticipated fell to decay, and it now became my duty to assist his unfortunate family – his wife has been dead many years, his children two girls are both dead and he has long been a vagabond about the streets, calling on me occasionally for a trifle of money which I have not the heart to refuse him.*

About this time a circumstance occurred which marks the mode of thinking and acting of people of narrow intellects and vulgar notions in all times towards those who are considered as their inferiors. The Landlord of the Crown and Anchor Tavern had lately taken into partnership a young man the son of a Glazier and Painter in Essex Street in the Strand. His father the Glazier was a wealthy man the son had been what was called well brought up. His family had been on good terms with my father and mother and I applied to him as well as others to give me some portion of their custom, he was the only one who did so, and he gave me his leather breeches to clean, about once a month for which I recieved 1/6 – He sent me a pair to clean just at the time that a working man had given me an order for a pair of corduroy breeches. I was unable to purchase the materials and was regretting my inability to complete the order when on turning out one of the pockets of Mr Willis's leather breeches to clean it, I found a half guinea. With this I purchased materials and on the saturday night following received a guinea for the Corduroy breeches. The moment I got the money I went to Mr Willis, told him the circumstance and returned the half guinea, the consequence was what I had predicted to my wife. Willis never again employed me in any way.

* August 16. 1833. He must be now nearly 70 years of age I saw him to day at Brompton and gave him as usual half a crown.

7 1791–1793

My brothers master to whom he had been bound apprentice died, and he had been some time since turned over to a Mr Hutchins a Wharfinger at the bottom of Water Street near Arundel Street. My brother was out of his time and was employed by Mr Hutchins as a general overseer of his business and not as a lighterman he having resolved never more to row in a barge and he never did. By him I was recommended to Mr Hutchins to fill a vacancy which was to happen on the following saturday; that of overseer of the Scavengers, Hutchins being a contracter for several parishes, to remove the dust and ashes and to sweep the streets. My business was to see that the men who swept the streets did their work in sweeping clean, and filling the mud carts properly – in seeing that the horses were cleaned and put up in the evening and that they and the carts were taken out at the proper time in the morning. To this employment I was to have gone on the following monday at half past five o clock in the morning. My wages were to have been eighteen shillings a week. On the friday however I was sent for by Mr Allison, I refused to go. Lingham had endeavoured to play me a trick by inducing me to confess to a combination of workmen and thus to be able to prosecute me for combination, and I suspected that Allison meant me no good. All my wife's supplications were useless Go I would not. At length she said, may I go? and after some importunity, I said she might go and get herself affronted. In a short time she returned, and let fall from her apron as much work for me as she could bring away. She was unable to speak until she was relieved by a flood of tears; she then said that Mr Allison expressed himself pleased to see her, and pleased that she came instead of me, said he had not used me well and spite of the other masters he was resolved to make me all the recompence he could, he then bid her hold out her apron and pushed from the counter into it the work she had brought home, telling her that he knew I should work very hard and grudge every minute I was not at work, that I need not therefore come to the shop myself, but that he would send to me daily or she might bring the work as it was finished, of which I should have as much as I could do.

The whole, or nearly the whole, of the eight months when I was not employed was not lost. I read many volumes in history, voyages, and travels, politics, law and Philosophy. Adam Smith and Locke and especially Humes Essays and Treatises, these latter I read two or three times over, this reading was of great service to me, it caused me to turn in upon myself and examine myself in a way which I should not otherwise have done. It was this which laid the solid foundation of my future prosperity, and completed the desire I had always had to acquire knowledge. Reading of Hume put me on improving myself in other ways. I taught myself decimals, equations, the square cube and biquadrate roots. I got

The Autobiography of Francis Place

some knowledge of Logarithmes, and some of Algebra. I readily got through a small school book of Geometry and having an odd volume the 1st of Williamsons Euclid I attacked it vigorously and perseveringly. Williamsons is by no means the best book on the subject, yet I am still of opinion that it is the best book I could have had, for the purpose of teaching myself. My progress was for some time very slow, I was perplexed between quantity and number and could not readily abstract myself from the consideration of numbers. I suspect that this has its baleful influence on all who learn arithmetic before they acquire any knowledge of Geometrical figures and diffinitions of them, which by experience I now know may be taught to children without much difficulty, and which being taught, assist the learner to a great extent when he comes to be taught Mathematics, as a science. Often and often did I find my self at fault and was as often obliged to turn back again, I was sometimes brought to a standstill, and at times almost despaired of making further progress. Williamsons Euclid is preceded by five dissertations, these I read carefully working the problems as I went on. I have no doubt that I should have had less difficulty had I not been impressed with a persuasion of the great difficulty of acquiring the information I sought. The volume contained the first six books of Euclid. With labour such as few would take and difficulties such as few would encounter I got through the six books, but not at all to my satisfaction. I knew no one of whom I could ask a question or receive any kind of instruction, and the subject was therefore at times very painful. I had acquired a good deal of information and was upon the whole well pleased with my progress. I was beginning the book again when Mr Allison sent for me and this for a time put an end to my studies.

As I read I hoped and expected more and more that some circumstance would occur for my advantage, I saw as I thought a certainty of success in the world if such a circumstance should occur. I was in no doubt that whenever it was possible to take a step I should be prepared to take it and should not let the opportunity pass by. I stated my opinions on these subjects to my wife, and used every argument in my power to satisfy her that we should not always be poor, but that by some means or other, not then visible but which must in time be visible I should get into business, that whenever that important step should be taken, I should do a good stroke of business, should get money and by the time I was forty five years of age should be able to retire from business. She thought me insane when I talked thus, and often afterwards when in different circumstances but before I was able to take a shop, I repeated my opinion, she used to say, that I was certainly mad on that subject. I however very nearly realized my prediction, as I

7 1791–1793

ceased all active interference in business before I was forty eight years of age.

It will have been seen that I was not religious, I could not believe otherwise than as I did, I could not persuade myself that their was either wisdom or honesty in attempting to stultify myself as I saw some did, but at times I doubted my reason, and endeavoured to have faith, but those were transient abberrations. Humes writings put an end to them for ever, all doubt vanished and I was ever after at ease on this subject.

Just before the death of our child my Father died in the seventy sixth year of his age, he had been confined to his bed for some time without any particular disorder, except gout which in his enfeebled state was not violent as it had formerly been, and scarcly deserved to be called gout, what he had of it was no longer confined to particular parts, but he appeard to have the consequences of gout and old age all over him. His stomach was never free from disease during his last illness and this it was which at length killed him

My poor mother was almost worn out by attending to him and her business which with all her efforts hardly produced them food.

After my fathers death my mother's fate was a little mitigated. My brother was out of his time, and he was about to be married, she had therefore only to provide for herself and my youngest sister who was now at liberty to assist her more than she had been.

A young man a shoe maker had paid his addresses to her, and offered to marry her, my father disliked him and his offer was not accepted he married another and became a respectable well doing tradesman. Two other young men had paid her some attentions, one was a Compositor named Roidhouse, the other whose name was Stimson had served his time to a butcher in Fleet market. My mother preferred the printer who was a steady sensible young man of respectable appearance, my sister on the contrary gave her preference to the Butcher, and this was matter of great grief to my mother, who was now fated never more to enjoy any thing like comfort. Spite of the advice and remonstrance of her own family and of every body who knew the butcher, and in opposition to a disposition which was mild and yeilding she obstinately withstood every effort to save her from certain destruction and married Mat Stimson

He was the only son of an old villain lately deceased who was formerly a butcher, and who with his wife as great a villain as himself had for many years kept a "fence" in Fleet Lane, it was in appearance an old Iron and Rag shop This was however a mere blind, and intended as a shew of the means of "making a living". The father had been tried at the Old Bailey more than once, and had been punished more than once. The mother had also been confined for criminal offences. Besides the boy there were two girls, one several years older than the boy the other about two years younger. The eldest was a common low lived, dirty, drunken woman of the town and a notorious thief. The youngest lived at home with her mother, and with the son assisted her in her business. My sisters marriage into this miscreant family, nearly broke my mothers heart, her distress, her loneliness – her age and inability, and want of business produced such a state of suffering as can scarcely be concieved. She was indeed a terrible example of the misconduct of others. Without any fault of her own, with every claim to consideration and respect she was at sixty four years of age deserted by every body, neglected and insulted even by her children. My eldest sister being herself nearly reckless, instead of soothing and assisting her misused and plundered her of some of the little property she had still preserved. My brother who had the means of serving her totally neglected her, and scarcely ever called to see her, and I was utterly unable to assist her in any way. The only mitigation of her sorrow was the affectionate attentions of my wife, who from the first moment of their becoming acquanted with one another, had never ceased to pay the most marked and filial affection and respect.

I interfered as much as I could. I remonstrated with my brother and sisters, this producing no good results, I reproached them, but all to no good purpose. I therefore discarded them. With my brother I had no sort of communication for several succeding years, until he got into difficulties and applied to me to assist in extricating him, which I did. With my eldest sister I never more had any acquantance or intercourse whatever.

My youngest sister lived in ready furnished lodgings near Fleet Market. Her husband was a go-between the thieves and his mother and was sometimes himself a thief.

Such was the state of myself and my relatives when Mr Allison again gave me employment.

CHAPTER 8

From my being employed by Mr Allison to My being employed by Mrs Barnes. London Corresponding Society. Family History

Temporary Prosperity. Work – from 16 to 18 hours daily – Clerk to several clubs – Condition of Working men. London Corresponding Society – Book clubs – Sisters husband, Mothers afflictions.

All difficulty and apprehension vanished on our being again employed by Mr Allison. We both went to work "with a hearty good will". The carpenters wife who was as well pleased as she could have been had she been our mother, was now employed to cook and wash for us, to keep our room clean and to get our things from the Pawnbrokers as fast as we could procure money for the purpose. We now worked full sixteen and sometimes eighteen hours a day sundays and all. I never went out of the house for many weeks, and could not find time for a month to shave myself. We turned out of bed to work and turned from our work to bed again.[1] My hair was black and somewhat curled my beard was very thick and my whiskers large, my face somewhat sallow, and upon the whole I must have been a ferocious looking fellow. A journeyman tailor, a poor workman and a poor creature, lived in a garret above our room, he was very young and had a wife a poor thing like himself, she had never seen me, but knew the person of my wife. Our window was opposite the backs of the houses in Holywell Street in one of which a man and his wife were quarrelling and making a great noise this caused me to put my head out of the window, and the woman who was above me and was looking down

---

[1] Place later found it impossible to maintain this regimen of work. 'The most painstaking, saving, industrious man is not free from the desire for leisure; there are times when he is unable to bring himself to the conclusion that he must continue working. I know not how to describe the sickening aversion which at times steals over the working man, and utterly disables him for a longer or a shorter period, from following his usual occupation, and compells him, to indulge in idleness. I have felt it, resisted it to the utmost of my power; but have been so completely subdued by it, that spite of very pressing circumstances, I have been obliged to submit, and run away from my work.* This is the case with every workman I have ever known.

* For nearly six years, whilst working when I had work to do, from twelve to eighteen hours a day. When no longer able, from the cause mentioned, to continue working, I used to run from it, and go as rapidly as I could to Highgate, Hampstead, Muswell-Hill or Norwood, and then "return to my vomit."' (*Improvement of the Working Class*, pp. 14–15).

The Autobiography of Francis Place

upon me saw my head and the hair on one side of my face and exclaimed to her busband, "the young woman below us has got a black man for her husband." This became a standing joke against me for some time afterwards. We soon recovered from our deplorable condition, bought cloaths, and bedding and other necessaries, a good bedstead and many other things which made us comfortable, my wife was again in the family way and as the time approached we removed to a much more convenient room in a small recently built house near the Angel Inn in the then open space at the end of Wych Street.

The form of the house and room was as below:

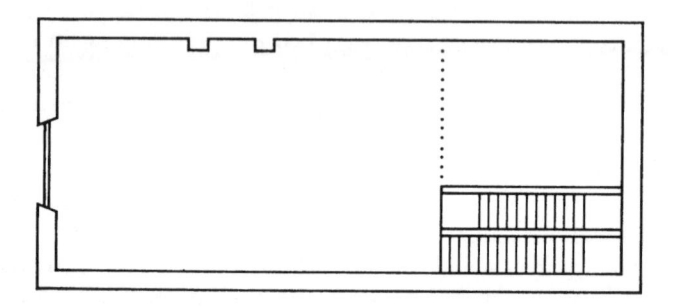

Along the space where the dotted line is placed we put an Iron rod close up to the cieling, on which ran a couple of curtains. We employed the wife of a hackney coachman who lodged in the Garret to Cook and wash and clean for us, we had plenty of work, and we worked hard, I bought a stove and had it set on a plan of Count Runfords,[1] our little furniture was good enough for our circumstances and the room was especially neat and clean. There was a small yard to the house and a washhouse, and these were great conveniencies. We had never before been so well off or had reason to be so well satisfied, I was able also to assist my mother. We used to work later than usual, on friday nights, and earlier than usual, on saturday mornings, so as to finish our weeks labour by three o clock, on the saturday afternoon and we ceased working on sundays. I used to clean myself and go to Mr Allisons to settle with him, and my wife and the coachmans wife used to put the room into the best possible order, we then put on our best cloaths if the weather was fine and took a walk. As we scarcly left our work for meals all the week we had a hot supper on the saturday, a beef steak or mutton chops. Our neat place, the absence of want, and the expectation of continuing to do well, the persuasion that our days of suffering were at an end, and our mutual affection made us,

[1] Count Rumford.

perhaps, as happy as any two persons ever really were. This state of prosperity was however of short duration. Allisons wife was a she devil, he a good natured silly fellow who was wholly under her control, he used to spend his evenings at the public house and she used to console herself with the Revd Mr —— and they sometimes got drunk together. She could not bear to see the change of appearance in me and my wife; like but too many others she disliked to see others happy and prosperous, and above all she disliked our receiving so much money as we did of her husband notwithstanding we earned it by our labour. She therefore contrived to have some of the work given to another man, and by the middle of april 1794 I had no more work given to me than I could easily do myself without any assistance from my wife. Some of the men who had failed in the strike of the preceding year had commenced another benefit club, it was really a benefit club and had no reference to a strike, the money was never to be used for any purposes but those of releving the sick and burying the dead members. To induce the masters to raise their wages a more perfect combination was necessary, provisions were enormously advanced in price and they who continued to make leather breeches were in a very bad condition. Some of them therefore applied to me – and I prepared a scheme for a tontine to continue for three years, it was however, well understood that the real purpose was to raise money for another strike. I had plenty of leisure to attend to the business, and became secretary and confidential manager. The first meeting was held on the evening of the last monday but one in the month of April 1794. A great many of the men joined it at once and nearly the whole of them came into the project in a short time, and paid their monthly money regularly. This combination produced an advance of wages in the spring of 1795 without a strike. The masters had done themselves much injury by holding out against the reasonable demands of the men in 1793. and they did not like to encounter another strike. As the fashion of wearing leather breeches was gradually changing most of the master had taken to making stuff breeches, Some however still continued to make leather breeches only, and this was the case with the two principal masters. It seems that during the former strike many of their customers had left them and employed their tailors to make breeches for them, they had however got them back again, and by the spring of 1795 had very greatly increased their number. The tailors could not then make breeches to fit as the breeches makers did, and such was the notion of fashionable men in favour of the Breeches makers, that they were able to charge, and did charge full half as much again as the tailors charged and their profits were enormous. These were advantages they did not like to put to hazard, and they therefore made an advance in the wages of the journeymen

The Autobiography of Francis Place

without waiting to have it demanded. The advance was quite as much as had been desired in 1793 and the men were satisfied The money which had been collected was distributed and the Tontine was put an end to. I was paid ten pounds a year as secretary, but when the money was divided my office ceased, and I was thought no more of. So far as I alone was concerned the advance of wages was injurious, it did not advance the wages of a stuff breeches maker and this was my employment. Had there been a strike, a Shop would have been taken in which the masters would have been undersold, I should have had the management of the shop and when the strike was ended should have remained in it on my own account, and thus have become a master tradesman.

Besides the Tontine among the Leather Breeches makers I formed another society among the Carpenters which continued for two years and ended by an increas of wages being given. I was secretary also to a benefit club of journeymen plumbers. Especial meetings of these clubs were called by printed notices filled up and left at each mans lodgings, for filling up and delivering these I was allowed to charge postage price. I drew up articles for several other clubs, and assisted in their formation, for all which I was paid, thus my income was kept up for some time and I had what was of much use to me more exercise than I had been accustomed to for many preceding months. I also got an occasional order from some of the men in these clubs. To gain the time necessary to attend to these clubs, I and my wife worked together as usual when we had any work to do.

On the 28 of April 1794 My wife had her second child a girl whom we named after her Elizabeth, we had been hard at work all day and I had been out at business in the evening, my wife had been putting the room in order when she was taken in labour, and when I came home I found her in that state. At her first lying in she was attended by a woman, but as we were not quite satisfied with her treatment, we resolved to have a man of some reputation, and one had been engaged, two guineas were laid by for him, and as good clothes had been provided for the child as any working man could reasonably desire. She was delivered at two o clock in the morning. Our room was on the second floor, the landlady of the house was with my wife, and I was invited to sit in the room on the first floor. In this room was a number of books, and among them every thing which had been published by Thomas Paine, all these I had read and cheap editions were in my possession; but here was one which I had not seen, namely "the Age of Reason Part 1. I read it with delight. It was the first deeistical book I ever saw, excepting the writings of David Hume. I had lived in the house about two months, but there had been no other communication between me and my landlord than a friendly salutation, but the quantity and kind of books I found in his room made me desirous of his acquaintance. He was an Irishman from the County of Antrim, a cabinet maker by trade, and what was very unusual he was a good workman. He was a mild quiet benevolent man. His wife was an ill bred, fat, dirty slovenly cockney, the daughter of a Glazier in the Strand. I knew her when she was a girl, like other such girls in the neighbourhood. They had each of them some money when they were married, but she was ridiculously expensive in her mode of living and he was but ill adapted to carry on his business as a shop keeper, and the money they had was soon expended. She now kept a green shop and he made cabinet work in a shed at the back of the house, for a customer when he could procure an order, at other times for the Brokers. They might have saved money but there was sad want of economy on the part of the wife, ultimately he died very poor and she with two or three children went to the workhouse

I continued working for Mr Allison, attending to my clubs and now and then making a pair of breeches or a waistcoat for a customer of my own.

My Landlord made me a chest of drawers of solid mahogany, so contrived that they might be taken in halves, and yet without the appearance in front of being two chests. He also made me a mahogany dining table. He was paid for these articles partly in money, partly in cloaths. We had now quite enough furniture for one room all good and nearly all new. We really wanted nothing now for personal comfort, and could this state of things have been continued we should have saved money and I should have become a master tradesman. But the hopes of a man who has no other means than those of his own hands to help himself are but too often illusory, and in a vast number of cases, the disappointments are more than can be steadily met, and men give up in despair; become reckless, and after a life of poverty end their days prematurely in misery. The misfortune is the greater too as it is only the better sort of persons to whom this happens. To the careful saving moral men and women who have set their hearts on bettering their condition and have toiled day and night in the hope of accomplishing their purpose. None but such as they can tell how disappointment preys on them, how as the number of their children increases, hope leaves them, how their hearts sink as toil becomes useless, how adverse circumstances force on them those indescribable feelings of their own degradation which sinks them gradually to the extreme of wretchedness. Others there are in much larger numbers whose views are narrower, they who hoped and expected to keep on in a decent way who never expected to rise in the world and never calculated on extreme poverty. I have seen a vast many such, who when the evil day has come upon them, have kept on working steadily but hopelessly more like horses in a mill, or mere machines than human beings, their feelings blunted, poor stultified moving animals, working on yet unable to support their families in any thing like comfort, frequently wanting the common necessaries of life, yet never giving up until "misery has eaten them to the bone," none knowing none caring for them, no one to administer a word of comfort, or if an occasion occured which might be of service to them, none to rouse them to take advantage of it. All above them in circumstances, calumniating them, classing them with the dissolute, the profligate and the dishonest, from whom the character of the whole of the working people is taken. Yet I have witnessed in this class of persons, so dispised so unjustly judged of by their betters, virtues which I have not seen, to the same extent as to means, among any other description of the people. Justice will never perhaps be done to them because they may never be understood, because it is not the habit for men to care for others beneath them in rank, and because they who employ them will probably never fail to look grudgingly on the pay they are compelled to give them for their services, the very notion of which produces an inward hatred of them, a feeling so common that it is visible in the countenance and manners in nearly every one who has to pay either journeymen, labourers, or servants.

We foresaw that at no distant period Mr Allison would be compelled by his wife to discontinue giving us work, we therefore made every effort we could to obtain money and to purchase with it as many useful articles and cloaths as would serve us for a long time and enable us to keep up our respectable appearance, a matter of the greatest importance to every working man, for so long as he is able to keep himself up in this particular, he will have resolution to struggle with, and frequently if not generally to overcome his adverse circumstances. No working man, journeman tradesman is ever wholly ruined until hope has abandoned him.

Our anticipations were soon realized Mr Allison ceased to give me work and upon my asking him the reason, he said he thought "we had been long enough together and had better part for a time", the truth was his wife had compelled him to discharge us. Mr Allison was a large fat heavy looking man, ignorant and weak, he had always been under the domination of his wife, who was much younger than he was, a square built, fierce shrewd woman, who would do as she liked. He had been in a bad state of health without any particular disorder, was often in low spirits and at times melancholy; within a few months from the time he discharged me, he was locked up in a madhouse in which I believe he died some years afterwards. Mrs Allison kept the shop for some time after her husbands death but what became of her afterwards I never heard, it is very probable however that she became very poor and ended her life in that state, for poverty kills apace. Those who having been

8 Dec. 1793–1795

once well off in the world fall into poverty seldom long survive their change of circumstances.¹

After being discharged from Allisons I procured work from three or four journeymen who sometimes had more work than they could do, these jobs, an occasional customer of my own, and the emoluments I received from the clubs enabled us to maintain ourselves decently, and to continue to assist my mother, whom we endeavoured to make as comfortable as we could. The work I procured was of a very precarious nature and very irregular, sometimes I had more than I could do, at other times I had none at all. Sometimes I worked all night long, at other times I had no employment for two or three days together, but as what I did was paid for at the highest rate of wages it was upon the whole very good employment.

The intervals the employment I now had procured me were not wasted I resumed my studies and made progress in them all. In this way I continued until the spring of 1795 when having a good shop of work offered me I removed for convenience to a lodging in Fisher Street Holborn.

My Landlord, the Cabinet Maker was a member of the London Corresponding Society, and at his request I also became a member. This was in the month of June 1794. On the 12 of May Thomas Hardy the Secretary was seized by order of the Government on a pretended charge of High Treason, and about the same time ten others on the same charge, Thomas Holcroft whom it was also intended should be seized avoided them and was at large till the time of trial approached when he surrendered himself.² The London Corresponding Society was like the Society of the Friends of the people and the Society for Constitutional Information established to provide a reform in the Representation of the people in the House of Commons.

[The London Corresponding Society, founded in January 1792 by Thomas Hardy, a shoemaker, differed from the other two societies mentioned by Place in that its members were mostly artisans and small shopkeepers. In his notes for a history of the Society, Place repeated Hardy's account of its origin: '"The

---

[1] The rough draft of part of this paragraph has been preserved. In it Allison is not 'ignorant and weak,' but 'utterly ignorant and of very weak intellect.' Instead of 'he discharged me,' the first draft reads, 'I left him.' In it, the tale of the Allisons ends tangentially: 'His wife and her foreman Richard Taylor carried on the business for some time; until the foreman married a girl from his own country who was in keeping by Sir William Manners. The foreman who had no money of his own took a large house in Bond Street which he fitted up at great expense, and became a master' (Add. MS 27808, f. 2v).

[2] The men against whom the grand jury found a true bill for high treason were John Baxter, John Augustus Bonney, Thomas Hardy, Richard Hodgson, Thomas Holcroft, Jeremiah Joyce, Stewart Kyd, Matthew Moore, John Richter, John Thelwall, John Horne Tooke and Thomas Wardle. They were soon called the 'twelve apostles.'

The Autobiography of Francis Place

Society began in the latter end of the year 1791, in consequence of a conversation I had with a friend respecting the unequal Representation of the People in Parliament. That conversation suggested the propriety of instituting a society with a view of ascertaining the opinion of the people on that question, by corresponding with other societies that might be formed, having the same object in view, as well as with public spirited individuals . . . The first meeting of the London Corresponding Society was held on 25 Jany 1792 it consisted of *eight* persons; who after arranging the form and terms of admitting members it was agreed in order to pay the expenses of stationary, printing and postage of letters that each member should pay one penny per week . . . The second week of meeting eight more members were added, and the week following nine. The whole number was twenty five, and the sum in the treasury was four shillings and one penny . . .

'"The first address and Resolutions which the Society Printed and which was published very extensively in the Newspapers and otherwise was dated the 2nd of April 1792. and from this time the society became known to the public. Societies were then formed in different parts of England, Scotland, and Ireland, in quick succession for the same laudable object – a constant correspondence was afterwards kept up with these societies. The London Corresponding Society was considered as the Parent Society, which induced Burke in one of his mad rants in the house of commons to call it, 'the Mother of all mischief'"' (Add. MS 27808, fs. 3–4). The quotations are from a letter Hardy sent, in 1816, to be read at the dinner celebrating the anniversary of his acquittal in 1794.[1]]

All or nearly all the persons apprehended were members either of the London Corresponding Society or of the Society for Constitutional Information

The violent proceedings of the Government frightened away many of the members of the society and its number was very considerably diminished. Many persons however, of whom I was one, considered it meritorious, and the performance of a duty to become members, now that it was threatened with violence, and its founder and secretary was persecuted. This improved the character of the society as most of those who joined it were men of decided character, sober, thinking men, not likely to be easily put from their purpose.*

---

[1] This letter is reprinted in his autobiography, *Memoir of Thomas Hardy*, 1832, pp. 105–11. For an account of the society, see E. P. Thompson, *The Making of the English Working Class*, 1968, passim and esp. Ch. 1; and Henry Collins, 'The London Corresponding Society,' in *Democracy and the Labour Movement*, 1954.

* September 7. 1833. In the rough draft of my memoirs I made a sketch of the London Corresponding Society incorporating it with other matters. I have here omitted the sketch and intend to make a seperate essay on the subject. [Place's sketch of the London Corresponding Society, contained in Add. MS 27808, fs. 2–117, is an amplified version of the account he gives in the autobiography. All footnote quotations from Add. MS 27808 are excerpts from this earlier draft.]

[In the rough draft Place wrote that those who joined at this time 'were men who possessed something decided and energetic in their characters and they became very active members' (Add. MS 27808, f. 3).]

8 Dec. 1793–1795

The Society assembled in divisions in various parts of the Metropolis, that to which I belonged was held; as all the others were weekly; at a private house in New Street Covent Garden. Each division elected a delegate and sub delegate, these formed a general committee which also met once a week, in this committee the sub delegate had a seat but could neither speak nor vote whilst the delegate was present. I was soon elected delegate and became a member of the General Committee[1]

In this society I met with many inquisitive clever upright men and among them I greatly inlarged my acquantance. They were in most if not in all respects superior to any with whom I had hitherto been acquainted. We had book subscriptions, similar to the breeches clubs, before mentioned, only the books for which any one subscribed were read by all the members in rotation who chose to read them before they were finally consigned to the subscriber. We had Sunday evening parties at the residences of those who could accomodate a number of persons. At these meetings we had readings, conversations and discussions. There was at this time a great many such parties, they were highly useful and agreeable.

The usual mode of proceeding at these weekly meetings was this. The chairman, (each man was chairman in rotation,) read from some book a chapter or part of a chapter, which as many as could read the chapter at their homes the book passing from one to the other had done and at the next meeting a portion of the chapter was again read and the persons present were invited to make remarks thereon. as many as chose did so, but without rising. Then another portion was read and a second invitation was given – then the remainder was read and a third invitation was given when they who had not before spoken were expected to say something. Then there was a general discussion. No one was permitted to speak more than once during the reading The same rule was observed in the general discussion, no one could speak a second time until every one who chose had spoken once, then any one might speak again, and so on till the subject was exhaustd – these were very important meetings, and the best results to the parties followed.[2]

[1] Each division also had a secretary and 'as many tything men as were tens in the division. All these officers were elected quarterly ... Each division was allowed to retain one shilling a week from the subscription received for current expences. Every member was allowed a copy of whatever might be printed by the order of the General Committee.' A division was to consist of about thirty members; when the number reached thirty-six, sixteen of the members were to branch off and form a new division (Add. MS 27808, fs. 16–17).

[2] This paragraph was added, on the verso of the preceding folio, after the fair copy had been written.

In the earlier sketch of the LCS Place said that the meetings were marked by a rigidity of decorum: 'Eating – drinking – & smoking were forbidden either in a

The Autobiography of Francis Place

Early in the month of october 1794. A special Commission was issued to try the persons accused of High Treason. To prepare matters for the approaching trials, several committees were appointed, of one of these I was a member,[1] and when the nine days trial of Thomas Hardy commenced, I used to attend daily at the Old Bailey from noon 'till night. Go to work when I came home, and again in the morning early 'till noon, and thus I contrived to do as much as an ordinary days work. I was very active and useful in directing others, and was well pleased to see the esteem in which I was held by those with whom I acted who were clever men in circumstances very superior to mine. When Hardy, Tooke, and Thelwall were acquitted and the others discharged, the society increased with great rapidity.[2]

In this year. 1794.[3] a sad affliction fell on my poor mother and my youngest sister. Her husband was apprehended on the charge of having

---

division or in a committee. No man in liquor was permitted to remain in any division or committee and habitual drunkenness was sufficient cause for expulsion' (Add. MS 27808, f. 10).

[1] The committee work entailed meetings with the accused in jail: 'In 1794 I was several times in Newgate on visits to persons confined for libel &c – one sunday in particular I was there, when several respectable women were also there – relatives of those I went to see. When the time for leaving the Prison arrived we came in a body of 9 or ten persons into a large yard which we had to cross – into this yard a number of felons were admitted, and they were in such a condition that we were obliged to request the jailer to compel them to tie up their rags so as [to] conceal their bodies which were most indecently exposed – and as I have no doubt intentional to alarm the women, and extort money from the men. When they had made themselves somewhat decent we came into the yard, and were pressed upon and almost husseled by the felons whose Irons and voices demanding money made a frightful noise and alarmed the women. I who understood these matters had collected all the halfpence I could – and by throwing a few at a time over the heads of the felons set them scrambling swearing and all but fighting whilst the women and the rest made their way as quickly as possible across the yard' (Add. MS 27826, f. 186).

[2] Place recalled this acquittal and the preceding trial years later when he addressed Lord Erskine, who had conducted the defence of Hardy: 'Your Lordship notices the well earned praise I bestowed on you for your eloquent, learned and manly exertions during the State trials in 1794, the bare mention of which brings to my mind an association of ideas the most exhilerating – and sends me back to the Old Bailey with the most vivid recollections of the men and things of that time, never can I forget the emotions I felt during the nine days trial, or the joy in which I partook on hearing the verdict Not Guilty pronounced on my worthy and excellent friend Thomas Hardy' (Reply to Lord Erskine, 1819, in Add. MS 35154, f. 25).

Place characterized Hardy, in the earlier version of the history of the LCS, as 'my friend, that peculiarly honest upright man, Thomas Hardy, whose manners are so simple that he never made a personal enemy in his life' (Add. MS 27808, f. 107).

[3] Place prefaced this section with the note, 'This is misplaced. See the date.' The date should be 1799.

8   Dec. 1793–1795

committed a highway robbery. He was Tried, Convicted and Cast for death.[1]

The Morning Chronicle.
London:
Tuesday, April 23, 1799.
Public Office, Bow Street.
Before J. Floud, Esq.

Matthew Stimson was brought in custody on a charge of committing a highway robbery on the person of Mr. Read, a Mealman, at Watford, Herts, who deposed, that on Saturday evening, about six o'clock, as he was passing through Burrow lane, near Hendon, in a chaise cart, he was attacked by the prisoner, who had a handkerchief over the lower part of his face, and who, presenting a pistol, robbed him of a half guinea and his pocket-book, containing a 2l note, and then rode off towards Hendon; that in a few minutes after the robbery he met some persons, whom he told of it, and who immediately pursued and took the prisoner with the note and money on him, which were produced, and also three loaded pistols found in his pockets.

The prisoner, on being asked by Mr. Floud if he would wish to say any thing in defence to the charge, replied it was very true, but said it was his first offence, and distress alone had prompted him to it, having a wife and two children without support; interrogated as to his former mode of living, said that he had been brought up to the business of a butcher in Fleet Market, but had failed. There being good reason to suppose that he has been guilty of other robberies, notwithstanding his protestations to the contrary, he was ordered for further examination on Wednesday next.

The Morning Chronicle.
London:
Thursday, May 9.
Old Bailey.

Yesterday the Sessions commenced before the Right Honourable the Lord Mayor, Mr. Baron Perryn, Mr. Justice Grose, Mr Recorder, &c. when eighteen prisoners were tried, five of whom were capitally convicted, viz. – *Matthew Stimson*, for feloniously assaulting John Field on the King's Highway, and robbing him of a pocket book, a two pound bank note, and other articles; *Susannah Harrison*, for stealing six silver tea spoons, and a number of other articles, the property of Daniel Wade, in his dwelling house; *John Beven* and *Richard Mills*, for feloniously assaulting Henry Kemp on the King's Highway, and robbing him of several halfpence and penny pieces; *John Vickers*, for stealing a ewe sheep, the property of Jonathan Passingham.

My sister was now with an infant obliged to go and live with my mother, doing what she could with her needle towards earning her living.

---

[1] In the manuscript, the following newspaper cuttings are pasted on a separate page before this paragraph.

The Autobiography of Francis Place

She was utterly subdued and never again lifted up her head. Stimson had robbed a farmer on the highway, he was a small weakly creature, a mere boy in appearance, the man he robbed was a tall stout active man who might have pulled him off his horse laid him across the pommel of his saddle and rode away with him. Mat Stimson was a great favourite among the thieves his companions, as well as with most of the turnkeys in Newgate, who were old cronies of his father and mother and he was therefore, "made comfortable." A scheme was devised to procure him a pardon, and the thieves and turnkeys and some City men of consequence* took pains in this matter. A petition was got up and was well signed, the story it told was plausible, it dwelt on his youth – his first offence – his wife and child, – his sincere contrition, and his friends being willing to establish him in business, this was sent to the Secretary of State addressed to the King. He also petitioned himself, promised to become an honest man and to take care of his family. The business was so well arranged and so well managed that a free pardon was looked upon as certain. He was however an atrocious incorrigible villain whom nothing could reclaim. If a pardon had been sent to him he would have gone to the club in Fleet Lane there had a feast with the thieves, drank success to the craft and laughed at the wisdom of those who had been imposed upon by the petition. He would have been again apprehended for thieving, and would inevitably have been hanged. Upon learning that he was likely to obtain his liberty I at once and without consulting any body went to the Treasury and saw Mr Ford the Magistrate. I told him who and what I was and the business I was upon, gave him a short history of Stimson and his family, explained to him the conspiracy of the thieves and turnkeys, related the case of Mat's eldest sister then under sentence of transportation in Newgate, and begged him to cause enquiry to be made. This he promised to do. I then earnestly solicited that Mat might be transported for life as the only means of preventing further mischief and saving him from the Gallows. In a few days Mat was ordered to be transported to Botany Bay for life. Somehow or other my interference became known among the thieves and turnkeys, and boasts were made of what they would do to me, I was threatened, was "to be done for". This sadly alarmed my mother and my wife. I therefore determined to put an end to their fears, and the threats of the thieves. I borrowed a pair of pocket pistols loaded them with ball and resolved to

* When a case was got up by the Turnkeys and people about the Goal to save a '*Pal*', the Old Bailey attorneys took the lead. favourable reports were made to the gaoler, then to some of the officers of the court, then to the City Officers and there were always influential men – past-Sherriffs aldermen and Common Council men who interfered in such cases and very many of the greatest miscreants were saved while smaller criminals suffered.

use them if necessary, thus armed with weapons and resolution, I went on the club night to the house of rendezvous and into their club room some of the thieves knew me, some did not. I soon made myself known to them all, avowed that I had been the cause of Mat's being transported, insisted that I had done him service, and saved his life. Much noisy disputing followed, and I adverting to their threats 'to do for me', told them there was not a man among them who dared attack me. They one and all disclaimed any such intention, but some of them abused me as unfeeling and unnatural in getting my own sisters husband transported. I shortly defended myself and left them in by no means bad temper with me. Mat and his sister were transported about the same time and I never again heard one word of either of them.

Before Mat was sent away from Newgate my sister was able to earn as much money as would in conjunction with my mother have maintained them decently, but she gave her money to her worthless husband and distressed my mother exceedingly.

After Mat had been gone some months, the young man before mentioned the Printer again visited my mother, then courted my sister and at length married her, we all hoped she would do well, but she was not now the same sort of person she was when she married Stimson. She was always sedate, and remarkably neat in her person, her sedateness had now become a settled melancholy, she was no longer neat, had no care for any thing, made home uncomfortable to her husband who fell into despair lost his sober habits and took to drinking. In a short time his health became impaired his business was neglected and he dropped gradually into a state of miserable poverty. My sister lingered on from melancholy to a state of perfect apathy and died miserably. I had much respect for her husband who was a worthy man, I pitied him advised him, assisted him and did all I could to comfort him – I was always fond of my sister, and my wife was kind to her in an exemplary way to the moment of her death. Stimson's mother had been dead some time and her youngest daughter finding herself possessed of several hundreds of pounds, married a man who lived in the Borough he was a dyer, and dyed for thieves and fences, she took my sisters child and brought her up. She grew up and is married to a man the owner of some stage coaches and is doing well.

The last time I saw my sisters husband was on the day when she was buried. Since that day I never saw nor heard of him, and was never able to hear any tidings of him altho I took much pains for a long time to trace him.

CHAPTER 9

From my removal to Fisher Street in 1795 to my removal to Holborn in 1796.
London Corresponding Society

Employed by a Mrs Barnes. – Godwins Inquiry – Resolve to become a Master Tradesman – Two rooms, – advice to Workmen – London Corresponding Society – State Trials in 1794. – Chairman of the General Committee – Treason and Sedition Bills 1795. John Ashley. Jno Binns – Government its difficulties – Sent as a Deputy to Birmingham.

The Shop I now worked for was kept by a widow woman named Barnes, her husband had been dead about a year, he had a considerable trade in Gloves – some leather breeches making and somewhat more of stuff breeches making than would employ a man constantly, this I was to undertake. Her business was conducted by two men who acted as foremen. One of them a very sedate respectable middle aged man cut out gloves and attended in the shop. The other who had the care of the breeches part of the trade, also attended in the Shop and on the customers at their places of residence. His name was McDonald an Irishman, who did not understand his business in any particular. He was well pleased at my undertaking the stuff breeches as he knew I should instruct him in cutting out and making the most of his materials. This I did, and when he found himself capable of going on without me, I became an object of dislike to him. This I had anticipated. I had had experience enough to satisfy me that a vulgar narrow minded person is ever uneasy when compelled perpetually to come in contact with a person from whom he has received assistance to an extent which he himself would not be willing to give to others, and I knew well that McDonald would do no one any service which he could avoid. I was not therefore surprised at finding him opposed to me taking every opportunity in his power to annoy me, and if possible to drive me from the shop. He neither understood me nor himself. I was very little annoyed by any thing he could do. I was endeavouring to procure customers of my own, intending as soon as I had procured enough to keep us from starving to give up journey work altogether. I was finally induced to come to this determination sooner than I should otherwise have done by reading Mr Godwins "Enquiry concerning Political Justice."[1] It is remarkable enough that almost

[1] 'I was determined to work my way up to a state of independence; which, from the moment I read Mr Godwin's Political Justice in 1793, I never once doubted I

9 1795–1796

every honest journeyman is deterred for a long time, and some forever from making an attempt to get into business, lest he should be *ruined*, notwithstanding, being ruined could only bring him back again to journey-work. This must seem strange to all who have not had practical experience on the subject. The fear of doing injury to others by contracting debts he may be unable to pay is a proper feeling, and when it is not indulged to an extent which prevents a man from bettering his own condition without doing injury to any body operates beneficially; but besides this reasonable apprehension, the fear of personal ruin operates to a very considerable extent, it did with me. The reason is that there is a sort of mystery in the matter an uncertainty which they who fear to do evil are not willing to encounter. Mr Godwins book extinguished this fear in me. It led me to reason on the matter and convinced me that a man might turn others to account in every kind of undertaking without dishonesty, that the ordinary tricks of tradesmen were not necessary, and need not be practised. This was to me the most grateful kind of knowledge I could acquire and I resolved to lose no time in putting it in practice I did so and followed it up as long as I remained in business. My resolution was however nearly set aside, at once, as will be related, and was contemplated to be set aside on another occasion, but neither of those cases induced me to turn aside from my purpose the main object of my life, which was adhered to with an inflexibility and under many disadvantages to an extent which has often made me pleased with and proud of myself, and encouraged me to persevere in and to accomplish purposes which they who have been associated with me, or conversant with the subjects have previously condemned as impossibilities.

I was perfectly convinced that if I continued to work as a journeymen and depended on the savings I might make, that I never should have the means of becoming a master, and should therefore remain a journeyman as long as I lived. I saw the certainty that I should have a large family, and that nothing but wretchedness awaited us, if I did not contrive to get into business. I knew that by purchasing materials at two or three shops, however small the quantities, and letting each of them know that I made purchases of others, each would sell to me at as low a price as he could, and each would after a time give me credit. I afterwards put this mode of proceding in practice, and whenever I had two things to purchase I bought one at one shop and carried it under my arm to another shop where I bought the remainder of what I wanted. In a little time credit was offered to me each wishing to have the whole of my custom

---

should attain to' (Letter to George Rogers, January 15, 1832; quoted by Norman E. Himes (ed.), *Illustrations and Proofs of the Principle of Population*, 1967, p. 315).

and each probably supposing it was greater than it was. From this time I always bought on short credit; instead of paying for the goods I put by the money, taking care always to pay for what I had before the term of credit expired. I thus established a character for punctuality and integrity with three mercers and two Woollen Drapers, and as I foresaw I should, if I could once take a shop have credit to any amount whatever. This was a work of time but of less time than I had calulated upon, I had supposed that it would scarcly be accomplished in less than six years, it was accomplished in less than four years.

The room in which we lived was a front room at a Bakers Shop, the house had three windows in the front, two in the room and one in a large closet at the end of the room. In this closet I worked. It was a great accomodation to us; It enabled my wife to keep the room in better order. it was advantageous too in its moral effects Attendance on the child was not as it had been always, in my presence. I was shut out from seeing the fire lighted the room washed and cleaned, and the cloaths washed and ironed, as well as the cooking. We frequently went to bed as we had but too often been accustomed to do with a wet or damp floor, and with the wet cloaths hanging up in the room, still a great deal of the annoyance, and too close an interference with each other in many disagreeable particulars which having but one room made inevitable were removed, happily removed forever.

I have before remarked that the consequences of a man and his wife living in the same room in which the man works is mischievous to them in all respects, and I here add as a recommendation to all journeymen tradesmen and other workmen who are much at home, and even to those who are only at home at meal times and after working hours and at other times, such as sundays, and when they have no employment, to make almost any sacrifice to keep possession of two rooms, however small and however inconveniently situated as regards the place of their employment, much better is it to be compelled to walk a mile or even two miles to and from their work, to a lodging with two rooms than to live close to their work in a lodging of one room. I advise them also to arrange them contrary to the usual custom of those who have two rooms, and to put the bed in the room in which as much as possible of the domestic work is done. A neat clean room tho it be as small as a closet, and however few the articles of furniture, is of more importance in its moral consequences than any body seems hitherto to have supposed.

THE LONDON CORRESPONDING SOCIETY

From the time when I became a member of the London Corresponding

9 1795–1796

Society I was punctual in my attendance at my own division, as well as at the General Committee to which I was continually elected. I was frequently appointed a member of sub committees, and was at length elected one of the five who formed the Executive Committee. I had attended this committee for some time before I became a member of it. The Secretary Ashley and the Treasurer Beck as well as the members of the committee were always desirous of my advice and assistance. I was also one of a committee who drew up a new constitution on a comprehensive scale for the society assimilating its organization as much as possible to what we concieved was the best form of Government for the nation. It was printed by the Society, and is I am still of opinion a striking proof of the talent and judgment of the men who were selected to draw it up.

Ministers, began their career by alarming the people they fortified the Tower of London, put out Proclamations and succeeded to a very great extent in frightening the nation so as to increase their own power. This was followed up [by] the trials of the members of the British Convention in Edinburgh & their transportation, by the seizure of Hardy and others; by reports of secret committees, and by the suspension of the Habeas Corpus Act[1] They could not however take away the lives of the men they had seized, but they scared the members of the Society of the Friends of the People at the head of which was the present Earl Grey then the Honorable Mr Charles Grey, Lord Erskine then the Honorable Thomas Erskine and a host of popular and eminent men, and induced them to suspend the meetings of the society.

The acquittal of Hardy and others dissipated to some extent the fears which had been excited, and vast numbers of the thinking part of the working people as well as many who were better off in the world joined the London Corresponding Society; as they did other reforming societies in various parts of England. So rapid indeed was the increase of the

[1] The arrest of Hardy and the others was followed by the suspension of the Habeas Corpus Act on May 22, 1794. In the earlier version Place added a footnote to his account of the suspension of Habeas Corpus: 'Apprehension of an invasion from France, wrought up as it was by Ministers either from real or pretended fear, and the fear of the republicans at home, which was also augmented by the conduct of ministers, threw into their hands unlimited power and augmented all their resources. 85.000 men were voted for the Navy. 40.000 for the land service 100.000 Militia, and 40.000 foreign troops were taken into pay. Voluntary Contributions were made. Volunteer troops of horse and foot were raised throughout the Kingdom, and Loans were made to subsidize foreign powers.'

In his text Place then continued: 'The alarm which ministers and their adherents thus created all over the country cannot now be either conceived or appreciated. The only body of persons which did not partake in any great degree of alarm was the London Corresponding Society which as was before observed immediately increased in Number' (Add. MS 27808, fs. 3v, 4).

139

The Autobiography of Francis Place

Society in London that the actual number of members who regularly attended in their divisions weekly were by the end of May 1795 reported at about two thousand.[1] The Habeas Corpus Act was still suspended and many persons were in close confinement in various prisons without any specific charge on which they could be brought to trial, and without any apparent term to their imprisonment, yet nothwithstanding these circumstances and the continual denouncements made against the Reform Societies, they all, with the exception of the Friends of the people who were afraid to assemble, increased the number of members, and in october there were in London upwards of seventy divisions of the London Corresponding Society which sent delegates to the weekly meetings of the General Committee

The number of delegates and sub-delegates with a few persons who were admitted to "the honour of the sitting", usually exceeded one hundred. The committee assembled in a very large room in Beaufort Buildings in the Strand, over the lecture room of Mr Thelwall.[2] The committee room was fitted up with benches and desks in the manner of a

---

[1] The Society continued to increase, and in July it reported: 'Our members increase with a rapidity unequalled at any former period, near eight hundred within this last month' ('A Letter to Sheffield, July 22, 1795,' in *The Correspondence of the London Corresponding Society* [1795], p. 35). A letter of September 23, 1795, stated that the Society had gained 1,500 new members since its last general meeting (p. 65). Place's estimate of 2,000 members and 70 divisions is much more conservative than that of his friend John Binns, who wrote that there were 12,000 members punctually paying the dues of a penny a week (*Recollections of the Life of John Binns*, p. 45).

[2] John Thelwall (1764–1834), a poet and elocutionist, gave public lectures on political subjects. He had been driven from one tavern hall to another as the landlords were threatened with loss of licence or with violence from thugs hired by anti-republicans. Finally, with assistance from rich radicals, Thelwall hired at Beaufort Buildings (now Savoy Court) a house which contained a lecture room and living quarters. The lecture room, which held 700 people, was often too small for the audience he attracted (Charles Cestre, *John Thelwall*, 1906, pp. 80–2). Thelwall, a member of the LCS, was arrested and tried for high treason along with Hardy and ten others. After his acquittal, Thelwall continued lecturing and writing for reform. His lectures, according to Place, 'were delivered in courses twice a week, on the Wednesday and Friday evenings. The price of admission was sixpence. The room was constantly crowded to excess. The lectures contained much loose declamation, they also contained many curious facts and statements but nothing which could be called either seditious or libellous, Thelwall entertained all the vulgar prejudices of the day ... These lectures had their share in producing and keeping up a state of irritation against the government' (Add. MS 27808, f. 36). Binns characterized him rather unfavourably: 'John Thelwall was one of the boldest political writers, speakers, and lecturers of his time. In his lecture-room, in a debating or political society, or at his desk, he was fearless; yet, in private, he was one of the most timid alarmists I ever associated with' (Binns, op. cit. p. 44).

Long after the close of his political career in 1797, Thelwall corresponded with Place. In 1832 he was complaining to Place that not enough people showed their appreciation of his services to liberty by subscribing to a fund for him (Add. MS 37950, fs. 131–2; see also Add. MS 37949, fs. 142–3, 257, 291).

9 1795–1796

school room. The presidents chair was in the middle of one of the ends, advanced a few feet from the wall it was a sort of pulpit the floor of which was raised about three feet above the room floor, there was a seat for the secretary in front of it raised about half that height, the treasurer and the members of the executive committee had seats at the sides of the President. I was for some time elected president by shew of hands president for the evening and on successive nights, and as it was found that I kept good order and dispatched the business in less time than most others who filled the office it seemed that I should be always elected.[1] The duty of the chaiman was arduous, frequently difficult, it required quickness to percieve and resolution to decide, joined with conduct which while it was preremptory and inflexible was not calculated to be offensive, and but few were competent to fill it with satisfaction either to himself or to the delegates, many of whom were unacquainted with the necessary forms of such an assembly.[2] The forms of the house of Commons were as nearly as possible observed. The business was divided into parts and called on by the chairman in due order. I was particularly careful in making minutes, and aided by the Secretary was always able to make the best arrangements to expedite the business. These arrangements were always in strict conformity with the Constitution of the Society, and I therefore never permitted any deviation from the course laid down. It was soon seen that my method accelerated the business and enabled the committee to go through the whole of its business which was sometimes not the case when the chair was occupied by another person.

In the month of August it was referred to the divisions as a constitutional question, whether the Chairman of the General Committee should be chosen every time the committee sat, or whether he should be elected for three months. It was determined that the president should be elected for three months. A ballot for chaiman was taken and on the third of September I was elected to the office by a very great majority. It was the post of honour and was eagerly desired by several members.[3] The quarter would have ended on the third of december, but as the Pitt and Grenville Bills, the Treason and Sedition Bills; were then in progress through parliament, no new election was made and I retained the office till these bills received the Royal Assent on the eighteenth; which made

---

[1] Earlier version: 'I was frequently voted into the chair' (Add. MS 27808, f. 29).

[2] In the first draft of this portion of the memoir, Place wrote: 'It may easily be supposed that among so many persons of various dispositions no small portion of whom were eager to make speeches, and impatient of controul that the office of Chairman was not an ordinary one, and that but few of the members were qualified to fill it' (Add. MS 27808, f. 29).

[3] Earlier version: '... and was eagerly desired by several others as well as by me' (Add. MS 27808, f. 28v).

The Autobiography of Francis Place

it illegal to continue the office of president or even to be present in any political assembly consisting of fifty persons. On these bills becoming law I vacated the office, and was re-elected president of the General Committee under a new organization of the committee conformably to the law.*

The part I took in the management of the affairs of the society brought me acquainted with all the leading members, and I became particularly intimate with many of the best and wisest of them, and there were many who were good and wise and virtuous men.[1]

Among these and others I picked up as many customers as with the work I still obtained from Mrs Barnes eneabled me to live, but I never once asked any member of the society to give me employment or in any way held out inducements to any one to do so. The whole of the employment I obtained as well from customers as from journeywork was not sufficient to enable me to save money, my wife had one child to attend to and was about to have another so that she could do little in the way of help to me and this was the less necessary as I could do all the work myself. I was obliged to charge very low prices to my customers, and my profit was consequently very small; profit was not indeed so much my

---

* Of the meetings and proceedings of the London Corresponding and other Societies during this period an account will be given in the Essay before alluded to. This has never been accomplished other occupations which could not be put off prevented it until I became unequal to the task by a complaint in my brain which made me unequal to the task. May 28. 1851

[Place's desire to see a history of the LCS written dated back to 1798 when he urged Hardy to write his account of the Society. Place's intention of writing the history himself arose at least as far back as 1815, for in that year Alexander Galloway wrote that he was sending some letters of a famous LCS member, Maurice Margarot, and apologized for not having written all that Place wanted (Add. MS 27816, f. 117). The next year Place wrote to Hardy urging him to get on with his account of the Society (Letter of December 8, 1816; Add. MS 37949, f. 45). In 1824 Hardy wrote to Place, asking if he had yet begun his history (Add. MS 27816, f. 233). Thirteen years later Place told a correspondent that he now had all the journals of the Society, all the papers of Hardy, etc. (Add. MS 27816, f. 305). These documents fill more than seven large volumes (Add. MSS 27808 and 27811–27817).

For a fuller explanation of the brain complaint which made him unable to write the history, see below chapter 14, no. 8, 'State of Health. continued.']

[1] 'The concern I had in the management of the society, brought me acquainted with all the leading members, with most of the cleverest men I was intimately acquainted, most particularly so with John Ashley the Secretary, Alexander Galloway the Assistant Secretary, Thomas Hardy, John Bone & Anthony Beck the treasurer, Thomas Harrison, Richard Wild, Colonel Despard, John Binns, Richard Hodgson, James Powell, Thomas Evans, Paul Thomas Lemaitre, John Fenwick' (Add. MS 27808, f. 30). Apparently with the intent to revise this list, Place drew a line, cutting off all the names except those of Ashley, Galloway, Hardy and Beck. He drew a series of slash marks through the name of Richard Wild.

9 1795–1796

object as quantity, as the means of enabling me to purchase at several shops and make myself known to those from whom I expected to obtain credit whenever I should be able to take a Shop. I did not make the society in any way subservient to these purposes, as I might, and now think I ought to have done, my notions of independence were somewhat absurd, and they prevented me from deriving all the benefit I might have received and circumstances warranted. I was however afraid of doing any thing which might prospectively debase me in my own opinion and I acted on the safe side. This notion with which I had long been familiar was confirmed by the reading of Mr Godwins book.

I had omitted no opportunity of improving myself in every possible way and had made considerable progress; as the way in which my advice was asked, the deference which was paid to my opinions and the being appointed as has been related to the office of Chairman of the General Committee assured me.

It was fron regard to John Ashley the Secretary of the London Corresponding Society that I was induced to take the room in Fisher Street which was next door but one to the house in which he kept a shop and parlour and carried on the trade of shoemaking. He was less scrupulous than I was and consequently had more customers among the members of the society and was much better off than I was. He was a serious thinking man of rather an imposing appearance, he was six feet two inches high of proportional bulk and had a manly countenance, he was a dark complexioned man with a clear skin and some colour in his face. He was a man of undoubted courage on all trying occasions, was honest and sincere. He was much attached to me and I to him. He was employed by, and acquainted with several persons who had considerable collections of books, of which he had the use and he supplied me with as many as I could use.

I was also well acquainted with a young man a member of the society whose name was John Binns, he was the son of an Ironmonger in Dublin who had given him what was then called a bettermost sort of education. He had been brought up without any trade and was at this time working as a plumbers labourer earning, or rather obtaining altogether, about a guinea a week. He was a very well informed man, on many subjects, but inexperienced, very desirous of increasing his stock of knowledge, but at times volatile as most Irishmen are. His working hours were in the summer time from six in the morning 'till six in the evening, and from day light 'till dusk in the winter time. When I had work to do I worked from an early hour in the morning till nearly eight o clock in the evening on those days on which I attended the business of the society out of doors, and 'till nine o clock on other nights, sometimes much later. Binns used

The Autobiography of Francis Place

to leave his work as soon as he could, and came to me to read, whilst I worked, and thus we both obtained knowledge at the same time.

The year 1795 was a year of extraordinary difficulty and needed such men as Pitt, Dundass and Grenville to carry on the Government, and yet sustain the bad proceedings which had been in progress since 1792. The members of the Corresponding and other Societies and a vast many other persons in all parts of the country were of opinion that Ministers would not be able to surmount the difficulties and would therefore be compelled to concede a reform in the House of Commons. I had no such expectation. I beleived that ministers would go on until they brought the Government to a stand still, that was until they could carry it on no longer it appeared to me, that the only chance the people either had or could have for good and cheap Government was in their being taught the advantages of representation so as to lead them to desire a wholly representative government; (this is still my belief) – so that whenever the conduct of ministers should produce a crisis, they should be qualified to support those who were the most likely to establish a cheap and simple form of government. I therefore advised, that the society should proceed as quietly and privately as possible. My opinion was shared by very few of my coadjutors, almost every body seemed persuaded that the House of Commons would be induced to consent to a radical reform in the state of the Representation and on this belief the society proceeded, public meetings were held of which I disapproved, but when after the propriety of holding such meetings had been amply discussed and decided I assisted to prepare the necessary arrangements, Resolutions Petitions, Remonstrances and Addresses. Many of the best men in the Society were afterwards of opinion that my view of the matter was correct; when they found that Ministers made these meetings pretexts to introduce the treason and sedition bills, in the month of November.[1]

[1] The ministers may have been alarmed by the number of people who testified to their desire for reform by attending these public meetings: At the public meeting of the London Corresponding Society on October 27, 1795, there were reported to be upwards of 150,000 people present. At the next meeting, on November 12, 1795, there were, according to the newspaper account, upwards of 300,000 (Add. MS 27808, fs. 37–8, 54). Even if these numbers are exaggerations (as Place thought the first was), they suggest that the actual numbers were impressively large.

To enable a large crowd to hear the speeches and resolutions, the General Committee had arranged to have three platforms. The plan 'was to pursue exactly the same course at each place, and as nearly as possible at the same time, so that there should be in fact three distinct meetings for one purpose. The mode of voting we recommended was this. After a resolution, or a petition was read the question was to be put in the affirmative by the holding up of a white handkerchief on the rostrum. The negative, by holding up a hat' (f. 54).

Place was careful to refute charges that this public meeting was disorderly: 'More order than was observed at this meeting was never observed at any meeting,

9 1795-1796

From the day on which notice was given and the Seditious meetings bill was read a first time the *Executive* Committee met every evening excepting the thursday when the General Committee assembled, I was constant in my attendance and was excused by my division from being present at their weekly meetings. A great quantity of business came before the committee, the correspondence was considerable, and every body who could and would assist was put in a state of requisition. Our sittings were continued 'till midnight and occasionally 'till two o clock in the morning. Being thus occupied at night and also during some part of each day. I was compelled to some extent to neglect my work which did me considerable injury.

The society had never substantially recovered from the state in which the state trials in 1794 had placed it.

[Place added the following footnote after 'recovered':]
* The State Trials of 1794 Concluded only with the year – and the Government took care not to give it as much time as became necessary for it thouroghly to renovate itself, this and its own want of prudence caused its present difficulties.

The first full meeting of the London Corresponding Society after the State Trials of 1794 was in Jany 1795 – on the 29th of October in the same year the Parliament was Assembled and Lord Grenville in the Lords and Mr Pitt in the Commons moved that an Address on the Kings Message be taken into consideration the nex day – this was agreed to. Witnesses were examined respecting an attack which had been made upon the King and proceedings were taken for the purpose of putting down Political Associations Lord Grenville gave notice of a New Treason Bill Mr Pitt of a new Sedition Bill – The Habeas Corpus Act was suspended and a considerable number of persons were apprehended, and committed to various Prisons.

[The events which provided immediate stimulus to the introduction of these repressive laws were the alleged attacks upon the king on the day he opened Parliament, October 29, 1795. The window of his carriage was broken by a stone thrown at it and, supposedly, someone tried to open the door of the carriage and assault the king. In the earlier draft of his memoir, Place gave an account of this day:

'It had long been the custom for the spectators to show their dislike of the proceedings of the court by hissing and groaning as the King went to the Parliament, and the practice still continues. The newspapers almost always say that the king has been most affectionately greeted by the people, this they do even when, from some particular cause he has been assailed with hisses and groans . . . Formerly the procession went through St James's Park and was comparatively but slightly guarded . . .

---

either within or without doors. I remained on one of the platforms after the business was concluded and saw the people disperse in the most orderly and quiet manner, in half an hour not one was to be seen in any of the surrounding fields' (fs. 54–5).

The Autobiography of Francis Place

'Every body expected that the King would be assailed by the clamours of the ill fed discontented people, and ministers might if they had wished have prevented it. Parliament might just as well have been opened by a commission as it many times had been, either on account of the Kings health or to suit the purposes of ministers, and this would probably have been done, on this occasion, had not ministers wished, that what did happen, should happen.

'On the 29 October the King went in state to open the session of parliament. An immense number of people had assembled in St James's Park who hissed and groaned as the procession passed along. The people continually called out. No Pitt, no War, Bread, Bread, Peace, Peace.

'When the state coach had nearly reached the House of Peers, one of the windows was broken, the spot where this happened was in the narrow part of St Margarets Street, between St Margarets church and Henry the 7th chapel. The Ordnance office was at this time a building at the eastern end of St Margarets church, and between this and Henry the 7th Chapel were some irregularly built houses, from a bow window in one of these it is supposed something was thrown against one of the windows of the state coach, made a hole in the glass and starred it. A pretense was set up that the King had been shot at and an inference drawn that it was the result of a plot to kill him. After the King had opened the parliament the House of Lords adjourned till 5 o clock when a sort of enquiry was made respecting the attack on the King.'

Several witnesses testified that they saw a small object hit the glass of the coach. Place summarized the evidence of the attack:

'The evidence amounts to this, that one or two things were thrown at the state coach in Margaret Street and that one of the windows were broken. That the glass was broken by something thrown and not fired from a gun may be inferred from its being seen. It is absurd to infer that a stone or a bullet thrown by hand would not make a small hole in a pane of thick plate glass. A pocket knife was once thrown through one of the panes of plate glass in my shop front which made a hole not much bigger than the cross section of the knife . . .

'Five persons were apprehended as rioters . . .

'The king as was his custom, soon after his arrival at the Palace at St James's, got into a private carriage and was driven through the Stable yard into the Park on his way to Buckingham House, as soon as the coach entered the park it was recognized by some of the people who set up a shout and run after it, the number of these persons was not great, one of the newspapers said 17 or 18. This was magnified into an immense mob which had attempted to seize the King. The Kings carriage it was said had been pursued by the mob which had overtaken it, and an attempt to open the door and drag the King out was only prevented by the lucky arrival of the horse guards, just time enough to save the Kings life.

'On the day the King went to open the parliament I was in the Park. I went there alone, simply as a spectator When the State Carriage came into the Park at St James's the crowd which was immense, Hissed and groaned and called out No Pitt – No War – Peace Peace, Bread Bread. I went as far as the end of the Mall whence I could see over the whole of the Parade and am certain nothing was done beyond what I have related, within the Park. On the return of the Procession I went with it from the Horse Guards to the Stable Yard the

9 1795-1796

noise continued the whole of the way, but no stones were thrown at the carriage, if there had been I must have seen them. When the private carriage entered the Park I was about 200 yeards from the Stable Yard gates, I heard the shouting and saw some persons running after a carriage, but I had no suspicion it was the Kings private carriage until I saw the Horse Guards Galloping towards it. The Guards rode through the crowd and reached the coach before any of the persons who were running.'

The London Corresponding Society barely escaped implication in this alleged attempt to open the door of the king's carriage:

'John Ridley a Bootmaker who kept a shop in York Street Covent Garden, was, with his brother who kept a shop in St Pauls Church Yard, coming from Knightsbridge they were on the path next the rails of the Green Park beyond the Stable yard, when hearing a shouting and seeing some persons running John Ridley who did not know that the carriage which was close to him was the Kings private carriage, or that there had been any tumult, stepped from the foot path into the road way the better to ascertain the cause of the noise and the agitation among the people, he was close to the side of the carriage, his foot slipped he was thrown towards the carriage and was in great danger of falling under the hind wheel, to save himself he thrust his hand against the coach door and pushed himself back so as to escape the wheel, the Horse Guards arrived at the same moment. All this happened in less time than the account short as it is can be read in. Ridleys dress was accurately described in a posting bill issued I believe from the public office in Bow Street. The Thousand Pounds reward promised in a Proclamation was understood to be offered for the apprehension and conviction of the person who broke the Coach window in St Margarets Street, and the man whom it was said, attempted to open the door of the Kings Private carriage. Had Ridley been apprehended he would in all probability have been hanged for attempting the Kings life, and as he was a delegate from one of the Divisions of the London Corresponding society, and occasionally assisted the Secretary in his department, no doubt would have remained that an attempt had been made to seize the Kings person and to murder him, or that it was a plot got up by the leaders of the London Corresponding Society. The facts are however, correctly and truly stated. Ridley changed his coat, and went about his business as usual' (Add. MS 27808, fs. 41-9).

A government proclamation issued shortly afterwards, attributed the attack to the public meeting which had been held at Copenhagen Fields. On November 6, Lord Grenville announced that he would bring to the House of Lords 'An Act for the Safety and Preservation of His Majesty's Person and Government against treasonable and seditious Practices and Attempts' (36 Geo. III c. 7). On November 10 Pitt announced his intention of bringing to the House of Commons 'An Act for the more effectually preventing Seditious Meetings and Assemblies' (36 Geo. III c. 8). Place recalled the witch-hunt atmosphere of that period:

'No adequate idea can now be formed of the actual state of the country after the meeting of Parliament and while the bills were pending. The affair was made the most of both by ministers and the exclusively loyal all over the country. The Newspapers hurled treason. The over loyal citizens of London

The Autobiography of Francis Place

took the lead in calling public meetings the trickery resorted to, and the fooleries which were played seem almost incredible. Loyal addresses were got up in every possible way. Petitions in favour of the bills were handed about, meetings were held to support ministers and to encourage them to establish if possible a perfect despotism. Threats, intimidation, persecution were all resorted to, all means were fair to persuade or to compel people to sign loyal addresses and petitions, while those who were known to be adverse to the conduct of ministers were calumniated in the grossest manner, and injured in every possible way, complaint was useless, redress in any way was hopeless, the Loyal talked and acted just as they pleased.

'Those who thought at all on public matters and were opposed to ministers, and who were not under some local influence came forward to oppose the Bills.

'The number of loyal addresses amounted at last to 579 — of these 90 were from Military bodies and 70 from the Clergy.

'The number of Petitions and of signatures as nearly as could be ascertained, were

For the Bills	Against the Bills
Petitions – 65 – Signatures 29.922	Petitions 94. Signatures 131.284'
	(Add. MS 27808, fs. 51–2).

The bills passed on December 18, 1795.]

It had [Place's text continues] paid off much of the debt it owed and might have paid the remainder had it not expended its funds on public meetings. Present circumstances caused a considerable increase of expenditure and notwithstanding every thing that could be done without expense was done and notwithstanding a vast number of persons now became members the income did not meet the expenditure and new debts were incurred.

When the Treason and Sedition bills became law and a different organization of the Society was adopted by which care was taken that not more than forty nine persons should ever be present at any meeting,[1]

[1] Early in December 1795 the LCS was reorganized: the metropolis was divided into four districts; no district was to have more than 45 divisions. There were to be district committees, but only one delegate or sub-delegate from each division could attend. The four district committees elected members to the general committee, there being one member for every five divisions. Since the district committees had no power, except to choose members of the general committee, the members soon ceased attending meetings of the district committees. Deputations were then sent from the general committee to divisions whose members slighted the district committees. Place, who had been elected to the general committee from the fourth or western district, recalled these visits: 'I remember having to attend in this way as many as three divisions on one evening, having to harangue each of them on their neglect and to urge them to a state of greater activity' (Add. MS 27808, fs. 68–70).

This duty devolved upon Place because he had been re-elected chairman of the general committee. At the time of his re-election and the change in organization of the LCS, 'a trusty person was appointed to keep the door [of the general committee], lest by some mischance the number should at any time exceed 50, and thus subject the whole to punishment' (f. 70).

As a result of the reorganization and the consequent poor attendance at district

9 1795–1796

the whole character of the Society was changed the number of members rapidly declined, and the whole of the labour and expense fell upon a comparatively small number.[1] The consequences were the same all over the country, the reformers were disappointed in their expectation no reform had been obtained, some thought it dangerous others that it was useless to meet again and the whole matter fell rapidly to decay. It had been resolved at a public meeting in Copenhagen Fields that deputies should be sent into the Country to obtain cooperation and assistance and it was now determined that a trial should be made. John Binns and John Gale Jones were appointed for this purpose, they had written instructions for their guidance and special directions to keep within the limits prescribed by the Law. Jones went to Maidstone Rochester &c[2] and Binns to Portsmouth, on their return they were sent together to Birmingham, this was early in March 1796. It was absurdly supposed that because Government had not interfered with their proceedings that they would not interfere and a notion pervaded the society that they would be able to reestablish the societies which had ceased to exist, to induce people to form new ones, and collect at least as much money as would pay their expences.[3] The deputies had addressed several meetings at Birmingham

---

meetings, 'many divisions got the reports from other delegates or remained in ignorance of what was going on, these things could not fail to produce dissertions and to drive away some of the best of the members' (f. 70).

[1] In his earlier draft Place described an instance of the labour and expense he encountered: 'On the 2nd December [1795] the society gave notice of a meeting to be held near the Jews harp house in Mary-le-bone fields, now the Regents Park. The reason for not holding the meeting where the two last were held was, that the money paid for the use of the field did not compensate the unavoidable damage done to it and the surrounding fields; by the immense number of persons who crossed them in all directions, making new paths, and gaps in the hedges, and treating down banks. It was with the greatest difficulty any place could be procured and much time which could be exceedingly ill spared from our ordinary occupations was consumed in waiting on different persons, to obtain permission to occupy one of their fields. All the active men on the committees were industrious men, very few of them were masters and many of them had families wholly maintained by the work of their hands, to such persons loss of time was not only a great pecuniary evil but also in the discomfort neglect of business occasioned at home. These circumstances reduced the number of those on whom the burthen fell to a small number. It may be doubted by those who are friendly to the people that it was wise in any man to make such sacrifices as the condition in which the society was placed demanded' (Add. MS 27808, fs. 58–9).

[2] He described the trip in a book which contains an unexpected mixture of travel gossip and reform history: *Sketch of a Political Tour Through Rochester, Maidstone, Gravesend, &c.*, 1796.

[3] In the first draft, Place stated that the plan to establish stronger communication with other parts of the country would have been prudent if the society had been large and growing, but was useless in the changed conditions. 'It happened however that we cajoled ourselves, and each other with delusive expectation which prove us to have been very silly people' (Add. MS 27808, fs. 71–2).

The Autobiography of Francis Place

when they were apprehended on Treasury warrants and sent to the Dungeon, on this being made known to the Executive committee I was dispatched to Birmingham and after some difficulty was allowed access to them in the prison.[1] I remained three days at Birmingham attended their examinations before the Magistrates who were assisted by Mr White the Solicitor to the Treasury who was sent to Birmingham for that purpose. I could not find persons at Birmingham, where we were all strangers, who were willing to bail them so I returned to London. Bail was procured and they were discharged out of custody. They were afterwards tried for having used seditious expressions Binns was acquitted and Jones was convicted but no sentence was passed on him.[2]

On the 27th of January 1796 my third child whom my mother named Annie was born,[3] I had been and was till the time I went to Birmingham badly supplied with work and Macdonald the foreman having discovered on what errand I was gone alarmed Mrs Barnes my employer, who evidently appeared desirous to discontinue her employment but did not like to dismiss me. I had never on any occasion disappointed her, and had done the work well, so she had no reasonable cause of complaint against me. Seeing however how the matter stood I ceased going for work and Macdonald ceased to send me any, and our connection was ended. As I had not had enough work from customers to maintain me I was again reduced to poverty, and again occasionally suffered from privation.

The quantity of business in the London Corresponding Society had increased greatly and was fast getting into arrears, and this induced me

[1] This was the first time that Place had ever been more than thirty miles from London (Add. MS 27143, f. 167). He travelled up to Birmingham on the same coach as Mr White, the Treasury Solicitor. With him he carried this letter from the executive committee of the LCS: 'March 18th 1796 – LCS Ex Committee Fellow Citizen

'Having received information from a friend in Birmingham that Citns [J]ohn Gale Jones, and John Binns our two Deputies to that Place were apprehended and taken to Prison but upon what charge we are as yet unacquainted; the Committee came to the resolution of Dispatching the Bearer Francis Place to render them all the assistance he possibly can in their present situation; As Citn Place is a stranger to Birmingham we have thought it advisable to refer him to you not doubting but you will cheerfully undertake to give him all the information and assistance in your power' (Add. MS 27815, f. 35).

[2] Jones was tried on April 9; Binns on August 15, 1797, some seventeen months after his arrest. 'Had Government brought them to trial at once,' Place speculated, 'there is no doubt both would have been convicted, but by delaying it till the next year they missed their point, Jones who was tried first was convicted, but his offence even after conviction appeared a more venal offence, Binns was acquitted' (Add. MS 27808, f. 74). Cf. Howell's *State Trials*, vol. xxiv,1818, cols 595–652. Binns' defence was led by Samuel Romilly. Soon after the acquittal Binns left the LCS (Add. MS 27808, f. 105).

[3] In the earlier version Place added: 'we had then two living, both girls, this tyed up my wifes hands and made my loss of time of serious consequence to me' (Add. MS 27808, f. 74).

9 1795–1796

after much solicitation to take the office of assistant secretary, for the quarter from Lady day to Midsummer day, and to take the quarters salary £3 2s 6d. This money I took with great reluctance, I had done business which if fairly remunerated would have not been overpaid even to a poor man like me with ten times the sum. Had I not been very poor I should have refused the money, as it was I often felt regret at having taken it.

The society now went on very absurdly in some respects. In July it commenced a Magazine which I and others opposed as much as we could, we saw clearly enough that instead of being the means of decreasing the debt it would be the cause of an increase, and so it turned out.[1] I was out of office at Midsummer and not liking the proceedings of the Executive committee I refused to be elected to it again as I did also to be president of the General Committee and became simply the delegate of the division to which I belonged.

Ashleys business had increased considerably and this induced him to take a house No 6 High Holborn near Grays Inn Lane,[2] he persuaded me to go with him, and take his second floor for which I was to pay him Sixteen Guineas a year an enormous sum for me to undertake to pay, but as he was satisfied he should be able to procure me many orders I concluded that I should find means to pay the rent. The rooms were rather large, it was an old fashioned house, and the front windows projected, so that we had a view up and down the street; they were light airy and comfortable

We were both weary and almost disgusted with the proceedings of the society and at the end of the year Ashley resigned his office of Secretary and became as I was simply a delegate to the General Committee.[3]

[1] *The Moral and Political Magazine of the London Corresponding Society* was published monthly between July 1796 and May 1797. Place criticized it more sharply in the earlier sketch of the Society: 'Another absurdity in which I however took no part was the setting up a magazine.' Instead of paying a penny a week for dues, the members were to pay 4½d per month and receive the magazine, 'a better contrivance to prevent the society paying its debts could hardly have been devised.' By the end of 1796 the expenses of the Society and its magazine had consumed the weekly dues and also £170 which had been contributed for the defence of Binns and Jones. The Society's financial report for the last half of 1796 showed a deficit of £185 (Add. MS 27808, fs. 75, 77).

[2] The move occurred at Michaelmas 1796. This house was 'opposite Middle row, six doors west of Grays Inn Lane' (Add. MS 27808, f. 75).

[3] After Ashley resigned as secretary of the LCS, the post was taken by John Bone. According to Place, 'he was an honest upright man, very religious, sedate and methodical but not well qualified for the office he filled.' Next was Thomas Evans, 'a fanatic of a peculiar description, ignorant conceited and remarkably obstinate. Such a man could only have been secretary when the society had proceeded a long way in its decline and had greatly changed its character.' Presiding over the LCS in its last days was Thomas Crossfield, whom Place characterized as 'a man of learning

The Autobiography of Francis Place

No 2 Joined the L. C. Soc in the month of June 1794[1]
    Hardy apprehended in may – & 10 other ⎫
    Holcroft ⟨reviewd⟩[2] then...................... ⎬ 12 –
Friends of the people................................No 3.
Society for Constitutional Information............No 1.

    Members all Frighted[3] by the Violence of the Govt – number diminished – but many Joined No-2 – all who joined were men who now joined it were men of high ⟨character⟩ well educated men

    Soc met in division in various parts of the metropolis – and correspdd with many societies in verdous places at a distance

    I was a member of the 27th division. each division was limited to 27 – but admittd – 45 when 18 branchd of[f] and formd a seperatie division. each division elected a delegate and subdelegate – These delegates formd the General Committee to which the sub delegates were admitted but could take no part in the procddings unless the delegate was absent – each delegate or sub delegate made a report to his division of what passed at the General committee – each member paid a penny a week and contributed whatever he pleased or could collect – Each division met once a week at a private house – public houses were interdicted – a small sum was taken for expences and the remainder was paid in weekly to the general comn I was soon electd delegate. In this society and especially in its general com – I met with may inquisitive upright men – with some of whon I soon formd an aquaintanc I may say friends with many of whom my acquatance continued until they died off only one now remaining.

    Early in the month of Oct 1794 a special Com was issued to try the 12 *apostles* for High Treason The trials commencd in October I attended at the Old Bailey every day for several hours – working in the night time, and early in the mornings – I was one of a committee to look after the witnesses and bring them up. and this I contend to do at every trial When the Trials came on and a true bill for Treason had been found Holcrofts he surrendered – Hardy – Tooke and Thelwall were tried and acquitted – Vast numbers joined the Society. These trials led me to acquaintane and respect of many men in circumstances very superior to mine. See their State trials 1785 – 5 –

---

and talents, both of which were most miserably misplaced, he was as his tombstone in Hendon Church Yard describes him a drunken harum scarum fellow' (Add. MS 27808, fs. 105–6).

[1] Unlike the rest of the autobiography, the material from this point on in the chapter consists of notes, in small manuscript, written on the back of an advertisement for a wine and spirit merchant.

[2] The undecipherable word signifies that Holcroft gave himself up after a true bill for treason had been found against him.

[3] The text originally read, 'Members of 1 & 3 Frighted.' As Place's notes indicate, No. 1 is the Society for Constitutional Information, No. 2 is the London Corresponding Society, No. 3 is the Friends of the People.

CHAPTER 10

Residence at John Ashleys

Embarrassments of the London Corresponding Society. – Absurd conduct of the Members – I resign my office of Delegate – Leave the Society – Public Meetings – Members seized – Ashley's conduct – Ashley's goes to France[1] – I contemplate going – My condition – Prospects.

Ashley I, and several other members of the General Committee did all we could do, to induce the committee to give up the Magazine which was a losing concern, and to make every possible exertion to pay the debts of the society, we knew that the very name of debt was enough to drive many members away and to prevent others from joining it. We were satisfied that there were members enough and spirit enough among them to raise the sum necessary and speedily to pay off all we owed; we knew too that we should be aided by money from persons who were not members and we had no doubt that when the debts were paid, the society would flourish. We therefore offered to pay a shilling a week instead of a penny, and to go round night after night to the divisions and persuade as many members as we could to increase their subscriptions. We made two propositions which were rejected and other schemes were adopted. Our propositions were.

I. That no money beyond mere current expenses should on any account be expended until all the debts were paid.[2]

II. That every member should be requested to increase his subscription, and that as many as could be induced to collect money from others, should be officially authorized to do so.

Money in sufficient quantity to pay the expenses of the prosecution of the deputies Jones and Binns had been collected, but had been expended to support the magazine and the Literary committee who managed it were made debtors for the amount. This constituted one of the principal items of debt. Many of the influential members were of opinion that if a public meeting was held, it would act as a stimulus, induce great numbers of persons to join the society, and others to assist it with money, and they had no doubt at all, that by this means the society would be soon in a flourishing condition. We on the contrary were as certain that a public meeting would ruin it. The matter was frequently discussed and it was at

---

[1] Changed from 'Ashley's conduct.'
[2] Also, that the Society's publications should be limited to addresses of no more than four octavo pages (Add. MS 27808, f. 78).

The Autobiography of Francis Place

length resolved to continue the Magazine and to call a public meeting. On this being resolved and notice by a placard given on the 23 March of the intention of the society to hold a public meeting, Ashley and I resigned our office of delegate were now simply members of the society, and attended no meetings excepting, those of our divisions.

Our efforts were now directed to raising money to pay the expenses of defending the deputies, there was a good deal of right feeling in the society on this subject and the money was a second time subscribed. This being accomplished and the society being still determined on holding a public meeting, Ashley and I at the conclusion of the quarter in June [1797] ceased to pay our quarterly contribution and were no longer members of the Society.[1]

On the 14 July the public meeting was advertised in the Newspapers and in Placards, to be held on the 31 in a field near St Pancras Church. It seems that some of the Middlesex Magistrates were of opinion that the meeting would be illegal, this opinion they expressed in a posting bill which commanded the attendance of all constables at the place of meeting. This led to a conference between some of the leading members and the Magistrates who refused to say why they thought the meeting would be illegal.

On the day of meeting three tribunes were as usual erected in the field, at the foot of each of which a Magistrate took his stand surrounded by a very large number of constables, said to amount altogether to nearly two thousand, and near at hand were large bodies of troops,[2] as well horse as foot. The business of the meeting was regularly opened and allowed for some time to proceed, when at length one of the Magistrates read the Proclamation from Pitts Sedition Bill, and immediately ordered the persons on each of the platforms to be seized. The persons taken into custody were   Richard Hodgson Hatter.
                                              Robert Cutler Fergusson Barrister.
                                              Thomas Stuckey.[3]

---

[1] Earlier version: 'As John Binns was the friend of both of us, as Jones was a very old acquaintance of Ashleys and rather an intimate acquaintance of mine, *and as both of us had concurred in sending them to Birmingham* we thought ourselves bound to render them all the assistance in our power and we did so, as well in the society as in private. Having secured them the means of defense; and finding the society resolved to hold a public meeting we gave notice in our respective divisions that we were no longer members of the society. This must I conclude have been at the conclusion of the June quarter as the Public meeting was held on the 31 of July following and I was not at the time a member of the society and was not at the meeting' (Add. MS 27808, fs. 79–80; my italics for words which Place crossed out).

[2] 'From 6000 to 8000 soldiers' (Add. MS 27808, f. 80).

[3] The *Morning Chronicle* (August 1, 1797) lists his name as Tuckey. It also lists one other man who was arrested: John Wibbie.

10   Oct. 1796–Sept. 1797

> Alexander Galloway Machinist.
> Richard Barrow Surgeon.
> Benjamin Binns Plumber.

The business of the meeting was to have been.

> I. An Address to the Nation.
> II. A petition and Remonstrance to the King.
> III. Certain Resolutions.

Ill timed as these proceeding were, the papers were drawn up with great talent.

The Morning Chronicle of the next day observed that on the persons before named being taken into custody, the Military were ordered on to the Ground where they galloped about for an hour.

The persons taken into custody were admitted to bail by the Magistrates after which they were drawn to their homes in coaches by the populace.

The bail was for their appearance at the ensuing session, but no bill was I believe ever preferred against any of them.

After this meeting the Society declined rapidly and by the end of the year was in a very low state.[1]

My removal to Ashleys did not improve my circumstances, he was unable to do much for me, and a circumstance occurred which soon made him unable to do any thing for himself.

He and his wife lived in the Shop and Parlour, having the use of a kitchen. The first floor was let to a woman and her daughter who were laundresses and had the care of chambers in Grays Inn. This woman took as a lodger a fine tall handsome woman named Lambert, she had been in high keeping and well versed in intrigues, she was about thirty three years of age. Ashley had all his life long been a sedate sober steady man, and was as simple with respect to what related to such women as a child. As it sometimes happens to such women she fell desperately in love with Ashley and he fell as desperately in love with her. Both became as silly as any raw girl and boy could be, they were never easy apart, and did all manner of foolish things to be in one anothers company. Ashleys wife was a short, square built, large boned, ill made woman, her manners were vulgar, and her temper intolerably bad.[2] She was quarrelsome and

---

[1] 'After I left the society [June 1797] it proceeded on its decline in consequence of its debts, the fear the government had produced and the mismanagement and misdirection of its leaders' (Add. MS 27808, f. 108). 'What now [January 1798] remained of the society was its refuse, with the exception of Galloway, Hodgson, Lemaitre and a few others who from what they considered conscientious motives still adhered to it' (Add. MS 27808, f. 106).

[2] Place's son crossed out this sentence and the following two, and marked 'Dele' in the margin.

The Autobiography of Francis Place

spiteful and morover some twelve years older than her husband. She was precise, saving very industrious and particularly clean in her person and her apartments; but in her temper she was a very devil and had in her frequent fits of utterly unfounded jealousy been a perfect fury. As might be expected Ashleys folly and his wifes impetuosity and abuse rendered all chance of reconciliation hopeless. He became reckless and she furiously crazy, business was neglected and ruin seemed inevitable. Ashley soon became ashamed of his folly, yet was unable to extricate himself, either from the embarassments of his business to which his wife would not permit him to attend as he otherwise might have done, neither could he muster courage to break with Mrs Lambert, to whom for solace, his wife was perpetually driving him, he was in a sad dilemma, and saw only one chance to escape; this he took, and resolved to leave both the women and go to France to seek his fortune. Ashley now made up his concerns when he found there was property enough to pay all he owed to leave him twenty pounds to carry him to France, and as many book debts due to him, as would maintain his wife for about a year and a half even if she did nothing towards maintaining herself. Mrs Lambert was much worse off. She had an annuity on which she had for some time lived and kept up her appearance Such however was her infatuation, that she spent her money to make a foolish shew when abroad with Ashley and got in debt to the greatest possible extent. She would have done any thing and every thing possible to make common cause with Ashley in the road to ruin.

Ashley made the best arrangements he could and went to France.[1] Mrs Lambert was soon afterwards arrested for debt and the last I heard of her was, that she was confined in the Fleet Prison. I assisted Ashleys wife to collect the debts which Ashley had assigned to her and did her all the service in my power. She had a sister lately become a widow who kept a public house at Hackney a well doing woman. Mrs Ashley went to live with and assist her in her business, and was here as comfortably provided for as a woman of her disposition could be.

[1] 'Attempting to go to France was at this time Treason,' Place noted in his earlier draft. 'But there was no great difficulty in going to Helvoetslays by means of smuggling vessels' (Add. MS 27808, f. 83v). Ashley's emigration convinced the government's Committee of Secrecy that he had gone to Paris as an agent for the LCS to obtain the assistance of the French army in overthrowing the British government (Add. MS 27808, f. 109). In the margin of the autobiography Place's son added: 'Ashley prospered in Paris – got a first rate business and became the Hoby of the place I knew him in 1816 – F P Jr He never returned to England & his wife died' (Add. MS 35143, f. 30; Sir Thomas Hoby was a diplomat, exile, translator of the *Courtier*). In 1829 Alexander Galloway, another LCS member, informed Place of Ashley's recent death. Because of Ashley's liberality and generosity to his friends, wrote Galloway, he left three of his four children unprovided for, though he netted £3,000 to £4,000 a year (Add. MS 37950, f. 58).

10 Oct. 1796–Sept. 1797

Ashley had urged me very strongly and very frequently to go to France with him, he had no doubt of obtaining assistance from persons whom he knew at Paris, and from others who had heard of him as Secretary to the London Corresponding Society; he said we could make common cause until we were both settled in some way of business and were able to maintain ourselves seperately, that my wife should share any money which might be obtained from his book debts, that she might live with my mother and do something towards maintaining herself and the two children until money could be raised to send for her. I was miserably poor at this time and was all but resolved to go, but when the prospect and probabilities came to be calculated and discussed with my wife, I gave up all thoughts of going to France with Ashley.

During our residence at Ashleys we suffered a good deal from poverty but it was not hopeless poverty. It sometimes happened, that we wanted food, when we had money laid by to pay a mercer or a woollen draper and dared not touch it, lest by not paying to time all hope of ever getting into business should be destroyed. Ashley knew how matters were with me and he occasionally fed the children. He was fond of children and especially of the eldest of mine. He used to have them with him at times, the eldest who was nearly three years old he had with him almost every day, and would frequently nurse the youngest which was just able to run about, for an hour at a time.[1] His wife disliked children and especially mine, they were in her way and she grudged the trifle the food cost, and when Ashley was from home if the eldest went into her parlour she sent her away. She had however some regard for my wife and no dislike to me; as I was always disposed to do her any services I could, and discountenanced Ashley's proceedings with Mrs Lambert.

The number of my customers was small, the prices I charged were very low, and what was worse some few got into debt with me and never paid their debts. My wife frequently importuned me to go again to Journey work, and offered to try to procure it herself if I would let her. I however resolutely refused, I insisted upon it that I should work my self into a condition to become a master tradesman and should then be able to maintain my family respectably, that no hope of my ever being able to do this in any other way existed, and that nothing should therefore divert me from my purpose. That our present privations were by no means so bad as those we had suffered, and that there was something like a certainty that they would at no very distant time be ended for ever; that as every day was a new day, the contemplation of the evils of

[1] Marginal notes: 'Betsey. Annie.'

The Autobiography of Francis Place

one day was as much as we ought reasonably to entertain, and that it was disgraceful not to bear the evils of one day with temper. This reasoning often repeated had its weight with my wife but it neither satisfied her nor reconciled her to her condition. Still we were not unhappy, upon the whole, we were comfortable, and at times very far indeed from unhappiness. There was however one bad result of our long state of probation and privation; it to some extent destroyed my wifes cheeful disposition, and made her apprehensive of misfortune, and she never recoverd from this entirely. Her situation was necessarily worse than mine on account of the two children, and her fears of our ever doing well were increased by her being again pregnant. Sometimes she almost despaired of ever being better off in the world, and at these times, she used to complain of my folly in thinking I should be able to take a shop and commence business, and as to my succeding and being able to procure money enough to live without business, she declared it was sheer insanity. These fits were however of short duration and were always caused by some great privation she and the children suffered and the shame she felt at the children being fed by Ashley.[1] The few good cloaths we had left were taken great care of, and when out of the house we always made a respectable appearance and were generally considered by those who knew us; as florishing people, who wanted for nothing. In fine weather on sundays we usually walked into the fields taking the children with us, our walk was frequently to White Conduit House and the fields beyond it towards Copenhagen House. Both these places were celebrated Tea Gardens and the number of persons who frequented them on Sundays was very great. We carried the children nearly the whole of the way and returned as we went never spending a single halfpenny.

An accident which would hardly in other circumstances be worth mentioning caused us considerable inconvenience and some privation. One Sunday morning having no means to procure a dinner I walked to Deptford to a Journeyman Mill-wright a customer of mine who owed me some money. He gave me a guinea and I hastened home at the end of perhaps half an hour I was detained talking to him, and his wife; on reaching home and putting my hand into my pocket the guinea was gone. I had lost it, I could not imagine how, so I returned to Deptford, hoping I might have left it behind me by slipping it beside my pocket, no guinea could be found and I walked home again to go without food, for myself and all the rest of us, that day and until means could be found to procure a small sum of money for the supply of our immediate wants, on the next day.

[1] In the first draft, Place added at this point: 'There were times however when we enjoyed a considerable share of happiness.'

Appendix to Chap. 10[1]
Age of Reason
Case of Thomas Williams
Conduct of Mr. Erskine

Towards the close of the year 1796 I projected the publication of a cheap edition of Paines "Age of Reason" I knew no one so likely to undertake it as Thomas Williams a book binder who dealt extensively in small publications. He was however too poor to purchase the paper and unable to obtain it on credit. I was in good credit with a paper maker in Thames Street, in consequence of having had some transactions with him on account of the London Corresponding Society and having usually made payments to him for the Secretary. I calculated the quantity of paper necessary for printing two thousand copies of the Age of Reason, and found that the two parts might be profitably disposed of at the publishing price of a shilling each copy, and I had no doubt that two thousand could be sold in the society. We therefore undertook to print them.[2] I was to find the paper and Williams was to get the work printed. An edition was soon ready, it was a Crown octavo on a good yellow wine paper and was well printed. The profit if any was of course to be divided between us. In about a fortnight from the day it was published Williams

[1] The appendix is dated 'October. 1824.'
[2] William Hamilton Reid, an ex-radical, suggested a closer connection between the LCS and the publication of *Age of Reason*. He maintained that the leaders of the LCS forced the members to accept Paine's doctrines: 'It is still fair to admit, that the adoption of Paine's Age of Reason was not agreed, to in the London Corresponding Society, without considerable opposition, especially in the general committee; but as zeal superseded judgment, in their discussions upon the subject, the epithets of d-m--d fool, and d-m--d Christian, ultimately prevailed; and a bookseller was soon persuaded by the heads of the party, to undertake a cheap edition of the Age of Reason, for its more ready dissemination through the divisions, at that time rapidly increasing in numbers every week: but after Williams, the bookseller just alluded to, was imprisoned for this publication, his family received much less assistance from the society, than from mere strangers' (*The Rise and Dissolution of the Infidel Societies*, 1800, p. 5). Reid saw further results of the LCS's adoption of Paine: 'The attachment of the party was carried so far, that the bare circumstance of having the Age of Reason in a house, was deemed a collateral proof of the *civism* of the possessor ... Bone and Lee, two seceding members, and booksellers by profession were *proscribed* for refusing to sell Volney's Ruins and Paine's Age of Reason; and that refusal construed into a censure upon the weakness of their intellects ... After these notions of infidelity were in a manner established in the divisions, it is natural to suppose, that in choosing their delegates, those persons were preferred who were doubly recommended by *their religion*, and their politics. However, from this period, when the leaders began to force their anti-religious opinions upon their co-associates, it is undeniable that their intestine divisions hastened their dissolutions more than any external obstacles' (pp. 5, 6, 9).

came to me and said he had as much money as would pay for the paper and if I would let him pay the paper-maker, it would do him service. I of course consented. He then went on to say that he should not expect me to bear any loss on account of the publication, but would take it intirely upon himself. I saw through this pretence and said, you know *Tom* that I am not covetous of profit, I see how the matter stands, you have sold the edition and intend to print another, well, take it all to yourself, I care nothing about it. The two thousand copies we had printed had all been sold and the demand continued. Williams not only wished to keep the whole profit of the two thousand copies, but he intended to print and did print a much larger edition. He sold a very large number; but at length the opinion of Mr Bayley, now Mr Justice Bailey was taken on the chance there was of convicting the publisher of a seditious and blasphemous libel. Mr Bayley's opinion was that the publication was one which might be prosecuted at Common Law. An Indictment was therefore preferred and a true bill found by a Middlesex Grand Jury. This was done at the instance of the "Society for carrying into effect his Majesty's Proclamation against Vice and Immorality." better known of late years by the name of the. Vice Society.[1] The whole of the proceedings may be seen at length in Howells *State Trials*, Vol 26,[2] with an Introduction giving an account of the publication of the Age of Reason, and the opinion of Mr Bayley at length. Williams knew nothing of the prosecution until the Bill was found, and then he came to me greatly alarmed and said WE are prosecuted for the Age of Reason. WE I retorted, no Tom, not WE – how can WE be prosecuted. YOU as soon as YOU found that money could be made by the sale of the book took care to exclude ME from any participation. YOU have printed and sold a very large number of copies on your own account and have taken the profit to yourself. YOU must therefore change your note and sing I, not We. There can be no WE now, but if I can in any way assist you I will. Mr Erskine was immediately applied to, to defend Williams, but he had been retained by the Vice suppression Society. There were several reasons why we should chuse Mr Erskine. 1. because he was suspected of being but a weak christian.[3] 2. because he was one of the founders, if not the projector of the "Society of Friends of the Liberty of the Press." One of the resolutions of which was. – "That *no* writing ought to be considered as a public libel, and made the subject of Criminal Prosecution unless such writing shall appear to be published

---

[1] The Proclamation Society, as it was originally called, founded in 1787 by William Wilberforce, was particularly interested in fighting the sale of Paine's *Age of Reason* (Muriel Jaeger, *Before Victoria*, 1967, p. 44).

[2] Vol. XXVI, 1819, cols. 653–720. Place's quotations from Howell contain some minor inaccuracies which do not alter the substance of the passages.

[3] This clause was marked for deletion by Place's son.

Appendix: Age of Reason

with a design to excite the people to resist the Civil Magistrate or to obstruct the execution of the existing Law."

Mr Erskine at the second meeting of the Society on the 19 January 1793 in expounding the principle on which it was to act condemned all societies which busied themselves in prosecutions for libels and asked, – "Where if such societies become prosecutors for libels is the accused to find justice among his peers"?[1] Meaning the Jurors before whom he may be tried, and the Grand Jury to whom the bill of Indictment may be presented. He explained all these matters and reprobated the interference of all associations. He utterly condemned such associations even when directed against actual crimes as – "Infecting the Courts not only with a *general prejudice*, but by a *pointed and* particular passion and interest." "We have – he said – further to remark that these objections to popular associations for the purpose of prosecuting crimes apply with double force when directed *against the press*, than against any other objects of criminal justice which can be described or imagined. – He declared – "that we will maintain and assert the right of instructing our fellow subjects, by every sincere and conscientious communication which may promote the public happiness." – and – "If in the legal and peaceable assertion of this freedom we shall be calumniated and prosecuted, we must be contented to suffer in the cause of freedom, as our fathers before us suffered, and like our fathers we will also persevere until we prevail" – "If this selection (of persons to be prosecuted) is to be transferred to self constituted assemblies of men agitated by a zeal however honest the press must be broken up, and individuals must purchase their safety by ignorance and silence." – "In the career of such a system of combination we forsee nothing but oppression and when its force is extinguished nothing but discontent, disobedience and misrule"

Mr Erskine read this and much more equally valuable matter from a paper he had drawn up. "On the motion of Mr Sheridan it was adopted as the "declaration of the Friends of the Freedom of the Press.", and as such was signed by "Thomas Erskine" as Chairman. "It shortly afterwards" received the signatures of above five hundred persons", many of whom were members of parliament, on their becoming members of the Society. "Ten thousand copies of the declaration were printed and distributed by order of the society."

It was therefore with some surprize that we found Mr Erskine had accepted a retainer for the Society for Suppression of Vice, we understood the situation of council as to the acceptance of briefs, but we could not persuade ourselves that Mr Erskine might not if he had wished, have

[1] Erskine's speech was published under the title *Declaration of the Friends of the Liberty of the Press*, 1793.

put the matter in such a light as would have prevented his being employed, by an obnoxious, and by him stigmatized society,* and if he could not accept a brief from us, at least have been neuter, and Mr Erskine as I well knew when the consequences came upon him was sorry he had not refused the retainer.

Mr Kyd a friend of Mr Erskine's was then retained as counsel for Williams.[1] Mr Kyd was an infidel and[2] a man on whom reliance could be placed, but he was of little importance at the Bar when compared with Mr. Erskine.

When the Trial was called on eleven *special jurors* answered to their names, when to the astonishment of every body Mr Erskine refused to "pray a tales,"[3] and the trial was postponed.†

Of these special Jurors[4] in public libel cases, it is impossible to speak with too much reprobation.[‡] That they were, selected-packed, and paid for verdicts, which any Judge recommended them to find, and which they knew would be agreeable to persons in authority was as well known to Mr Erskine as to any man living. Mr Erskine knew well that the special Jurors appointed to try such causes as he had undertaken to conduct were for the most part, *ignorant, illiterate men*, who made special juries a trade. What is very remarkable and very reprehensible, is the

* That we were not unreasonable in our expectations is proved by Mr Erskines subsequent conduct, as will be shown in the sequel
† Howells *State Trial[s]*. Vol. 26. p. 660.
‡ Vide Sir Richard Phillips on the Office and Duty of Sherriff [*A Letter to the Livery of London Relative to the Views of the Writer in Executing the Office of Sheriff*, 2nd edn, 1808] [and] "On the Law of Libel with strictures on the Self-styled Constitutional Association", a pamphlet, (by Francis Place) Published by John Hunt 1823
[In this pamphlet Place distinguished between common juries and special juries: A common jury was composed of housekeepers. Nominally they were summoned by the sheriff, who took a street or two in a parish and ordered forty-eight housekeepers to appear on a certain date. For their jury service they received a shilling for each case with which they were connected – usually about 30s. for a term of jury service. Special juries, theoretically, were composed of freeholders drawn from a list on the sheriff's book. It was assumed that as freeholders they would be persons of superior intelligence and education who could decide questions of difficulty. In fact, special juries were drawn from a list made up by the secondary, who took recommendations from other special jurymen, attorneys, and the sheriff. It was a small list of persons most of them neither freeholders nor householders, who served over and over, for a guinea a case, hence their name 'guinea men' (pp. 33–43; Add. MS 35144, fs. 254–9).]
[1] Stewart Kyd, like Thomas Hardy, was one of the 'twelve apostles' who were arrested for high treason three years before, in 1794. Erskine had then been counsel for most of the defendants, including Kyd (Howell, vol. XXIV, 1818, cols. 215–20).
[2] Place's son crossed out the words 'was an infidel and.'
[3] A 'tales' (from the phrase *tales de circumstantibus*, 'such of those standing about') is a writ summoning ordinary jurors or bystanders to fill out a deficient jury.
[4] Marginal note: 'Special Jurymen Special Rascals.'

Appendix: Age of Reason

circumstance that eleven special guinea men did attend, and yet Mr Erskine was afraid to trust the case to these men with one "common juror".[1] I do not believe that another case can be found in which eleven jurors, special jurors attending the counsel for the prosecution refused to "pray a tales". When however the Trial came on Mr Erskine gave a reason why he refused to take a single uninfluenced person on the Jury, and in doing this he committed the unpardonable offence of endeavouring to influence the Jury by the gross and utterly untrue description he gave them of themselves.

He said. "May* it please your Lordship: – Gentlemen of the Jury: the charge of blasphemy, which is put upon the Record against the publisher of this publication is not an accusation of the servants of the Crown, but comes before you sanctioned by the oaths of a grand jury of the country. – It stood for trial on a former day; but it happened, as it frequently does, without any imputation on the gentlemen named in the pannel,† that a *sufficient number* did not appear to constitute a *full special jury*, I thought it my duty to withdraw the cause from trial, till I could have the opportunity of addressing myself to you who were originally appointed to try it.

"I pursued this course, from no jealousy of the common juries appointed by the laws for the *ordinary* service of the court, since my whole life has been one continued experience of their virtues; but because I thought it of great importance, that those who were to decide upon a cause so very momentous to the public, should have the *highest possible qualifications* for the decision; that they should not only be men, *capable from their education* of forming an enlightened judgement, but

---

* *State Trials.* vol. 26. p. 660

† He should have added in Libel cases in which the Church or State are concerned, because the "special men" must be kept in good humour, but in other cases between man and man, Mr Erskine has often enough been unsparing of imputation on negligent jurors, and I have heard the Judge order fines to be levied on them for non-attendance as ought to be done in all cases.

[1] Why was Place so hostile to Erskine? Erskine's taking the wrong side in this trial scarcely accounts for Place's rage. Place had much experience of reformers turning conservative; and other such defections did not provoke anything like this detailed attack. Place was probably enraged at an attack Erskine had made on the London Corresponding Society a few years before Place wrote this appendix. In 1819, after the Whig candidate Lamb had defeated Place's friend Hobhouse, Erskine issued a pamphlet entitled *Short Defence of the Whigs against the imputations attempted to be cast upon them during the late Election for Westminster.* Erskine charged that in the trials of 1794 it was the 'criminal and dangerous licentiousness of the bolder reformers that produced these state prosecutions.' Erskine also accused the reformers 'of almost wholly keeping out of sight the tumultuous meetings and the alarming mass of publications which led to the state trials.' Place wrote but never published an angry refutation (Add. MS 35154, fs. 16ff]. Years later, in 1836, Place wrote of Erskine to Mrs Grote: 'I knew him well, he was like all his whig associates a charlatan' (Add. MS 35144, f. 358).

that *their situations* should be such as to bring them within the *full view* of their country, to which in character and in estimation they were, in their own terms to be responsible"

There is indeed in this false excuse, and paltry fulsome flattery peculiar baseness. Mr Erskine knew that many of the regular special jurors very very poor, very obscure very ignorant men who followed the trade of "guinea-men" to eke out a maintenance. He knew that some of them had received no education at all. He knew that servants of noblemen had been placed on the special Jury lists, He knew that of all men their notions of responsibility to their country was of no importance whatever. He had refused to trust his case to one man in twelve chosen indifferently as all jurors ought to be, he had been blamed for this, so he made the best excuse he was able, And miserable and false and disrespectable enough – and more than enough it was.

He said – "Nothing that I have ever said either professionally or personally for the liberty of the Press do I mean to day to contradict or counteract." Yet he had carefully suppressed the knowledge he had that the prosecution was brought by one of those associations which he had stigmatized as instruments of injustice and had utterly condemned as oppressive, and tending directly to deprive the person prosecuted of a "fair trial by his peers", and he did his best himself to aid the Society in their attempt to prevent the man he was employed to persecute from having a fair trial. He worked hard to aid them in the bad cause, to help a society which he had truly said was, "destructive of liberty and tending in an eminent degree to destroy knowledge, to extinguish integrity and to produce nothing but oppression and when its force is extinguished nothing but discontent disobedience and misrule" – he lent himself for this bad purpose and as good means could not be used to arrive at the bad end, he adapted himself to the circumstances of the case and put himself upon a par with it, if indeed he did not take the lead in the scandalous business

But Mr Erskine did not stop at concealment, he went further and endeavoured to mislead. He said "the charge," was not an accusation of the servants of the Crown" that is, it was not an obnoxious *Ex Officio Information*, filed by the Attorney General,[1] "but comes before you (the

---

[1] *Ex Officio Information*: 'A criminal information filed by the attorney-general *ex officio* on behalf of the crown, in the court of queen's bench, for offences more immediately affecting the government, and to be distinguished from informations in which the crown is the nominal prosecutor' (Bouvier's *Law Dictionary*). There was strong feeling against such such informations; in a list of political abuses an LCS document couples them with abrogations of the jury system: 'Unconstitutional and illegal INFORMATIONS EX OFFICIO, that is, the arbitrary will of the king's Attorney General, usurping the office of the ACCUSING Jury; and the interested

Appendix: Age of Reason

Jury) sanctioned by the oaths of a Grand Jury of the Country." He took care however not to tell the Jury how the bill came to be presented, or by whom it was presented, he did not say the bill had been preferred at the instance of an association, "which will infect the court – prevent justice – extinguish the press – produce nothing but oppression and end in discontent, disobedience and misrule;" but by distinguishing it from an *ex officio information* he gave it a character of respectability, and went out of his way in his eagerness to obtain a verdict, to find an excuse for a jury whom he knew wanted no excuse, who wanted indeed nothing but an indication from the Judge, of the verdict which would be most agreeable to him. Mr Erskine knew this, but he had an eye to something beyond the jury and that was the public, his object was therefore to mislead the public, to whom he had said the moment before that "he would neither contradict nor controvert any thing he had ever said either personally or professionally for the liberty of the Press." This declaration with the concealment that the "Proclamation Society," as it stiled itself, were the prosecutors he hoped would effectually blind the public. He deceived himself, as men who flounder about in the support of evil in public matters generally decieve themselves.

Mr Erskine laboured diligently in his disgraceful vocation, he made two speeches, one in opening the case and one in reply to Mr Kyd, by far the best which have ever been made either before or since on similar occasions to procure a conviction; but the loose matter they contain, the nonsense, and which he knew to be nonsense about the Constitution and the Laws, and more than all about the oath,* taken by the packed special jury, an oath which if abided by would have prevented them finding a verdict of guilty is a disgrace to a man of his knowledge and talents.

---

oath of a vile common informer, with the judgment of as vile a common trading or pensioned justice, substituted in the room of our birth-right, an impartial trial by our country' (*Address to the People of Great Britain and Ireland*, 1794).

* The Jury mans oath is as follows. "You shall well and truly try the issue joined between——(the parties)——and a true verdict give, ACCORDING TO THE EVIDENCE – so help you God." It is by no means uncommon for the judge in other cases to tell the jury to put out of their consideration all, or part of what has been said to them by the counsel, and attend ONLY TO THE EVIDENCE, and he then reads the evidence from his notes. He then shews the bearing of *the evidence*, and the proof it contains of the breach of some law, but in libel cases the Judge does just the contrary, he passes over the oath, taken by the Jurors, he says nothing about evidence of the breach of law, but he substitutes the *opinions* of the counsel to which he adds his own, and he directs the Jury to find a verdict in direct contradiction to the oath they have taken, to *find a true verdict according to the evidence*, of which he says not one word, because there is no evidence on which to ground a verdict of guilty. In other cases if an attempt were made to conduct them in this way the Judge would nonsuit the prosecutors from want of evidence on the ground that there was nothing before the Jury of which they could take cognizance.

The Autobiography of Francis Place

On reading the trial again at this instant (June 1824) for the purpose of again calling the particulars more accurately to my recollection, and after having recently gone over the whole matter with Thomas Williams, I have felt deep shame aye and pity too for Mr Erskine whom I cannot cease to admire for what he on many occasions did, for the benefit of mankind. Mr Kyd's defence was as good as under all the circumstances of the case he could make it and when Mr Erskine had ended his vehement reply, Lord Kenyon summed up the matter of opinion, *not the evidence*, which had been delivered. He summed up the opinions by giving his own, and then he called upon the Jury to give their opinion by saying guilty [or] not guilty of an legal offence, not guilty of any defined crime proved before them *viva voce*, but guilty of differing in opinion with them, matter of opinion and nothing else being before the court, thus deciding contrary to the oath they had taken to Judge only by "the evidence".

On the 27 November Mr Erskine moved for Judgment on Williams – he said – "My Lords with respect to the prosecution, I felt it at the moment of trial as I feel it now, of infinite importance to the public; there is *no transaction of my humble life my Lords which I look back upon with such heartfelt satisfaction*, as the share I had in protecting the interests of religion and morals". I knew at the time this was said that it was utterly false and that so far from Mr Erskine "feeling heartfelt satisfaction" he was really heart sick. He went on boasting that if the nation could be polled it would be found, "that no proceeding that ever took place has given more satisfaction than this conviction has done," this making some allowance for hyperbole was probably true. Just as any person among any particular sect who attempted to persuade people of other sects of the folly they committed and the impositions practised on them would be condemned by those to whom he had addressed himself; but it would give nothing like "heartfelt satisfaction" to a philosopher to know, that he who had been the cause of an honest mans condemnation and certain imprisonment, was applauded for his conduct, by ignorance and absurd superstition.

On the third of february 1798 Mr Erskine still the tool of the Society whom he had denounced as the enemy to mankind, as the "promoter of ignorance and the destroyer of knowledge", moved for the Judgment of the Court upon Thomas Williams, when after having again praised the Special Jury he was constrained to admit, that "*the prosecution had been so much arraigned in different quarters*, it is therefore necessary that I make a few observations." He then entered on a lame justification of what could not be justified in his own conduct, and stated as of his own knowledge, "that an affidavit made by Williams in mitigation of punishment was true." He had been so much annoyed in various ways in con-

Appendix: Age of Reason

sequence of his conduct in this prosecution, that he had called upon Williams several times, and but, that he could not in the face of the world recant and eat up his own words, he would willingly have become his advocate.

It happened that a lad named Hayward was a sort of clerk to Mr Kyd whom Mr Erskine very frequently visited at Chambers, and as but little caution was observed, Hayward heard all that passed respecting the prosecution of Williams, and he repeated to me the subject of every conversation he heard. Haywards father was an intimate friend of Mr Kyd's, and he was told by Mr Kyd from time to time many circumstances relating to the prosecution and these he communicated to me. I availed myself of all occasions, and they were many to make the best use I could of the information I recieved, for the annoyance of Mr Erskine in the hope that he would at length become so uneasy as to exert himself to prevent a severe sentence being passed upon Williams, in this I was successful and so far as his notions of consistency, and fear of public censure could operate on him he did exert himself to prevent a severe sentence being passed, and came at last to the resolution he should have adopted at first, to return the retaining fee and have no further concern with the society.[1] In a letter inserted at the end of the trial – p. 714. from Lord Erskine to the Editor – dated the 7 february 1719 [1819] is a statement of the circumstances which induced him to decline proceeding to move for judgment, and to return the retainer. After expressing some good feelings in which I have no doubt he was sincere, he says. "Such a voluntary society, however respectable or useful, having received no injury could not (it did) erect itself into *custos morum* and claim a right to dictate to counsel who had consented to be employed on the part of the king (in the name of the King a law fiction) for the ends of justice only."

[1] Erskine, as counsel for the Proclamation Society, had, on June 24, 1797, presented the case against Williams, obtained a guilty verdict, and, on February 5, 1798, asked the judge to have Williams brought to court for sentence. Before the appearance of Williams for sentencing (on April 28, 1798), Erskine wrote to the Proclamation Society, urging that they could best show their 'charity and Christian forbearance' by asking the judge to consider the time already served as Williams' sentence. The Society unanimously rejected Erskine's appeal for mercy (Howell, XXVI, 713–14). At this point Erskine returned the fee the Society had given him and withdrew from the case. In commenting on the sentence passed, the *Morning Chronicle* (April 30, 1798) noted that the court could not have given a lesser sentence unless it had been asked to exercise leniency. The *Morning Chronicle* disapproved of the 'reverend prosecutors' refusal to 'vindicate Christianity' by showing the 'sublimest aspect of Christianity' – mercy.

Place has argued that Erskine withdrew because of fear of public censure, part of which Place had instigated. Certainly, the liberal *Morning Chronicle* had given ample space to the trial on three or four occasions (half of the space of the whole paper on October 21, 1797, was devoted to the trial) and had taken a strong stand for mercy.

The Autobiography of Francis Place

"The bar, had indeed, in my own experience, rejected a retainer of that anomalous description". He then relates a case in which having accepted a fee in the name of the first regiment of guards to defend one of its officers – the attorney on the other side represented to him that it was no retainer, this was left to the decision of the bar, who agreeing with the Attorney that it was no retainer, he was obliged to accept that of the Plaintiff, and obtained a verdict for him. He then continues thus. "Upon the present occasion, therefore, I made up my mind to act for myself, and not only not to pray judgment, but to cancel the *Irregular retainer* altogether by striking it out of my book, and judgment being afterwards prayed by another counsel the defendant as must have been expected was sentenced to a *severe* punishment, but Mr Perry to his great honour exerted himself for this helpless family, raised a considerable sum of money for their support without which they must have perished.["] So far Mr Erskine appeared to be himself again. But he only told a part of the truth.

On the 28 of April 1798 Mr Justice Ashurst passed sentence on Williams. "A mild sentence": *as he called it,* – "a severe sentence" *as Mr Erskine called it.* A mild sentence it certainly was if we compare it with many others of a more savage nature, mild too as to duration and in some instances even as to privation with some and those a large number passed by the Privy Counsil and under which many persons were suffering without any specific charge made against them, without trial, and without any means of relief under the Habeas Corpus Suspension act,[1] but the sentence of a "years imprisonment in the house of correction in Cold Bath Fields there to be kept to hard labour" – and to be as was the custom of the prison, to be denied the use of books of pen ink and paper, and for a considerable time to have these privations strictly enforced, not to be allowed to have any one to come in to him not even his wife, but to be compelled to speak to her through a grating and at two yards distance, was a most cruel, as it was a most shameful, and illegal punishment. Mr Erskine however knew well enough before he became the tool of the prosecutors that this or something worse would take place, and he had reason to believe that he would be the instrument of a much more severe punishment, in the length of the confinement, if not also of a fine far beyond the means of the persecuted man to pay.

On receiving his sentence. Williams asked if he might have a bed? When Lord Kenyon who was on the Bench said, "I cannot order that." I dare say you will be treated properly, I wish to have it understood that this sentence is a very great abatement of the punishment, as in *modern*

[1] A reference to the mass arrests of April 19, 1798, described in the next chapter. The persons arrested were imprisoned from 1798 to 1801 without trial or sentence.

Appendix: Age of Reason

times, within the period I have sat in Westminster Hall,* three years imprisonment has been ordered for an offence of much less enormity than this, for the publication is horrible to the ears of a christian."† Yet at this time as there had all along been there were many different editions of the Age of Reason on sale, as there was for a long time afterwards. until the demand declined, but the book has never been out of print, and never has there been a time when any difficulty to obtain copies existed.

In the letter from Lord Erskine to the Editor of the State Trials before mentioned is a statement of the circumstances that induced him to decline proceeding to judgment, and among others a pathetic tale of Williams and his family partly true and partly false, and on that account deserving of attention. He says.

"Having convicted Williams, and before he had notice to attend the Court to receive judgment I happened to pass one day (1) through the Old Turnstile from Holborn in my way to Lincolns Inn Fields when in the *narrowest* part of it (2) I felt something pulling me by the coat, when on turning round I saw a woman at my feet (3) bathed in tears and emaciated with disease (4) and sorrow, who continued almost to drag me into a miserable hovel in the passage (5) where I found she was attending upon two or three unhappy children in the confluent small pox (6) and in the same apartment not above ten or twelve feet square (7) the wretched man (8) I had convicted was sewing up *little religious tracts* (9) which had been his principal employment in trade (10), and I was fully convinced that his poverty (11) and not his will ha[d] led to the publication of the Infamous book, (12) as without any *stipulation of money on my part, he voluntarily*, and eagerly engaged to find out all the copies in circulation, and to bring them to me to be destroyed (13)"

1. Williams's house was not in the narrowest part, it was in the wide part, just before the place were the narrowest part commences.

2. It is altogether untrue that any such circumstance occurred or could occur. This according to Lord Erskines account was the first, and it may be fairly inferred from what he says the only time he was at Williamss house. The truth is he went to William in consequence of the annoyance he met with and was complacent and kind to him, he called

---

* Lord Kenyon was appointed to the office he held – on the 7 June 1788 – the period therefore to which his observation relates is ten years, but it ought to be confined to a shorter period.

† And so, according to this man dignified by a seat on the Judicial Bench thinks that words which may be "horrible to the ears of a Christian," a reason to justify persecution – in his state of horror real or pretended he probably did see that what he pronounced from the judgment seat would if could justify the proceedings or rather the sentence upon Williams, justify every persecution of every kind and extent ever committed by mankind on their fellows.

upon him three or four times; thus he became known to Mrs Williams, who until he called had never seen him.

3. This is equally untrue – Mrs Williams was not diseased nor emaciated with sorrow, she was a somewhat slovenly person, rather short and thin, but very lively, and talkative, she had no appearance of being diseased.

4. It follows of course that if the circumstance related never occurred that there could be no pulling into the Hovel, neither could a house which was three stories high be a hovel.

5. The small pox – is an enormous exaggeration, Williams had but two children, and only one of them had the small pox when Mr Erskine called, and it was not confluent but inoculated.

6. The apartment – the indication here is that they had but one small room, there was however a shop not much larger but somewhat larger than the apartment described by Lord Erskine, and there was a small parlour behind the shop, in which they did not sleep. The house had three stories above the shop, and the upper one was a good light garret which served as a workshop, and in which I sometimes, when I had nothing else to do worked with Williams at Book Binding.

7. The wretched man. Williams was just the reverse of a wretched man. He was a remarkably fat man with a good brad jolly face a good natured laughing countenance, and he was as jolly and as merry as he looked.

8. Was sewing up religious tracts. This is a pure piece of invention.

9. His principal employment. Not it indeed – Williams would sell anything, but selling religious tracts was with him out of the question, he had no connection to enable him to sell such tracts, and the profit of retailing them must have been next to nothing. He sold old books and Political Pamphlets in his shop which was attended by his wife, and he bound books, up in the Garret, he had a fair good business, and might have saved money for several previous years but he was fond of good living, and he knew very well in what good living consisted, and so did his wife, and well indeed they lived and spent all the money which came to hand quite as fast as it came, neither of them had any notion of economy and no desire to save. He must have cleard at least a hundred pounds by the sale of the Age of Reason.

10. It is not likely that Mr Erskine was at all convinced that it was 'his poverty and not his will which consented' He knew all about Williams and his circumstances.

11. Mr Erskine certainly did not consider the book – an "Infamous Book."

12. This is a mere flourish, Williams had sold at the least seven thousand copies; Mr Erskine knew that some thousands had been sold,

Appendix: Age of Reason

and to talk of receving the copies in circulation is a piece of deceit, as Lord Erskine very well knew when he wrote the letter.

The truth is Williams never discontinued the sale of the Age of Reason as long as a copy remained, but he ceased to sell them openly in the shop, and only supplied the trade, or let persons whom he knew have them.

After Williams was sentenced Mrs Williams received some money from Mr Perry of the Morning Chronicle and a guinea a week during the whole time Williams was in prison. I understood at the time and so did she that the guinea a week was allowed her by Mr Erskine. Mr Erskine called on her several times during her husbands confinement, and as often as he called he gave her some money.[1]

On the verdict being given Lord Kenyon said. "I have observed several persons from curiosity taking notes of what passed here. This publication is so shocking that I hope nobody will publish this: I mean that a general detail of it will not make any part of that publication. Nobody who has any regard to decency, nobody who has any regard to their own interest will endeavour to disseminate this publication by publishing what has passed to day." Lord Erskine however corrected his speech for the Morning Chronicle and it was of course published the next day. The Morning Chronicle however gave only a general account of what had been said by Mr Kyd. Mr Kyd therefore wrote out his own speech and printed it with those of Mr Erskine.

It was printed in 12o – in a cheap manner under the title of. "The Speeches at full length of the Honourable Thomas Erskine and Stewart Kyd Esqr. on the trial of Thomas Williams for publishing Paine's Age of Reason together with Lord Kenyons charge to the Jury. On the 24 June 1797.["] London

There was no publishers name to the pamphlet and none were I believe sold except by Williams. I had a large number of copies sent to me, which I distributed.

[Place pasted the following newspaper clipping in his manuscript and beneath it wrote his comments.]

May 11, 1798.
The WIFE of THOMAS WILLIAMS, the BOOKSELLER, to the PUBLIC.

THE WIFE OF THOMAS WILLIAMS, with the most profound veneration for the Laws of the Country, begs leave to submit her situation, and that of her Infant FAMILY, to a Humane and Considerate Nation. The Public

[1] The newspaper cutting given at the end of the chapter was pasted into Place's manuscript at a point roughly opposite the end of this paragraph.

The Autobiography of Francis Place

are acquainted with the circumstances of her Husband's case. He was not the original publisher of the Pamphlet entitled 'The Age of Reason,' but some time after its first appearance, when a Right Reverend and Learned Prelate thought it worthy his pious labours to publish a refutation of the Book, thereby bringing it again into discussion, it was sold by her Husband in the same way as by many other Booksellers in town and country.

Mrs. WILLIAMS owes eternal gratitude to the Honourable Thomas Erskine, who gave his professional services to the prosecutors for the suppression of the book, but whose truly christian temper refused his countenance to punishment beyond the necessities of justice. She does not presume by this remark, to insinuate the severity of the judgment, as applying to the Judges who pronounced it, but to lament that the prosecutors should not have interposed that mercy, when the objects of the prosecution had been obtained, which, without their consent, the Court could not administer; more especially when upon the entire submission of her Husband to the direction of Mr. Erskine, their own Counsel, in every thing he might think necessary to public atonement, that Gentleman, upon seeing the miserable distress of their Infant Family, caused it to be signified to her, for her comfort, that he had advised the prosecutors to be satisfied with the imprisonment her unfortunate Husband had sustained in the interval between the terms before the judgement was pronounced.

A generous Public will sympathize with her in the shock she received in finding that this humane representation of their own Counsel had been rejected by the Prosecutors, in consequence of which her Husband was condemned to Hard Labour in the Prison of Cold bath-fields, and thereby cut off from the means of supporting his Family, who must actually perish in want, but for the benevolence of the Public.

By their seasonable succour she is in hopes of being enabled to carry on their little Business in BOOKBINDING, and in the SALE of STATIONARY, at their Shop in Little Turnstile, Holborn; where the ORDERS of Ladies and Gentleman shall be executed with the utmost punctuality, and she will be grateful for their kind favours. – Little Turnstile, Holborn, May 7.

The above advertisement was written by Mr James Perry and Printed in his Newspaper the Morning Chronicle on the day of the date. The purpose was to whitewash Mr Erskine.

The expressions put into the mouth of Mrs Williams are perfect absurdities, but of which she was incapable of judging.

CHAPTER 11

From my Removal from Ashleys in Sep. 1797 – to my removal to Charing Cross in April 1799. London Corresponding Society

My condition – Learn French – Committee of the London Corresponding seized and imprisoned. O Quigley Jno Binns Thos Evans – United Englishmen James Powell, Colonel Despard – Treatment of persons seized – Subscription for their families – Willam Frend – Coln Bosville – Richd Wild, correspondence relative to a partnership with him – Borrow some money – go into business at Charing Cross. History of the London Corresponding Society – Toleration – Morals – Delegates.

On Ashleys leaving his house I removed to another, ten houses to the westward No 16 in high holborn. It was a very large very old house. It had eight rooms on a floor, I had four en suite upon the second floor for which I paid sixteen pounds a year. The four rooms formed one half of the floor from front to back. The front room had a large window in Holborn, the back room was fitted up as a kitchen and was supplied with water by a pump the two intermediate rooms were intended for bed rooms and had no light but what was borrowed from the front and back rooms. There was a communication with the stairs from the front and back rooms, the rooms were therefore very convenient, we intended to lodge some respectable single man and thus reduce the amount of the rent which was more than my circumstances warranted me to undertake to pay without such aid.

I made some extraordinary efforts to increase the number of my customers and succeeded in obtaining at times as much work as I could do, sometimes more and then my wife assisted me, my employment was however very irregular sometimes sinking down to almost nothing – at other times all I had to do was wanted at the same time.

I was obliged to give credit even in my small way and to charge low prices. I could not from want of capital enlarge my trade beyond the point to which I had brought it. Had I increased the number of my customers and consequently the credit I must have given I should have gone deeper into debt, and should not have receivd payment from my customers fast enough to enable me to make my payments to the mercers and drapers as regularly as I had hitherto done, and thus have injurd my credit and put an obstacle in the way of my getting into business as I wished. Had I enlarged my business I should have had to purchase the

The Autobiography of Francis Place

things to fit up the garments for ready money, as I had all along been obliged to do, as the quantities were small, and I should have been also obliged to employ a journeyman occasionally. These things were beyond my ability. As it was, the increase of trade I had obtained embarrassed me very much at times, it was with the utmost difficulty and by means of great privations that the money to pay for the goods I purchased was scraped together. I should in time have overcome this difficulty, but it would have been a painful process as capital would have increased very slowly. All the increase of business I found went into my books. Fifty pounds in money would have established me in a business quite sufficient to have put me beyond want, and the fear of want, beyond indeed all apprehension for the future. But fifty pounds or any sum beyond five pounds a sum I did occasionally borrow from a member of the society named Thomas Harrison a careful honest sensible man, was all the assistance I could command, which I was willing to accept. Very few whom I knew could afford to lend me money. Jew King[1] would willingly have made an advance at which he hinted more than once, but to have accepted any thing from him would have been downright baseness, so I remained in poverty, sometimes wanting food. In this state I remained until I left Holborn. My wife had always been the cash keeper, and when I wanted sixpence which was very seldom I asked her for it, neither of us spent any money or ever tasted any liquor stronger than small beer. It happened more than once as it had happened before that we wanted food when she had several pounds by her which we dared not touch lest it might lead to irregularity in my payments to the mercers and drapers, my future chance of prosperity depending on the strict regularity of my payments. My wife who had become pretty well reconciled to my determination to get into business in a shop did every thing she could to forward my purpose. She found two or three shops in streets which ran into Holborn, from the window of any one of which she thought I could scarcly fail to sell as much as would pay the rent and perhaps do something more, but my ambition had risen considerably and I no longer contemplated a shop in a bye street. I now looked forward to a shop in a principal thoroughfare or in a street of good name where a large quantity of business might be done. In this I persisted.

I was in my twenty sixth year my wife was not quite twenty four, we had as before related two children living and another about to be produced we were both strong and healthy and there seemed a moral certainty, that we should have a numerous family. As I could not doubt of success whenever I should get into business, so I was resolved to give my children the best possible education which my circumstances would

[1] For an account of John, or Jew, King see below pp. 236–9.

11 Sept. 1797–April 1799

afford, I also resolved as much as possible to put my self in a condition to assist them while they were young, and to judge of their progress as they grew up. I therefore determined to obtain some knowledge of the French Language, but how to accomplish this was a great difficulty on account of the expense. It was however overcome. There was in the London Corresponding Society a man named Hitchins, a strange creature in his appearance and odd in his manners, very profound and pompous, which so ill suited his short squat figure as to make him appear ridiculous, he used to talk with great self complacency of his skill in teaching and he was well qualified to teach as far as the acquisition of such learning as he was acquainted with went, he followed the old method of giving a task but no explanation, if it was learned by rote all was well if not he became angry. To explain and remove difficulties was beneath his dignity. He had never once reflected on the truth that it is of little importance by what means the learner acquires the information he stands in need of, and that it is in the power of the teacher frequently to convey as much information in a few minutes as an ignorant scholar might be a week in acquiring without assistance. His notion was the old one, that unless the learner did every thing for himself, he did nothing, and he was therefore a bad teacher. This I did not previously know and he was the only person I could find who was willing to teach for so small a sum as I could afford to pay. With this Mr Hitchons I made an agreement to receive an hours instruction twice a week in the french language, provided I could procure four others to join me so that he should receive half a crown a week for his services. I found four. One was the late Mr Richard Hayward, then a very young man and very poor. The Thomas Harrison before mentioned he was a watch face painter about my own age. Richard Wild a man about ten years older than myself a tailor who was foreman to Mr Croft in Fleet Street, and Richard Fenton a gun maker, a remarkably ingenious mechanic and very clever workman. They were all members of the London Corresponding Society and all of them confidential friends of mine and mostly so of one another. I used to plod at the French Grammar as I sat at my work, the book being fixed before me I was diligent also in learning all I could after I left off working at night. My progress was rapid and I soon discovered that our teacher was not well qualified to teach us in some particulars. We therefore resolved to procure a frenchman if possible. After some seeking we found an Emigrant Priest a kind considerate attentive man, a scholar, who was well calculated to teach; we all of us progressed rapidly under his guidance. I usually when I had done with my french, read some book every night and having left the Corresponding Society I never went from home in the evening I always learned and read for three hours and sometimes longer,

The Autobiography of Francis Place

the books I now read were french; Helvetius Rousseau and Voltaire. I never wanted books and could generally borrow those I most desired to peruse. I borrowed french books from two members of the Society a Mr Webbe,[1] was one, his father and I believe he himself – was a musician, a musical composer as I heard, he was a very precise careful young man who occasionally employed me. The other was a Mr Williams a Law Student, he lent me books but never employed me. In March Richard Wild came to lodge with me, he like many others had led a loose dissolute live until he became a member of the Society, he was now altogether a reformed man, he was abstemious and remarkably industrious, he was of a sedate reserved and somewhat suspicious disposition and therefore not a very amiable man. He had the room next to the kitchen to sleep in and was accomodated at a cheap rate.

Thus stood my affairs and thus was I circumstanced when on the 19 April 1798 the whole committee of the London Corresponding Society were seized by a general warrant, or by no warrant at all, by some Bow Street officers and Kings Messengers at the committee room in Wych Street. The room in which the committee met was a noble room on the first floor at the top of a spacious stair case. It was part, at one time of the residence of the Earls of Craven and afterwards the Club room of a tavern called the Queen of Bohemia, the spot on which it stood is now partly occupied by a place of public entertainment called the Olympic Theatre.

The apprehension of a French invasion had been pushed to the utmost. Mr Dundass[2] had brought a bill into the house of commons, "to enable his Majesty more effectually to provide for the defence and security of the realm, and for indemnifying persons who may suffer in their property by such means as may be necessary for that purpose." On the 27 March Mr Dundass said "the object of the bill, is to have the power of knowing in case of emergency, who are ready to appear in arms in order to co-operate with the existing power of the country, and to enable them who were so inclined to be put into that situation which may be most answerable to giving effect to their inclination."[3] A sort of general arming was going on, and people in all ranks, all over the country, were offering their services to Government. On the 5 of April the propriety of offering the services of the London Corresponding Society was discussed in the General Committee, in consequence of two of the divisions having recommended that measure, many objections were made to the proposal and the question was adjourned to the next meeting. On the twelfth it was

[1] Spelled 'Webb' in the earlier version.
[2] Henry Dundas, M.P. for Edinburgh, secretary of state for war.
[3] *The Parliamentary History of England from the Earliest Period to the Year 1803*, vol. XXXIII, 1818, p. 1357.

11 Sept. 1797–April 1799

again discussed and again adjourned. It was brought for final decision before the committee on the 19th and was about to be dismissed, from the several obstacles which stood in its way if carried, and from the fullest persuasion of the committee that it would not be accepted by the Government, which never would consent to put arms into the hands of the members of the society as a body.

A french invasion was deprecated by the members of the society, and especially by the committee, and it was therefore agreed to recommend the members of the society individually to join some corps in his own neighbourhood. Just at this instant the whole of the members with all the books and papers in the committee room were seized. The whole of the persons present were taken before the Privy council and after some unimportant questions were asked of them, they were sent to different prisons.

This stroke extinguished the Society, which never made any attempt to meet again, not even I believe in any division, the members dispersed and wholly abandoned their delegates.[1]

In the month of January 1798 O Quigley came from Ireland and was introduced to several members of the London Corresponding Society. He was understood to be a member of the Society of United Irishmen and a catholic priest, but it was not known that he was on his way to France as a delegate.[2] I saw him three or four times and liked him much. He was a tall stout good looking man of remarkably mild manners, kind and benevolent, he was supposed to be a man of property and there was therefore nothing remarkable in his being in London.

Benjamin Binns the brother of John Binns, a man of much meaner understanding than his brother, and Thomas Evans who had become secretary to the London Corresponding Society, made an attempt to form a society of United Englishmen. Evans was a strange creature, with very contemptible reasoning powers, a sort of absurd fanatic, continually operated upon by impulses and capable of undertaking any folly of which

[1] The society was officially extinguished a year later (July 1799) when it was prohibited by name in 'An Act for the more effectual Suppression of Societies established for Seditious and Treasonable Purposes; and for better preventing Treasonable and Seditious Practices' (29 Geo. III c. 79; Add. MS 27808, fs. 110v–11). The societies prohibited by name were the United Englishmen, United Scotsmen, United Britons, United Irishmen, and the London Corresponding Society. According to the act, these societies had been formed in order to engage in a 'traitorous Conspiracy . . . to overturn the Laws, Constitution and Government.'

[2] A month later (February 1798), as he was embarking for France, the Rev. James O'Coigly was arrested at Margate, tried for treason, and in June executed at Maidstone jail. John Binns was arrested with O'Coigly, but acquitted. Binns claimed that he was not fleeing England but arranging transport for O'Coigly (Binns, *Recollections*, pp. 80ff; cf. Place's account in Add. MS 27808, f. 105).

he could make himself one of the leaders.[1] These two found some ten or twelve other foolish fellows who joined them, and having learned from a man who was much with Quigley the organization of the United Irishmen, went immediately to work, collecting people and preparing papers. The object of this association was to produce a revolution. A more absurd and ridiculous project never entered the heads of men out of Bedlam. I attended two or three meetings when about half a dozen persons were present, and pointed out to them the extreme folly of their proceedings. They did not however desist and I am fully persuaded they were prompted to continue their follies by government spies employed for the purpose.

The Report of the Committee of Secrecy of the House of Commons exaggerated their proceedings in a most scandalous manner.[2] It says, "it appeard that about *forty divisions* of United Englishmen had been formed in London about twenty of which had their regular days and places of meeting." This was wholly false, there was *not one such division*. The society was only in an incipient state. An attempt was to be made to establish a society of United Englishmen and a meeting was held on the 18 of April for that purpose There was nothing secret about the matter, many persons were invited I among the rest. With some who were invited I had a conversation, we agreed that the project was equally absurd and mischievous and it ought to be put an end to. I was for doing this by sending for B. Binns and Thos Evans, and an easy silly fellow their coadjutor named James Powell, and frankly telling them, that if they attempted to proceed we would openly proclaim them, and thus prevent them from involving others in mischief and disgrace. This was objected to particularly by Colonel Despard, who proposed that we should go to the meeting and there expose its mischievous tendency.[3] To this I at once objected on the ground that they were prompted by

[1] According to Place, about 1811 Evans and others propagated the rumour that Place was a government spy. Discussing this charge Place commented on Evans: 'Thomas Evans – a brace maker in Newcastle Street Strand – was some years ago saved from ruin by me – and his family supported principally by my exertions during his imprisonment of 3 years – when charged on suspicion of High Treason – to whom about the year 1806 I lent twenty pounds to produce necessaries which he used for a dishonest purpose, and was in consequence forbid coming to my house – ' (Add. MS 35152, f. 63).

[2] *Report of Committee of Secrecy*, 1799, p. 26. This lengthy report describing the allegedly subversive societies went through four or five editions. Place owned and annotated a copy which had belonged to John Richter, one of the 'twelve apostles' arrested in 1794.

[3] In the earlier version Place said that he proposed they threaten to go to Mr Ford, the magistrate at the treasury, and tell what they knew about the United Englishmen, but that this scheme was objected to on the ground that it would appear dishonourable (Add. MS 27808, f. 92).

11 Sept. 1797–April 1799

emissaries of Government who were well informed of all their proceedings. I therefore refused to go. I said that I had already exhausted all the arguments I was master of to no purpose and would use no more. That I was sure they could not succeed and would never be able to hold another meeting, that I knew some who were going who would do all that we could do to put an end to their proceedings and that there would be nothing but disputing and vexation at the meeting. Government were as well informed on this subject as I was, and as they concluded this would be the last meeting it would not answer their purpose to let it terminate quietly in an abortion, they therefore caused the whole of the persons present to be seized. On Evans was found a copy of the test, and another in a different form was found under the table where it had been thrown by Powell.[1] Two of those who had been apprehended escaped, Powell was one of them. Powell absented himself from home for two or three days when finding it was known that he had been at the meeting, that he was one of the persons who had escaped, and that his house had been searched he came to me almost in despair. He was a man whose relatives were gentlefolks, well informed respectable people, but he was an only son, had been indulged and spoilt and made a man of before his time and had therefore become a boy with the age of a man. He was maintained by his mother and kept a small neat house near Pentonville.[2] There was no absurdity no sort of proceeding among them that Powell did not eagerly go into nothing which any villainous spy could suggest that he would not adopt, and he was therefore the most dangerous man among them. Had Powell been taken and questioned he

---

[1] The proposed oath for the United Englishmen, found in the pocket of Thomas Evans: 'I——do Truly and sincerely engage to defend my Country, should Necessity require; for which Purpose am willing to join the Society of True Britons, to learn the Use of Arms, in order that equal Rights and Laws should be established and defended.' The alternative form of the oath, found on the floor of the George, St John Street, Clerkenwell: 'In the awful Presence of God, I A.B. do voluntarily declare, That I will persevere in endeavouring to form a Brotherhood of Affection among Englishmen of every religious Persuasion; and that I will also persevere in my Endeavours to obtain an equal, full, and adequate Representation of all the People of England.

'I do further declare, that neither Hopes, Fears, Rewards, or Punishments, shall ever induce me, directly or indirectly, to inform or give Evidence against any Member or Members of this or similar Societies, for any Act or expression of theirs done or made, collectively or individually, in or out of this Society in pursuance of the Spirit of this Obligation.
So help me God'
(*Report of Committee of Secrecy*, 1799, Appendix, p. 75).

[2] The earlier version contained more and different details about Powell: 'His father had been a clerk in the Custom House a man of property – his mother was a well bred Gentlewoman . . . He had been married to a woman of the town who had left him and he was now living with a young woman at a small house near Battle Bridge' (Add. MS 27808, f. 92).

would have told all he knew, and altho he knew no more than any spy and not so much as the spies had reported, since there can be no doubt that they exaggerated as usual, still it would have been from the mouth of one of themselves, and as he would have been led on to say almost any thing, or at the least to say what might be twisted to mean any thing, – the Government would have been able to make a much better case with than without his evidence they were able to do, and to increase the false alarm they excited. Powell was honest, but silly.[1] Government had nursed the United Englishmen and when it was found that they could not be pushed on to any actual breach of the law, seized them as conspirators, as they did the committee of the London Corresponding Society. They had no specific charge with which they could go before a jury but alarmed as the people were it answered their purpose to make a pretended shew of danger. Wretched employment this for the ministers of a great nation. It was therefore of some importance that Powell should be prevented falling into their hands. It occurred to me that the safest place in which Powell could be put was my apartments. It never would I concluded be supposed for an instant, that he would seek concealment with a person so liable to be apprehended himself, as I was, and that unless therefore they came to seize me, they would never look for any one else in my lodgings. I therefore having once got him, detained him and took care that no one who came to me should see him. With the assistance of his friends I procured him a passage to Hamburg. I made him a suit of half military cloaths – such as Volunteer Officers wore and sent him to Harwich, from which place he and his wife who joined him at the moment he left London in the evening coach proceeded to Hamburgh.[2]

The whole number seized at both places amounted to twenty seven or twenty eight. So as far at least as numbers went the number was perfectly insignificant. Both were actually in every respect insignificant this the Government knew well enough, notwithstanding the importance given to them and the parade made about them in both Houses of Parliament, with their formal proceedings and reports of Secret Committees. Of the twenty eight half a dozen at the least were not members of any society but persons who went to the meetings to persuade the parties not to think of going on with the propositions before them. The number of persons taken at the committee room of the London Corresponding Society was I think thirteen, so that the formidable and terrible society of United Englishmen could not exceed ten including Powell who had escaped.

This is a pitiful showing of the British Government.

[1] Powell was really a government spy (P.C. 1. 42. A. 143).
[2] In the original version, it was Powell's mistress, not his wife, who joined him.

11 Sept. 1797–April 1799

The persons seized were put together without distinction conspirators or committee men, they were all equally harmless and no distinction was needed. Richd Hodgson Alexander Galloway Paul Thomas Lemaitre – Hasseldon – members of the London Corresponding Society, and Benjamin Binns the leader of the United Englishmen were sent to Newgate; put on the State side of the Prison, allowed whom they pleased to visit them all day long, tolerably well lodged well fed and respectably treated by the Gaoler. Others were committed to the House of Correction in Cold Bath Fields commonly at that time called the Bastile, and were subjected to the regulations adopted for the treatment of convicted felons, for whom the Prison as its name imports was built,[1]

These persons were for some days not permitted to see any body, and when afterwards their friends were admitted, it was only on two days a week by an order from a magistrate and at the distance of two or three yards seperated by gates between which a turnkey was placed. For some days they had nothing but the Gaol allowance. Afterwards they were allowed to receive provision sent by their friends. They were not allowed the use of pen or ink nor to receive any letter addressed to them – all sorts of provisions sent to them were searched, yet paper pens and ink were conveyed to them.[2] Means were also found occasionally to receive papers from them.

The difference in the treatment and kind of confinement was not caused by any difference of conduct of the persons who were confined, yet one set were merely confined and made as comfortable as persons in prison could well be made, whilst another set were suffering the heaviest penalty which could be inflicted on the most incorrigible felons, who were condemned to suffer it as punishment for the crimes they had committed.

As soon as I could ascertain how the persons seized had been disposed of, I called a meeting of half a dozen men who had been or were members of the London Corresponding Society, and suggested to them the propriety and necessity of raising money by contributions for the support of the families of the persons who were imprisoned, but such was the terror the proceedings and disposition of the Government produced and of the habeas corpus act being again suspended that no one would either act

---

[1] Committed by the Privy Council 'to Tothill Fields: Naylor, Probyn, Rogers, Davidson, Massie, & Barnes; to Cold Bath Fields: Keir, jr; Thos. Evans, Despeard, Bone, Ebsworth, Purnell, Webb, Edwards, Goodluck, Roberts, Neagle, Clay, Crank, Campbell, Fushard, Cowle, & Humphreys; to Newgate: Binns, Moore, Lemaitre, Hodgson, Phelps, Heseltine, Savage, John Galloway, Alex. Galloway' (*Morning Chronicle*, Monday, April 30, 1798).

[2] 'In large quills, carefully pushed into the meat close to the bones' (Add. MS 27808, f. 95v).

The Autobiography of Francis Place

as secretary or consent to have his name and address taken down. I was therefore compelled to act as secretary. Memorandum books were purchased, headed and signed by me, authorizing the bearer to receive subscriptions. The books were numbered and registered and a designation instead of a name and address was inserted in the commitee book. Thomas Hardy on my application consented to act as Treasurer.[1]

I had long known and during the preceeding two years had been well acquainted with Mr Wm Frend,[2] and I now therefore applied to him to assist in procuring money for the families of the persons in prison. He readily undertook to do so and said he would assemble some of his friends at his chambers in the Temple on the following saturday for the purpose. I attended the meeting, and it was resolved that each of the persons present should collect money from his friends, meet every saturday at the same place and pay the money to Mr Frend who would pay it to Thomas Hardy, who was instructed to honor any check I might draw, on the friday in each week. I to lay an account of the receipt and expenditure before those who came to Mr Frend's chambers on the saturday. I also attended at a meeting of the persons who had taken the memorandum books on the monday evening and furnished them with a copy of the account.

Having made these arrangements by which some assistance was secured for the families of the imprisoned persons, and having got Powell into my possession, which greatly pleased those to whom the information could be confided. I went to Sir Richard Ford at the Treasury told him who I was, and that I was come to ask him if Government intended to make

[1] Hardy, the founder of the LCS, had not been active in the Society since his acquittal in 1794 on charges of high treason. In 1794, Hardy's pregnant wife, greatly distressed by his imprisonment and by the government's searches of their home, gave birth to a stillborn child and herself died two weeks later. Hardy believed that her death was caused by the political oppression. This personal tragedy may account for his withdrawal from LCS activities. Later Hardy gave in to Place's entreaty that he should write a history of the LCS. The document he wrote (and later published as *Memoir of Thomas Hardy*, 1832) stops sharply with the events of 1794.

[2] William Frend (1757–1841), was a fellow of Christ's College, Cambridge, who became a Unitarian and was later banished from the University for writing a pamphlet criticizing the abuses and liturgy in the Church of England. He then settled in London, retained the emoluments of his fellowship, and added to his income by teaching (*DNB*). Frend, like Hardy, Lemaitre, Jones, Galloway and other radical acquaintances of the 1790s is mentioned in later volumes of Place's papers. In 1807 Frend was one of the Westminster electors attending a meeting to promote the candidacy of Sir Francis Burdett (Add. MS 27850, f. 68). In 1823 he started a subscription for the support of Thomas Hardy. He wrote to Place: 'I have great pleasure in adding your name as an annual subscriber to our worthy friend T. Hardy of five pounds & the more so as yours is the first subscription I have received without a personal application on my part' (Add. MS 37949, f. 138). Place himself took over management of the relief fund from Frend in June 1827 (Hardy, *Memoir*, p. 93).

11 Sept. 1797–April 1799

any provision for the families of the persons they had imprisoned, he good naturedly said I might think myself well off that I was not also sent to gaol, and asked me if I was not afraid to come to him. I said I did not consider I was well off simply because I was not ill treated, that if I were sent to prison I should consider myself as very ill treated, and I added that there had been no selection of persons, and therefore I was not seized, that Ministers wanted a new alarm so they seized men indiscriminately and had succeeded, and as no purpose could now be answered I knew very well they would let me alone. He said he would attend to what I had suggested and there the matter ended – at the end of about two years a weekly allowance was made to each of the families.

The committee at Mr Frend's, and the conference with Sir Richard Ford, reassured those who had taken books and induced others to lend their assistance, these things also convinced Powell that he was safe, as he thought it very unlikely they would molest me, and would not suspect him of taken refuge with me.

Having made these arrangements, I schemed a table containing the names of all the persons confined, prison in which each was confined – the wife – the children the other relatives supported – the means every one had towards supporting his family, and scales of relative proportions for the relief of each. This I put on a single page of foolscap paper. The scale was calculated at the rate of six shillings a week for each man, four shillings for each wife and two shillings for each child – valuing the income any one had by the same scale and deducting it. It was easy to add to or diminish the amount on the scale pro rata as the means might be more or less. I sent the Table into Newgate to the only persons with whom free intercourse was permitted. I requested them to inspect it carefully and to correct it if it needed correction. I had however seen the relatives of every one of the prisoners had questioned each of them as to the amount of income or the want of income and had gained such correct information that no alteration was made in the table. I accompanied the table with a letter, in which I said, I expected a good deal of money would be collected, but that unless the sum greatly exceeded the expectation of those concerned in collecting it, the weekly allowance to any one would not much exceed thirty shillings a week. That I knew very well, if the amount in the treasurers hands should be a considerable sum they would not be satisfied to receive it weekly but would want to have it all at once, that if this should happen they might be once for all assured, I would do all I could to prevent it, nothwithstanding any thing they might say or do for the purpose of obtaining the money. They were offended at the supposition, but were all of them well pleased with what I had done, and the way in which I had done it, the effect it was likely to

The Autobiography of Francis Place

produce and the fairness and equality of the scale for distributing the money which might be obtained.

We were soon able to pay 12/ to each man 8/ to each mans wife, and 4/ to each child; thus a family as large as mine then was, received 28/ a week. Two of them received 30/ and one 31/6 every week. The mony which came from my earnings for the support of my family did not average more than twenty shillings a week. Thus matters stood when on the 28 June 1798 my eldest son Francis was born.[1] After the birth of our first child as has been related we employed a medical man in good practice, he had two guineas for his first attendance and a guinea for each of the succeding two. This guinea was always carefully saved and immediately paid. As my wife was young strong and healthy, as none of the absurdities of nursing and feeding were indulged in, as there were no curtains to the bed, no candle, nor heating and stimulating messes we had no occasion for a regular nurse, some assistance was indispensible and this was easily procured. My wife remained in bed not more and seldom so much as two days, on the third day she got up to dinner and in a few days went about as usual, only refraining from any laborious employment.

The wives and other female relatives of the persons in confinement came to me at noon on the saturdays to receive their weekly allowance, the weather was hot and the bed had been removed into the front room in which there was light and air, I was turned into the kitchen

The women when they came for their money got into the front room and there in a body annoyed my wife sadly, would not desist and when requested to leave her would not depart, the consequence was, that I turned them all out. This was an offence never to be either forgiven or forgotten, and they afterwards annoyed or endeavoured to annoy me in every possible way. Mrs Hodgson was not of the number who misbehaved she was an amiable respectable woman, better bred than any of the others, and she sent her eldest daughter for the money generally in the afternoon. I cared little for the annoyance and continued to pay them as usual, my wife could not however treat the affair as I did, and she therefore disliked them exceedingly. She could not patiently see me paying them sums above our own income and receiving nothing in return but ill usage from them, this was soon remedied to a considerable extent, the money for each was put up seperately in a piece of paper and the amount and the name of the person was written on the outside, all they had to do was to recieve the mony and put their initials to the amount in my book very few words being said on either side. The offence given to the women was told to the men, by each woman who had access to her

[1] This son, Francis, corrected the text to give his birth date as June 22.

11 Sept. 1797–April 1799

husband, in her own way, and the men were persuaded that I had treated them very ill. Some sent me notes containing complaints and upbraidings. I gave them a general answer, that I was not conscious of having done any thing, or said any thing which deserved reprehension, and that I could say no more as it related more to matters between man and wife than to me. I promised to continue to do them all the service I could without any expectation that I should be able to please every one, but thought they ought to give me credit for good intentions. Here the matter dropped but the ill will which had been engendered was not extinguished. There was nothing peculiar in the conduct of the women, nothing which would not have occurred under any similar circumstance with women in any rank of life, and of this I was so well convinced that I was very little annoyed at it.

About Michaelmas, the sum exceeding the weekly payments had for some time been upwards of One hundred and fifty pounds, the money collected weekly continuing to exceed the sum paid, by a trifle, and the persons who were in Newgate became desirous to have the money in hand divided amongst the families of those in confinement, this they told me one day when I went to see them. I put them in mind of my letter I sent with the Table, in which I had anticipated the demand, and of their being offended at my presuming to think it possible they could be so silly. I told them of the determination I then expressed not to accede to any such request. I argued the matter with them at great length – shewed the folly of the request, pointed out the injustice it would be doing to those who were confined in Gaols, with whom we could not communicate on the subject, and concluded by assuring them that if every one of the persons in confinement were of the same opinion I would still oppose the proposition to divide the money and do all I could to prevent it, as I was certain it would disperse the two committees put an end to the subscription and bring distress upon all their families. I did not however satisfy them and in a few days I received a formal demand in writing, accompanied with reasons why the money should be distributed. I laid the letter before each of the bodies which assisted to procure subscriptions, when it was unanimously agreed not to comply with the demand. This determination I communicated to the writers in a letter telling them, I had, as I promised I would, done all in my power to prevent their demand from being complied with. This produced a remonstrance accompanied by threats of exposing my conduct. This I disregarded, and the consequence was, a formal protest against my conduct and the decision of the two committees, the paper also contained a notice that a copy would be sent to each of the newspapers. To this I replied, pointed out the injustice of doing any think likely to put an end to the subscription, told them that we could not be induced to do any thing which to us appeared to have such a tendency, and espically at the request of less than one third of the number of persons for whose support the money was raised, that such a publication would ruin the subscription, but would have no influence whatever on me, and would after all not effect the purpose they wished but would make it more than ever our duty to distribute the money carefully and in reduced allowances in proportion to the injury they did to the subscription. My inflexibility, or as they called it, obstinancy, caused them to desist and the matter was dropped. After some time I went to see them when it was agreed, that I had done what I thought was for the best, as they thought for the worst, but that as I meant to do what was right however mistaken I might be, there was no good purpose to be obtained by disputing any more about it. It was agreed amongst them that I was too obstinant and self willed, and that as I could neither be persuaded nor intimidated to do what was right, and that as I had the power and would use it, it was of no use to be other than friends as usual, and there the dispute terminated. When however after some time the subscription fell off and little remained in the Treasurers hands, they agreed in confessing that I was right and had done them service by my pertinacity.[1]

I continued to act as secretary until I left Holborn when Thomas Harrison became secretary and continued in the office until the state prisoners were released in 1801.[2]

[1] 'From causes which I do not know,' Place wrote in the earlier draft, 'the subscriptions fell off and gradually declined until about the middle of the year 1800 when all the money was expended and the subscription had wholly ceased, as the subscription declined the allowance to the families of the men in prison was reduced, and they were all brought to a state of distress; at length Sir Richard Ford in consequence of representations made to him, procured from government an allowance for those families which was I believe regulated much in the same manner the payments from the subscription were regulated, and this was continued as long as any of the persons who had been seized remained in Prison' (Add. MS 27808, f. 104).
[2] Place recorded the last act in this drama of treason and sedition: 'On the 2 March 1801. all the persons confined under the suspension of the Habeas Corpus act were brought to London from Shrewsbury, Reading and other Gaols and they as well as those confined in the Cold Bath Fields Prison being taken to the Duke of Portlands office, were discharged on entering into their own recognizance. But Coln Despard, Alex Galloway, Richard Hodgson and Paul T. Lemaitre refused to give any recognizance. They demanded a trial, which being refused they claimed to be set at liberty unconditionally this was also refused and they were sent to Tothill Fields Bridewell here I visited them. They said they would enter in no recognizance lest doing so might prejudice them in the actions they intended to bring against ministers and others for false Imprisonment.' In the end 'they were turned out of Goal on a promise to appear if called upon to do so.' To prevent such suits as these men intended, the government passed a bill to indemnify all those arrested. 'This after all the pretensions of danger, and all the charges of treason and sedition' (Add. MS 27808, f. 112). The *Annual Register* Chronicle recorded that when the state prisoners were brought to the Duke of Portland's office, 'the whole were treated

11 Sept. 1797–April 1799

My acquaintance with Mr Frend became more close in consequence of the business we transacted together. He used occasionally to call upon me, and gossip with me for an hour whilst I worked. I had always some questions to ask relative to language or science, and he was always desirous to give me information, and thus he became to me a most valuable instructor.[1] As I knew a little of mathematics and something of astronomy, Mr Frend took pains to teach me as much as he could of these two sciences, he also put me forward in Algebra, and had I remained in Holborn, or been so circumstances as to have been at leisure to receive his instructions I should have become a tolerably expert mathematician. Removing to Charing Cross put an end to his instruction.

Another person who in like manner visited me was Coln Bosville he was a very kind man, rich and willing to part with his money, whenever he thought he could do good to any deserving person, or to promote parliamentary reform which he greatly desired to see accomplished.[2] He used to request me to make enquiries for him when he was disposed to give money to persons, and I was generally employed to give the money to those he intended to serve; he never offered me money for my own use, he never knew that I wanted money to purchase necessaries. He once hinted something about my taking a house and thought that about four hundred pounds might enable me to do so. I however stopped him and requested him never again to hint at any thing of the kind. My notions of independence were somewhat absurd I could not bear the thought of

---

with civility and attention.' Those who lived in the country were given five pounds to pay their expenses home (p. 7, quoted in Add. MS 36628, f. 73).

[1] Place remembered with gratitude these visits from Frend and a few other educated men who had come when he lived in mean quarters: 'When I first knew Mr Holcroft [1795–6], I was not in circumstances which enabled me to visit any body, or to let any body visit me, unless, for the purpose of occasional conversation, and they who were willing to visit me for this purpose were compelled to be contented to talk with me, as I sat at work. Very few therefore of those whose circumstances were more affluent than my own visited me. It was a mark of respect, and as it regarded me, of my importance also, that, any man who was well off in the world, and well instructed, condescended to visit me at all. I lived on the second floor, in a room in which many of the concerns of the family were carried on by my lately deceased, and most dearly beloved wife, without assistance from any one, and notwithstanding the peculiar care she bestowed upon the place and the children, and herself; as to neatness and propriety, it was not a place which many persons would chuse to frequent. I was however visited by some remarkable men. Mr Wm Frend, Coln Wm Bosville Colonel Despard, visited me frequently, and frequently conversed with me for considerable periods, several other highly respectable and worthy men also visited me occasionally, and those visits were very advantageous to me in intellectual and moral points of view' (Add. MS 35145, fs. 28–9).

[2] William Bosville (1745–1813) – Harrow, Coldstream Guards, Whig – supported reform but dressed like a courtier of George II (satin suit, powdered hair in a queue). He visited Cobbett in prison and gave him £1,000 (*DNB*).

selling my independence to Mr Bosville, as I conceived taking his money would be. This was sad folly, and I have often when I have thought of it been ashamed of my self. Mr Bosville had an income he could not spend, gave away much money and was defrauded of more, four hundred pounds were not to him an object of much concern and would probably have been the making of me. I did well without his money, but this does not lessen the folly of refusing his money which was an absolute good, for a precarious chance, of which chance even at that time I had not even a glimpse.

After I was in business alone for several years Mr Bosville used to call upon me and was always pleased at hearing of my success.[1]

Richard Wild who has been before spoken of continued to lodge with me and we were close friends. He was a painstaking, careful, plodding man, and very industrious. He was frequently visited by his brother who was many years younger than himself, this brother had lately come from the country and was a porter at very low wages to a tradesman near Covent Garden, at length he took his supper occasionally with us, and as I was utterly unable to feed him at my own expense I spoke to Wild on the subject and requested him to pay me the value of the food his brother had eaten to this he demurred and I remonstrated, Wild was earning some forty five shillings a week, and I was scarcly able to purchase food for my family, his meanness was therefore reprehensible and I told him so; he paid me, and then for some time became sulky, this I also noticed to him and supposed that he would remove, his brother continued to come and sup and he paid for it, he however remained with me and was not sulky but there was a difference in his behaviour which was not pleasant. This however was put an end to one evening when we met at Richard Fentons the Gun Maker where Wild again assumed his usual conduct and manners. A conversation occurred on that evening which induced me to write the following letter.

March. 7th. 1799.

Dear Wild.

The conversation at Fentons on thursday has made a considerable

[1] Besides Frend and Bosville Place named Col. Despard as one of the remarkable men who visited him (see p. 187 n1). Edward Despard (1751–1803), had a distinguished army career and was superintendent of his majesty's affairs in Yucatan until he was recalled because of allegations of cruelty and illegal actions. In 1792, after a wait of almost two years, he was told there were no charges against him. As Place indicated, Despard was caught in the government raid of 1798 and imprisoned until March 1801 (see p. 186 n2). In November 1802 he was arrested on charges of high treason; he was convicted, and on February 21, 1803, hanged. According to government spies, Despard had plotted to win over some of the soldiers of the guard, then to seize the Tower and the Bank of England, to assassinate the king, and to stop the mails from leaving London (*DNB*).

11 Sept. 1797–April 1799

impression on me, that and some other circumstances which have occurred have induced me to make a proposition to you. But before I do so, it is necessary to settle forever, the differences which have existed between us, these would have been passed by and left no trace behind had they occurred with an ordinary person. I give my confidence to very few, but when I do give my confidence I give it wholly, and as in your case, I have no reserve, and conceal nothing, take no pains to appear other than I am, and therefore expect to find similarity of conduct. When two men are placed in these circumstances it is the duty of both to be perfectly sincere. In this state I considered you and I were placed. It was in consequence of this that I felt your conduct so keenly. I was hurt at finding myself disappointed, and sorry to see you fall of[f] so much in my estimation, in which I had hoped you would always stand equally high. I attributed the disposition you evinced to the mode of thinking your fathers extreme severity had produced in you and partly from the necessity of reserve, as mentioned by you, which you thought it was necessary for you to observe when you first came to London to guard yourself from imposition. To these causes I traced your conduct, and assure you that after an attentive examination of all the circumstances I never attributed it to any badness of heart, or as you seemed to suppose any wish to do me injury, or to cause me uneasiness. I have very much regretted the differences which took place because I wished you to stand in the situation my notions of friendship had placed you. I have been very desirous to ascertain your opinion respecting these differences, and unless I greatly mistake it must be much the same as my own. These remarks ought to be made on their own merits, and without regard to any other consideration. They are not now made with any sinister view, this I conclude you will readily believe. If I am correct in this, let all that has passed be forgotten If I am incorrect read no further as the proposition I am about to make ought not to occupy the attention of either of us one moment.

It is not my habit, and this you know, to court an acquaintance with any man, whom I do not very much respect, I can bear any thing with equinimity from any one whom I think unworthy of my friendship, or whose character is unknown to me, and is not therefore intitled to my particular regard. To such persons I never explain any part of my conduct, whilst to him to whom I have given my confidence I am always ready to explain myself in every way.

What it was, that introduces the subject of a partnership between us, I did not understand, it was I believe Fentons suggestion, you seemed to be pleased with the notion, and I observed that if you and I could take such a shop as the Linen Drapers in Holborn opposite to our lodgings we could soon do a good trade in it. Your reply has appeared to me significant, you said you knew two persons who had taken a shop in Henrietta Street Covent Garden as Tailors and Leather Breeches makers and were doing well.

I have thought much of this, and it is very remarkable that the Linen Drapers shop is shut up to day and is to be let. The next house to it is also to be let. Now my proposition is this. That you and I take one of these shops or some other house and go into business together. I have as much business as will feed my family, and you can probably procure as much as will be equal to it. If I were to sell my furniture and collect the money due to me I could raise from forty to fifty pounds, but I can have no money if I retain my goods and my customers, and consequently I shall not be able to advance any. I can however have every thing necessary for carrying on business at a fair credit. You would therefore have to advance some money, for which you might recieve interest. All I should require would be a bare subsistence, the money due to me as it came in would supply me and my family with cloaths for some time. As to economy I shall say nothing. Of industry I shall say nothing. You know as much of me in every respect as you can ever know, and can therefore form your own opinion without further aid from me. You will believe, I trust, that I do not make the proposition merely because I have a family, and am willing on their account to risk you on the chance of serving myself. I am particularly desirous of the welfare of my family, as you also know, but no desire to serve them, would I am sure, induce me to do any thing which I could not contemplate without pain, or that any man ought to be ashamed to acknowledge. So far indeed am I, from having any wish to induce you to do any thing you may not think advisable, that unless you should really desire to adopt the proposition on your own account, I would much rather have your refusal than your acceptance. I have however endeavoured impartially to estimate the good consequences likely to result to us both. I have carefully considered the proposal in all its bearings and you have the result.

There are some matters of detail which you will no doubt attend to should you be disposed to accept the proposition, as for instance, the inconvenience of my family, always however remembering that no one of them should on any account have any thing in any way to do with the shop, or business, but be kept to their own apartments.

I send you this view of the business in writing that you may think of it at your leisure, and examine it in all its bearings. Should you from any cause find the proposition inconvenient to you, you need make no formal

11 Sept. 1797–April 1799

objection, you have only to take no notice of it and it shall never be alluded to by me

Yours truly
Francis Place

This letter led to a conversation and I wrote as follows

March. 11. 1799

Dear Wild

According to my promise I now proceed to state some of the circumstances relative to our intention. First as to the money for the support of my family. I shall take as little as possible, should the money which is due to me exceed the sum necessary to purchase cloaths I shall expand the surplus for food; and take so much less from the business. Second you can take as much out as I do, and if you do not use it advance it on interest for the use of the business. Third every sum drawn out, and every sum put in to bear or to be charged with interest. Fourth, we must have a day book a Ledger a cash book, an order book, and a stock book – The Cash Book must contain every item received or expended. Fifth – All the books must be examined by us jointly, every week, compared with the bought book, or book containing an entry of every thing purchased for money or credit, and with the bill book. We should thus have a clear view at all times of our accounts. of the actual state of our business and of our ability to proceed with it in the best possible way.

There is one matter which you, probably, have not considered, I mean the expense of Coals and Candles. My notion of this matter is, that these should be a joint charge If for instance I had no family we should be obliged to have fire and candle in much the same quantities. You should therefore as to these matters consider yourself as a housekeeper and not as a lodger, for suppose again the house to be taken either by you or I seperately, you or I would then have to pay these expenses, and so, if we take it together we should take the expense together. This is however on the supposition that one fire will be sufficient for all our purposes. If I required another fire, I of course should pay for it. You to be boarded and lodged* – by me for fourteen shillings a week.

Yours truly
Francis Place

*That is found with bed bedding – &c – for one room.

Wild now seemed to be very desirous to get into business with me, yet there were symptoms of reluctance to come to a close. We talked over all the details. We calculated the chances of success thus. If we take a house

The Autobiography of Francis Place

in a good situation we shall scarcly fail to succeed, for we have business enough between us to feed and clothe us, and the sale of Gloves, Slings, Breches balls, Boot garters[1] waistcoats, and an occasional customer which a Shop cannot fail to bring will certainly pay the rent and taxes. We were both satisfied there was no great risk. But then he would say how is the money to be raised to get into a house, his repeating this led me to expect I had miscalculated his means, and at length induced me to ask him how much money he could command, he said not more than twenty pounds, I was surprised at this. I thought he had saved at the least a hundred pounds. I therefore examined my accounts, and concluded that on such an occasion I might collect twenty pounds from my customers. Having thus satisfied ourselves that we could raise forty pounds, we went in search of a house towards the west, and having seen several we at length found one, No. 29 Charing Cross which was just the thing for us, if we could obtain possession of it. The rent was only fifty pounds a year, but for the lease, fixtures, and conveyance of the Lease eighty four pounds were demanded, the house had a good front and needed only outside painting. The rent was very low the house was small, it was rated low in the Parish Books, but how to raise the Eighty four pounds was a question not easily solved. Borrowing was the only chance we had, so we set to work at it, Wild amongst his acquaintance I amongst mine. I collected twenty four pounds from my customers, from debts due to me by them, and obtained promises of small loans from several of my friends, Wild did the same. We then went to all those persons and collected from fifteen of them as much as with his twenty pounds, and twenty two pounds of mine made up the Eighty four pounds which we at once paid on an agreement and took possession of the house. Whilst the assignment of the Lease was being made, we went together to such Mercers and Woollen Drapers and Trimming sellers as either of us was known to. To these persons we made known what we had done, and how we intended to proceed. We then asked each of them if he was willing to give us credit, and all but one immediately consented, the man who refused was named Hardisty, he was rich and had taken more money from me than any other, and had never hesitated to give me the credit I required, After we had been sometime in business he solicited us to deal with him and offered as liberal terms as any other Draper and Mercer, but we would not now leave dealing with those who had unhesitatingly given us credit to deal with one who had refused us credit. Hardisty's refusal was of no importance to us, so many others were willing to give

---

[1] Sling, a leather strap for carrying a rifle; breeches ball, a composition ball for cleaning breeches; boot garters, straps attached to the boot, circling the leg above the knee, outside the breeches, to keep the boot in position when riding.

11 Sept. 1797–April 1799

us credit, and to so large an amount that we could want neither mercery goods, cloth nor trimmings to enable us to make a shew in the shop and to supply any number of customers we might obtain. We wanted however Gloves and Slings, these sold in various forms and at very high prices, with enormous profits, we wanted also some kinds of Manchester Goods which if purchased wholesale would make a great difference in the price to be paid for them. To obtain these we went to wholesale houses in the City looked out the goods we wanted bargained for prices at the usual credit, then told our story and referred them for character to the Woollen Drapers who knew us had consented to give us credit and knew something of our habits. Not one of these persons refused us credit, and on the 8th of April 1799 we removed, to the House the goods we had purchased were sent in the next day and the shop was opened.

My furniture consisted of very few articles, and excepting two or three pieces were of a very mean description. As we were going into a respectable neighbourhood, as the Shop had been nicely painted, and our names put along the front in large gilt letters, so as to have the appearance of means to do business in good stile; as the goods we had purchased would enable us to make a handsome display in the windows we were desirous to conceal the proofs of our poverty which the furniture would have given if exposed by day light, A small cart was therefore hired, the goods were packed in convenient pieces and at dusk were put into the cart. My Brother, Wilds Brother Richard Hayward, myself and Wild were all there and in a few minutes the goods were carried into the shop and we were in actual possession of a house and a shewey shop almost to our own surprize, in which I anticipated great success my wife great fears for the result.

The house was in excellent condition but very dirty, so on the next sunday, Wild his brother, myself and my wife all set to work early in the morning and scowerd it from the top to the bottom as well the wainscot as the floors, and finished by whitewashing the Kitchen cieling.

Thus for the first time in our lives, or rather I should perhaps say since we were married I and my wife enjoyed a truly comfortable residence in which we had rooms enough intirely to seperate our domestic concerns, and get rid of the many inconveniences which had hitherto annoyed us.

Up to the time that I collected the money due to me from my customers to take the house I never had been at any time since my birth in possession of five pounds which I could fairly call my own.

When we got into the house at Charing Cross we had but one shilling and tenpence among us all, but we had a well digested plan to obtain and carry on business, we had health and knowledge, abstemious habits

The Autobiography of Francis Place

great industry, a shewy shop a good stock of fashionable goods and a determination to succeed let what would happen

Before we went into the house and after I had resigned the office of secretary to the subscription for the persons in confinement I wrote to them a short narrative of their proceedings, and my own, and took my leave of them. I thought then I think now that the London Corresponding Society was a very useful society. Its purpose was a reform in the house of Commons on the basis "of *annual parliaments and universal suffrage*,"[1] the plan had sone years before been laid down by the Duke of Richmond and fully developed in a letter from the Duke to Colonel Sharman.[2] And had been followed up by corresponding societies consisting of Noblemen and Gentlemen in many Counties and Cities and conducted by their deputies who proposed and gave reasons for their proceedings. At one of these meetings of deputies when it was resolved to petition for annual parliaments there were present

Sir William Plomer Lord Mayor of London in
the Chair

Earl of Surrey	The Duke of Richmond
Viscount Mahon	THE HON WILLIAM PITT
Henry Duncombe	Sir Cecil Wray
James Martin	Thomas Brand Hollis
the Revd C. Wyvil	Dr John Jebb
John Cartwright	John Wilkes
Brass Crosby	Sir Wathin Lewes – and others.

When it was determined to agitate the question of reform all over the country, that the sense of the people might be taken.

The meeting was held on the 18 May 1782 and was only one among many meetings of delegates in committee or convention, as may be seen in Mr Wyvils collection of Political Papers.[3] (The Society was also guided by and proceeded on the declaration of the Society for Con-

---

[1] This quotation is from the address which was read to every delegate on his election to the general committee of the London Corresponding Society (Collins, in *Democracy and the Labour Movement*, p. 112).

[2] Charles Lennox, *A Letter From His Grace the Duke of Richmond to Lieutenant Colonel Sharman, Chairman to the Committee of Correspondence appointed by the Delegates of forty-five Corps of Volunteers, assembled at Lisburn in Ireland*, 1792. This extended (16 pp.) letter, dated August 15th, 1783, went through several editions between 1783 and 1817. It was read in full at the trial of Thomas Hardy in 1794. Erskine, Hardy's attorney, read from a copy which was handed to him in court by the Duke of Richmond himself (Howell, vol. XXIV, 1818, cols. 1047–57).

[3] Christopher Wyvill (ed.), *Political Papers, Chiefly Respecting the Attempt of the County of York, and Other Considerable Districts, Commenced in 1799, and Continued During Several Subsequent Years, to Effect a Reformation of the Parliament of Great-Britain*, 6 vols., 1794–1802. Place derived his data on reform movements from vol. I, pp. 424 and 228–44.

11 Sept. 1797–April 1799

stitutional Information established in 1781 by about two hundred Noblemen and Gentlemen to procure Annual Parliaments equal representation and universal suffrage.[)]

And finally by the committee and sub committee of Westminster which was composed of Noblemen Gentlemen and Tradesmen, of which Mr Fox was sometime chaiman and under whose name as chairman a report was published and very extensively circulated recommending Annual Parliaments, Universal Suffrage and voting by Ballot with a division of the country into electoral districts each of which was to return one person to parliament. This was in May. 1780. and no expectation was or could have been entertained that proceedings which went beyond any thing the London Corresponding Society proposed, which were composed of and supported by the most eminent men in the country without let or hindrance, would in their case be imputed as the most atrocious of crimes, and when so imputed; that they were to succond and betray the cause they had embarked in simply because they were unjustly treated, was not to be expected by any rational man.

The London Corresponding Society was not calculated to do mischief in any way,[1] all its acts were not well judged, but when did an assembly of men act with discretion on all occasions; when indeed for any length of time did either the House of Lords or the House of Commons act discreetly in all things. If it be objected that this is a reason why such Societies should not exist the answer is, go a step further back, take away the causes which make such societies necessary and there will be no such societies, but so long as the causes remain, so long as the House of Commons does not fairly and fully represent the whole people by members chosen for short periods, so long will such societies be necessary to demonstrate to the people their own energies, and influence their rulers to concede to them some part at least of their reasonable requests and by the manifestation of the opinions of the people prevent the country being plunged into anarchy and confusion. But say objectors, Government should not itself be governed by clubs, true, and it never can be, for it will either concede the necessary reforms, or drive the people into insurrection against its abused authority, clubs will continue from time to time to be forced, to be formed, spite of any law to prevent them until the Government is so far reformed as to make them unnecessary and then they will cease to exist, Clubs then if they be an evil are an evil of less magnitude than the abuses which cause them to exist, and perpetuate their continuance.

[1] In the earlier version Place was at pains to deny charges, made by the Committee of Secrecy, that the LCS was directed by 'secret machinations' and that its purpose was to establish a republic with the help of France (Add. MS 27808, fs. 106–9).

The Autobiography of Francis Place

If, as I hope I shall, accomplish my intention of writing a history of the London Corresponding Society an account of the principal political Societies from the year 1780 and a view of the Political conduct of Government from 1792 to 1801 I shall be able to demonstrate that these societies which have been so much abused and vilified were highly useful, that they furnished the means of much right thinking, much political information; that they promoted an increase of moral conduct, and assisted mainly in improving the great body of the people. That Clubs will continue there can be no doubt until the people being fully convinced of the folly of being governed by a king a house of Peers and an established Church; when they will revert to a representative system in all respects. But they may be much restrained and limited, by such reforms as may be safely conceded if the governments shall ever become wise enough to concede them and thus introduce the great and unavoidable changes gradually and safely.

All the leading members of the London Corresponding Society were Republicans, that is they were all friendly to a representative form of Government,[1] but their leading men were none of them Anarchists, none of them hot headed revolutionists but sedate men who sought for representation through the Government itself by such steps as might bring about the changes they wished by degrees, and not more rapidly than an instructed people could bear them.

A great majority of the members of the society were also Republicans, but not men who sought to overthrow the Government at once and at all hazards reckless of consequences, I have heard it declared in the General Committee of the Society when more than a hundred delegates were present, in opposition to the imputations cast upon the society in parliament, that sudden change in the form of the Government was not desirable, as it would not be the consequence of correct reasoning, but "a Revolution brought about by our Vices instead of our Virtues," would lead to enormous evils, and that no change which was not the result of a thorough conviction of its utility could be permanently useful." I have heard this sentiment expressed in the committee more than once and have heard the speaker applauded.

Some of the members were simply reformers who thought the Parliament might be induced to make a reform as extensive as that which they desired, Others again not only beleived that the parliament would concede the desired reform, but that the reformed house would speedily

[1] Place's earlier draft had an additional sentence at this point in the text: 'This they were taught by the writings of Thomas Paine, and confirmed in them by Mr Winterbottoms history of the United States of North America a work which was published in numbers and generally read by the members' (Add. MS 27808, f. 113).

11 Sept. 1797–April 1799

set aside the King and the Lords. Some were of opinion that no reform would ever be obtained by the concurrence of the King Lords and Commons, but that the Government would be carried on, the abuses continually increasing "until corruption had exhausted the means of corrupting" when an explosion would be caused, and a representative Government spring out of the Chaos, they who thought thus were strenuous in their exertions to have the people well instructed in the principles of Representative Government and this it was which led to the drawing up of the Constitution before mentioned and the printing of it in large numbers. I and my most intimate friends, were of this opinion. Some and they were few were desirous of confusion, they were for all sorts of absurd and violent measures,[1] they had no weight in the society and very few of them continued to be members of it for any considerable period.

It is worthy of being remarked, that notwithstanding the vigilance of the Government, and the attempts made by their atrocious spies to induce the committee to do acts which would bring them within the reach of the law, that no really illegal act was ever committed, nor amidst the continual prosecutions for libels did the society ever publish a line on which the Attoney General could fasten a charge of libel, which he could venture to place before even a packed special jury.

Government did to be sure prosecute some of its members soon after the formation of the society but nothing was really proved as an act of the society which had not been done repeatedly in the most open manner, by the first men in the Kingdom with impunity. Government did trump up a charge of High Treason in which even during the reign of terror, it was signally defeated. Government did seize and imprison some of the members twice and disperce one of its meetings but it was not able to bring forward any specific charge and therefore discharged the persons it seized and imprisoned without bringing any one of them to trial, excepting John Gale Jones, and his conviction was so clearly improper that he was never called up for judgment. Government bestowed epithets enough on the members of the society, it made many threats of vengeance it did many ourageous and illegal acts, but after the State Trials in 1794. It never dared to commence legal proceedings against it, or against its officers – either for sedition or libel. These circumstances may be safely taken as proofs that the society did not, and could not deserve the character which was given to it.

If ever Toleration,[2] in its widest, sence prevailed any where, it was in

---

[1] Earlier version: 'A very few were for using violence, for putting an end to the government by any means foreign or domestic' (Add. MS 27808, f. 114).

[2] In Place's original draft, this paragraph started with four sentences not retained in the final version: 'Nearly all the leading members were either Deists or Atheists – I was an Atheist, That is I did not believe in a God because I could not discover the

The Autobiography of Francis Place

the London Corresponding Society. No man was questioned about his religious opinions, and men of many religions and of no religion were members of its divisions and of its committees. Religious topics never were discussed, and scarcly ever mentioned. It was a standing rule in all the divisions and in the committees, that no discussion or dispute on any subject connected with religion should be permitted and none were permitted. In private – religion was a frequent subject of conversation. It was well known that some of the leading members were Free Thinkers, yet no exception was ever made to any one of them on account of his speculative opinions, nor were ever brought into discussion. Thomas Hardy was a serious religious man, John Bone a good honest man, sometime assistant secretary, was a saint, and a busy man privately in his endeavours to make converts, many others were very religious men, of various denominations. The Society was stigmatized, as an association of Atheists and Deists, whoue object it was to rout out all religion and all morals; as every other body of reformers was stigmatized, the charges against the society were general and vague, but so strictly was the exclusion of religious subjects maintained that no specific charge founded on evidence was ever made against it. Even the Reports made to the Lords and Commons in their committees of secrecy, false and scandalous, as they were in many particulars, never ventured to make a clear and specific charge on this head against the society of an open or covert design, "to take from us our holy religion."[1]

The moral effects of the Society were considerable. It induced men to read books, instead of wasting their time in public houses, it taught them to respect themselves, and to desire to educate their children. It elevated them in their own opinions, It taught them the great moral lesson "to bear and forbear." The discussions in the divisions, in the sunday evenings readings, and in the small debating meetings, opened to them views which they had never before taken. They were compelled by these discussions to find reasons for their opinions, and to tolerate others.[2] It

---

existence, or conceive the possibility of such an existence as I was called upon to believe without proof. I was told a number of nonsensical things by men and I read a number of others in books, but I found that none of these persons had any more knowledge on the subject than I had myself, that is that we were all profoundly ignorant, and I could not consent either to worship their ignorance or my own. In the absence of all proof I could not believe. This was also the opinion of many others. There were however a number of very religious people. If ever Toleration . . . ' (Add. MS 27808, fs. 115–16).

[1] The Act of 1799 suppressing the LCS and other societies charged them with printing papers 'of an irreligious, treasonable and seditious character, tending to revile our holy Religion.'

[2] 'It is 37 years since I became a member of the London Corresponding Society, the very best school for good teaching which probably ever existed' (Letter to George

11 Sept. 1797–April 1799

gave a new stimulus to an immense number of men who had been but in too many instances incapable of any but the grossest pursuits, and seeking nothing beyond mere sensual enjoyments. It elevated them in society. Of all this among multitudes of other proofs a very striking one occurred on the anniversary of the acquittal of Thomas Hardy on the 5th November 1822 at the Crown and Anchor Tavern in the Strand, at this dinner about two hundred persons were present. I attended the first anniversary in 1795 but had never been at any other between 1795 and this in 1822. In 1795, I was a journey man breeches maker. In 1822 I had retired from business. At this meeting I was recognized by no less than twenty four persons who had been delegates from divisions and members of the General Committee of the Society when I was chairman. I had not seen more than one or two of them for upwards of twenty years several I had never seen since 1797 – or 1798 all of them recognized me, but I could not recognize many of them until names and circumstances were mentioned. The greetings were mutually agreeable, of these twenty four men, twenty at the least of them were Journey men or shopmen at the time when they were delegates to the General Committee of the Society, they were now all in business all flourishing men. Some of them were rich most of them had families of children to whom they had given or were then giving good educations. The society had been to a very considerable extent the means, and in some of the cases the whole means of inducing them to desire to acquire knowledge the consequence of which was their bringing up a race of men and women as superior in all respects to what they would otherwise have been as can well be concieved. It is more than probable that a circumstance like this never before occurred. That so many persons from among the delegates alone should still be alive, in good health and in good circumstances and should from sympathy assemble in one room is a very extraordinary circumstance, a plain and positive proof of high moral conduct and right feeling which never was surpassed, if indeed it ever was equalled. But if twenty four such men were found in one room at one time, how many such men must there be in the whole country. It must be concluded that compared with the whole number of delegates and even with the whole number of members the number of persons of the same sort must be very large. I know many well doing men who were members but not delegates, and yet my acquaintance with the members out of the committee was not large. Every such person with whom I ever conversed has acknowledged the benefit he derived, and the knowledge he obtained from having been a member

---

Rogers, January 15, 1832; quoted by Himes, *Illustrations and Proofs of the Principle of Population*, p. 315).

of the society, whilst I never heard of any one man who was made worse in consequence of his having been a member of the society.

Vague declamation against the society should then go for nothing, nor should any attention be paid to the accusation of any one be his rank or condition whatever it may, unless he can shew that as much evil was done to individuals and to the public as I have shewn good was done. This is however impossible and I may I am sure safely affirm that the London Corresponding Society was a great moral cause of the improvement which has since taken place among the *People*.

CHAPTER 12

From my Removal to Charing Cross on the 8 of April. 1799 – to my return to it on the 8th of April. 1801

Partnership with Richard Wild – We do a great business. Wild marries – His Wifes character and conduct – His conduct – Arrangement with our Creditors. I remove from and return again to Charing Cross.

We opened the house at Charing Cross with a handsome shew of choice mercery goods, and in a few days some very fashionable waistcoats were placed in the Shop windows. At this time there was no shop at the West-end of the Town which exposed first rate fashionable articles of dress for men in the windows, and we sold a considerable number of waistcoats at a high price. Pantaloons ornamented with silk braid had not then become common they were worn by very [few] persons excepting Cavalry Officers. We ornamented some very finely and hung them in the windows, several persons came in to look at them but as the fashion was not yet set and they were very shewey, they had not the courage to give orders for them, but we generally succeded in getting an order for some garment of of those who came in, and after some little time we received orders for laced pantaloons.

For articles of fashion which were somewhat out of the common way we obtained high prices, but for coats and other common things, we thought it advisable to charge low prices, that is low prices as compared with those charged by the leading tailors. At first we both worked at sewing, but in a few weeks we had so much to do in attending to customers, superintending the trade, cutting out and keeping the books that there was no time for any thing else. It was our custom to have every thing done which could be done before we closed the business for the day, and this frequently occupied us from six o clock in the morning till twelve o clock at night. In the morning after breakfast one of us used to wait upon the customers, see every garment we made put on, shew patterns, or specimens of new articles, and new fashions. No one was either neglected or disappointed, a thing very unusual at that time. This conduct was steadily pursued and the consequence was that before the winter commenced we were obliged to raise the roof of the house and convert the whole of the garretts into a workshop

We were often pushed into difficulties by the sudden increase of business from want of money to pay current expenses and wages, and it

The Autobiography of Francis Place

sometimes happened, that we could not pay the workmen their wages, some were paid half some less on the saturday night and the remainder in the course of the next week.

We procured a very clever man as foreman named Viggears, and a young man who understood the trade as shopman. We went on increasing our business continually and at Christmas 1800 we had thirty two tailors at work and three or four Leather Breeches Makers. No such rapid increase of business had ever been known. We had before us, the prospect of one of the largest businesses in London, and a certainty as we thought – of making a rapid fortune. The house was too small, and proper accomodations for the trade we were doing could not be made in it. The next house was a large house, a well built lofty, and somewhat elegant house, well adapted in all respects for a large and genteel business. This we had partly agreed to take from lady day 1801, My partner was about to be married and it was agreed between us that as I had a family I should remain in the house and he should take lodgings in a house nearly opposite This was a judicious arrangement and had it been acted upon so that we could have gone on together as we ought to have done, we should have made, large and rapid fortunes. We had calculated on this, we had estimated the great increase of profit when we should be able to buy for ready money, and the rapid increase of capital when we should be able to withdraw it from the business and add the income not only of the annual sum withdrawn from the business yearly but that which arose from the money withdrawn and laid out in some advantageous way. The cupidity of my partner put an end to these calculations in an instant.

I had three children when we entered the house another was coming, my wife attended the children washed for the family and did the household work

Towards the end of the year 1799 – this was no longer necessary so she hired a servant. In the summer of 1800 Mr Wild told us he should shortly be married and he frequently spent his evenings from home as had not hitherto been his custom. In the week preceeding Michaelmas he said he should be married on the sunday following, and the arrangement respecting his lodging on the opposite side of the street was mentioned. He said that the person he was about to marry had no furniture he wished us to board her as well as himself for a week or two to enable them to purchase some furniture and that he would then remove at once to the lodgings over the way. I did not like his bringing a wife into the house, but as the house was as much his as mine I made no objection, but consented to board his wife as I had done him. He had never told us who the lady he was about to be married to was. He now said she was a dress maker and miliner and lived in Mary le Bone, a very respectable clever woman, that her name was Atkins and she was the sister of a builder in a considerable way of business near Sloane Street. My wife and I had no reason to doubt the correctness of the description, and we therefore expected to see a genteel woman about thirty years of age. My wife made the best preparation she could to receive them and as many of their friends as might accompany them. We put some of the best furniture we had into the second floor for their accomodation. We waited in expectation of seeing them all the afternoon and until eleven o clock at night, when Wild came home bringing with him a woman upwards of forty years of age, a large, fat woman – as vulgar and as much at her ease though they came alone as any woman of any kind or description could be. We were greatly disappointed and foreboded no good as likely to result from my foolish partners extraordinary marriage. The lady fell to boasting of her business which she said she should continue notwithstanding her marriage. I was not to be imposed upon thus, I saw at once what she was, and was resolved to enquire till I had made out her history, I did so and in a few days discovered, that she was born at Bath and when a Girl worked in the Brickfields, but having a good face had turned it to account as a common prostitute. She had since lived with several men and had latterly been supported by an old man who lived in Sloane Street whose name was Martyr, and had I believe been a Lottery Office Keeper. She was no dress maker, could not make a gown for herself or any thing else. Her brother the builder was I found a jobbing bricklayer living in a little house in a lane at the back of Sloane Street. Part of the information I obtained by rather an odd circumstance. A few days after she came home I saw her in deep conversation with a master carpenter in an unfinished house in St Martins Lane, I knew the Carpenter who when I spoke to him about her laughed heartily at the joke of her being married to Wild, said she was a damned old —— with whom he had once for a short time lived. My wife and I agreed to take no notice of the information we had received, but to treat her as respectfully as we could and as soon as possible to get Wild to remove as had been agreed. His removal was however put off until we should get possession of the house we were in treaty for, but by this time he had resolved to stay where he was as the sequel will shew.

With such a woman it was utterly impossible to be at peace, her language and manners were gross in the extreme, she was suspicious, insolent, drank too much and was a thief, robbing the shop frequently, though she wanted for nothing. She soon became scandalously abusive to my wife, and made her very uncomfortable. At length I mentioned the matter to Wild as gently as I could, and suggested to him the propriety of seperating the families, which he affected to be pleased with and said it

The Autobiography of Francis Place

should be done as soon as we had settled for the House at next door. We agreed to do all we could to prevent the annoyance in a quiet way, and until the proposed arrangement was carried into effect to bear quietly whatever might happen. Thus we went on 'till Christmas day. Just before noon on that day when Wild and I were making up the books, he after some hesitation and a shuffling sort of conduct which excited my surprise, in a faultering tone which showed that he was labouring under considerable doubt and apprehension, said he had been considering the propriety of taking the next house and thought the house we were in might be made to answer our purpose if I would remove. I saw the whole matter at once. He knew as well as I did that it was impossible to make the necessary arrangements for our business in the small house we occupied. I looked at him steadily and said. Wild I hope you are not going to be a rascal. The manner in which I addressed him utterly confounded him. Giving him no time to recover himself, I said – and if I do not remove you will do – what? – He could not answer me – so I went on – try to get the house to yourself? – he muttered – yes. – and you have taken the necessary steps? – yes. – and have applied to Mr Light? – yes. I was more nearly overcome with feeling than I ever remember to have been, but I rallied, and said firmly, – Wild I am sorry for you. That you of all men, you who have always been treated so handsomely by me, and been so cheerfully and well attended to by my wife – you who have been benefitted so much by my acquaintance, and are now in the high road to fortune which but for me you could not have been, – that you should have deliberately contemplated my ruin and done all in your power to accomplish it is as surprising as it is dishonest and lamentable; but we will not quarrel. It is impossible for you and I to go on together any longer, and we will therefore part immediately. Arrangements can easily be made, they need not occupy many days. But tell me what said Mr Light to you? He replied "send Place to me". I. Then said I let this matter rest 'till tomorrow moning and I will go to Mr Light, and have the business arranged as soon as possible. This was all that passed between us. A more miserable wretch than Wild was during this colloquy I never beheld.

The matter was of so much importance to me that I immediately wrote down the words as they have been related. It was my dinner time, and knowing the effect it would have on my wife I intended to say nothing about it until I had seen Mr Light, but I never had any secret in any thing which related to my domestic concerns and I could not dissemble, I could not conceal, and felt I could not conceal from my wife that something extraordinary had happened. I had succeeded in subduing my feelings to a considerable extent, still this was so unexpected and to us so

12   April 1799–April 1801

very serious a matter, that I could not be easy and placid. I therefore told my wife what had occured and read my notes to her. The effect as I had anticipatd was terrible, neither tongue nor pen can describe her anguish. She saw nothing before her but destruction there were the three children and another coming. She was sure we should all be turned into the street, industry was of no use to us, integrity would not serve us, honesty would be of no avail, we had worked harder, and done more than any body else, and now we were to suffer more than any body else, I made no attempt to soothe her, I knew it would be useless and my feelings were too much in accord with hers to permit me to do much, more than participate with her, it was undoubtedly the bitterest day of my life. She dreaded the horrid poverty she now saw before her and she felt the more acutely, since she had thought that her troubles and difficulties were ended, and that abundance and happiness was before us. I was the more affected as I did not see my way before me. I had a full and very lively presentiment of the difficulties before me, and could not calculate the means of encountering them. I was much hurt at being obliged to abandon, and that too all at once the uncommonly successful course I was steadily and cheefully pursuing, and in an instant give up the advantages of which I had all but obtained full possession.

Mr Light was a very respectable and intelligent gentleman an attorney in the Temple, he had been a customer to Mr Croft in Fleet Street to whom Wild was Foreman, and was now a customer to us. We had not asked him for his custom, no one who dealt with Mr Croft was solicited to become a customer to us. Mr Light had brought a brother of his a captain in the 25 Regiment of foot to us as a customer and he was at his brothers chambers when I called. Mr Light asked of me if I had had any conversation with Wild about the lease of the house? I said I had, and about our business generally. I then related to him what had passed between us, and read my notes to him. I then gave him a copy of the notes. He said, "Your partner of whom I entertained the best opinion is I see a great rogue and a great fool set on by somebody to work his own ruin. He came to me several times and asked my advice about a dissolution of your partnership which I supposed was desired by both of you. He said your wives could not agree and it was necessary for you to separate. I who had observed how industrious you both were, and how competent you both were, thought it was a pity you should put your well being in jeopardy, recommended a reconciliation, and suggested that one of the families should remove from the house, to this Wild assented, but on wednesday he came to me with the lease of the house in his hand, and said he wished to know how that could be made his. I said as the lease was assigned to you jointly, he must have your consent to a

The Autobiography of Francis Place

transfer. From the manner in which he behaved, and the reply he made I began to suspect that you were unacquainted with his proceedings and I therefore desired him to send you to me." But said Mr Light "how came you to challenge him with having been with me if you had had no previous conversations with him on the subject?" I replied that I knew he had been to your chambers very often, and had made what at length appeared to me to be absurd pretences for doing so, and knowing the man thoroughly, no sooner did he allude to his purpose than I concluded he had consulted you. Mr Light said "I had better send Wild to him and he would endeavur to make arrangements to prevent a dissolution of our partnership unnecessary, and protect against future disagreements".[1] On my return home I told Wild what had passed at Mr Lights, and added that if he chose to go to Mr Light, let him draw up articles of partnership and at once remove from the house as had been agreed. I would forgive what had passed and go on again as usual. He said he would not go to Mr Light, but would give me an answer in the afternoon. He did not however give me an answer, but the next morning he said he was resolved to remain in the house. Then said I, you have resolved to keep the house to yourself – cost whatever it may? He said he had, and I might do as I liked. I said well be it so, you are more a fool even than a rogue and I have no doubt about the result. Only let matters stand as they are for two days whilst I make the books complete and then we will fight it out fairly. He said he would, and I went to work upon the books.

Notwithstanding my mind was made up, and my resolution to see the matter out manfully. I could not so far master myself as to be tranquil, I felt my situation acutely. I knew that we should be obliged to assign all our effects to our creditors, and notwithstanding I knew that there would be enough to pay them all, still I could receive nothing until they had all been paid, and as this could hardly be accomplished under eighteen months and might even extend to two years, I had the prospect of being left without a shilling and therefore without the means of again getting into business.

The customers I had before we came to Charing Cross had all left us, and our new customers were gentlemen who would not deal with a man in a garrett, and even if any of them should be disposed to do so, the having left a good shop and gone into poverty would be conclusive evidence that I was a rogue. Thus I saw myself cut off from all chance of recovering myself, but I was not subdued. I had never shrunk from any difficulty had never gave way to despondency never succumbed in the

---

[1] Sentence snarled in revision. Originally Place wrote '... he would endeavour to make arrangements which should make a dissolution of our partnership unnecessary, and prevent future disagreements.'

12 April 1799–April 1801

least, and I now took a resolute sturdy course. Wild knew me well and he feared me much but he had concluded that I should find myself helpless and should be palsied in my exertions by my adverse circumstances. His conduct was equally dishonest treacherous and cruel.

I had not been at the books many hours when our principal creditor, William Gustard of Tavistock Street Woollen Draper, a shuffleing - snuffleing narrow minded man a very slave to those by whom he profited an insolent tyrant to those who could not escape being dependent upon him came into the shop and with an air of insolent command asked me how the accounts stood. I asked him why he made the demand so rudely, because said he you have behaved ill to Wild, and I want to know on what I have to depend for the seven hundred pounds you owe me. I said to him very calmly. Mr Gustard, this is the second time you have behaved yourself insolently, you got rebuked on the former occasion and you can expect nothing else now. I don't care for you said he. Mr Wild has friends and money and you are nobody, so tell me how the accounts stand. I told him to take himself off quickly or I would assuredly kick him into the street, and I got down from the desk, intending if he did not retreat to do as I had said I would. He went away muttering, "we shall know what to do with you at the meeting on thursday." I had heard of no meeting but Gustards words alarmed me, so I went immediately to some others of the creditors, and found that Wild and his brother had been round to them all, told their tale and left a notice with each of them appointing a meeting at a Tavern nearly opposite our house to be held on the evening of thursday the 1 Jany 1801. when *he* was to shew them the state of the accounts and give them security for all the debts. He should he said carry on the business as usual on his own account. As he alone addressed himself to our creditors and I had not been to any of them appearances were against me and nearly all the creditors were prejudiced in his favour and disposed to think ill of me. This proceeding was in the true spirit of a cunning silly rougish man, it was as base as almost any conduct could be. I now went to each of the creditors and satisfied most of them that I had done and would do nothing wrong. This was on the tuesday afternoon and the wednesday before the meeting on the thursday. I then went to Mr Light and told him what had passed, he said I should not be born down, that he would be my friend, and his brother to whom I had never spoken three times said he would lend me £300 if I wanted it. He had he said been talking the matter over with Mr Seawell who would also lend me £200. Mr Seawell was a customer himself and had recommended us to several others, he was a very worthy gentleman and had a multitude of friends, he came to the Shop to me the same day and offered me the money which I declined to take until I knew how

The Autobiography of Francis Place

I should be circumstanced. My situation was now wholly and suddenly changed, and my prospects were as bright as they had 'till that moment been obscure, these were as sudden as they were extraordinary changes.

When the hour of meeting had arrived – I asked Wild if he was ready to go to it, observing that we might as well go together. He either was or affected to be surprised that I had heard of it, and he preremptorily refused to go to the meeting which he had himself called. I went alone and requested the creditors to appoint two of themselves to go to Wild and bring him to the meeting, that I was fully prepared to lay the whole matter before them in the clearest and simplest way but thought it ought not to be done unless he was present. Two were appointed, and after some difficulty they prevailed on him to come to the meeting. I then stated the whole case to them, and called upon Wild to shew that there was either exaggeration or mistake in any part of it. He sat mute, some of the creditors called upon him to say whatever he might think proper, he would not speak, some reproached him, but not one word would he utter. I therefore proposed an immediate assignment of all our estate and effects, save only my furniture. This they thought was handsome conduct, sone were of opinion that so flourishing a concern ought not to be broken up and wished a reconciliation. I satisfied them all that this was impossible, and that the only thing which could with propriety be done was an assignment to them the creditors of all we had. One of the creditors had brought his attorney with him who drew up an agreement, to three of the creditors as trustees for the whole and for us, and after some reluctance Wild signed it. Gustard as our principal creditor was one of the Trustees. He had been acquanted with Wild when he was foreman to Mr Croft. I had never dealt with him on my own account, and never saw him 'till Wild took me to his shop. The trustees were to sell every thing – in the best way they could and to collect the debts due to us, the Lease of the house was to be taken by one of us, at a single bidding by tender. As Wild was quite ignorant that any one had offered to lend me money he concluded that I should be unable to bid for the lease, and he should therefore, have the matter all his own way, he was therefore pleased upon the whole, and the next morning was so insolent that I was obliged to promise to thrash him well if he did not behave himself better. A day was named when the creditors were to meet again, I was to lay before them a correct balance sheet of our books, to surrender the books, and all other documents relating to the business, our tenders were to be put in and he who bid the highest was to have the lease, and of course possession of the house. When I read the balance sheet and exhibited the books, they were so clear and satisfactory that several of the creditors again urged us to go on together, this was however an absurd recommendation. It was agreed that the lease and good will was worth to either of us not less than £350 and he who bid the most above that sum was to be the purchaser The value of the good will was greatly inhanced in the opinion of the creditors by the accounts I had exhibited, and two of the creditors Mr Savage a Leather seller of Chiswell Street, who had known me from the time I was apprenticed and with whom I had laid out on various accounts many hundreds of pounds, and Mr Richard Richards a trimming seller in Drury Lane with whom I had dealt from the moment I had any dealings, urged me to bid £800 for the lease, and offered to advance the money for me. I did so, but when the tenders were opened it was found that Wild had bid £1000, two hundred pounds were immediately paid as a deposit and I signed an agreement to assign the lease whenever it should be presented to me for that purpose.

I had taken the precaution to hire, or rather to borrow a house, the meeting of creditors terminated late in the evening and very early the next morning I quitted Charing Cross.

These were singular vicissitudes to happen in the short space of nine days. On Christmas day in the morning I had before me the almost certain prospect of a handsome residence, the half of a large and very profitable business and of being able to retire from business altogether in a few years as rich as I desired to be. At noon the prospect seemed to be wholly blasted, and I was once more cast abroad without a shilling and by no means certain that I could borrow fifty pounds. I knew that the creditors would be satisfied with nothing short of an unconditional surrender of all we possessed, and that until they were paid I could not receive a shilling. I knew well enough how estates were managed by trustees, and doubted much that with their management and the paiment of law charges which they would necessarily incur that any thing would be left for me. I had therefore no hopes of receiving any thing from the business. I had twenty two pounds when I came to Charing Cross, it now seemed almost certain I should leave it without one.[1] I was fully convinced, that Wild must have found the means of raising money or he would not have behaved as he did. I had therefore much to fear and little to hope. I was astonished at his baseness but I lost not a moment in exerting myself to the utmost to save myself from the impending ruin. In two or three days afterwards – I had £500 offered me from men on whom I had no claim of any any sort, and no expectation of assistance. I went to every person I could think of who was at all in any way likely to be persuaded to lend me five pounds and obtained promises of assistance for more than £300, and on the the ninth day from

[1] Originally: 'without a shilling.'

the commencement of my troubles, I had a further offer of £800 to purchase the lease, Thus I had the unexpected command of upwards of £1600.

I had all along preserved my integrity, had never acted meanly towards any one, was I think I may say more than usually sincere, and they who knew me well placed great reliance on me in whatever I undertook for or with them I was cheered and delighted at the countenance I met with and the assistance which was offered to me now when it had become so necessary and when I had no security to offer to any one. I considered it the result of my own conduct and the character I had obtained and was not a little proud of myself when under circumstances which necessarily put to hazard whatever money any one should lend to me, to find that of the many persons to whom I made application not one refused to do something for me, and several offered to lend me larger sums than I requested.

I soon discovered that the Mr Martyr, who had lately kept Wilds Wife was the person on whom Wild depended for money, and that he did actually advance him much more than a thousand pounds.*

The house to which I removed is at the corner of Russel Court in Brydges Street near Covent Garden. It was lent to me by John Ridley a Boot Maker in York Street who had long been a member of the London Corresponding Society

When Wild and I had signed the agreement to seperate our concerns I asked Viggears the foreman in the presence of Wild with whom he would remain, and he at once said with me. He had been an old and close acquaintance of Wilds, and they had led a dissolute life together, he told

---

* Sep. 1833. Both Wild and his wife were living in March last, and are probably both living now. He being seventy two or seventy three years of age, his wife nearly seventy. After we parted he reduced his business at Charing Cross in such a manner that he was obliged to leave the house. He then took a house in Craven Street in the Strand did a small quantity of business and let lodgings. Here he became a Bankrupt. He afterwards took the benefit of the Insolvent act Twice he compounded with his creditors, and was so reduced at last that I with others was applied to for a few shillings to save him and his wife from starving, when I last heard of him he was receiving aid from St Martins Parish. His brother died in the West Indies, many years ago.

In November 1833 – an attempt was made to raise a weekly sum to keep Wild and his wife from the workhouse; and to this I contributed – It did not succeed beyond a very short period. Wilds wife died in wretched poverty, and he went into St Martins Workhouse where he shortly afterwards died.

[After reading this chapter of the memoir, Mrs Grote told Place that he should never have done Wild another kindness. Place replied: 'Wild came and worked for us in the Westminster election of 1818. I had long before forgiven him. Eighteen years were too long a period to cherish enmity, he worked well, and was obliged to give me an account of what he did to me, he was embarrassed and when I gave him my hand, he was releived from a load' (Add. MS 35144, f. 357).]

12   April 1799–April 1801

Wild that he was a damned rogue and would have nothing to do with him. The young man who attended in the shop wished also to go with me so I engaged them both. I offered the foreman the wages he had received from us – namely two guineas and a half a week his cloaths and some perquisites. He however refused to receive more than two guineas a week of me until he saw how the business went on. He was a large fair haired Lancashire man about thirty six years of age, but an old man in constitution, he was a good looking man, rough in manners but with such an evident desire to give satisfaction as to gain the good opinion of all who came to the shop. He was a journeyman of the old blackguard school, had given in to all sorts of dissipation to the full extent of his power and his means and had injured himself past recovery. He was one of the most diligent men living, and when business was brisk, frequently came to his work at four o clock in the morning and sometimes even earlier. He was an invaluable man to me, he had my welfare greatly at heart and made uncommon efforts to promote it. He was never treated by me as a dependent but always as an equal. As his health declined, he often regretted that he had not known me earlier, he should then he said have been a strong healthy man. He was the first man employed by Wild and me, at two pounds a week he was to cut or sew or assist in any way he could, but as the business increased he was taken into the shop and wholly employed in cutting out, and attending to the customers when neither of us were at home. The second man engaged by us was named Price, he remained as a common journeyman till nearly the time when Viggears died, In anticipation of that event, Viggears took him under his direction and carefully and assiduously taught him all he knew to enable him to succeed him when therefore Viggears died in   [.] Price became foreman, and continued in my employment until I left off business he is now employed by my son as is the third man whom we employed and three others have been in our employment upwards of twenty years.

It was greatly to my disadvantage to live in Brydges Street, it was an out of the way unfashionable place, yet I had ten men at work. As I could not go on without some money I borrowed eighty pounds of Mr Savage and thirty pounds of Mr Richards, these were the only sums I borrowed.

I was very desirous to obtain a house at Charing Cross and I made continual inquiries for one. Early in March one was offered to me, it was a good but rather a small house nearly opposite to the house I now live in. The rent was £120 a year, the premium for the lease £200, the alterations and fitting up would have cost £250 more at the least, and it was on the wrong side of the way. I was however so very desirous to have a house at Charing Cross that I had nearly concluded a bargain for it, when

The Autobiography of Francis Place

I heard that I might have a shop and a parlour with a room on the first floor and other conveniencies, with a large light workshop at the back of it, this was in the old fashioned and very old house No 16. It was an excellent situation very commodious, and well adapted for all my purposes. I therefore at once signed an agreement for a lease and on the eighth day of april 1801 – exactly two years from my first removal to Charing Cross. I took possession of it with my family and have lived in it ever since.

CHAPTER 13

From my return to Charing Cross in 1801 to the year 1816. My Business – my Family

State of the house No 16 Charing Cross – I fit up the Shop   The street – Feelings – Practices – Business how conducted – Reflections – Westminster Election 1807 – Books – Men – Fire at the next house – Mr Tapster – Lease renewed in 1816. Business its maximum – Miss Atkinson and her school.

The house No 16 Charing Cross had for many years been known as the, "Royal Bagnio," It is probable, that it really was the "Bagnio" attached to the palace. It is called the "Royal Bagnio" in the lease I afterwards took of it. It had been a house of ill fame for more than a century but had fallen into such a state of decay and dilapidation, that no person would take it on a repairing lease. It was therefore let in tenements. The front was as at present, the back was in a court which some years before I took the house was a thorough fare from Charing Cross to Scotland yard along the western wall of the Duke of Northumberlands Garden

The back house which contained the Baths was let to a man named Thorpe who plundered it of some leaden tanks and of every thing he could sell and then ran away without paying his rent. The front house was still used as a house of ill fame. The basement was paved with red tiles, and the vaults were groined. These vaults were let to a Green Grocer, the Shop to a Barber, the entrance to the vaults was by a broad brick staircase under the shop window. The tenants were all poor and not very honest and as the landlord could not obtain payment of the rent he turned the tenants out and shut up the house. This was its state about the year 1795.6. It was then an infamous neighbourhood. There were some highly respectable persons living there but there were also a much larger number of very disreputable people. There were Five notorious houses of ill fame – three of which were in the main street. Seven public Houses, three of which were gin shops, all of them frequented by common soldiers and common women of the lowest description, and other vagabonds. The Court, at that time, and for many years afterwards called Angel Court* had fourteen very old houses in it, and almost every room in every house was rented by a poor prostitute, It was a den of the lowest and worst description. The houses were lofty, and were built in the old fashiond style of brick work in a very expensive manner, they had

* Now. Trinity Place.

The Autobiography of Francis Place

Pilasters and Capitals of fine red bricks, at regular distances. They had been originally remarkably well built, and probably when built overlooked part of the Royal Gardens

About 1798 A great change took place, the barbers Poll which stuck out at a shop a few houses below that in which I live was taken away, three of the public houses were soon afterwards converted into shops. The flags in front of the Crimping houses were taken down, and a progressive improvement took place until the street has become what it has for the last twenty years been.* (1835)

When the house No 16 was shut up Mr Stephenson who kept the Craven Hotel, then called the Globe in the Strand, agreed to take the whole of the premises, excepting the Shop and parlour, and a large room on the first floor now my kitchen, at a yearly rent of 80£. He let the back premises containing many rooms and a seperate staircase with the large and noble cold bath, the hot baths sweating room and other conveniences to his waiter Stephen Tapster, at a very low rent to preserve them as he said from total ruin.[1] In each of the three large rooms in the front house he put a Billiard Table and employed a man as a marker to look after them. The entrance to the house was by a door full four feet wide at the south end of the front, and a broad passage leading to a large very old fashioned Staircase, at the foot of which just beyond it was another very large door with a circular top and six large panes of crinkled glass in it. The street door was a massive gate nearly four inches thick – near the top of it was a strong iron grating, and in the middle of it a very small iron grating as all such houses had to peep through It was as strong as a gaol door. The door at the foot of the stairs had Iron bars across the lower panes. A large old fashioned lamp hung in the passage and shed a dim light as did three or four other lamps on the staircase these lamps were kept burning all night, to enable the gamblers to find their way up and down it had a most forbidden villainous look, yet a great many people attended the Billiard Rooms.

The house and premises were freehold held by a very old gentleman named Parke – and one of his sons who had failed in business, but now was a clerk in the Tax Office. He had the Shop the parlour and the room on the first floor before mentioned, these with a large building, the front of which was in Angel Court[2] I took of Mr Parke Junr at the rent of sixty pounds a year – the whole was in very bad condition. Mr Parke paid his

---

* See Appendix [i] at the end of this Chapter: 'The Street Charing Cross.'
[1] This is the sentence Place wrote originally. Later he crossed out and added words to produce this sentence: 'back the premises containing many rooms and a seperate staircase he let them to his waiter with the large and noble cold bath, the hot baths sweating room and other conveniences to his waiter Stephen Tapster, . . . '
[2] Place wrote 'Johnsons Court' above this name.

13   1801–1816

father forty pounds a year and there was an understanding between them, that he was to hold possession or to let them in any way he pleased so he secured the payment of forty pounds a year,[1] he sold prints in the shop. I took the shop and his room on an agreement for seven years. I pulled out the Shop front, closed the doors in front *under* the shop to the vaults and paved the places were there were wooden flaps in the footpath in front of the Shop. I put in a new front as elegant, as the place would permit, each of the panes of glass in the shop front cost me three pounds, and two in the door, four pounds each. the whole of the work as well the front as the fitting up inside was done in fourteen days, the painting &c were finished in two days more and on the 8th of April 1801 exactly two years from the day I first went to Charing cross I opened my new shop,[2] such shop fronts were then uncommon, I think mine were the largest plate glass windows in London if indeed they were not the first. the goods were also of a superior kind and I sold from the windows more goods for about three years than paid journeymens wages and the expenses of housekeeping. This ready money business made it unnecessary for me to borrow money of any body. I expected that it would be so, and I was not mistaken. I calculated every thing as well as I could, and was fully persuaded that the expensive shop front which almost every body thought was extravagant, and some utterly condemned as a proceeding which my circumstances did not justify was the means of at once putting me at ease as to money matters and of greatly increasing my business. My expenses were very heavy fitting up the Shop, cost me nearly three hundred pounds to be paid at the ensuing Christmas. I gave my foreman in money and perquisites full three guineas a week – I engaged a second foreman, an expert Leather Breeches Maker at thirty six shillings a week, and the young man before mentioned as shopman at about twenty two shillings a week, my expenses for assistance and rent were full two pounds a day. There were five large argand lamps[3] in the shop besides candles, to make the windows and every part of it as nearly equally light as possible. I was fully satisfied that display in every way in which it could be made was necessary to enable me to procure as large a share of business as I required. It looked well that there should be several people employed about the shop, and

[1] In the margin, Place's son wrote: 'Initial must be used here some of the family still live – 1873 P jr.'
[2] Responding to Mrs Grote's comments about his memoir, Place recalled that on the day before he opened his shop he 'was miserably poor ... had scarcly any furniture and hardly a change of cloaths' (Add. MS 35144, f. 355).
[3] Oil lamps of great brightness, invented in 1784. They differed from earlier lamps in having two currents of air; the later addition of a glass funnel over the flame increased the brilliance.

The Autobiography of Francis Place

it was to me essential that I should be at liberty to attend to the customers. I was myself no tailor, I could not cut out a coat as it should be cut nor make it up as it should be made up. I never thought it was worth while to learn to do either. I knew I could procure competent persons for these purposes, and that the most profitable part for me to follow was dancing attendance on silly people, to make myself acceptable to coxcombs, to please their whims, to have no opinion of my own, but to take especial care that my customers should be pleased with theirs. It was all matter of taste, that is of folly and caprice. I knew well that to enable me to make money I must consent to submit to much indignity, and insolence, to tyranny and injustice. I had no choice between doing this and being a beggar, and I was resolved not to be a beggar.

Scarcely, any man has any reserve before his barber or his tailor, it is not usual, for a man to practise his customary hypocrisy towards people so far beneath him in his own estimation, such is the opinion of all men, of the barber and the tailor. It is caused by their attendance about the persons of their customers. The best, the mildest, the most considerate men I ever knew, were not altogether free from the practice of this offensive conduct. I have seen men of large and comprehensive understandings, men who made the most acute and accurate observations give in to this very reprehensible conduct to a great extent without ever observing or in the least suspecting they were guilty of it. I never yet knew a man who did not think he was behaving respectfully towards his tailor when his conduct was of a very offensive description. But the general run of men who wear good cloaths would scorn to have it thought, that they could condescend to take any pains about "the fellow;" contumelious behaviour is by such men alone thought the proper treatment for him. The folly and vexation, and passion displayed by men who ought to know better, when from some slight cause not adverted to by themselves, they become agitated it is a very deplorable infirmity, but it is common. When thus excited they exhibit their own superiority over the poor tailor by finding faults where there are none, and by making displays of bad taste and bad humour which would not if related be believed by themselves, and not in many cases even by others as likely to have occurred, but I can imagine nothing except being a footman or a common soldier as more degrading than being either a barber or a tailor.

How often have I felt shame for a man, how often pitied him when he has said and done things in reference to me by which he disgraced himself without ever reflecting on his own folly, meanness, and injustice, and which had I not pretty well understood my self and my position, as well as my customer, would have degraded and humbled me in my own

13 1801–1816

opinion. How often has a fault been found and resentment been shewn merely from a vile habit. How often have I taken away a garment, for a fault which did not exist and which I of course never intended to rectify, how often have I taken back the same garment without its ever having been unfolded, & been commended for the alteration which had not been made, and then been reprehended for not having done what was right at first. How often have I been obliged to take back a garment and sell it to a jew for not much more or any more than one third of its price, because a man or his wife or his mistress disliked it when it was made up, how often on the most trivial, or frivolous pretense been obliged to do the same thing, as for instance because there was one button on the front of a coat or waistcoat more or less than he or she at the moment thought would make the garment more becoming. How often have I done this and on a subsequent order from the same person for a similar garment taken home the rejected one which has been highly approved. How often have I attended at the command of a customer, at a distance of two or three miles on a wet day, been kept waiting in the Hall for half an hour or an hour, and then either been told that the customer had forgotten me, or could not see me, and I must come again at a time named, and when kept by one person so long that I was five minutes beyond the time named been rebuked for negligence by another. In short, a man to be a good tailor, should be either a philosopher or a mean cringing slave whose feelings had never been excited to the pitch of manhood. One or the other he must be, if he start poor, and hope to succeed in making a considerable business. He who is niether the one nor the other, will never be any thing but a little master and will probably die in debt.

I had three things continually in my recollection.

The first and by far the most important was to get money, and yet to avoid entertaining a mercenary money getting spirit, to get money as a means to an end and not for its own sake.

The second was to take care that the contumelious treatment I had to endure should not make me a sneaking wretch from principle to those above me, a tyrant to those below me.

The third was, to beware of presumption, that I did not become arrogant. I had no doubt of success and therefore felt most strongly, the necessity of watching and guarding myself, in the hope that when I had realized as much money as I deemed requisite to a state of independance, my habits and manners should not be such as would exclude me from what is called good society, if at that time I should desire such society, should occasionally be cast into it, or should not exclude me from the acquaintance and even friendship of the better sort of men of genius and talents. These notions which I had early cherished were much strength-

The Autobiography of Francis Place

ened by "Godwin's Inquiry concerning Political Justice," and they tended in no inconsiderable degree to promote my happiness.

I was now in my thirtieth year and looked forward to realize as much as £20.000 by the time I should be forty-five years of age this being the sum and the age which I had predicated as necessary to my becoming independent, the notion of which when expressed had at times caused my wife some annoyance, and induced her to say I was mad in that particular. I thought the road to fortune was now straight before me, My wife could not bring herself to think as I thought. The miseries of poverty had made such an impression upon her, her hopes which had been raised pretty high and had been blasted by the conduct of Wild, had made her apprehensive that she should never long together be free from misfortunes, she always expected some catastrophe, something she used to say would happen to reduce us again to poverty, and her dread of being so reduced has never left her, and probably it never will leave her*

Business increased and I was greatly in debt. The capital embarked consisted of the credit I obtained which at the end of three years was upwards of £7000 yet I never dishonored a bill, nor ever kept any one a single day beyond that on which money was due to him without paying him. The business had increased so fast that I was very early able to charge a good price, and my profits were large. I never lost a minute of time, was never on any occasion diverted from the steady pursuit of my business never spent a single shilling – never once entertained any company, the only things I bought were books, and not many of them. I adhered steadily to the practice I had adopted, and read for two or three hours every night after the business of the day was closed, which never happened till half past nine o clock. I never went to bed till twelve o clock and frequently not till one but I indulged a little in the morning by lying in bed till seven. I had long since obtained the power of abstraction to a considerable extent, could dismiss a train of thought, at pleasure and take up another, could leave any business of any kind, and go to something else without, any reference to the subject I had left and when I had concluded the new thoughts or finished the new business could revert to the old thoughts or the business and take them up again where I had left them. I used wholly to dismiss all thought of business when it was closed for the day, and could therefore go to my book quite unoccupied with any thing else.

I adopted a mode of doing business which differed from the usual practice, which saved time and money and secured a supply of the best articles. It was never to buy any goods in a mans warehouse, nor any

---

* It never did to the day of her death, though it had been so much weakened as not at any time to make her uneasy.

13   1801–1816

where but in my own shop. Mercers and Drapers were willing enough to send goods to me on approbation. They who knew the sort of goods which suited me, were constantly running a race with one another to serve me. I never drove a bargain, this I never could do, and had I attempted to purchase goods in the way others did I should not have bought them so cheaply as I did. My mode was this, to buy of those who charged the lowest price telling them I should shew their bills of parcels, to whoever offered me goods and should give the preference to those who charged the lowest price. When therefore persons came to solicit orders, I shewed them the goods I had, and the invoices, and said beat that and I will give you an order but unless you can serve me better than I am now served, I will not leave those who serve me well. I never would lose my time either in going about to look for goods, or by long conversations with talkative people who came to sell their goods. The competition I encouraged was sure to have the desired effect and I bought at as a low a rate as any one could sell. The only article I did not buy in this way was black superfine cloth. This I had from a manufacturer in Gloucestershire, and for which I always paid ready money, it was of a very superior quality, and was high priced, but it was, as black cloth in particular should be, a very choice article. I could have bought good black cloth in London at a somewhat lower rate, but I could find none which I liked so well, or of which I could be certain of obtaining of the same quality always. My son still deals with the same manufacturer.

I made every one with whom I dealt either send a bill with the goods or make an entry in a memorandum book. At the end of every month an account for the month was delivered, and no orders were given after the third day of the month to any one who had not delivered his account of the preceeding month until it was delivered. These accounts were all pasted into a guard book and indexed. At the end of the year a general bill was also delivered. All these accounts were checked, and the General yearly bill was pasted into the guard book at the end of the monthly bills, and thus all source of dispute was avoided, and during the whole time I was in business I never once had a disputed account. I found that £7700 in credit had saturated the business with capital, and I therefore concluded that I might now safely reduce the length of credit I had hitherto taken; and that I might go on shortening the credit until I could buy for ready money, and when I had accomplished this, I might draw the surplus as it arose, out of the business. It however required nearly ten years to enable me to purchase all I wanted for ready money; that is, I paid every month for the goods I had purchased in the preceeding month, those whom I dealt with preferring to be paid monthly, to being paid for every parcel of goods. My capital therefore at the end of ten years consisted of my book debts, stock in trade and the value of the lease I had taken which was not less than £1500 but I had by this time laid out about £700 on the premises. As I reduced the credit I took I purchased at lower prices and the difference went to profit, after I was able to purchase for ready money it frequently happened that I gained as much by buying as by selling, and thus my profit was sometimes doubled.

[In a letter to Mrs Grote, Place gave a supplementary account of his method of doing business:

'My business was attended to in a way in which no such business had ever before been attended to . . . no one employed by me was permitted to be irregular in any thing. I gave to every one more wages than he asked upon condition that he never asked and never accepted any money or other thing as a present from any one, for any matter which related to the business. Every person from whom I purchased goods was told of the arrangement, and he was desired not to give any thing to any one of my people. That if he did and I found it out I would cease to deal with him, and discharge the man who accepted his present. My people were therefore highly respectable.

'My good able worthy foreman died in my service, leaving me his executor to his property gained in my service. I paid his widow about twenty pounds a year during her life and at her death divided the principal as he had directed among his brothers children. He was the first man I ever employed as a journeyman. The man who succeeded him was the second man I employed, and when I retired from business I left him, with my son. He was carefully taught by my first foreman who when he found he was not likely to live much longer, took pains to provide me a man to fill his place.

'My other managing man was for his station in life a perfect gentleman. He was the most polite and by far the most polished man of a journeyman I ever knew, he was a remarkably discreet conscientious independent man, he was highly respected by every one of my customers who noticed him, they always addressed him as Mr Kingsbury and they paid the same respect to him when speaking to me of him. He was the first acquaintance I made in the trade when I became a journeyman, he was about ten years older than I was. He was the delight of all my children, he loved them and they loved him. He died a batchelor leaving me as his executor to rather more than [£]700 all of which he had accumulated in my service, the money was divided among his relatives.

'The young man who went with me when Wild and I parted was pushed into business by me and has done well for himself and his family

'My shop boys were good boys, most of them left me to better themselves.

'One is a navy surgeon –

'Another has long been steward on a large estate

'Another has long been in business and brought up a family respectably.

'One a very worthy young man died in my service.

'It was well understood that I was never to have to complain of anything twice, and that I never would complain three times.

'I gave unusual indulgences to all my people and did them many important services, but nothing of this kind was allowed to interfere with any matter of business so as to produce irregularity, every thing was made to give way to the

13 1801–1816

business, and no excuse for any thing relating to it was admitted. I did every thing myself that any one else did, even to sweeping the shop and the pavement outside of it. No one therefore ever hesitated to do whatever was required of him.

'I recommended my journeymen to better places and helped several of them to become foremen to other master tailors, I did them other services and the best and steadiest workmen were always desirous to work for me.

'My account books were arranged specially to suit the trade and were regularly entered and posted.

'My customers were looked to with great attention and the debts due to me were regularly and carefully collected. The largest book, *not the thickest*, was my bad debt book, it was ruled in twenty columns intended for as many years. There was a large amount in it when I left business, but I cannot say that I lost a shilling by bad debts. The costs and charges of every kind were accurately made out and apportioned to every garment I made and a per centage was laid on to cover the charges and the loss by bad debts. My losses by bad debts did not amount to the per centage ...

'This may be taken as the history of my life from the time I returned to Charing Cross to the year 1817 it was by far the most quiet period of my life' (Add. MS 35144, fs. 349–51).]

I steadily followed the plan I laid down, and stuck to my business until I found it so firmly rooted that it could not be injured, this I did for about six years when circumstances induced me to interfere with a Westminster Election and this again caused me to become a politician – that is an active interferer with public matters.

I however still continued to act with the utmost reserve towards my customers many of whom were men in the public offices. I never made free in conversation with any of my customers and when any one of them made free with me, I always let it pass by with as little notice as was possible. I wished that none of them should know any thing of me, but as a tailor, for I was well assured that if it became known that I was any thing more than a mere tailor many of my customers would cease to deal with me. This was proved in several instances. When I found myself so circumstanced that I was quite certain of success I ventured again to interfere in matters of a public nature and many circumstances, as will be related under another head, cooperating to that end I in 1807 undertood to manage a Westminster Election for the purpose of returning Sir Francis Burdett to Parliament.[1] I did not intend to be publicly known in

[1] Burdett (1770–1844), a popular independent political figure, having lost £100,000 contesting elections, refused to spend his money on another election. Place, with his fellow electors of Westminster, by electing Burdett managed to break the Tory–Whig 'gentleman's agreement' whereby the two factions shared the seats. Burdett became estranged from Place in 1810 but their acquaintance was resumed in 1819, and when people like John Gale Jones wrote to Burdett for money, he sent the letters on for Place to deal with.

The Autobiography of Francis Place

the matter, but I was, and the consequence was that several customers left me, among them was my Landlord, Thomas Parke, who not only took away his own custom, but induced such of his friends as he had recommended to me to leave me. This was at the time of very little consequence, a little diligence soon replaced them. On another occasion in the year 1812 I lost a pretty large and valuable connection. At this time I had a small room in the second floor uniformly fitted with library shelves, and in it were about a thousand volumes of books. One day when I was from home on business, a customer came to try on a pair of pantaloons, and my foreman, incautiously took him into my room; he expressed much surprize at the number of books, the fitting up, and the library table though there was nothing in the least expensive but it was all neat and in keeping. his remarks were sarcastic and he was evidently displeased,* I waited upon him in a few days when some trifling omission being discovered, he told me, he supposed I was thinking more about my books, than about his orders. He was one of my earliest customers, a good one, he had taken some pains to serve me by recommending his friends to me. From the moment the foreman told me what had passed I saw I should lose him as a customer, and I told the foreman so. The evil was done, and I resolved to try an experiment. I took no notice of his conduct but prodigious pains to please him, that I might the more accurately observe the workings of the evil spirit in him. All would not do he could no longer bear with himself – he could not bear to think of me, my presence was excessively obnoxious to him, he took away his custom, and thus ridded himself of much of the annoyance, but he could not forget me his pride was hurt, and his meanness could only be satiated by doing me injury, and he took away some of the best customers I had. Other somewhat similar instances occurred as some of my customers learned from time to time, that I was a "bookish man", and had made acquaintance with other "bookish men".[1] Had these persons been told that I had never read a book, that I was ignorant of every thing but my business, that I sotted in a public house, they would not have made the

---

* Sep. 1833. This feeling still subsists, and has been exemplified continually in Newspapers and Magazines and especially in Blackwoods Magazine. Last year only the Professor of Morality, in Edinburgh, Wilson – at a large public meeting took occasion to boast that he should not be deterred from his purpose by any man 'no not even by Mr Place the Tailor of Charing Cross" yet we were utter strangers to each other.

[1] 'The prejudice against a man having books was very great. In my own case, even in 1812, I lost as many customers as paid me for the goods they had to the amount of 500*l*. a year, on a gentleman discovering that I had a room full of books. I was so well aware of the feeling, that I suffered no one of my customers to know that I had a book, as far as I could avoid it' (Place's testimony before the Select Committee on Education. *Parliamentary Report . . . on Education*, 1835, p. 69).

13 1801–1816

least objection to me. I should have been a "fellow" beneath them, and they would have patronized me; but, – to accumulate books and to be supposed to know something of their contents, to seek for friends, too, among literary and scientific men, was putting myself on an equality with themselves, if not indeed assuming a superiority; was an abominable offence in a tailor, if not a crime, which deserved punishment, had it been know to all my customers in the few years from 1810 to 1817 – that I had accumulated a considerably library in which I spent all the leisure time I could spare, had the many things I was engaged in during this period, and the men with whom I associated been known, half of them at the least would have left me, and these too by far the most valuable customers individually.[1]

To return. In 1802 Mr Parke Senr. agreed to grant me a lease of the whole of the premises, at a rent of £120 a year and at Midsummer I became his tenant I agreed also to pay to Mr Parke Junr – twenty pounds a year for the remainder of his term. I was very desirous of getting Mr Stevensons Billiard tables out of the house, but as he had waved his preference to the lease in my favour, I could not refuse him an underlease of the upper part of the front house. He soon however shewed a good disposition to accomodate me and in 1803 – he gave up the first floor to me, on my reducing his rent twenty pounds a year, this was very handsome. In 1805. I pulled down the old enormous stack of chimneys which ran up the front house and projected nearly four feet into the rooms and in a very few days built up a new stack with the old materials, Cleared out from the first floor the very old, small pannelled wainscoating, covered the old floor with a new one made a new cieling, put up a small temporary inclosed stair case in the wide passage – made a chimney piece out of the marble slabs of one of the baths now no longer used, made a capital water closet on the first floor, shut out the great stair case with a partician, made a good kitchen of the room which had till now been our bed room and had five rooms on the first floor all modern all neat and good in a very plain stile. I made cloaths for furniture to two very respectable men, my clothes and their furniture being the best that could be made, and like every thing else the furniture was plain and strong. I

---

[1] 'Tradesmen are to a very great extent in the power of the aristocracy and of them who are subservient to the aristocracy and who make a parade of that subserviency by following the example of the titled and the rich, namely in taking away their custom from those who put themselves forward in political matters in opposition to either of the factions... It will be seen when I come to relate the transactions of 1807 1818–1819 and 1820. that so inveterate was the hatred produced by my conduct on the opposers of the people that nearly one and all of my customers left me and that my losses in consequence amounted to many hundreds if not thousands of pounds. April 18. 1826' (Add. MS 27849, fs. 163–4).

The Autobiography of Francis Place

had now as handsome a suite of apartments as a man with moderate views could well desire to have, The only thing not in keeping was the new stair case which was very steep, and too narrow for more than one person to pass up or down.

My old partners brother[1] who was a great rogue as himself had in the year 1803 gone into partnership with another man and had opened a shop two doors below mine as a Cheesmonger. In feb. 1804 this house, was found a[t] about two o clock in the morning, to be on fire, it was soon burnt down as the fire proceeded from the kitchen and apparently from under the staircase, Mr Thomas's my next door neighbour was also burnt down and my house was very much damaged it was saved by almost incredible exertions The party wall was condemned and as the time which would be occupied in taking it down and rebuilding it, would be considerable, and as during this time no use could be made of the Billiard Rooms, I persuaded Mr Stevenson to give up the second floor on my taking off, another twenty pounds a year from his rent, leaving him the third floor at twenty pounds a year. Thus I obtained possession of the second floor which I thoroughly repaired and made modern. I made a new and handsome small staircase from the first to the second floor, and shut out the large stair case from this floor. I planned the stair case and made a working drawing for it. It has been admired by almost every builder and surveyor who has seen it. I had now plenty of room for all my family which consisted of four children. My wife attended assiduously to all her duties in the exemplary manner she had always done, but it had not for some time been at all necessary for her to do the drudgery, and this was a great comfort to me I was as much attached to her, as any man who had any thing good in him must have been to such a woman and her ease and comfort and happiness constituted a very large portion of mine.

I was still very desirous to get the remaining Billiard Table out of the house, not only because it inconvenienced my family by the noise people made in going up and down the large stair case drunk or sober and at all hours of the night, but because I thought it disreputable to have it on the premises. At length in 1812 I gave Mr Stevenson a hundred pounds for his under lease and thus became possessed of the whole of the premises, which from back to front occupied one hundred and forty two feet, and contained upwards of thirty apartments.

Mr Tapster Mr Stevensons waiter became my tenant in 1802 and continued to be my tenant 'till Michaelmas 1810 when he took the Ship Public House nearly opposite to my House at Charing Cross. He was a sober industrious careful man, his wife a careful steady well disposed

[1] Marginal note: 'Gregory Wild.'

13 1801–1816

woman, she looked after the Baths, and kept every thing in the best state such a very old place permitted. They paid me fifty pounds a year, punctually and were excellent tenants. I had no expectation that I should ever again obtain such tenants as they were, but as an opportunity offered of putting them in a way of providing for their family which might never again happen I thought it was my duty to assist them. I therefore advanced the money necessary for Tapster and became his security for six hundred pounds, he conducted the house in the best possible manner, turned out the vagabonds who resorted to it, and made it respectable. On the death of Mr Stevenson some few years afterwards he succeeded him at the Craven Hotel where he is now a flourishing man.* Tapster was not the only person I assisted to get into business as well as in other ways. Some whom I assisted did well and behaved well to me. Some who did well behaved ill towards me Some did ill some turned out bad people and I lost many hundreds of pounds, by them.

I let the Baths to a relative of my wife's who was a waiter at the Salopian Coffee House, he wanted tact and his wife was a daudler. they let the premises go rapidly out of condition and paid me no rent, at the end of three years, they removed and I let them to a man who was noisy troublesom and dirty, he so mismanaged the Baths as to drive away his customers I could obtain very little rent from him, Thus the matter went on until in 1816 I obtained a new and long lease from Mr Thomas Parke who was his fathers successor and I then pulled down the whole of the back premises.

It has happened all my life long, at least from the period when I became a journeyman, that I was continually placed in circumstances which enabled me to do services to others, and I am not aware that I ever refused, at least to endeavour to serve any one who applied to me, to do any thing which an honest man might do. It may appear an odd or an extraordinary matter that at the very poorest of times, when I was utterly unable to serve myself, I was continually serving others. When for instance I was in the deepest poverty in Wych Street, I improved several men in the art of cutting out and preparing leather breeches, and instructed them wholly in cutting out stuff breeches to enable them either to become small masters or foremen, and from this time I was seldom without the case of some to whom I induced others to do service. I had many matters brought to me for adjudication, arbitration or

---

* Mr Tapster like some others to whom I did important service was what is called ungrateful. From the time he took the Craven Hotel he never recommended me a single customer, but he recommended another tailor whom I understood gave him a per centage which he could not ask of me as he knew I never would do any such thing, nor ever would give money to servants, as but too many did.

arrangement, I hardly know the time when for three months together I have been free from this kind of interference.* I have seldom grudged either the time or trouble altho in the settlement of some mens affairs where the conduct of the man has been absurd or where some of the creditors have been more than usually perverse I have had much trouble and consumed much time. I however do not know a single case where a man was willing to give up all the property he had that the creditors did not come to an agreement to discharge the debtors even when his conduct had not by any means been what it ought to have been. I have, as every body else has, heard much of hard hearted and vindictive creditors, but I never met with such an animal. I have seen many who have been very severe and some who have expressed themselves in a way which might be called malignant, and there is often but too much cause given for vindictive feelings, but I never yet found any man who did not at length agree to take what he could get and discharge the debtor. In many cases where no imputation laid against the debtor, I have witnessed the greatest desire to serve him, and several have been kept up, saved from ruin by their creditors and have gone on well again.

I gained much knowledge in many ways and on many subjects by these interferences, for which I never made any charge, unless, the matter related to an association or large body of men, in some such cases I have accepted a sum of money equal to that which the other arbitrators were paid, In three or four instances where the parties were found to be rogues, or where the trouble was occasi[on]ed by bad feelings on both sides I have made charges, as I did not think that rogues and evil disposed persons had any claim on my time because they had misbehaved themselves

My business continually increased till the year 1816 when it reached its maximum the net profits of that year considerably exceeded three thousand pounds.

My eldest children were now grown up or were growing up.† I kept my two eldest daughters at a boarding school until the eldest was twelve and the next ten years of age I then took them home and sent them to a day school in Palace Yard Westminster. I soon found that they were making rapid progress in their own and the french Language and upon

---

* This was written in 1824. since which until my removal from Charing Cross, these matters increased very much upon me. Since my removal in March 1833 I have had two matters to arbitrate and am pledged to undertake another where it is a question of legacies to the amount of some thousands of pounds.

May 1834.

† Elizabeth was 22 years of age
  Annie----- was 20----
  Frank----- was 18. ----
  Mary------ was 12. ----

13 1801–1816

enquiry learned that it was caused by a young lady who was a teacher in the school, a Miss Atkinson. I soon made her acquaintance, and found that she was not conscious of half the merit she possessed but was wasting her time on a miserable salary. With much trouble I succeeded in persuading her to take a house and commence business on her own account. I guaranteed her against loss and undertook to procure her pupils. Not one of those in the school she had left was solicited, yet in a short time she had as many as her house could contain, or she wished to have. Her terms were two guineas a quarter besides extras. Here my two eldest daughters were well grounded in Languages, and then I employed the best masters I could procure as well for book learning as for accomplishments. They were well instructed in French and Italian, Arithmetic Geography – some Astronomy, Algebra Mathematics and History, Needlework of all kinds and the making of their own cloaths.

My wife who had never been regularly taught any thing had wonderfully improved herself in many things, she was not only a capital dress maker and miliner, but she could catch a fashion at a glance and instantly adapt it to any purpose she wished. She was an excellent judge of the value of articles used by females, and she was clever at purchasing. Every thing was bought in the best way and made up at home, the females were therefore enabled to dress well at a comparatively small cost.

My eldest son who had not in any way been neglected, as soon as the General peace was made was placed in the Banking house of Messr Mallett at Paris, here he perfected his knowledge of the French language which he spoke as well as a native, this accomplished I sent him to Dresden where he acquired some knowledge of the German Language and returned home in November 1816. At this period I had nine children living. In the following year my wife had twins two boys these were the last she had, one of them died in infancy leaving me ten children to be maintained and educated.[1]

Appendix i
The Street Charing Cross

The state of London may be somewhat guessed at, by a short discription of the fine open street from the Statue at Charing Cross to the commencement of Parliament Street.

On the eastern side and not far from Northumberland House was

[1] In this year, 1817, Place's son Francis took over the shop and Place retired from business.

The Autobiography of Francis Place

Johnsons Court. There were 13 houses in this court, all in a state of great dilapidation, in every room in every house excepting one only lived one or more common prostitutes of the most wretched discription – such as cannot now be seen in any place. The house excepted was a kind of public house and a Crimping house of the very worst sort.* The place could not be outdone in infamy and indecency by any place in London. The manner in which many of the drunken filthy young prostitutes behaved is not describable nor would it be beleived were it described.†

A little lower down was the long celebrated Brothel the "Rummer Tavern", it was a large back house, now occupied by Mr Clowes as a printing office and there were doors through the walls, at the back part of my house which communicated with the Rummer – They both had signs, and the large iron bolts which held them are still in my house, projecting from the wall. For some years after I took my house there was an immense wooden Rummer[1] some five feet high fixed against the front of the next house, a silversmiths shop, behind which was the Rummer Tavern. Beneath my house were brick steps from the cellar to the street, The cellars to which those steps led were occupied as milk cellars. At the next house No. 17‡ was a small back house, to which access was gained by a very narrow passage – this was a crimping house and low brothel. Behind No 22 – was another such house occupied in the same way. Behind No 28 was another, this was an authorized crimping public house, and had a large union Jack standing out from the house in front. At No 19 – was a barbers shop with a striped Poll in front – below No 30 were some three or four houses with their gable ends towards the street. Their ground floors were about 6 steps below the foot pavement, they were very old and inhabited by very low dirty people

No 24 was a dirty Gin Shop – as was also another house a few doors lower down, those were frequented by prostitutes and Soldiers I can remember the crimping house No 28 being gutted, and a drummer who was active in the Riot being hanged in front of the house in the open

---

* I remember the gutting of this crimping house, a poor young man had been crimped and confined in one of the garretts – Here he fell sick with the small pox and in his delirium, broke the bars of his window ran out upon the top of the house, and along the top of another house, from which he fell naked into the street. A mob collected and destroyed every thing the house contained. This put an end to the trade of crimping there and the house was afterwards occupied like the others.

† There was nothing new in the conduct of the miserable prostitutes in Johnsons Court – Their conduct had been the same for many years and was put up with until the houses were pulled down

‡ Mr Thomas the Butcher who kept No 17 – says that when he first took the house, he has seen as many as 13 Sedan Chairs in the middle of the day belonging to Noblemen and Gentlemen, waiting outside the Rummer for their masters – The arms of the owners were on the chairs and the chaimen wore their liveries.

[1] A drinking glass.

Appendix i: The Street Charing Cross

Street.[1] Scotland Yard where Whitehall Place now stands, was covered in part with old wooden buildings, one of which was used as a kind of barrack or guard house for soldiers. This place was called the Tilt yard. Along the front of Privy Gardens, where there is now an iron railing there was an old wall, against which, early in the morning and late in the evening Saloop[2] was sold, in the day time the wall was covered with ballads and pictures; some of these were such as could not now be exhibited any where. Miserable daubs but subjects of the grossest nature

At night there were a set of prostitutes along this wall, so horridly ragged, dirty and disgusting that I doubt much there are now any such in any part of London. These miserable wretches used to take any customer who would pay them twopence, behind the wall.

On the opposite side of the way was a range of miserable looking low buildings with high tiled roofs – there were goverment offices[3] and reached from Downing Street to the old Treasury. From the place where these ended, along the front of the treasury and the Horse Guards, the Soldiers going on Guard in the morning were shaved, weather permitting – had their heads well greased and flowered – and their pigtails tied. No description can convey to any one the scenes exhibited here. Immediately in front of the Horse Guards, were a range of apple stalls, and at twelve at noon every day two very large stalls were set up for the sale of "Bow Wow pie." This pie was made of meat very highly seasoned. It had a thick crust around the inside and over the very large deep brown pans which held it. A small plate of this pie was sold for three-halfpence, and was usually eaten on the spot, by what sort of people and amidst what sort of language they who have known what low life is may comprehend, but of which they who do not must remain ignorant. It is no exaggeration to say that so excessively gross were the language and manners of soldiers at this time an the horrible women their associates, that when *compared* with them, the soldiers of the *present day* are gentlemen, and the women decent.

The house on the south side of Buckingham Court, now part of the Admiralty – was a public house for the accomodation of soldiers and their women, as was also the Ship a few doors to the Northward – There was a public house of a somewhat better sort next door, on the north side of Drummonds Banking house.

It seems almost incredible that such a street could be in the condition

---

[1] Most of the twenty-one people executed in 1780 for their participation in the Gordon Riots were hanged at the site of their crime.

[2] A hot drink made of powdered salep or sassafras, milk and sugar.

[3] Marginal note: 'Board of Control &c.'

The Autobiography of Francis Place

described, but so it was – people were not then as now offended with grossness – dirtiness – vulgarity – obscenity – and atrocious language.

I can myself remember every fact I have mentioned.

I need hardly notice how highly respectable the street is now

There were several bulks – coblers stalls, here; and a great many such in the Strand.

Appendix ii
Gun Lock Improvement 1804–1807[1]

In the year 1804 I made a considerable improvement in Gun Locks. It was occasioned thus. Two persons, named Tatham and Egg. were in partnership at Charing Cross as Gun Makers. &c. Tatham was a man of the world[2] and like most tradesmen not too scrupulous in the means used to get money, by any means, not *disreputable* among the general run of such men. He was a plausible smooth faced man, very precise, affecting great loyalty and saintship, judging of others, without judgment as loyal saints should always do. Egg was a Gun maker with great pretensions and very little knowledge He was an ignorant german, very narrow minded full of suspicion, and, where he suspected, very malignant. Tatham had been shopman to a Gun maker but was no mechanic. They quarrelled and I was requested to interpose to set matters right between them. I liked neither of them and least of all Egg. They had however a good business, which was likely to be ruined and certain to be injured by thier dissentions. I therefore consented to act as Eggs agent and accountant. Tatham employed a Mr Snow a regular accountant and paid him for his time and trouble. I did Eggs business without pay. Mr Snow and I went on very agreeably during the seven years the partnership continued and from the time when I first interfered in it. We so far reconciled the parties as to enable them to continue their partnership profitably.*

Egg was always "fadding", that is attempting to make improvements, but he was so utterly devoid of science and mechanical genius, that he made blunders only; yet his blunders served him and increased his business, he spoke broken english, was very confident, and had pre-

---
* Egg was a customer of mine before I interfered in his partnership concerns. When this expired Mr Snow and I made up the accounts and divided the property. Egg took a shop at the end of piccadilly and Tichbone Street. I did him some important services, for which he rewarded me as others have done. When he found that he could do with out my aid and was getting money he paid me his long standing account and took away his custom.

[1] This appendix is dated 'Dec 1825 Sep 1833.'

[2] Place's son crossed out the rest of this sentence and marked 'Dele' in the margin.

Appendix ii: Gun lock improvement

sumption and insolence in his manner, which would not have been born for an instant in an englishman, in him it was taken as proof of talent and knowledge, he was continually telling me of his projects and inventions, and I as continually shewing him his folly. At length he pretended to have discovered a method of simplifying the Gun Lock. Upon which I said I could construct a much more simple Gun Lock than he could, and it was agreed that each of us should produce a lock simplified as much as each of us could simplify it. He never produced one I however was resolved to attempt to put into practice some notions I had formed on the subject. As I had no time to spare from my business I employed myself after nine o clock at night in making drawings, and the sundays in filing up modles in wood and pewter, when I had proceeded to a certain extent I was induced to take out a Patent, but by the time the patent was completed, I had still further improved the lock and at length it became the simple strong and safe lock exhibited in the sketches annexed[1]

Fig. 1. Is a lock at half cock. A. the Tumbler. B the Sear. C. the Sear-spring. D the Trigger E the main spring. Two desirable objects are obtained in this lock 1. Great additional strength. 2. perfect security at half cock. The periphery of the tumbler of the half bent is perpendicular to the sear screw, and cannot therefore by any accident or violence be broken, nor can it ever be worn out as it is in common locks, and especially in musket locks.

The tail of the sear rests upon the horizontal part of the trigger and cannot by any force or concussion be detached from the tumbler. The gun cannot therefore be made to go off at half cock. The Sear Spring C. has in proportion to its length scarcly any motion and cannot therefore be broken, its whole motion at the end next to the sear is not more than its own thickness, though it might with safety be moved th[r]ough the space of half an inch In the common lock the bent sear spring is the weakest part of the lock, in this lock it is one of the strongest parts and can never be deranged.

The Bridle is denoted by the dotted line, and is secured in its place by the side screw – the Sear screw – and the trigger screw.

In the common lock the bents in the tumbler are merely notches and are liable to be broken off or worn out, so is the nose of the sear, this is necessary to allow a slight action of the trigger to pull the lock off. In this lock both the bents are deep notches and the sear nose is three times as large as in the common lock. In the common lock the strain of the tumbler on the sear nose is across it and this makes it weak and liable to be broken. In this lock the pressure of the tumbler is perpendicular to

[1] These sketches have disappeared.

The Autobiography of Francis Place

the Sear screw, and cannot break of the sear nose. If the sear could wear at all, it would wear to shape and could never therefore become weak.

The bridle may be dovetailed into the solid piece thus It may be said that in this lock there is but one screw, namely the Sear screw. All locks have a pin for the Triger and a pin would do equally well for this lock, but a screw is a more workman like finish to the lock, and is much stronger than a pin

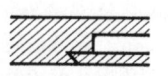

Fig. 2. Is a lock at full cock. The periphery of the Tumbler is as at half cock, perpendicular to the Sear screw. When at full cock the sear nose has been carried further from the center of the tumbler than it was at half cock, and the tail of the sear has been carried beyond the horizontal part of the trigger. The trigger being now pulled it will draw the sear away from the tumbler and the lock will go off. The action may be made as fine as a hair trigger simply by the form of the angle of the trigger. It may by the same means be made as palpable as may be desired for the coarse hand of the common soldier.

The lock is not more simple than it is safe; yet it would not be an easy matter for any one to concieve the trouble and difficulty I had to get a lock made It put the workmen out of their usual mode of working It was the invention of a person who had no sort [of] business to interfere with their trade, and they would not make it. I was not however to be put from my purpose, so I got the plate of a lock rough filed by a man who was a government lock contractor in East Smithfield – I marked the holes in it, got them tapped and the screws made. I got, the sear, the sear spring the tumbler and the trigger forged, and on the following sunday morning I went to the mans shop very early, and filed them up myself. I paid no regard to finishing but I fitted the parts accurately. The men were now ashamed and one of them immediately made me a couple of excellent locks, of the common size of a musket lock I had them put on two pieces of walnut tree wood abut a foot long made of the form and size of that part of the stock of a musket on which the lock is placed, and had the wood cut away so that the action of the lock could be seen I then shewed one of them to Capt Drewry a very respectable man, who had the management of the Artillery Office at Messr Cox and Greenwoods the Army Agents. He at once expressed his admiration of the lock and promised to mention it to some of the best informed officers of the Artillery and Engineers. He did so – and in a few days a tall good looking swaggering soldier like gentleman marched into the shop and seating himself on the end of the counter, with an air of supercilious dignity said to me. "Oh you have improved the musket Lock, so Mr Drewry tells me? *A* Yes I have made a very simple lock which is secure at half cock.

Appendix ii: Gun lock improvement

Q. Eh! have you made it of cloth.? *A.* yes. and that's more than you could do. Q Well then let me see it? *A* yes, if you will tell me who you are? Q. Why then my name is Bloomfield. Q the son of ⟨Colonel⟩ Bloomfield? *A* Yes. Well then I am glad to see you for as your father is a scientific man and has busied himself in such matters, I shall also conclude that his son is a clever fellow and understands a gun lock when he sees one.["] I then gave him the lock, he took in both his hands and instanly sprang off the counter, exclaiming "By God, here it is, done by a tailor, my father and I have all our lives long been trying at it, and have failed and now it is done by a tailor." We were now pretty well on a level and very sociable. He asked me if I would meet him and some other persons at an hotel in Albemarle Street in the afternoon I said I would and I did meet Major, now Sir Benjamin Bloomfield. Colonel Hadden the Surveyor General to the Ordnance Mr Drewry and two other gentlemen. They all examined the lock and all praised it, at length Bloomfield wrote a note as follows,

> Dear Congreve
> Examine this lock and pass sentence upon it.
> Yours &c &c
> B. Bloomfield

I took the note and saw Mr. now Sir William Congreve at his Chambers in the Temple.[1] He examind the lock took it to pieces and put it together again, with a little instrument I had made for that purpose, he was very much pleased and shewed me a small and curious instrument he had made for projecting straight lines either perpendicular, to any baseline, or as radii from any center. He then gave me a note to Major Bloomfield with these words written in it. "The lock is invaluable."

In a few days I received a note requesting me to attend at the Ordnance Office I there saw Colonel Hadden who appeared to me to be, and was a very clever man, and a man of business. I left one of the locks with him, and attended by order several times. After some time consumed in this way I was requested to attend at the Master Generals, Lord Moiras, house. Here I met Colonel Hadden Lord Moira, the Duke of Gloucester and several other persons. The lock was examined I was questioned and much commended and directed to call on the superintendant at the Tower. This superintendant whose name was Noble was a Gun Maker, and a clever man, he had orders he said to make any thing for me I might

[1] Congreve, the first inventor to suggest armour-plate for warships, had recently developed rockets. Congreve's new rockets, which enabled the British to capture and burn Washington, D.C., in 1812, are celebrated in the national anthem of the U.S.A.

wish, and also to make some muskets with the new lock to them, if I had no objection to his doing so, these muskets were to be sent to several regiments to be used and reported on. I did not object to his making as many as he pleased for experiments I requested him to make one for me and to stock it with a short barrel. He accordingly made one for me, and I believe some for experiment. He told me after he had made mine that he could make tools with which children could make such locks as mine as they were so very simple. These transactions took up much time and as I had my own business to attend to I paid but little attention to the Gun Lock. After a time Colonel Hadden called upon me and asked me to go with him to the Tower, here I found Lord Moira and several other persons all seated behing a large table. The superintendant and several of his working Gunsmiths were called in, the locks made by them were produced and I was desired to point out the advantages they possessed I said it was what such a piece of mechanism should be – safe at half cock, simple and cheap, and that was praise enough, and all that need be said unless some of the workmen could shew the contrary in some particular. They were questioned, and all said they had no fault whatever to find in it, and when further questioned they confirmed all I had said. These were judicious proceedings I was again and again requested to attend at the Ordnance office in Pall Mall and was more than once offered a large contract for muskets. This I refused saying I did not wish to embark in any new business being well off in my own and having as much on my hands as I could attend to, and I thought it would be much more advantageous to Government to give me a sum of money and have the muskets made at their own manufactory and by their old contractors, especially as they were now making more than a thousand muskets a week in their own shops in the Tower. That I was neither a greedy nor a needy man, and would be contented with any sum a fair man of their own chusing should say was a reasonable compensation. I then gave Colonel Hadden two offers of contracts, from Gun Makers who were making locks for Government, to make my locks one at fourteen and the other at sixteen pence per lock under the contract price at which they were then making Government locks Colonel Hadden said the matter was of considerable importance and should be attended to. Time passed, on, I had several interviews with Coln Hadden but nothing was definitevely settled. At length Colonel Hadden said he was authorized by the Board of Ordnance to settle with me the compensation I was to recieve and he requested me to name a sum. This I declined, saying I should not dispute about the sum, but would take whatever the board thought would be a fair remuneration, that putting the value of the improvement out of the question, the saving in the expense of manufacturing would exceed six

Appendix ii: Gun lock improvement

thousand pounds a year, and might probably be eight thousand pounds a year. but I was not going to drive a bargain. Colonel Hadden was pleased paid me some compliments for the manner in which I had behaved, and said I should hear from him again, and I did. Colonel Hadden after some time sent for me, and named Mr George Ridge the Banker at Charing Cross, an ingenious mechanic himself, as the person who should name the sum I ought to receive to this I at once assented. Mr Ridge had from the first been well acquainted with the project and process of the lock. He came to me and said actual compensation was out of the question since I should obtain nothing like it, that three years savings ought to be given to me, but he thought if I would consent to receive Ten Thousand Pounds I should get that sum without any difficulty. I said I was willing to take that sum and should be satisfied, but that as a good deal of time had been consumed and I had had much trouble I hoped there would be no further delay. In a few days I was again sent for by Colonel Hadden who told me I was to have the sum named by Mr Ridge.

I was then told to come on the following monday when I should be introduced to the Board, and the matter would be settled. I had never yet been before the Board nor had any communication been made to me in writing. I believe however that every thing was fair and honorable, and that the long delay was merely the ordinary way of doing business by the Board. The monday on which I was to attend was the 27th of April 1807. but on the sunday preceeding it Mr Powell Mr James Paulls attorney called on me and said Parliament would be dissolved the next day.

I kept my appointment at the Ordnance Office but could not obtain an audience, the parliament was about to be dissolved, the Whigs were to be turned out of Office and Lord Moira was to be displaced from his office of Master General of the Ordnance.[1]

The Westminster Election of May followed in which I took an active part. When the elections were all over and the new Ministry were comfortably seated in office. Lord Chatham as Master General I renewed my application I was respectfully attended to and an appointment was made The appointment was made for twelve at noon I attended and waited till the Office closed at four o clock, and was then told the Master would not come, the appointment was renewed three several times. and three times did I attend and was dismissed after several hours waiting in like manner as at first. I was told that the Master was a lazy negligent fellow, who would neither get out of bed nor attend to his business in any way, and

[1] Moira held various important appointments in England between 1783 and 1813, when he became governor-general of India and commander-in-chief of the forces in India.

that he signed papers in bed. I could not however understand why his presence was necessary to any arrangements with me as the other business of the Office was done without him, so I wrote a letter stating my attendances, shewing that the matter was of more importance to the Board and to the public than to me individually, and that unless I received an appointment to attend for a specific purpose I should not again be seen at the office. No notice to me was taken of the letter and there the affair ended.

I have since learned that during the next ten years the number of muskets, carbines and pistols, made was so large that upwards of £100.000 would have been saved by the adoption of my lock.

I never made a single shilling by the lock.

Appendix iii
John King[1]

Among the persons with whom living with Ashley brought me acquainted was John – alias the notorious and infamous Jew King[2] – he had for some time been making friends among the reformers, and particularly of the Leading Members of the London Corresponding Society. Of Ashley and Hardy he bought boots and shoes of Richard Hodgson hats. I sometimes made an article for some of his livery servants, other members of the Society were employed by him in the same way, and with each of us he used to converse at our shop or lodgings. I knew a great deal of him and his proceedings as well privately as publicly, as in courts of law. I disliked him much and always suspected that he contemplated some iniquity. Some thought he meant honestly, some though[t] he was a Spy. Ashley Coln Despard and myself thought his object was to take advantage of any circumstance and especially of any commotion caused by an invasion or an attempt at invasion to enrich himself.

The alarm of invasion had become pretty general and was kept up by the Government. King was assiduous in persuading people to arm themselves, to be able as he said to repel invasion and assist the civil power in London should the army and volunteers be called to the coast. To some who wished for invasion or any thing else by which confusion might be brought about, King held a different kind of language, he pursuaded several to purchase pikes, and to keep them openly, that is hung across

[1] Next to this name Place's son pencilled in large letters 'Dele'; and beneath it he wrote 'Not to be printed.' Below that, in what appears to be the same handwriting is pencilled 'I agree to this – .'
[2] In the margin Place dated this acquaintance '1796–7.'

Appendix iii: John King

their apartments so as to be seen by all who entered and to learn the use of them. I saw several, they were eight or nine feet long, and they were in the possession of those who were not members of any political society as well as of some who were members. King meant to turn these people to account in some way if he could. He thought there would be an invasion that the Government would be broken up and that he should be able to have considerable influence and power which he intended to use for his own purposes. He endeavoured all he could to make people pleased with him and to rely upon him, he practised all sorts of tricks to accomplish this purpose, among others he invited them to his house in small numbers classing them according to his own notion as each might appear likely to be useful to him. I with much reluctance attended one of his dinners at a house near Manchester Square. John Ashley Richard Hodgson, Alexander Galloway and two or three others were of the party. He gave us a sumptuous dinner of three courses and a dessert all served on plate, the table was attended by men in livery and one in plain cloaths. This disgusted me utterly and when after dinner King dilated on the probability of an invasion and a revolution and the great advantages these would produce to the country, I told him I did not believe there was any probability of either invasion or revolution, but that if either was likely to occur I should be exceedingly suspicious of him. This led to a fierce dispute with Hodgson whose opinion differed from mine, and who was willing to give King crdit for honest opinions and good intentions. King reasoned the matter calmly and justified himself as well as he could. I told him I knew a great deal of his history was well acquainted with his practices and could have no confidence in him. He admitted that he might have done wrong, but not to a hundredth part of that which had been scandalously imputed to him, that he had done much good which greatly overbalancd all the evil which could have resulted from his mistakes. I denied the statement and the inference and contended that the balance was on the other side. King insisted that I was mistaken and had been grossly imposed upon, and added that even if what I said was true still he was entitled to crdit since it was evident, if he had ever been so bad as I was willing to believe he had been, he was now at any rate a reformed man. As such even it was hardly fair to charge him with dispositions he certainly had not and acts which he did not commit. Suppose said he a woman had once in very uncommon circumstances committed a faux pas but had been reclaimed and led an irreproachable, aye an exemplary life, would you point her out, and call her whore, would that be acting either wisely or justly, and does not this even on your own shewing apply to me." I said well be it so, time will shew and if at the end of two or three years you shall appear to me to be what you say you are, I shall then entertain the opinion of you which you will deserve. Here the matter ended and here my acquaintance with King ended. My companions were somewhat offended with me, and especially Hodgson, they objected to my telling a man at his own table to which I had been invited, such matters as I had told King. I said I would not submit to be so egregiously imposed upon as King intended to impose upon me neither would I leave him to suppose I had been imposed upon, and that I should not have been there at all but for the persuasions of Ashley and Hodgson

King had three illegitimate sons, two of them were all but men the third was some years younger, the eldest was named George and was the only one with whom I was acquainted though I knew the two others. The second son had been or was a Midshipman, his father used to keep him without money and he pawned some of his fathers plate. This was known to us and King had been adverting to it, he said that his son had shewn signs of contrition, but he had replied. I shall not take your word, but will judge of you by your conduct and if at the end of a year or two I find you are changed I shall believe so.

King's house was a large one, he had several servants in livery, two not in livery one whom he called his steward, he kept a coach, a curricle and a gig, and yet he had nothing at this time, but what he got by his wits.

He was an atrocious villain. If a circumstantial accont of his conduct were written it would not, as it could not be credited. It could not be believed that any man would ever have attempt to do many things which he did, without incurring punishments which would put it out of his power to commit other offences. It would not be believed that people could be found who were so foolish as to be imposed upon and robbed to the extent they were robbed by King, much less would it be believed that such persons abounded to the extent his practice shewed they did. It would not be believed that people when robbed as he robbed them would put up with it, as numbers of persons did. It would not be believed that any man could have turned the laws to his purpose as he did. Neither would it be belived that he could command the grossest perjuries to be committed for years as he did without ever having been caught in his own trap. Least of all that the way he was spoken of by counsel in the Law Courts, and by Judges on the Bench, by the newspapers and by special publications, should have apparently, if really have done him no harm, or at all impeded his practises or warned fools against his roguery.

King seems to have calculated on three things. 1 – the fear. 2. the cupidity. 3. the folly of mankind or at least of a sufficient number to answer his purposes. His business was fool catching he knew that many were fools from cowardice, and that most cowards could be made fools,

Appendix iii: John King

that such persons were very generally rogues or capable of being made rogues even to the cheating of themselves, and he acted accordingly. He was a man of uncommon sagacity with respect to other mens understandings and leanings, and no one ever knew better how to lead them than he did, when once they could be brought to repose any the smallest portion of confidence in him, and thus it was he deluded and cheated such vast numbers of persons out of their property.

His son the Midshipman being pushed to extremities shot himself at a window in a house opposite to the back of his fathers house at the moment he had attracted his attention to him. So the eldest son told me.

When George came of age he had no business or profession he could follow, his father employed him in various nefarious ways, but paid him badly. This he did not like so he revolted, his father then caused him to be arrested for a debt he said he owed him. He was however released and put on board a ship bound for Jamaica, then – as his father told him to fill a situation of profit which he had provided for him. When however he was clear of the coast he found he had been tricked, he was turned among the sailors and fared as they fared, he was landed in Jamaica with very few cloaths very little money and no friends. Here he suffered greatly, and at length worked his way home as a sailor. He came to me at Charing Cross in a miserable plight, and exceedingly unwell. I gave him some money and heard no more of him for some months, when one day he came to my shop, well dressed, and in good health. The first words he said were these. "I am going to damn my soul for that old rascal my father." He then told me that soon after I gave him the money he was again arrested for debt by his father, that he was in poverty and misery so he made his submission to his father who supplied him with cloaths and money and employed him in various ways, – "in all manner of rascally things" – and now said he I am on my way to the Court of Kings Bench to swear to a mans writing, whom I never saw write, and whose writing I never saw till last night,[1] As no one suspects this will be done by me, and as I know the man, it is concluded that no one will be prepared to question me, my story is very short and I am not to deviate from it on any account. I saw him afterwards when he told me he had proved the hand writing and had not been questioned at all. He continued with his father some time, then left him and became a perfect vagabond. The last time I saw him was in 1819. he had just returned from Brussels in good plight. I asked him how he lived, and he said he could not tell how, but that he contrived to live pretty well

King is I believe living in Splendour at Paris – he is now a very old man.[2]

[1] At this point in the text there is an erasure of about two inches, possibly the victim's name. [2] At the end of this appendix is the date 'October. 1824.'

CHAPTER 14[1]

NO. 1.[2] CAMPBELLS LETTER TO BROUGHAM

Early in the month of february 1825. Mr Thomas Campbell wrote a letter to Mr Brougham recommending an University to be established in London; This had been a favourite project of Mr Campbells for some three or four years and we had frequently conversed together on the subject. Campbells letter to Brougham appeared in the Times Newspaper on the 9th of february and in it were the following words in allusion to me.

"There is such a thing as wealthy ignorance in London, which cares not for being laughed at. The sum of this ignorance, or, rather of uneducated talents may be greatly exaggerated by ridicule, but why should it exist at all. There are prejudices, too (be it spoken without offence) against a man of business amusing himself with literature and science. As an instance which falsifies this prejudice, I wish I could name without appearing to be personal and indelicate, an individual known to us both, who is on many subjects one of the best informed men in the kingdom. That highly respectable man rose to his present independence by sheer industry. He wrought many a year as a journeyman workman, – struggled with many difficulties, and had a numerous family. yet amidst all his difficulties, he educated his children well, and taught himself several sciences and languages. He has now retired from business with a competent fortune, sits in a library of his own purchasing that contains many thousand volumes, and is devoting the remainder of his life to his favourite studies. That highly laudable person, and others who could be mentioned, shew that a man may rise to fortune even amidst unintellectual pursuits; but how few men of business have really been, or are likely ever to be ruined by study; and how many have been made bankrupts by habits which reading and study would tend to avert."

This induced me on the next day the 10 feb to write as follows. Mr friend Campbell in his letter to Brougham has suffered his partiality to lead him into error.

I do not know several languages, nor indeed any one language to which the word *know* can be properly applied. I regret I do not, I have often felt the inconvenience which has resulted from my ignorance in this

---
[1] Chapter 14 is not a continuous narrative like the previous chapters. It consists of a series of documents (some unrelated to each other), composed over a period of twenty years, dealing with Place's personal life. See above pp. xxviii–xxix.
[2] This document is dated 'Feby. 1825. Aprl. 1835.'

240

14.1 Campbell's letter to Brougham, 1825

as well as in other matters. It was not possible for me to learn languages *accurately* until the time came when I was able to leave my business intirely, and then at my age, nearly fifty, it seemed to me that systematically to learn languages would consume more time than the knowledge I should acquire would be worth. I then thought I still think, that *accurately* to learn languages is of less value to me, and less likely to be useful to others, than those matters in which I have been and am still likely to be engaged. Thus it was, and thus it is; all I desired, all I still desire to attain can not be attained, and the learning of languages has not therefore been systematically pursued. Besides what I know of the English Language, and from some etymological reading which has been less useful to me than it would have been, had I been a scholar, I can not be said to have any knowledge of Languages.

I can read and translate french as I read it with ease, but I can not speak the language so as to maintain a conversation. I can read law latin, and law french, sufficiently well for any purpose I can desire, and can understand enough of saxon for my own use, but I cannot read any latin classic, my knowledge of the latin grammar is very imperfect, while of the Greek grammar and Language I know nothing. Of the Italian language I am but indifferently acquainted with the grammar, and not much better with reading in that language. I have looked enough at the Grammar of the German Language and conversed enough on the subject with well educated Germans to ascertain the difficulties of attaining a competent knowledge of that Language, and these have deterred me from attempting to acquire that knowledge, though I have several times made a feeble attempt, and more than once all but determined to accomplish it, but other matters have determined me to pursue a contrary cource.

Of science – I really know very little.

1. Chemistry. I know as much as is necessary to keep me from committing gross errors – I have read a good deal – talked a good deal, and seen and assisted at some experiments. This can not be called understanding chemistry.

2. Geology – my knowledge of this science is very general and superficial. (1838 I have since 1825, attended a good deal to this science

[3. Omitted]

4 – Natural history the same – Botany much less, or rather none at all.

5. Mathematics, here again my knowledge is very limited, I know some little of Trigonometry – and Conic Sections. – These after I had plodded hard at Euclids elements, have never appeared to me to be difficult subjects. I have gone on with them, as far as I have gone and also with algebra without much difficulty – and think I could make any *requisite* progress rapidly.

The Autobiography of Francis Place

6 Machinery – I have a competent share of knowledge of the construction and uses of machinery, and have assisted in simplifying more than one complicated machine. I was always delighted to be among machinery. Have had an extensive acquaintance with some of our principal London Engineers and been freely admitted at all times into their factories. I have also had a rather large acquaintance with other ingenious mechanical men as well practical as scientific. – Of the art of ship building and rigging I have as much information as can ever be necessary for me to possess – From mere childhood this has been a favourite subject of enquiry.

7 Law. This has never with me been – "a dry subject." I have read much for an "unlearned" man, conversed much with "learned men", and attorneys. and have a competent share of information, on this subject especially as I think – in relation to more ancient english law – and parliaments.

8 I have taken every opportunity I could to obtain information respecting Jurisprudence, I have pursued it as far as I could, it was for this and for the knowledge I desired to have of Law that I learned the law languages of former times.

9. Political Economy. I read Adam Smith when I was very young and more than once afterwards, the whole of his Wealth of Nations – and made notes which have not been preserved. Since 1817 this subject has engaged much of my attention. My acquaintance with Mr Ricardo and the discussions we had previous to his publishing his work[1] convinced me that I had a great deal to learn. I believe that I now understand as much of this 'sciencee' as almost any one. Under this head I include Population and Taxation.

10 Metaphysics, was for some years my most important study, other subjects were read of and thought of in a more desultory way, but this was studied as assiduously as my avocations permitted. I attribute much of the knowledge and utility I possess to this science. It has taught me nearly all the knowledge I have of myself. It has caused me to question myself, at times to subject myself to a rigid examination, I think I can trace conclusions to their premises with considerable approximations to impartiality and sometimes to see pretty clearly the consequences likely to result from certain causes, more accurately and to a much greater extent than I should otherwise have been able. It has enabled me to understand the reasoning powers of other men, to see their limits and thus to avoid on the one hand the waste of time, and on the other hand to obtain all sorts of information to the greatest extent of

[1] David Ricardo's *Principles of Political Economy and Taxation* was published in 1817.

14.1 Campbell's letter to Brougham, 1825

their knowledge. It has greatly influenced my conduct and made me both a more useful and a better man than I could have been had I remained in ignorance of those things which such a course of study supplies. It has made me understand my own ignorance by enabling me to understand more correctly the actual boundaries of knowledge, and kept me from wasting my time in speculative enquires where nothing could be learned. Many years since it put me at ease on subjects which annoy and distress, and corrupt and destroy mankind – the vain enquiries engendered in the imagination and then reasoned upon and acted upon as realities. It has I think enabled me to understand the true doctrine of motives, a matter of very great importance which few clearly comprehend.

11. I have been and am now somewhat intimately acquainted with several painters three of them eminent men, and have known two or three sculptors and several architects. I have sat for characters and gathered whatever information I could. I can model a head indifferently, can sketch a simple object, and know the outlines of perspective. These were matters among others which occupied my attention when my children began to require instruction that I might to some extent be capable of estimating their progress.

12. Astronomy as I science I know nothing – I however understand as much of popular astronomy as most men who have not pursued it as a science.

13. Geography. I have a very competent knowledge of geography, I was early taught to desire information on this subject, and have all along attended to it – have read much on the subjects worked many problems, and read a large portion of voyages and travels. Have conversed much with well travelled men, some of whom have imparted to me more knowledge than they themselves were aware they possessed. I think I am pretty well acquainted with the positions and forms, climates, dresses, manners religions, &c of most nations and people.

It is inconceivable to those who have not by practice ascertained the fact, how much on this and on other subjects they may gain from ignorant people, and how easy it may become in most cases to detect false accounts intended to impose upon and decieve the auditor. If a man will patitently hear the relater, and not interrupt him, and then put questions respecting particulars, thanking or praising the relater for any real information he may communicate, he will assuredly obtain all the information which can be obtained and as surely detect, any attempt at imposition. I have pushed some enquiries to a great extent in this way on subjects I did not well understand, with all sorts of people, both will and ill informed, have used the information as I obtained it to elicit more and have acquired, by this mode, much valuable instruction.

14 Phisiology. I know as much respecting the sciences which may be classed under this head as can be necessary to be known by a non professional man. I have read and studied several systems of Anatomy – have visited museums – attended at dessecting rooms and heard some anatomical lectures, and have etched with a pen, not very correctly, all the bones in the human body – and some of the muscles.

This is I believe a fair, and as clear as I can make it, account of what I do and what I do not know, in Arts and Sciences, and Languages. Others there are who know better than I do the amount of my acquirements and of my ignorance, but among these assuredly must not be classed my excellent friend Thomas Campbell.

The subject on which without pretension I have prided myself most, is the power I have possessed of influencing or governing other men individually and in bodies. I am sure I may say truly, by honest means, and for what at the time always appeared to me to be useful purposes. This has always been to me, a test of the information I had acquired, and had I not succeeded as I have done, I should have been disappointed and turned back to enquire why I had failed. I have never interfered in any way, in any one single instance out of my business for the purpose of any personal advantage whatever except intellectual advancement. In all public matters in which I have been engaged, I have either been *the* leader or one of the leaders, and I am not aware of any one instance in which I did not obtain as much, and in some instances considerably more credit than was due to me.

In the numerous cases in which I have interfered in the concerns of others, I have never in a single instance done any one act with a view, as I might have done, and as many others did, to promote any purpose of my own, either as to present emolument. or what is called getting on in life.

Like other persons I have generally had to do with the common run of men, but even when acting with more enlightened men, who better understood the reasons for their own actions, I have, I think I may fairly say, found myself leading – and not following. Though I have followed many individuals, most cheerfully and lea[r]nt much from them. In many difficult, cases, some of much importance I have after a while found myself treated with marked respect, and sometimes by those who at first were disposed to think contemptuously of *the tailor*. I have often thought that I merited the distinction, since whenever circumstances have increased in difficulty, and become also disagreeable, I have taken upon myself as far as I could whatever was most difficult and most disagreeable. I have never shrunk from any fair share of responsibility and have sometimes taken the whole upon me, and I have almost always succeeded in my undertakings. I never put forward any claim to merit,

14.1 Campbell's letter to Brougham, 1825

and yet I have been judged of in a way which I know was far above my due. Circumstances have at times occurred which have induced people to give me so much more credit than I deserve that I have felt excessively ashamed.

I have however had enemies; almost all of them have been men to whom I had done services or on whom I had conferred favours. There is hardly a crime of which I have not been accused – of this some proof has been given in the account of the West London Lancasterian Schools – in the British and Foreign School Society – And in the account of the inquest on Sellis.[1] Others will be noticed. These however never did me any harm, but some good as they enabled me to appreciate my own weaknesses. I have to be sure been pretty well black-guarded, by some of the miscreants of the press, but this vulgar abuse is what every man who endeavours to make himself publicly useful ought to expect and to disregard.

[When Place, in his only published book, *Illustrations and Proofs of the Principle of Population*, recommended contraception as a means of controlling population, he was accused of immorality. Perhaps the most offensive of the attacks on Place for his stand on contraception was that in *The Bull Dog*, a short-lived satirical magazine. Its 'Letters to Notorious People. No. 3, To Mr. Francis Place,' contained expressions like this: 'I have perused your soul polluting pages . . . you and your catamite gang . . . You, Francis Place the elder, of Charing Cross, are the author of the following most foul and devilish attempt, at corrupting the youth of both sexes in this country; an attempt at no less than making *catamites* of the male portion of the youth, and of the females, *prostitutes*. . . You, Sir, are an old man, a nasty old man . . . Your offence is aggravated by the fact, that had not the very aristocracy, whose assassination you are attempting to cause, having allowed you to build their breeches and waistcoats, you would at this moment be the inmate of a workhouse' (September 9, 1826, pp. 85–7).

[1] The most persistent of the accusations against Place was the charge that he was in the pay of government. In 1810 Place was foreman of a jury investigating the death of Joseph Sellis, valet to the most unpopular of the king's sons, the Duke of Cumberland. The rumour that the Duke had murdered his valet was contradicted by the jury's verdict of suicide. Two days after this verdict, Place wrote, 'Colonel Wardle called upon me. He said every body was dissatisfied with the Verdict and that Sir Francis Burdett was among the number. That it was reported, I was in the pay of Government and had procured the verdict improperly' (Add. MS 35144, f. 21). Burdett, who was then in the Tower, became convinced that Place's treachery had brought him there. He nurtured this notion, and in 1814 demanded that Place be expelled from the West London Lancastrian Association (a group supporting education for the poor) on the ground that Place was a government spy. Believing that he could no longer be useful in the Association, Place resigned (Wallas, pp. 54–5, 107–8). In his *Memoirs* Henry Hunt repeated the insinuation that Place was bribed for his verdict at the Sellis inquest: 'It is said that, since that period, Mr Place has been a very *rich man*; but that, before that time, he was a *poor, very poor Democrat*' (1820, II, 424).

The Autobiography of Francis Place

In the same year, 1826, the *European Magazine,* in a character-study of Place, described him as the fountain of the philosophy of Bentham, Mill, Birkbeck, etc., and after quoting Burns's 'A man's a man for a that' continued, 'so say we of Mr. *Place*; for whether it be sung or said, spouted or written, the mere vomitory from which it proceeds has no more influence upon the thing itself, than the brazen stop-cock used in drawing it has upon the wine in the cask' (n.s. II, 231–2).

At a later period *Fraser's Magazine* employed the same kind of attack: 'This hero was found, we believe, in a dust-pan, upon the steps of a house in St. James's Place, about sixty years back, by an honest Charlie, who forthwith conveyed him to the next workhouse, where (for these were unenlightened times) the little stranger was kindly taken care of' (XIII (1836), 427).]

Had I been disposed to turn my opportunities and my influence to account in the way most men do, I might have accumulated a considerable fortune. I could have increased the value of my estate to at the least double what it was, I might have been worth £40.000, but respect for myself and the hope of operating beneficially on my family instead of accumulating money to make them neither gentlefolks nor tradespeople, were with me more powerful persuasions than mere wealth.

In one respect I do not think I have been overrated and that is in a character for decision and acting up to that decision which with a small portion of judgment is of more importance in the active concerns of life than almost any other single acquirement. Few decide at the right moment, and still fewer act promptly and effectually on their decisions. Thus it is that matters of the greatest as well as the smallest moment linger on, or are altogether neglected. Thus it is that the affairs of the world move on slowly when they ought to move rapidly, and mankind comparatively ignorant and unhappy when wisdom and happiness ought to prevail.

All overestimates of individuals, are however dangerous and frequently pernicious, as they produce conceit and pride of which I have often discover I had[1] a pretty large share. How far I have been able to control these propensities, has no doubt been decided by the few really wise men whom it has been my happiness to have as friends. What they think of me I can only conjecture from their conduct on ordinary and extraordinary circumstances.

Some circumstances as marking the opinions of others on this subject are rather curious examples, more particularly those which arise from my having been a *tailor* and still living at the *tailors* shop.[2] This is a mark

[1] Snarled verb phrase because Place emended his fair copy which read, 'I often discover I have ...'
[2] When Place was depicted in satiric cartoons, it was usually as a tailor. One such cartoon, in *The Bull Dog*, shows Place holding a long pair of shears and is titled 'Viscount Snip and Baron Bodkin, of Charing Cross Place.'

14.1 Campbell's letter to Brougham, 1825

not easily to be obliterated. A man with not half my imputed knowledge, or a tithe of my independence. who was able to make a decent personal appearance, had never followed any sort of business, or been in any way useful, would be invited to rich mens tables and exhibited as a very useful and extraordinary person. I know several such. But! the *Tailor!* spoils all. I have often been asked where my country house was. Mr Place of Norwood, or Hampstead, or Stamford Hill might on some occasions be endurable – he might be almost forgotten as the '*tailoring creature*'. But I have no country house, and never shall have a country house nor any other probably than that at Charing Cross. '*Tailoring creature*' I shall probably remain to the end of the Chapter.

The various public political and Parliamentary matters in which I have interfered have brought me acquainted with many great men, and caused me to be most graciously invited to call upon some of them. This I have never done, unless something which related to others made it necessary, and this happened very seldom It was a rule with me from the first never to call on any great man in any other case, and I do not believe I have seen so many as half a dozen Lords and Commoners at their own houses, excepting Burdett – Hobhouse and Hume,[1] and not even either of them unless on business. To all invitations I have replied, that I was at home till eleven o clock in the morning, and after four o clock in the afternoon, was always ready to attend to any suggestion, and to cooperate in any project which was likely to be useful and especially if it related to the working people. With those public men who called I always communicated freely. Several have expressed a desire to become better acquainted with me, but this I always declined as our circumstances and habits of life differed greatly and I could not consent to be patronized, or to be a "humble friend". To come when I was sent for and to go when my presence was not quite agreeable, and to take care not to be in the way when other great men or women were there. To those who wished to be better acquainted, I said you can be as much

[1] John Cam Hobhouse, Baron Broughton (1786–1869), a friend of Burdett (and of Lord Byron) ran for Parliament as a reform candidate from Westminster – unsuccessfully in 1819, successfully in 1820.
  Joseph Hume (1777–1855), M.P., first voted as a Tory, but was converted to radicalism by James Mill, a former schoolmate. Mill urged Place to take Hume in hand. At first Place was not impressed: 'I found him devoid of information, dull and selfish ... Mill said, "Work on with him and he will come out; there is much in him that will grow by good nursing ... " Our intimacy brought obloquey upon both of us, to which he was nearly as callous as I was. He was taunted with "the tailor his master," without whom he could do nothing. I was scoffed at as a fool for spending time uselessly upon "Old Joe," upon "The Apothecary." ... Mill's predictions were realized. Hume showed his capabilities and his imperturbable perseverance, which have beaten down all opposition; and there he stands, the man of men' (Letter to Mrs Grote, 1836; Add. MS 35144; quoted by Wallas, pp. 183–4).

better acquainted with me as you please, by calling here when you have any thing to do for the public good in which I can in any way assist,[1] but as their notions of what was for the public good, very often differed from my notion of what was for the public good, as almost the whole of them made party politics their rule of action, as I disliked both the great parties and as my notions were well known to be republican a few interviews were generally sufficient for their purposes, and our intercource as generally ceased, sometimes to be renewed again sometimes not.

Since the death of the Queen in 1821. there has been no strong nor decided political feeling on any subject,* the most important of all, as it includes all, Reform of Parliament, seems to have been abandoned as hopeless. The present Ministers have been more liberal than the whigs were, this is seen by the people who are therefore quiescent under their controul. They are pleased with the removal of restrictions on trade and commerce, with the amendments and consolidation of some of the laws, as for instance the modification of the Navigation Laws – the exportation of wool – the repal of all laws against combination of workmen to regulate their wages. Repeal of the laws against emigration of Artizans, repeal of the laws against extensive partnerships in Ship Insurances, the annihilation of the Levant Company. The consolidation of the Bankrupt laws, the proposed consolidation as well as the useful alterations of the Custom and Excise Laws, more particularly those of the Customs as suggested by a Gentleman in the Custom House named *Hume* into whose arrangements no lawyer has been permitted to stick his cloven foot. These and similar proceedings with others contemplated and avowed, lead the people to conclude that notwithstanding the ultra toryism of the administration, it is less exceptionable than any former administration and upon the whole, one which does not make a change in favour of the whigs desirable. The people know that the present ministers cannot live for ever, that they cannot as they die off be replaced with even such men as themselves, that the more the present ministers do, the more must be done by any set of men who may succeed them, and that it is therefore better to incourage them to go on with the amendments they are disposed

---

* 1825.
[1] In discussing the need for meeting places, Place spoke of those who called upon him: 'When I lived at Charing Cross a considerable number of persons from the poorest of the Hand Loom Weavers to now and then a Lord of Parliament used to call upon me.

'My Library which was a room built by me up two pairs of stairs in what was formerly a back house lighted by a large sky light, warmed in the winter in part by heated air, and made as to temperature as comfortable as it was quiet.

'My library was a sort of gossiping shop for such persons as were in any way engaged in public matters having the benefit of the public for their object, and it was well frequented' (Add. MS 35154, f. 195).

14.1 Campbell's letter to Brougham, 1825

to make, on the persuasion they entertain that the Whigs would not even do so much. This quiet state of things has made it less necessary for Noble Lords and honourable gentlemen to give themselves much trouble about me, and my connection has dwindled down to a pretty close connection in political and parliamentary matters with Mr Hume, a less close connection with Mr Hobhouse, occasional visits from Mr Grey Bennet[1] and a look in now and then by half a dozen others.

My being a *tailor* has been eminently serviceable to me by keeping my political acquantances in their places and me in mine, preventing too close an intimacy which would inevitably have destroyed my utility, be its value whatever it may. I have been much more able to obtain the concurence of parliamentary men in such parliamentary matters as their cooperation was essential. Than I could have done had I been on such a footing as would have endangered their popularity by an open participation, or had I been on such a footing with them as would have made me a dependint without any influence whatever.

My being a *tailor* has prevented all but a few of them inviting me to their tables. Many have shewn an apparent desire to do me services which I never needed and never accepted, many have proferred their friendship but scarcly any one of them has ever asked me to dine with him.

The[2] ladies too, of some of my grand acquaintances, condescended when we met in the country to be on familiar terms with me. but we never met in town. Had their husbands been so silly as to have invited me to dinner, and had I been so silly in such a case as to have permitted him to introduce me to the company in the drawing room, the breach of decorum would have caused the utmost dismay, and made the lady all but unable to perform her duty at the table. Dinners have been given by some whom I have greatly assisted, and who professed especial friendship for me and have afterwards taken especial pains to conceal from me that they had given such dinners to the persons who were present, while some of these persons have taken as special pains to let me know they were present; who besides were present and what had passed. Others again have taken as much pains to conceal from me that they were present. These matters never discomposed me. I know that it must be so, that it could not be otherwise while the present notions respecting genteel company prevails, and the present mode of thinking continues. To such an extent does this aristocratic folly prevail, that some of these people are not at all conscious there is the least disrespect in it, and would be surprised if any one were to hint that there was. It could never

---

[1] Another M.P. whom Place advised.
[2] A half page preceding this paragraph has been cut off.

The Autobiography of Francis Place

enter into their heads that any one who was a tradesman, or like me still preserved the semblance of a tradesman, and especially a *tailor*, that he should be invited, still less that any one of his rich *friends* should expect him to give him such an invitation.[1]

My good old friend and master Mr Bentham[2] is almost the only man among my *genteel* acquaintance who has never shewn this feeling. He is however too good a judge of others not to have perceived it, and he has frequently mentioned it and sometimes ridiculed it, he used to annoy some of his friends by praising his friend *Place the tailor*. In 1817 when I was with him at Ford Abbey and Sir Samul Romilly[3] with his wife and daughter, with their carriage and servants were at Bath, Mr Bentham invited them to spend a fortnight at the Abbey, but in doing this he thought it necessary to inform them that I was there and to ask them if that would be such an objection as to keep them away. These are pretty strong evidences. Gentlemen cannot associate with tradesmen. No nor even with a particular tradesman be his character whatever it may, much less with a *Tailor*.

[1] Two and a half pages have been cut out of the text after this paragraph. Place numbered the page containing the last half of this paragraph as page three; the page containing the next paragraph he numbered as page six. Opposite the first paragraph of the excised material is a footnote which he later tried to obliterate by writing over it. Unobliterated is the date, '1835. April.' The first two words can be made out: 'Mr Mill.' The thoroughness with which the four lines have been made illegible suggests that the note was an instance of Mill's discrimination against Place.

[2] 'Whenever I can turn again to my memoirs I will endeavour to do justice to my dear old master Mr Bentham. His fame and his character must live in his works, but so far as I can do him justice, it shall be done, I owe a vast debt for what is good and of high value to him, and I hope I shall not die without doing my best towards discharging that honourable debt' (Letter to Mrs Grote, 1836; Add. MS 35144, f. 354).

Place had met Bentham in 1812, and in the summer of 1817 he spent two months with Bentham and James Mill at Ford Abbey. Place, like other followers of Bentham, assisted in composing Bentham's notes into readable books. Place worked with others on the *Book of Fallacies*, the *Plan of Parliamentary Reform*, and *Chrestomathia*; alone he edited Bentham's *Not Paul, but Jesus*. So close was the friendship that Place in his diary for 1827 recorded, 'Visits from and to Mr Bentham have not been hitherto mentioned, as each of our houses were as frequently entered by either as his own' (quoted by Wallas, p. 80).

According to Holyoake, 'Bentham, who lived in Queen Square, Westminster, took his utilitarian walks with Place, and accompanied him on his business calls to take orders from his customers, or deliver the garments he had made for them. While Place was engaged within, Bentham would walk outside until his friend emerged again, when they would continue their walks and their political conversation.' One day when Place was detained in a house, Bentham tired of standing outside and sat down on the step to wait. A kindly passer-by came up and offered him a shilling (George Jacob Holyoake, *Sixty Years of an Agitator's Life*, 1892, I, 215).

[3] Sir Samuel Romilly (1757–1818), law-reformer, had long been associated with Bentham and with liberal movements. In 1797 he had been defence attorney in John Binns' trial for using seditious words at a Birmingham meeting (Binns, *Recollections*, p. 75).

14.1 Campbell's letter to Brougham, 1825

The party came. Sir Samul Romilly was, Mr Bentham said, more loquacious than he had ever known him to be – Lady Romilly was quite at her ease and was in all respects amiable, admirable – her daughter about 20 years of age and my daughter Annie nearly of the same age were capital friends, Miss Romilly and I played at shuttlecock and battledore in the grat Hall for exercise, but she had no suspicion who I was, she was much pleased with me, and as she concluded I was no less than a gentleman and a member of parliament she observed to her mother that she had never noticed any of my speeches. Her Mother did not at that time undeceive her.*

This account may hereafter be useful as marking the aristocratical spirit which domineers in all ranks, there will probably be material alterations in time to come, when these markings may be thought more curious than they are now.[1]

NO. 2. [LETTERS] TO JAMES MILL ESQR[2]

Charing Cross 15 Augt. 1827.

Dear Mill

I have been in somewhat anxious expectation of a call from you during the last three mornings, and have intended to call upon you at the India House, but I have been prevented, so do not to delay what might if delayed cause you some inconvenience I write to let you know why I cannot go to Dorking, to you, or indeed leave home at all.

My poor wife is in a deplorable state. When Mr Lawrence had performed his operation, he told me that if he had known the extent of the disease he would not have recommended an operation. I thought he

---

* NB I had written out several instances which had occurred much more curious than this, but upon a revision I cancelled them.

[1] After 'these markings may be,' Place originally had a different ending for the sentence. Later he wrote over these four or five words in order to make them illegible.

[2] Place met James Mill in about 1808, at a period when Mill used to come to London once a week to dine with Bentham. 'Our acquaintance,' Place recalled, 'speedily ripened into friendship, and he usually called on me on his way to Mr Bentham's, when we spent an hour together' (Add. MS 27823, f. 84; quoted by Wallas, p. 66). When Mill was not coming to London he and Place exchanged long letters, and Mill would demand that Place give him news of all the children. Place, in his turn, sent his family's greetings to Mrs Mill. When Mill was absent from London for long periods between 1814 and 1818, Place managed his money affairs (Alexander Bain, *James Mill*, 1882, p. 79). According to Holyoake, Mill's opinion of Place was so high that he asked Place to take charge of the political development of the mind of his son, John Stuart (Holyoake, *Sixty Years of an Agitator's Life*, I, 216).

The Autobiography of Francis Place

meant the extent to which he was obliged to procceed. I now however understand what he meant. It seems that true Cancer unless it be very early extirpated by the knife cannot be cured at all, and that when operated for after it has proceeded so far as to have affected the pectoral muscles or the lymphatic glands in the axilla an operation aggravates the disease. Both these circumstances had occurred in my wifes case, early as we thought the operation was performed it was too late. The disease has advanced and is advancing with such rapidity that she cannot live much longer. The swelling containing large hard lumps has proceeded quite across her chest and up the right side of her neck, so that she sometimes swallows with difficulty, her right arm is as large as two arms, and her right breast notwithstanding the amputation is larger than it was before the operation. By causing an artificial opening pain is mitigated. and this is all that can be done for her. She is well aware that she cannot live, but she is neither aware of the terrible suffering she must endure nor of the very short time she can remain alive. She has little confidence in any one but me, and were I to leave her she would at once sink down into a state of horrible despondency. She is not appalled at the thought of dying, but she grieves on account of her family, and it is my duty to remain with her and alleviate her sufferings, both bodily and mentally as much as I can by every means in my power.

You see how impossible it is for me to leave her for even so short a time, and our arrangements must therefore for the present be laid aside

Yours truly
Francis Place

Dorking 3d. Sept.

My Dear Sir

I should be sorry to ask you to leave home, if you think your presence of importance to Mrs. Place either as to mind or body – but if an absence of a few days would do no harm, & I fancy there is nothing so urgent in her case to make it otherwise, the weather is now so fine, that I wish to tempt you. Saturday & Sunday next, the Grotes are to be here again, & bedding will be scarce – but all other days are good, & I shall be here for three weeks.

Ever yours
J Mill

4 Sep. 1827

Reply.

My poor wife is in a sad state and getting worse every day. Her right hand and arm are useless to her, she is scarcely able to feed herself, She

14.2 Letters to James Mill, 1827

suffers greatly and cannot leave the house, she is so weak that she can scarcly leave her room. She mopes and imagines all sorts of miseries which greatly distresses us all. I cannot leave her, my absence would increase her truly unhappy condition.

I am peculiarly circumstanced just now. Annie has arrived from Buenos Ayres, last from Rio de Janeiro with her two sons and is expected every day to have another child born. Fred goes off to Buenos Ayres next week, and John has nearly sawed off the top of one of his thumbs. Thus I have a numerous family about me of great and small persons, and were I to go from home there would be no one with sufficient authority to keep them in order, and want of order would have a terrible effect upon my poor wife.

Fred's Departure being sudden needs my presence, and the Miers's[1] the miserable dishonest Miers's are giving me much trouble. The malignant Old Man who married Sophia Miers in Chile has been doing all in his power to annoy me and to get me into a Court of Law or Equity and I have been obliged to draw two cases one for Mr Bickersteth and am compelled to proceed with great caution, since in the present state of the law an inadvertence in serving these bad people, and I cannot give up my trust, might injure both me and the legatees whose scandalous conduct, since I must continue my trust, does not in the least make my determination to do them full justice one jot less than it has all along been.

Their affairs are however so nearly closed that I shall ere long make a final division of the estate among them, reserving only such things, and so much of the property as may be necessary, and taking such securities as under the direction of Mr Bickersteth I have been able to compel them to give.

You can now pretty well judge how I am circumstanced and how unlikely it is that I shall be able to come to you and enjoy with you the beauties of the neighbourhood of Dorking which never in the least pall on me.

Yours truly
Francis Place

NARRATIVE

Shortly after this my poor wife imagined that she should be more at ease if she were removed to Angmering in Sussex to the home of a very good

[1] Evidently relations of his son-in-law, John Miers, who married Annie Place. In his diary Place often complained of these troublesome family connections.

The Autobiography of Francis Place

Woman named Knight, and as soon as preparations for her removal and accomodation could be made she with her daughter Mary took up their abode at Mrs Knights. It was an open pleasant place which she had previously visited and to which as well as to the people she had become attached, and here on the 19th of october she died. No one supposed she was so near her death, nor was she herself at all aware at the time that she was dying. Her death was indeed so sudden, that happening to have no one of the family with her but Mary, there was no time for any one to reach her, the account of her expected death, and of her death reached us in London at the same time. She was buried in Angmering Church Yard. On the day of her funeral. I suffered more than I had ever before done and more than I believed I could suffer on any occasion, more I am sure than I can again suffer. I held up against it all I could. – I resisted as much as man could do, but it was useless, and I was utterly subdued, so much so indeed that I could willingly have died also. The retrospect which I was compelled to contemplate was too much for me, as I am sure it must under such circumstances have been for any one, and all that was in my power was hiding myself in a barn to indulge my sorrow. Go to the funeral I could not, I had no power left equal to such a purpose, and here therefore in the barn I remained a sad example, of a man who had successfully resisted many of what are esteemed very trying events, and thought that no event, nor any number of untoward events could subdue him; here he was a mere child without a particle of resolution or self controul left in him. Yet surely if ever man had cause for Grief I was that man, surely if ever man could be excused for indulging it I may claim that excuse. I had lost, and for ever my *friend* my long cherished *companion* in all my various changes of life, she who had my entire confidence, she who gave me hers, and had loved me most sincerely during Thirty Seven years, she who was guileless when we were married and retained much of her simplicity to the time of her death. The mother of my nine living children, She but for whom I never could have advanced in life as I did, She whose conduct had been most exemplary, cut off just at the time we were contemplating modes of enjoying ease and quietness for the remainder of our lives.

Such was the impression on me that for some time after her death, I frequently thought I heard her moving along the passages of the house, or in the rooms, these noises were made by others, yet I very often, looked up expecting to see her. I do not mean that knowing she was dead I continued to expect to see her, the expectation was a momentary flash, but the association of the noises and her presence came quicker than the recollection, that she was dead, short indeed as must have been the time.

14.3 Letters to son-in-law and daughter, 1828, 1829

NO. 3 LETTERS TO MR JOHN AND MRS ANNIE MIERS AT RIO DE JANEIRO

7 March. 1828.

My Dear John.

In your letters 3 and 4th of december last, you observe that I have discontinued to write to you on all sorts of matters and at the length I used to do. This is true but then your wife is doing it for me. When she leaves England again I will recommence gossipping, and even now I will not abstain, from doing so.

In the way some things are related to you as well by Annie as by Mary and Jane you cannot avoid coming to incorrect conclusions, and I have no doubt that in the long letters which you will receive by the packet which will bring you this, you will heare much about me, partaking more of feelings than of facts. This cannot fail to mislead you unless I anticipate it. If this letter should happen to be first read, and you should not have been previously informed of the subject you will say. – well what is the story?. Answer, a love affair and of me. There is nothing however very remarkable in so common an occurrence.[1] I John, loved my wife as well as ever man loved woman. I loved her as well at the close of Thirty six years after our marriage as I did on the day we were married. When young she was a most beautiful figure, my delight and consolation under all kinds of difficulties, and privations. She was good tempered, kind, considerate, abstemious and singularly industrious. She was all in all that a man in my circumstances could wish she should be, and more than any man could reasonably expect to find. No wonder then that I loved her dearly. As we were very poor she endured more than I did, this in all such cases is necessarily the womans fate. She seldom repined at her hard fate, she never made her condition matter of reproach to me, she was sometimes unhappy but this was transitory, and when we were not in actual want we were happy. At times we were supremely so, and but for her I never could have got forward in the world as I did.

Unfortunately her mild and kindly temper and disposition were not to continue for ever. As the elder children grew up, as my circumstances improved, and as I used the means I possessed to have them educated in a manner superior to most mens children in my rank of life, so my wife found herself, going far behind them in all sorts of school learning, and she conceived that as they advanced in knowledge, of this kind so they

---

[1] Place's son drew lines through the letter to this point and marked in the margin, 'Perhaps Dele.' On the opposite page he provided this substitute for the material he was deleting: 'In a letter to his son in law Mr John Miers at Rio de Janeiro he writes . . . '

The Autobiography of Francis Place

became less and less respectful to her, and at length she became fully persuaded that she was an object of reproach from wanting similar information. She never however, notwithstanding this persuasion objected to my either employing masters to teach them nor to the heavy expense this occasioned, but it had a bad effect upon her temper, made her sometimes give way to passion and made her as you know at times greatly agitated. Poor thing this was a weakness she had no power to controul. I do not pretend to say that on all occasions I was as calm and acted as judiciously as I ought to have been and done. Yet I did privately, i.e. between ourselves make many sacrifices, to soothe and persuade her, to be tranquil, and as she possessed the means to indulge in rational recreation, to make herself happy in all respects. Unfortunately she could not command her feelings in respect to the children, and she sometimes told them that if she and I were alone, or if none but the youngest were with us, we should never hear a word spoken in anger by the other.[1] We were not however upon the whole uncomfortable. My greatest pleasure was to have her as my *companion*, my delight was to see her and hear her voice, and as you well know I should have been happy to have spent more time with her than I did, had she at all times been willing to accept attentions, but she was not at all times ready to recevce proffered kindnesses heartily and I could not consent that they should be received in any other manner. She was necessary to my happiness, this arose from the sincere and ardent affection I had for her and our long continued uninterrupted intercourse, and especially from the association of ideas which made her a partner in all my concerns and projects whether real or imaginary. The only relaxation I really either coveted or courted was her society. This was my solace my recompence, and [had] she been fortunately able to appreciate this correctly and fully, we must have been the happiest of human beings.[2] A man may be the friend of another man, a *woman* alone can be his *companion*. It has been well remarked by a wise man, that he who is literary or studious and is also a man of the world needs the intercourse of the woman he loves, more than most other men do, and is more capable than most other men of the exquisite enjoyment of this converse – I beleive this to be strictly true. Certainly, so far as I can judge it is my case, as I know it is that of some others. When therefore my poor wife died I was much more distressed than I had supposed any circumstance could have made me, and yet I

---

[1] Extracts of letters from Place to his wife are quoted on pp. 260–2 below.

[2] Place's son crossed out the rest of the letter. On the page opposite this he wrote, 'So purely domestic and uninteresting out of the family that it had better be cut out.' Opposite subsequent pages of this letter he noted, 'As previously remarked upon,' 'The same remarks apply,' and 'Dele.'

14.3 Letters to son-in-law and daughter, 1828, 1829

thought I had reasoned the matter to a correct conclusion, this was proved to be an error. No one can imagine how wretched I was, any more than any one can form an accurate idea of the efforts I made to recover myself. So completely was I thrust out from, all which to me was most dear, that I knew not what to do. I had no society unless I sought it abroad, and I could not go abroad to seek it. No one remained with whom I could hold unlimited social converse. Frank will not talk, he will not trust himself in conversation. Mary takes but little notice of the circumstances which surround her, and makes no account of passing events. Jane is taciturn with a coldness which has the *appearance* of sulkiness. John is a coarse fellow now 5 feet 10 inches high, and still growing rapidly, he is quite a journeyman carpenter in his manners. Tom is a harum-skarum sort of a fellow and Caroline and William are children. Caroline is somewhat perverse and William poor fellow has for months had the St Vitus's dance.[1] Much as I love my children, desirous as I am to do them every possible service, it was and is quite out of my power to find among them the society which to me is necessary to my comfort. I cannot like many other men go to a tavern, I hate Taverns and Tavern company. I cannot drink, I cannot for any considerable time consent to converse with fools. I dislike set formal dinners, at which a man must either shew off, or be voted a bore, and shew off to very little purpose after all, to come home in the middle of the night discontented. I was utterly uncomfortable. I read and wrote all day, and almost all night. I had some matters of laborious research in hand, and I went on doggedly with them. I thought I might become reconciled to my circumstances. I endeavoured to persuade myself that a woman as a companion was not essential to my comfort, or at least that I might contrive to make myself cintented without one. In this however I totally failed. After hours of hard reading intense thinking and close attention while writing I went to the drawing room, and there instead of an agreeable woman as a solace to me I was entertained with the non-chalence of Jane – the oddities of Mary who notwithstanding is one of the very best creatures on the face of the earth. The jarrings and noisiness of John and Tom and Caroline, and the great uneasiness this occasioned in Mary. I had no one to converse with no one to talk over as I had been accustomed to do the occurrences of the day, no one to whom I could unreservedly communicate my thoughts no one to sympathise with me in any thing I was doing, and my thoughts were therefore turned in upon myself, and upon my poor deceased wife. I then went solitarily to my Sopha – I could not sleep in the bed and had discarded it from the day of my poor wife's death – there to endure the thoughts I could not dismiss, there to suffer

[1] Frank was 29; Mary, 24; Jane, 20; John, 17; Tom, 15; Caroline, 13; William, 11.

The Autobiography of Francis Place

as I had never before suffered. I assure you John that during many nights, I never slept at all. I had no desire for sleep, the torture I endured acted as a stimulus to the bodily organs and drove away all desire for sleep. I wasted away and at the end of three months had lost nearly twenty pounds in weight.

I bore this as long as I could, I had made the greatest efforts to overcome my chagrin by reasoning but I did not succeed, it was not to be overcome in this way. I became convinced that I must do one of two things – namely – either mix much in society, or find a female friend. The first I feared would not answer the purpose intended, and was besides inimical to all my habits. The last was to me on every account the most agreeable. I had taken a strong liking for a lady whose name you will have heard from Annie and others of the family.[1] I do not mean that I was conscious of any feeling of love for her, though that was sure to follow. She came occasionally as she had been accustomed to do, and visited us. My desire to be in her company increased, I began to pay particular attentions to her, and found solace in doing so. Our intimacy increased, and she who has much feeling and a lively imagination soon became considerably excited and I could plainly see she would if she had not already be prepared for an offer of marriage. I thought the matter over and concluded that I must not make the proposition. Unwilling to lead her too far, and then to disappoint her, I told her, that as she was a woman who had seen something of the world and possessed a good understanding, knowing too as she did as much of my habits and character as she could well know it was quite unnecessary for me to proceed with her in any but the most free and candid manner, that I had concluded she would not reject from me an offer of marriage, and that I was disposed to make it, but if she would examine the whole matter, and carefully look at all the circumstances present and prospective she would probably be compelled to conclude, that I ought to remain single, and that to place any woman at the head of so large a family as mine; among sons and daughters of such various ages, and dispositions would be altogether improper. That with respect to herself I was compelled to conclude it would be inimical to all her habits, that it would probably produce great disquietude if not unhappiness, to her, and if it did, great evil to my family would be the result. I treated her with the utmost

[1] Her name, which Place never mentioned in his memoir, was Louisa Simeon Chatterley. She was an actress at Covent Garden, having made her debut there in 1821, playing Miss Hardcastle in *She Stoops to Conquer* (John Genest, *Some Account of the English Stage from the Restoration in 1660 to 1830*, 1832, IX, 155). Born in 1797, she married the actor William Simmonds Chatterley in 1813 or 1814. In 1822 he died of drink (William Oxberry, *Dramatic Biography*, v, 1826, 271; *DNB*). She lived until 1866 (W. Davenport Adams, *A Dictionary of the Drama*, 1904, I, 277).

14.3 Letters to son-in-law and daughter, 1828, 1829

candour, put the matter into every form, reasoned it out in every way, and took my leave for three days. It was a very painful effort to me, to her it was much more painful. I began seriously to regret I had made any advances to her. They were not premeditated, but were produced by a number of odd coincidences as such matters generally are. At the end of three days we had another conversation. We were I beleive perfectly candid. She said she had no mercenary views in any respect, had an income above her expenditure, was slowly accumulating money, and was perfectly independent of every thing except of her profession. This indeed I knew as I had had her affairs in my hands nearly three years ago. She was sorry our acquantance should have gone so far, as to cause the pain it had done, and she would make the necessary effort to recover her tranquility. She was proud and pleased to acknowledge that I had been the best friend she ever had in her life, and had done her the greatest services when she was in difficulty and in sorrow. That my conduct towards her had then been so consoling and delicate that it was impossible for her not to be gratified when I paid her more than usual attention. That at this time of need my wife had paid the most generous and unexpected attention to her, cherished and consoled her and she loved her most sincerely, and all her children, every one of whom had been kind to her. That having thus discharged her debt of gratitude as far as she was able she hoped I should see the necessity there was that our acquaintance should terminate, at least for some time, and that it might possibly happen that at the end of six months we might meet again as we had formerly done. For six months then, said she I must decline seeing you. There the matter ended. There at the moment I thought it would end: but this was not possible, I could not wait six months, no, nor six days, so at the end of three days I wrote to her, and told her another conversation was necessary, and I gave my reasons for saying so, and said that unless she sent me a refusal to see me, and such an one as should leave no doubt as to her determination I should wait upon her the next morning. I did so and this led to a second and a third conversation and at length it became probable that we should be friends and companions until other arrangements could be made. She is very much to my taste, she has a very neat house, and every thing about her is rather elegant than otherwise. She lives in a very frugal manner maintaining her mother and her son, spending little, wasting nothing and saving something. She is cheerful and remarkably good tempered, and is I believe incapable of deception or meanness. If we do not long continue to be the best of friends it must be her fault. I shall treat her with marked consideration and respect. One main ingredient in my character is constancy in every thing, and certainly not least in such a case as this.

The Autobiography of Francis Place

There John, there is what you never expected from me, and you would not now have had one line of it, were it not that you must have heard and will continue to hear from others more of feelings than facts on the subject.

You can read this to Annie when she rejoins you at Rio.

Don't for a moment suppose that I impute the least blame to any one who may write to you on the subject. They cannot put themselves into my situation, and they must look on my conduct with apprehension.

1st as to what they will think of my bringing a wife home.

2nd as to what they will think my weakness, in which it is probable they will decide correctly.

I confess my weakness to a considerable extent, and only wish I was what no one ever was, strong at all points, at all times and under all circumstances.

Yours truly
Francis Place

[Place's letters to his first wife provide evidence of his love for her, of his concern for their family life, and also of their quarrels: he started a letter to her, on one of his picturesque excursions,

'Thou hast known me and my habits so long art so well acquainted with all my desires feelings and propensities that any of the common place expressions of endearment would appear like flattery to the best ever *friend* Thomas claiming the previledge of that name will be gratified with a perusal of my letters, as his severe and critical disposition will not permit him to spare me one single jot, I must out of fear of him and to shew what a docile fellow I am, use some term that may be deemed fit for his delicate ears to hear, that will not too rudely shock his nerves – Oh! I had all but made a grand mistake see what a dreadful thing it is to leave the beaten road, I had almost said my *dearest love* – dearest love indeed would he say, pray who then is the cheapest, sly dog! wicked critic! but I will disappoint him he shall not at my expence shake his fat sides, – no – I will use a term so true (as thou knowest) that all his carping shall be put to defiance his expectation baulked entirely – here it is –

MY. ONLY. LOVE'
(August 2, 1811; Add. MS 35143, f. 180).

Two years later, on another outing, Place again opened a letter to her affectionately:

'There, accuse me again if you dare – say I do not pay the little attentions so dear to women – you did not expect a letter, – but you see how true it is – that . . . "thou art present, whereso'ere I go."' (Sept. 24, 1813; Add. MS 35143, f. 235).

During his prolonged absence at Ford Abbey in 1817, he wrote two letters which reveal his unhappiness at their quarrels. The first, written on August 28, started by asking her for a letter:

14.3 Letters to son-in-law and daughter, 1828, 1829

'Never having been from home for so long a period, I am anxious to hear from you, – and there is enough about the house and the people in it to say, to make a good tough story – Now you see very plainly I have been thinking of you, but you are not to suppose it a mere casual, transitive thought, for it is only transitive in being committed to paper, for I think of you very often, and shall be gratified no little when I come home to SEE you – All the brats great and small pass in review before my minds eye, each gets estimated, and the peculiar traits of character belonging to each is carefully examined with a view to direct them to some purpose capable of producing, understanding and happiness ... Now I think I hear you say "Yes if he would be always so kind, "*Well But*" – now this well but is the thing that gives a turn to the reasoning and feeling, and is like ⟨Prassers⟩ prayers a sort of excuse for not having been quite so considerate or kind as you might have been yourself – So – a challenge – after another period of 5 or 6 weeks – spent in distant courtship with an occasional love letter, let us see who will be the least to blame; not the most to blame, in disturbing the Honey Moon – I shall carry off the prize in this – Not you indeed – "WELL BUT" I shall, now mark you that – so take all the pains you can, after this notice.'

A page later he ends the letter with some timeless domestic concerns:

'You must tell me how you like the carpet & if it covers the floor up to the oiled cloth – after it had been some days ordered I began to fear it was not wide enough ... you must also tell me how Fred and Mary and Jane behave themselves ... and, at what time in the morning – or day – Frank crawls out of his nest'. (Add. MS 35143, f. 294).

A few days later Place received a letter from his nineteen-year-old son Frank, saying that though he had arrived home early every night his mother was constantly annoyed with him: 'so minute and so redundant, are her feelings, that she falls out with me for the veriest trifles.' This letter prompted Place to make a sombre addition to a general diary-letter he had written. The page is marked 'Private':

'I was obliged to leave off before I had gone more than a twentieth part of my journey, because I found it impossible to finish it, without sacrificing a subject of more importance, and more intimately connected with the happiness of us all – I mean our conduct, so far as regards temper among ourselves. If happily this could be so clearly understood, as I think it might be, no human beings need be happier than we, it is a subject which has often preyed upon my mind, many have been the attempts, I have made to come to an understanding on this subject, and as many have been my failures, do not however for one moment suppose, I intend to insinuate reproach, I have your comfort too much at heart to intend saying or doing any thing which may have a tendency to cause you an uneasy thought, but notwithstanding, this you may, and probably will be somewhat hurt at what I am saying, only beleive me however to be actually as sincere as our long intercourse has proved me, and be just as willing to forget every former cause of discomfort as I am, to suppress all ebulitions of anger, to forbear, making hasty, conclusions and we shall soon be able to converse on disagreements in temper in ourselves and the children, as we are on other subjects and if this be really accomplished, the business will be done ...

The Autobiography of Francis Place

'When I say that hastiness of temper. Which prevents, reason and deliberation, that vehemence of expression, and an expectation of unlimited, unconditional submission to this hastiness, and vehemence, are your faults, you must give me credit for a plain statement of a fact, which even to think of gives me pain, and is not produced by any [sic] the slightest feelings of any sort but regret, regret, not produced by dislike of you, not by even the most distant approach to indifference, my love for you has never in the least diminished, but is as ardent after some 25 or 26 years of the day of our marriage, as it was on that day. and never have I seen the woman, who could when compared with you have had any permanent influence on my mind, or who could have commanded my affection, and what but, the strongest desire to see you happy beyond all human beings, could induce me, to write thus to you, and what but this could have induced me in almost unexampled scenes of distress and difficulty, to persevere as I did, silently, steadily, and unceasingly, pursuing the painful road I had to travel, and surely now that it has been sometime past, and we are in possession of the means of comfort, without our affections being decayed, we may if we chuse enjoy the remainder of our lives, and reach as our health and strength promises us a happy old age – This is now the great object of my existence, other objects formerly occupied my mind, because they were necessary to this, to rise from poverty was one – to gain money as a means of knowledge and comfort was the next, much has been effected, these objects I have obtained, and do but work with me, in that now to be obtained as you have done for the attainment of the others, and suffer me to guide in this as I have done in the others, and doubt not it will certainly be also obtained' (Sept. 15, 1817; Add. MS 35143, fs. 298–9).]

To Mrs Annie Miers at Rio de Janeiro – 12th September 1828.[1]
Extract.

– I too have my hope – it is that John will be able to make money – he is now approaching the time when he will begin to become an *old fellow*, and I hope that before he actually becomes one he will have placed himself in such circumstances as may leave him at ease as to money matters for the remainder of his life, with leisure to enjoy himself in such literary and scientific pursuits as will be dear to him and are a never failing source of pleasure; and I hope too, still more ardently do I hope, that he will not be unfortunate as I have been, and lose his wife when she has become more than ever necessary to him and when his situation is such, that his prospects of ease and comfort for the remainder of his life appear much brighter than they ever did before, when indeed with some few exceptions he may reasonably conclude that his wife as well as himself. and every one of his family has reason to calculate on being as comfortable, or even more comfortable than the general run of persons in tolerably easy circumstances and moderate desires can be.

I have written thus much in sorrow, I do not think that I am more

[1] Place's son crossed out this letter and the following one, marking them 'Dele.'

14.3 Letters to son-in-law and daughter, 1828, 1829

selfish than other liberally thinking men are. I do not think I am so selfish as indeed most such men are. I would be as little so as possible. I had calculated on years of that steady plodding life to which my habits had been formed. I hoped and wished, for so long a period, and so often, that my hopes and wishes had become expectations that your mother would be the longest liver of the two. My life was a good one, and she too enjoyed such sound health and such unimpaired strength, was so little approximated to an old woman, at 50 years of age that it seemed but reasonable to anticipate a long life for her. I was bitterly disappointed and you well know the affliction I endured. Do not conclude that I am unhappy. I am by no means so, yet I do at times suffer much, this is undoubtedly the result of weakness which I cannot always conquer. It is a weakness I did not suppose belonged to me to any thing like the extent I have experienced. I have made great efforts to overcome it; but a man at 56 years of age, however vigorous he may be in body and mind, does not either easily or readily reconcile himself to a change which reverses all his habits, and I feel assured that I never shall be perfectly reconciled to the circumstances in which your poor mothers death has placed me. I have to be sure every thing that I can have under these circumstances but I have emphatically speaking, no home, for she who made home, home, is gone. We had our differences of opinion, and her tastes differed widely from mine in some respects but they did not clash, as each persued what was most congenial and left the other unmolested. She was averse to all speculation, and I in matter of much moment was speculative; if I had not been so I must have remained a journeyman Breeches Maker. She was however in all respects perfectly honest and spoke her thoughts freely and fully, on all occasions. You know well how the children as they grew up made her uneasy, and but too often caused considerable irritation, but she had a thousand virtues and was the only woman in the world who could have been my wife, the only woman I ever knew with whom I could have gone on in poverty and what is usually called and would with any other, have been, misery, and with whom I could have been so thoroughly satisfied when in affluent circumstances. Had she lived we might and probably we should in a short time have been at ease in every respect. I had attained very much to this state, even as it regarded the children we should have been so, all of them excepting William are approaching a time of life, when they will be able to provide for themselves, at least to a considerable extent.

I have had a strong inclination to burn this letter, but having taking a turn and determined to send it, I shall not stop here, but will tell you the whole story about myself, to prevent mistakes which at the distance we are asunder takes many months to rectify. My course of life is this. I rise

The Autobiography of Francis Place

as usual about 7 a m and generally remain at home until after dinner and then go out. Once in about 10 days I go out before dinner, the weather being fine, and now and then I go to the Play-house, but as this going to the Play is more for professional than mere pleasurable purposes so far as respects the Play-house, I go but seldom and am always home before 12 o clock at night. These goings out are with my female companion.[1]

Whether or not I would have a female companion was not matter of choice, I had no choice, I was unable to chuse not to have one. That I should have found one, so well adapted to me is much more than I had reason to expect. You have read what I wrote to John on the 7 March on this subject, and if I were to write again I must repeat what I then said It is six months since, and I have reason to beleive that I underrated my companions good qualities. I have every reason to be satisfied. But I am not at home as I used to be. I am not as I should like to be in my own room among my books, I am not along with John and Tom, and Caroline in the evenings at all.[2] This is matter of much concern to me. I shall now endeavour to be at home sometimes of an evening, as the days become shorter and colder. My being at home will be useful to the children, now that they have no mother.

How changed indeed is my state. Here am I constantly in all weathers walking more than two miles home almost every night between ten and eleven o clock, and what may seem still more surprising, I have become reconciled to it, and think little of it as a trouble. I who hardly ever went out of doors after dark, I who spent every evening in my room have scarcly lighted my lamp these three months. I have been twice with Mr Mill at Walton upon Thames, once for 2 and once for 6 days. I have recovered as much flesh as I wish to have and am in good health. and excepting now and then am in good spirits.

You see my dears Annie and Jane with what confidence I speak to you, how plainly and barely I lay myself open to you, and you can both judge how widely my situation differs from that which I should prefer.

My circumstances taken altogether are untoward – very multifarious and partake sometimes of disagreeable cogitations. I do next to nothing in any literary matters. My mornings are occupied in many affairs of my

---

[1] Place's short-lived avocation of play-going had started about 1824 or 1825. Writing in 1827 of his exertions in connection with the OP (Old Prices) riots at Covent Garden in 1809, he said, 'I was not a play-goer. In the course of the last three 3 years I had seen most of our best acting Tragedies and Comedies some of them twice or thrice, and did not care if I never saw an other performance, of either sort' (Add. MS 35145, f. 4).

[2] He was also away from home in the daytime: he recorded that he heard three youths discussing the solar system in Green Park at 11.00 a.m. on Sunday, August 10, 1828, as he was walking from Charing Cross to Brompton, where Mrs Chatterley lived (Add. MS 27827, fs. 95–6).

14.3 Letters to son-in-law and daughter, 1828, 1829

own or those of other peoples of whom I never have any lack. My evenings are spent abroad, so that except the reading I there obtain, that is either reading aloud or being read to, I read nothing, and do not see how I am to find time to write any thing. But it is useless to repine, and I shall bear whatever I must bear with a good grace. I will not be *again* unhappy as long as I live let whatever may happen, the greatest cause of unhappiness to me which it was possible [to have] happen has happened and nothing even approximating to it can hereafter happen. Of living at all I have perhaps somewhat odd notions. As it regards myself only, I care very little about it, I never did care much about it, and but for those about me, I should not repine if I were now going to bed with the certain knowledge that I should never rise again. What would however appear a paradox to the generality is that notwithstanding this notion I have as much of chearfulness as most men, while they cannot but imagine that he who can think so little of the fear of death must be both melancholy and unhappy. But for the circumstances alluded to I should be as I have long been one of the most cheerful of men.

I had no intention when I commenced this letter to say any thing on the subject of which you have been reading, but there it is, Frank has read it and thinks it should be sent.

Yours truly
Francis Place

To Mr John Miers at Rio de Janeiro

London Jany 7 – 1829

----------In your letter to Frank speaking of me you say –
"It is notwithstanding a strange alteration in his pursuits and as you observe, the chief cause of regret that will no doubt be felt by himself is, that the change of habit and taste and of pursuits will be to render him of less importance than he has long been considered with persons whose opinions he must value". – There is a passage in Annies letter of similar import. I know as well as you and Frank and Annie and Jane and Mary or any one of you, how very much each desires that I should be happy, and esteemed, and I cannot but persuade myself that you not only think, I do, but that I really do possess many claims to esteem, and I assure you that I am very much gratified by a passage in Annie's letter in which she does me justice, respecting my wishes my exertions and feelings as they relate to my family, I seldom make professions, hardly ever draw the attention of any of you to what I have done or intend doing hereafter. I am contented that my actions shall stand in the place of professions and among such well informed and well disposed people as I have the happiness of knowing you all are, I shall I dare say be properly appreciated.

The Autobiography of Francis Place

You are all mistaken as to the regret you suppose, or rather have concluded I shall feel, in the way you have put it. I shall never feel the smallest portion of such regret. I know the world too well for that. I value it too justly to permit regret to lay hold on me. I do feel some regret however and must be contented to feel it in respect to my children, from the want of their mother, none other I again assure you. I know no one for whose opinion I have any regard who is not much more likely to commend than to censure me. I shall never do any thing which any one of those persons will ever be inclined to condemn.

I have been singularly circumstanced. I may say without vanity for I am only speaking in relation to facts which are not secrets, that my case is a somewhat extraordinary one. I do not believe that any man who has made his way in the world and obtained as much of what is called respect has obtained it in the same way. I have deceived no one, never practised the common tricks of a tradesman, not even those which are esteemed as quite unexceptionable, are even commended, and by means of which I might have obtained very considerable sums of money. In all my intercourse with men or as it is vaguely called the world, and this has been constant, and in very varied circumstances, not only have I acted disinterestedly but no suspicion to the contrary has ever attached to me. And then as to the assistance of others, I cannot be said to have accepted much, though I have given much to others. Never but twice in my life have I requested any and those were when I went into business at Charing Cross. Even on those occasions I *asked* but little and accepted less though on the last of those occasions much was offered. In no circumstance which I thought of moment in relation to myself or any of my *own* concerns, and very seldom even in the concerns of others have I asked the advice of any one, and no one has ever presumed to offer it. Thus have I acted for myself and have compelled respect, that respect which I long since observed was gained more by compulsion than voluntarily granted. I shall lose none of this, but if I lost it all I should not repine. One only reason there is, why it should remain, and that is, that if I lost it, my power to be useful to others would be somewhat abridged. They who want my services are not very likely to quarrel with me on matters which do not concern themselves. But there are others who may be placed between these and my particular friends, these are persons of some taste, some fashion, some consideration, all these will remain as they are. None of these have any claim upon me for more than the common courtesies of life. as practised among well bred men and women. Be assured that I shall lose no esteem that I would give a straw to retain, and that whatever of esteem I may have will stick close to me because the parties are all interested in esteeming me. I never indeed

14.3 Letters to son-in-law and daughter, 1828, 1829

either courted or cared to have the esteem of the vulgar high or low, and what is more I have made my resources to lie so much within myself, and my pleasures so much my own, and depend so much upon myself that none but myself can destroy them. But were all your predictions verified to me it would be of no consequence whatever. Rest assured that my reputation will remain much as it is.

I have more and more reason to be satisfied with my friend who has no one habit that I can reasonably disapprove of; but on the contrary very many to commend. If ingenious conduct as to past matters and a strong disposition for improvement, a strong love of repose and quiet, – carefulness – neatness – cheerfulness – a fair share of industry and a good temper, ought to make me satisfied, I should commit unpardonable injustice were I to be silent on such matters.

         Time has expired so adieu
         and believe me to be as usual
      Yours Francis Place.

[In another volume of his papers Place included two pages narrating the events of the next two years of his life:

'1830

July–1830 to July 1831 } time when written at many intervals

'At the close of 1829 I had detached myself very much from my political *friends*, and at the commencement of the present year, I had very few matters belonging to any body on my hands.

'I was to be married to Mrs Chatterley [the name has been crossed out] as soon as my family arrangements by the marriage of my eldest son and some other family matters were accomplished. I would fain have remained at Brompton where to build a room for my books would have cost me less than putting my house at Charing Cross to rights was likely to occasion.

'Mrs Chatterley's [name crossed out in text] home No 15 Brompton Square was neat in good condition and rather elegantly fitted up and furnished. The square was occupied by genteel quiet people, and was nicely kept. The House was well situated the front in the Square, the back looking over a small garden had an uninterrupted view as far as Chiswick, and was so circumstanced in respect to situation that it was not at all likely it would be built in. It is in the neighbourhood of Hyde park and Kensington Gardens, and the walks in almost every direction are clean and pleasant, but here I could not remain without greatly deranging my family, so we agreed to remove to Charing Cross.

'It was utterly impossible for me to detach myself from the business of others if I resided at Charing Cross. So I at once abandoned the schemes I would willingly have indulged, and more especially the attempt I had long since contemplated of writing a history of North America, and for which I

The Autobiography of Francis Place

have collected upwards of 600 volumes, and at once reconciled myself to my old way of consuming time

'Mr Hume was pressing on some subjects. Mr Hobhouse on others, they would however soon have ceased to expect much from me, if by remaining at Brompton I had made it inconvenient to them as well [as to] others to come to me. Mr Hume had promised to bring a motion before the house of Commons for a repeal of the 60 Geo. 3 c. 9. commonly called . . .' [Here Place's narrative ends] (Add. MS 35146, fs. 105–6).

Two other events of this important year in Place's personal life were the deaths of his youngest son, William (in 1829), and his youngest daughter, Caroline (in 1830). Of Place's fifteen children, eight were now dead.[1]]

May 1851. This was in relation to my intended marriage. I married and all was as good as I had anticipated for upwards of 12 years a family quarrel then took place which changed my wife wholly. Her Mother who lived with us died, he[r] only son turned out a finished rascal of the meanest kind and made his mother very unhappy during some years, but as he behaved and worse, she was led to consider him the more and – took all sorts of means to save him at my expence – this led to reproch that to a diabolical disposition my means diminished her carfulness became extravance – ill temper to a most extraordinary degree, – robbery to save her worthless son now carried to an extent which with my diminished means will be my ruin as her infatuation and ill temper, however injurious to herself appears to be her intention. and the law allows it.

[In 1851 Place separated from his wife and went to live in Hammersmith with his married daughter, Annie. His books and papers were brought in a wagon and stored in a dry stable. Two years later he took a house in Foxley Terrace, Earls Court, with his two unmarried daughters, Mary and Jane. On the morning of January 1, 1854, he was found dead in bed (Wallas, pp. 397–8). His wife returned to the stage; she is listed in programmes for plays at the Olympic Theatre in 1856 and 1858 (Adams, *A Dictionary of the Drama*, I, 277).

Place's entry for 1851, recording the collapse of his marriage is written on two pages. On the verso opposite the first part his son, Francis, pencilled 'Hear Hear.' Opposite the last part, he pencilled, 'a terrible finale.' At the end of Place's entry his son added an extended comment in pencil:

'Mr. Place's connection with the woman he took for 2nd wife was the only false step that can be laid to his charge – It was a terrible fallin off from his former ridgidly virtuous life – a bad example to his family and the numerous young politicians that crowded around him for teaching and worldly wisdom – It is inconceivable how he could have made so false a step and belied all the moral teachings of which he was a living illustration – An ordinary unknown man might in obscurity have been guilty of so much laxity and the world none the worse for it, but in FPs case it was an outrage upon the class he lived in,

[1] See Place's list of his children on p. 298, below.

14.3 Letters to son-in-law and daughter, 1828, 1829

indeed upon all society – It brought its consequences upon him in the wildness of his younger sons – in the anguish it caused his deploring and well disposed daughters – in the diabolical conduct (his own term) of the woman and in the utter desolation it brought upon him.

'It is painful to ⟨record⟩ so much injurious error of a parent to whom all his children are so much indebted – he was lavish in the means for their education which gave them material for future success in life he was indeed their idol but this sad dereliction from duty on his part caused a complete revolution and [word illegible] of feelings and actions among them

'My two sisters and myself now aged people are all that are left of his own numerous family – we are all I am happy to say in easy circumstances to the attainment of which we cannot but feel that we owe much to his generous conduct & his glorious example during our mothers life and great was our consternation and grief when the noble edifaction of his fine character became a wrick' – *Francis Place* Jr (Add. MS 35144, fs. 130–1).

Place's children may have disapproved of Mrs Chatterley because of the unfavourable publicity resulting from her friendship with Mr Christmas, a banker's clerk. The following version was given by Oxberry, who said that he learned these details directly from the concerned parties. The first sign of trouble occurred when Mr Christmas' wife applied for a warrant against Mrs Chatterley's mother (Mrs Simeon) for assault. It turned out that the trouble had started when Mrs Christmas threatened to 'immolate' Mrs Chatterley. The Christmases were separated; he gave his wife £120 a year from his salary of £500. At a party Mr Christmas had met Mrs Chatterley, then visited her, and done some business for Mrs Simeon, who lived with her. Presently a physician prescribed country air for Mrs Chatterley, who was in bad health. 'And here,' wrote Oxberry, 'the act of imprudence commenced.' Mr Christmas proposed that they combine their incomes, and hire a house and carriage together. This they did. Mrs Chatterley advanced her average income of £700; and Mr Christmas contributed about £400. They occupied separate quarters in the house; the servants thought of Mrs Chatterley as his sister; and Mrs Simeon paid the servants' wages. The extra money Mrs Chatterley received from her benefit nights she gave to Mr Christmas to invest; he gambled it in stocks and lost it. Presently Mrs Christmas wrote to her husband's employers, pointing out that her husband lived more lavishly than his salary warranted. Upon investigation the bankers discovered a mistake of £600 in one of Mr Christmas' accounts. Further inquiry revealed that he had gambled in stocks for nine years, 'partly on his own account, and partly for a lady of rank and title.' He had gambled £968,000 'in *time* bargains!!!' but had lost only £7,000 of it. 'This affair,' noted Oxberry, 'bore an aukward colour.'

People thought Mr Christmas had been led to gamble because of infatuation for Mrs Chatterley. Before going abroad Mr Christmas wrote a letter, which was published in the newspapers, in which he denied that Mrs Chatterley was responsible for his speculations. At her first appearance after these events were made public, the audience received Mrs Chatterley 'without disapprobation, but without any extravagant testimonials of applause' (Oxberry, *Dramatic Biography*, v, 271ff).

The Autobiography of Francis Place

This scandal was before the public for at least two years: *The Times* of October 6, 1823, reporting a peace warrant taken out against Mrs Christmas by Mrs Chatterley, indicated that they had been in the news (if not in *The Times*) before: 'Mrs. Christmas, whose unfortunate dispute with Mrs. Chatterley, the actress, has been so repeatedly before the public, is a prisoner in St. Martin's watchhouse, at the suit of that lady. It appears that the jealousy of Mrs. Christmas is undiminished; or rather, it has gone on increasing until Mrs. Chatterley felt that her person was in danger.' The climax of this affair, the trial of Mr Christmas, was reported in *The Times* on September 16, 1825. Mrs Chatterley was in court when the twenty-nine-year-old bank clerk was tried and sentenced to be transported for fourteen years. *The Times* scarcely minimized her notoriety by describing her as 'the lady alluded to by the prisoner.'

Eight months later Mrs Chatterley began to appear in Place's diary. On April 25 and April 27, 1826, she came to ask Place to help her regain some papers, presumably from Christmas. She returned for more advice on her affairs on both May 8 and 9, and she continued to solicit his help for the rest of the year. On October 20 Place and his wife walked to Mrs Chatterley's house in Brompton Square to see a letter from Christmas. This entry, and most of the entries about Mrs Chatterley, are heavily written over to obliterate the original words (Add. MS 35146, fs. 15v, 16, 19, 22v, 27, 47, 47v, 49, 50).]

NO. 4. MY OWN REVOLUTION[1]

Wednesday 27 feb – 1833

When I on the 13 feb – 1830 married my present wife my actual net income was about [£]1050 per annum – she had an engagement at Covent Garden Theatre which after paying all theatrical expenses left her about, £320 per ann.[2] We expected that she would be engaged for four seasons beyond the current season, and we reckoned our joint incomes at £1300 a year, we knew that there would be a loss from her house in Brompton Square while it was untenanted and that putting my house into condition would cost a considerable sum, which must at all events be expended on it, as nothing had been done to it for many years, but when all had been done and we were settled, still there seemed good reasons for concluding that our income for the next four years would not be less than £1300 – and then if she left the Stage that we should have at the least £1100 a year and perhaps £1200 a year. We calculated that

---

[1] On the page opposite the opening of this document Place's son wrote, 'It is questionable if this also ought not to be left out – FP.' The handwriting is not that of Francis Place Senior.

[2] In the mid 1820s her salary was 12 gn. a week (Oxberry, *Dramatic Biography*, v, 272).

14.4 My own revolution, 1833

when my two sons John and Thomas should be on their own hands as they were likely to be at the end of 1833 – and when her son had been apprenticed and all expenses relating thereto were paid, that we might live in comfort, and have all the conveniencies we desired, and our children be as comfortably provided for as ourselves at the expence of about £800 a year and that therefore at the end of 1833 we might save £300 to £400 a year, as a fund to establish the children in the world, or to be added to capital. This still seems to me to have been a reasonable calculation. It has however turned out a most erroneous estimate.

From my marriage to the end of the season at Covent Garden Play House, the net proceeds of my wifes salary were £160 – the net proceeds of the next season £330, but new arrangements were made at the Play House and she could not obtain a renewal of her engagement for the usual terms of three years – neither could she obtain an engagement at Drury Lane – or the Haymarket and of course all income from her exertions ceased.

Then came my losses.

1. Loss – Removal fitting up my house – loss of Rent at Brompton and additional expenses in respect to the family generally with law expenses – say 600

2. Loss. This was occasioned by the negligence of my attorney in not registering a deed relative to a Mill and some land at Erith – say including Law charges 1400

3. Loss This also was occasioned by negligence or something worse of my attorney at whose instance I had advanced money on a house at Kentish Town and on eleven houses in Staining Lane in the City of London – The house at Kentish Town required more money to put it into repair than it was worth and the Lease was surrendered – The 11 houses in Staining Lane where charged with Ground rents to the Cooks Company – Rates Taxes and Tithes amounting to a larger sum than all the rent which could be collected amounted to and after a while they were reconveyed as a gift to the man from whom I had them, – loss say..................1600

Over   £3600

4th. Loss. This was occasioned by the ill health of a man at Norwood to whom I lent money to enable him to increase his business for which he gave me two small houses as security, not worth half the money I lent him. He is an honest man and but for his ill health would have paid me. I had to put the houses in repair and they have at times been untenanted.

Another house at Norwood has cost me much money and loss whilst shut up by the roguery of the representative of the man to whom it had belonged, who being a man of straw put me at defiance and compelled me to get possession by law – these matters, caused a loss of............500

5. Loss – this was occasioned by the conduct of my former attorney Richard Hayward,[1] whom I had helped from his boyhood – put into business – and made a business for him. He induced me to advance £4999 on an Estate to which he must have known the possessor had no legal title.

The total loss of principal and interest – is...............................4.471

       Total loss of Capital..................£8.571

       ....of Income.................. 650

Leaving me – about.........£470. – This is all that now remains and this will from several causes decrease and at the end of 10 years if I should live so long will not probably exceed £300 per annum. The last loss was confirmed only the day before yesterday when I signed the agreement to take 5/- in the pound on £6971. this being at the time the amount of principal and interest due to me.

The unavidable cost if I remain in my present residence will continue to be as follows. Viz

	£
Rent and Taxes	45
Repairs, mendings, windows, cleaning &c &c	25
Servants	80
Postage, Stationary &c &c	16
Fire Insurance	11
Coals and Wood	28
Oil Candles Soap &c	14
Washing – Out, and sundries for the Kitchens, Breakage	12
	231
Unavoidable expenses Children in money	252
	483
More than Income	13
	£470

And nothing for eating & drinking Clothes &c &c

What then must be done[?] This. Let the house at Charing X if possible, by which 100£ a year may be gained – and this will make my income – 570£ a year and ultimately 400£ a year, on this we must live,

---

[1] Place's son tried to cross out the name with pencil.

14.4 My own revolution, 1833

and pay all the expenses of the family. And this my mind is made up to, and I will do it – cheerfully no matter whatever the privations may be

Now then for a speculation respecting contingencies. To my wife I shewed a statement of the case last night. It is well known that it requires more courage and good sense than one in a thousand possesses, to go at once from a higher to lower grade, Pride, false shame, want of real honesty all concur to induce people to keep up their stile until the last shilling is gone. Not so my wife, she at once said she had contemplated the change, and had made up her mind – we must go at once into a small house and reduce our expenses to our means. That if Mr Morris of the Hay-Market Theatre would not engage her she would go to one of the Minors – but this she shall not do – she shall not work herself into ill health for the low pay she would obtain at a Minor. If she can obtain employment at one of the principal Theatres well! If not – well! We will do without it.

If I would turn sycophant, be a tool and a rascal I could soon obtain employment under Government – This I will not do.

I am strong, active healthy and a better man than most at 61 years of age, capable of many things – and willing to undertake some one or more things, and if opportunities should occur. I will embrace them. At present I see nothing likely to be useful in this way, so I must wait.

NO. 5. 1833-4

My eldest son took the house at Charing Cross at the annual rent of 250£ 'till the expiration of the lease which had twelve years to run from March 1833.

I took the house No. 21 Brompton Square on a lease of 7-14-21 years at the annual rent of 60£ – and 3£ for the use of the fixtures. The house had been let at 80£ a year but it was sadly out of condition and the putting it into condition – the expense of removing fitting up the library, carpets &c cost me 360£

I calculated that my income would be sufficient to enable me to live comfortably tho' somewhat meanly and also enable me to meet the occasional demands of my family but I was mistaken.

Circumstances occured respecting the family which put me to very considerable expenses, and two small, tho excellint annuities which had produced to me 80£ a year were paid off – and reduced my income 32£ a year, some of my tenants ran away the houses were for a time empty, and expence was incurred in making them tenantable I had calculated on reciving from the estate on which I estimated a loss of [£]4471 – a sum of

The Autobiography of Francis Place

1500£ but to this day. 3 Nov. 1834. I have not received one shilling and do not see any chance of ever receving much if any thing. This further reduces my income – say – £75 – and I cannot therefore calculate on an income exceeding £370 a year.

I could live well enough on this sum but for the unavoidable expenses which some of my children and my wifes son will from time to time occasion. I could take a smaller house sell some of my books and bring my expenditure within my income, and this I will do if I cannot find some honorable source from which to increase my income.

In August 1833 my wife had the Cholera, her escape with her life was all but miraculous, and the effects of it are not even yet 3 Nov. 1834 interely removed. All chance of any employment at one of the Theatres at a salary which would more than pay all her expenses has passed away.

Nov. 3. 1834

I am this day 63 years of age and able to do almost any thing I ever was able to do, and many things much better than I could have done them some years ago, when any thing by which I can earn money is likely to occur,

1835–8[1]

A circumstance occurred which bid fair to enable me be useful to both myself and the public, in the office of Secretary to the Pure Soft Spring water Company – I entered on the business on the 18 Nov. 1834 and resigned the office towards the end of January 1835 – in consequence of the projectors being sad rogues.

For particulars – see Narrative of the pure Spring water company.[2]

1835

Occupied in reading &c respecting Municipal Corporation Reform – for particulars. see the Parliamentary and other papers. Backed –

Municipal Reform.[3]

NB. I lost the whole £6971 not one farthing in the pond was ever paid on that sum

Sep. 24. 1838

---

[1] Place's son drew lines through this entry and the next (1835). Next to these entries he noted, 'of no consequence.' Presumably the page was retained because of the final sentence on Place's financial losses.

[2] The company, organized to supply London with water from artesian wells, fell into the hands of City company promoters. For his services Place received £100. His narrative is in Add. MS 35145.

[3] These papers are lost. Place was particularly occupied with reform of city and borough corporations in 1835 because the Report of the Municipal Corporations Commission was presented to Parliament in March and a Corporation Bill was introduced in the House of Commons in June. Place may have helped write both these documents. In addition, he edited a weekly, *Municipal Corporation Reformer*, which ran for five issues (Wallas, pp. 341–3).

14.6 Early recollections, 1825

NO. 6. EARLY RECOLLECTIONS
State of my health   Narrative apud.
                         1776–1838[1]

Looking at the first volume of my poor friend Holcroft's[2] *life* page. 2. I read. "Most persons I believe retain through life a strong impression of very early childhood. I have a recollection of being played with by my parents when very young and of the extreme pleasure it gave me." – This turned my thoughts to the subject. I can remember when quite a child, I suppose under four years of age that I and my brother who was nearly two years younger than I was lying in a bed, by the side of that in which my father and mother slept. How much earlier than this period I laid in this bed or how far back my recollection extends I do not know, but I know very well that at this time I used to be troubled with a dream which frequently occurred and was very distressing. I dreamed that I was lying on the ground, pressed down to it and unable to move, while a huge mass of a brown colour, having a hole in it which shewed it was filled with fire of a red heat, was just rolling over me and about to crush me. The horror I felt was excessive, It generally produced groaning, upon hearing which my mother used to take me out of bed and set me down naked on something cold, "to bring me to myself,["] and as I came to myself I used to utter incoherent expressions of fear. This vision troubled me during several years, but as I grew older and had a more accurate conception of form, the mass about to crush me appeared to be a huge globe of which on account of its size I could see but a very small portion and as it came rolling on slowly towards me produced inexpressible terror. When I grew up and joined with other boys in Bullock hunting the vision ceased and in its place came another, of a "Mad Bull" being at my heels and about to toss me, sometimes I was pursued by more than one, never could I escape, sometimes I have been at an open door frequently at the door of some chambers in the temple seldom could I enter, at times I have been able to run up the stairs, the Bull was always close upon me, but always at the moment he was about to toss me just as his horn touched me I always awoke. My fear of a wild ox in my dreams was the more remarkable as I never had any such fear when I was awake. Dreams of this kind

[1] This document is dated 'August 28, 1825.' The inconsistency between this date and the 1838 date ('Narrative apud. 1776–1838') results, most probably, from Place's writing the first part in 1825, when he was composing the first thirteen chapters of his autobiography, and later – in 1838 – recopying and supplementing this account of his health. The colour of the ink and the style of the handwriting are uniform throughout the document.
[2] Place said he met Thomas Holcroft in 1795 or 1796, but felt unable to invite him to the single room where the Places lived and worked. Their friendship developed after Holcroft's return from the continent in 1804 (Add. MS 35145, f. 28).

The Autobiography of Francis Place

have not even now 1825* entirely left me, but they have become more varied and do not occur so often as they did during many years.† Sometimes I have been hanging from a second floor window by my hands, scarcly able to hold on and always with iron spikes beneath me, once I fell upon the spikes. but awoke at the instant. I have noticed that no dream produced pain, It seems to me impossible that it should as no pain was actually felt, and the sensation – pain – cannot I conclude be produced by dreaming. All that could thus be produced is the apprehension of pain.

One of my most annoying and during several years the dream of most frequent occurrence of this class of dreams, was, that I was at a considerable distance from home in the country or in some distant part of London in the day time naked to my shirt in a heavy shower of rain, always perplexed to know how I came there or why I should be thus naked. A few months since I dreamed that I went along the passage to my library and into it, every thing was disarranged and there was no carpet on the floor, stooping down to pick up a book, I could not rise again, something pressed me down and kept my face near the floor. I soon ascertained that it was an immense hand which covered the back of my head and shoulders, the fingers spread over me and I endevored to grasp the thumb but could not move. The oppression was dreadful and I have no doubt that if it could continue for a few minutes I must die, I conclude that the sensation however long it may seem in the dream is momentary. Frequent dreams such as these were indications not to be neglected, they were one among other reasons for my making a will as soon as I had any thing to leave behind me worth willing to any one.

When about 12 years of age I was occasionally afflicted with – "sick headache", the fit usually came on with a dimness of sight, or rather by a peculiarity of sight, I could only see the right side of the face of any one I looked at or the right half of any object which was not large, and only small portions of buildings or other large objects, and turn my head in any way I could, make whatever effort I might to see more of large objects or the left side of smaller objects I never could succeed. This was soon followed by partial numbness in one or both of my hands generally of my thumbs, and very frequently of the angles of my mouth, these symptoms were unattended by any pain, but they were soon succeeded by intense pain inside my skull, against which in every direction my brain seemed to press with great force, this was accompanied by a much more distressing effect, an aberration of intellect, or suspension of the power of reasoning, so as totally to prevent me from being able to connect any two words, my hearing was at these times very acute, and

* Nor even now 1838.   † They are less frequent and less intense 1838.

14.6 Early recollections, 1825

when I have heard a person named, that is his or her christian and sirname, I never could connect the two together, nor cease repeating them mentally but incoherently for a long time. The power of speech was also affected, I could not collect words together to form a sentence, and if I could have done so, I should have been unable to utter them so as to make sense of them. Emetics were the spediest remedy, the immediate consequence was debility followed by sound sleep for 3. 4 or 5 hours this was followed by hunger and that being appeased I always felt unusual vigour and sound health. These head aches were more or less frequent as I was able to take more or less exercise in the open air. During several years when I earned my living by sewing I was scarcly ever free from headache, and had often to endure terrible attacks: but from the time that I became a master tradesman in 1799 and had out of doors business to attend to, till the year 1818 I never had an attack, yet when I again became sedentary they returned and about every three months I had a severe attack. I now left off all fermented liquors, ate no green vegetables, and scarcly any fruit, took no soups, and scarcly any warm liquids, and ate less food, lately however by the advice of a medical friend I have generally taken a very small quantity of spirits in warm water late in the evening, and under this regimen, though I have not done myself full justice in taking regular exercise I have not been troubled with headaches.

After the death of my most excellent wife, I fell off in health and strength in a way and to an extent which I had beleived was impossible under any circumstances, and was impossible under any other circumstance, my head aches returned and during the two years which followed I had to endure their attacks very frequently and very intensely. These when I married again made me lessen the quantity I ate and leave off also all fermented liquors, save only about one third of half a pint of porter at dinner, my wifes mother having half a pint but drinking only two thirds of it mixed with water,[1] she is now *1838* in her 82nd year. During the last seven years I have not had the headache more than three or four times.

In August 1835, I had a severe attack of Sciatica brought on by walking in the Thames up to my knees about the distance of 200 yards only on a very hot day.

In 1836 I took the Influenza and was for the first time since I can remember, *ill*, I knew what pain was, but I did not know what illness was, I learned it now, for during a week I was quite disabled from doing any thing and yet could not tell what was the matter with me. This was followed by Gout in my right hand du[ri]ng 3 days.

[1] Place later emended the sentence, replacing 'but' with 'I.'

The Autobiography of Francis Place

When I was about 23 years of age I had a sore throat

In the Autumn of 1820 I had a touch of Sciatica

The worst complaint I ever had was in November 1825, I was at this time exulting in my health and strength. I had been standing during several hours in the yard of an Engineer to see some machinery put together and was chilled through. The place was four miles from my house and I returned home about 4 p.m. as rapidly as I could walk, but with all the exertions I could make I could not get warm. On my arrival at home I was seized with intense paid in the abdomen on the left[1] side, I had eaten nothing since the morning, I took some hot tea eat nothing and went to bed, I soon procured a profuse perspiration and concluded that all was well, but at 4 o clock in the moning I awoke with intense pain in my left[1] side the abdomen was swollen and was very tense, I lay still for some time, feeling my side and ascertained that it was sore internally over a very considerable space and that the swelling increased rapidly as did also the pain. I sent immediately for a doctor and requested him to bring his lancets which he did, and bled me to sincope, as soon as he was gone I put a number of Leeches to my side and when they came off I put a large warm poultice on, by which another large quantity of blood was taken away. I knew the nature of the complaint and what I could bear, this with some physicking and starvation for three days put an end to all bad symptoms. The Peritonitis was driven away and I was well again without any apparent diminution of strength.

The little knowledge of anatomy and of diseases I had obtained probably saved my life on this occasion. My wife wished me to take some hot brandy and water and to wait till day light, she did not like my being bled as I never had been bled; had I taken the liquor and waited some few hours, with the disease proceeding rapidly and promoted as it would have been by the hot liquor it is by no means improbable that I should not have been cured.

NB. These with occasional Colds, of which I have probably had more during the last seven years. than in any one of the three preceding periods of twenty years are all the illnesses which have afflicted me.

Christmas Day 1838.

NO. 7. AT MR MILL'S RESIDENCE, COTTAMOOR
WALTON UPON THAMES

Thursday 4 Septr. 1828. *Narrative*

The day being very fine I took Mr Mill's three eldest daughters with me

---

[1] Originally, 'right.'

14.7 Visit to Shepperton, 1828

on a walk to Shepperton. I have before observed that my father when he lived in Ship and Anchor Court near Temple Bar, used to go occasionally to Angle at Shepperton, and on two or three perhaps more of these excursions he took me with him. I was a very small boy at this time. I lived with him at a public house near the Church, and he took me with him in the Punt in which he and his companions fished. I had I thought a distinct recollection of the Public house and the Church and their relative position, the place whence we took water, and one or two of the places where he used to angle. I recollected that the public house was a low brick house with a high pitched tile roof on the right hand side of the road going towards the river, and when we came in sight of it, I knew it at once. I knew the two roads the Church and the landing place altho it must have been more than Fifty years since I had seen these places. The sign of the house was the Kings head. It is rather a small house. On a bench at the landing place sat an old man in the dress of a fisherman, we seated ourselves on the bench which would scarcely hold us all. I began a conversation with him He told me he was 82 years of age, that his wifes father Mr King kept the Kings Head 50 years ago, that his own father had also kept the same house, that each of them had kept the house about 50 years 100 years in succession between them. I told him that my father had for several years in succession been two or three times in the season at Shepperton fishing, that it must have been about 50 years since he was last there. That he sometimes staid a week sometimes a fortnight and always put up at the Kings Head, that he always had a horse and chaise, and that he must have known him, but had probably forgotten him. The old man asked his name, I said Mr Place – Simon Place – that he wore a grey coat a large flapped waistcoat with narrow gold lace on the edges.

I remember him said the Old Man, he was a fat man had a big belly I remember him well Sir. I said he had a friend, who was sometimes with him; his name was Baldwin. I remember Mr Baldwin said the Old Man, he Printed the Daily Advertiser. I could also remember Mr Baldwin, he was a tall thin man, and like my father had the Gout, but I never before knew that he was a printer

A multitude of pleasant associations crowed upon me, as I looked around me, at the water – the house – the landing place – the fishing punts – the Old man – the Church &c &c – and thought of my childish days – Some more grave associations when I reflected on the great number of persons who were now no more, and of the many who in a comparatively short time would be no more.

On questioning the Old Man respecting the company which frequented the place, he said it was quite another thing – formerly – many years ago a considerable number of gentlemen came to fish, now only one or two came together and these not often. Then many gay people came and dined on the water, or on the grass on the islands up the river – now none came.

I said I thought I could remember that my father and his party in some two or more punts, went to a place where the water was smooth and deep and where under some Shrubbery and Willow Trees they were sheltered from the Sun, and that they angled for many hours dining in their punts

I remember them well said the Old Man, it is a little higher up the River, and he pointed in the direction of the place.

He remembered my father slipping into the water between the head and stern, or rather the ends of two punts, holding on to each with one hand his fishing rod being also in one of them and his being laughed at by his companions for having two pair of eyes (spectacles) and yet not being able to see his way, but must tumble into the water.

The Old man was tall robust and had the appearance of a man under 70 years of age. I am said he – the oldest Fisherman upon the River.

NO. 8. 1841–1847 STATE OF HEALTH. CONTINUED

Narrative

Early in 1841. I had a severe cold which caused considerable irritation of the trachea, violent coughing great expectoration but no pain. It continued until the middle of the summer, and returned again in September when it affected the lungs, but still without pain. It departed as the summer came on, but returned again in the autumn, but left me early in November. At this time a schism was apprehended in the Council of the Anti Corn Law League. Its success was at this moment somewhat impeded and as is usual in all such cases some difference of opinion respecting the mode of proceeding had been expressed. A meeting of deputies from many places had been summoned to meet at Manchester on the 17th of November. The Committee of the Metropolitan was requested to send three or four persons. Of this, (the business) committee I was chaiman and was very much pressed to make up the number four. I did not think I was in a proper state of health to undertake the mission and therefore declined the office. The Business committee consisted of nine members some of them were old associates of mine and some when the committee was first appointed were strangers. All had now become

14.8 State of health continued, 1841–1847

special friends, all were able men, all men of business, all stout hearted strong headed men.* We had a large intricate, and difficult busines to conduct It was well attended to and well conducted as its rapid success shewed. I had been much connected with societies and their committees, but I had never known any committee which was altogether composed of men so well qualified for their special business as this was, and to their earnest solicitations I at length consented. The case was this. The Council did not at this time very clearly comprehend as it has since done either the principles of Free Trade, nor how to conduct so large a matter, as all were becoming, satisfied they must become before there could be any chance of success. The conference had therefore been called for the purpose of comparing opinion in various parts of the Country and to concert general measures to set the various parts of the Kingdom actively in motion.

We in London had from the day the Metropolitan Association was formed, seen the necessity there was for preventing any extraneous matter being mixed with our proceedings, "the Total and Immediate Repeal of the Corn and other laws which prohibited or impeded the introduction into the country, of articles of Food for the People.["]

It was therefore declared in the resolutions then adopted, that this was our sole object and that no other could be entertained by the committee This resolution was afterwards confirmed by the Association and made applicable to the whole body.

The Council of the League had not made any such declaration and Mr Joseph Sturge the Rich Corn Factor at Birmingham, one of its members, operated upon, by the for a moment inefficiency of the League, had resolved at the Conference about to be held, to propose to add to its proceedings, others for the purpose of promoting, measures to procure Universal Suffrage in the Election of members to serve in Parliament, with all its concomitants.†[1] A correspondence had taken place in which it had been shewn to him that among the members of the League were men of all parties, and every shade of Politics, and that were to adopt any special political scheme would break up the League. and thus, probably

---

* The men who composed the committee were
    [names never filled in].
† These were 1 Universal Suffrage.
         2. Annual Parliaments.
         3. Equal Voting Districts
         4. No Property Qualification.
         5. Voting by Ballot.
         6. Payment of Members.

[1] Sturge was a Quaker reformer active in several causes besides repeal of the Corn Laws.

for many years to come put an end to all exertion to procure the repeal of the Corn Laws. Mr Sturge could not however be put from his purpose. He also proposed that Mr Villiers should on the first day Parliament met propose a bill to the house of Commons for the Total and Immediate Repeal of the Corn Laws. On this subject there had been correspondence between Mr Villiers[1] and Mr Sturge in which Mr Villiers shewed Mr Sturge that the forms of the House would not permit him to bring in a bill as proposed, but Mr Sturge could not be put from his purpose. He was represented to me, not only a very obstinate man, but as one wholly impervious to reason in respect to any opinion he had formed, and that he possessed the bad habit of putting an end to all attempts to move him in such cases, of saying that arguments used for the purpose were not according to the light which was in him. The matter was of much importance, and to Manchester I went on the 16th of November by the Mail train. I arrived there at 9 p m and put up at the York Hotel. I had not been there long when Mr Sturge whom I had never before seen came to the same Hotel accompanied by a son of Mr Scholefield M.P. for Birmingham with whom I was acquainted and by whom Mr Sturge was introduced to me. We were friends in a few minutes, and in less than an hour Mr Sturge had consented not only to abandon his intention, but insisted upon my consenting that at the Conference on the morrow morning I should declare the renunciation of his intention and ground that renunciation on the conversation of the previous meeting, this was done before the business for which the meeting was called had commenced

One hundred and twenty persons were said to be present, they came from many places and especially from the large towns in the North All matters not intimately connected with the purpose of the meeting were previously dispatched and among them was the matter relating to Mr Sturge, respecting this matter it was resolved, that as soon as the regular business of the day was concluded and the Conference had been formally dissolved, as many as pleased should be requested to continue and have a conversation on Reform of Parliament To be opened by Mr Sturge stating his views on the subject.

The busines of the conference, interrupted for about $1\frac{1}{2}$ hours by a grand dinner given at the Adelphi Hotel, continued until 8 p.m when the meeting was dissolved

About 60 persons remained and I was voted into the chair a conversational debate on Reform of the House of Commons then commenced

---

[1] Charles Villiers, one of the founders of the Anti-Corn Law Association and chief spokesman in the House of Commons for free trade.

14.8 State of health continued, 1841–1847

and continued till 11. p.m. The conversation was lively and agreeable and the company dispersed in great good humour.*

There had been three days of intensely hard frost, a rare occurrence in November, it continued until noon of the 18th, on the morning of which at 10 o clock I started on my return to London. I arrived at the Terminus near Eaton [sic] Square at ½ past 9. p.m in one of the heaviest and coldest showers of rain I had ever witnesses. All the cabs in attendance had been taken by friends of expected passengers by the train and I had to wait in the cold and damp for full half an hour, when a small old racketty Cab returned from having taken a passenger to his home and I was put into it. Its bottom nearly touched the ground, both the windows were broken it was miserably damp and uncomfortable. In less than ten minutes my Bronchitis returned with redoubled violence and I was all but suffocated; so much indeed did I suffer that when I reached home I was all but helpless. I recovered to some extent next day but I was not [free] from the attack until the middle of June 1842. It returned again on the 1st of September with much violence which continued to increase till the 15th of the same month when it was so very bad that I became nearly reckless of consequences from any attempt I might make for relief.

I had heard of several Old fellows who had been cured of similar complaints by the Cold water system. I had seen and conversed with one of them. I therefore determined to try an experiment and with a fit of heavy coughing and expectorating I went to my bedroom, stripped myself naked stepped into a large hip bath, dipped a large spunge into cold water and squeezed it on the top of my head, this I did three times dried myself as rapidly as I could dressed and came down stairs. There was great reaction I was in a glow all over and somewhat relieved. I went up early to bed and and again repeated the ablution. Next morning after my wife had left the bedroom I repeated the experiment, and thus I proceeded during the nine following days when all my bad symptoms had departed. It seemed to me to be a desperate attempt in which I could not expect any one to concur, and was ashamed also to let any one know how I was proceeding but when I found myself comparatively well I told my wife how I had been acting. I then borrowed a shower bath which I used three times a day for a week, then night and moning for another week, then once a day as soon as I rose in the morning during the whole winter and had no return of the complaint. Dr Arnott now determined

---

* So strong was the desire of Mr Struge [sic] for interfering the movement going on under the appellation of Chartism, that it induced him to abandon the League, to which he had been a very liberal contributer, and to set up a society for Reform of Parliament, under the Title of "Complete Suffrage" to the increase of which he gave up much of his time and money. Some account of his proceedings will be found in the Guard Books, backed. Reform. Working People.

my complaint to be Asthmatic. I continued the bath but towards the close of the year the complaint returned again and was not so readily driven away by the shower bath as in the case mentioned and I continued to be better and worse until May when it again left me. I was now satisfied that I was much injured, my breath was short my strength reduced considerably. and upon the whole I was much debiliated. I went on much in the same way until the Autumn of 1844. when all the bad symptoms excepting some shortness of breath again left me, and so I continued until the 2nd of November when I was afflicted with a severe fit of sick headache, I had been wholly free from this complaint for a long period, but it was now intense. It had never before continued during more than 12 hours but in now continued day and night until the moning of the 5th when it was worse than it had ever before been, I had abstained from the use of the shower bath since the commencement of the head ache and the Asthma had returned. I was satisfied that I was now attacked to an extent I [was] unable to sustain and I told my wife so and she immediately sent for Dr Arnott, but in less than 10 minutes I was senseless on the floor, to utter dismay of my wife who was the only person with me. I recovered as suddenly as I had fallen, utterly unconscious of having been taken as I had been or that I had for a moment lost my consciousness. I found myself on the floor propped up by the knees of some person whilst another was holding me. I soon found the two persons were my next door neighbour Mr Hill and a surgeon Mr Pollard who lived at the botton of the Square. I was in an instant aware of my condition and asked how long I had been on the floor and was told full one hour. My neighbours said they must carry me up to my bedroom, but as I had ascertained I had the use of all my limbs and that my speech was not at all affected, I demurred to being carried and desired to walk up. The Doctor administered a draught of some kind which caused me to vomit, and as both my attendants insisted upon carrying me I submitted on reaching the first landing place on the stairs I relapsed vomited again and was again releived. I was then carried up to the second floor and was put to bed. Dr Arnott arrived soon afterwards, I had seen him on the previous day when he had no expectation of my being affected as I had been. He heard the case ordered me to remain in bed, to be quite composed and wrote a prescription, and thus was I for the first time in my life confined to my bed. Nothing which had ever before occurred having kept me there during 24 hours.

Dr Arnott said the fit had been brought on by derangement of the nervous system. The Doctor had some months previously advised me to read and write and think less than I had been accustomed to do and especially to abstain from the small close writing in the quantity I had

14.8 State of health continued, 1841–1847

been doing for the Delhi Gazette of which my Son. F.W. was the principal proprietor and Editor. This advice I neglected to take, and the Dr now said that as too close thinking for too long a time together had brought on the derangement so an attempt to continue the practice would produce the worst possible consequences.

The Dr might now have ceased to caution me for I was too much deranged to be able to occupy myself as usual. The immediate effects of the derangement were that I saw with each eye seperately. This was very annoying every thing in the room was seen double every small thing in two places and every large thing overlapping itself, whilst things near were sometimes sadly confounded with things further off. Another curious effect was that whenever I shut my eyes as I wished to do continually to avoid the disagreeable effect of double vision, was to me a very strange phenomenon, whilst my eyes were closed I had constant visions. I saw objects as clear as bright and as distinct as I had ever done with my eyes open One of these visions which repeatedly occured was that of a person passing before me at a very short distance a man, a woman or a child, but never more than one at a time though there were several in succesion. A man in a jacket a common workman would pass before me towards a kind of shop counter going from left to right but when he reached the counter he and the counter would disappear and another person a well dressed woman for example who would disappear as the man had done when she had passed the same distance as the man had done, there was no appearance of a counter excepting only when the man appeared this succession would continue until I opened my eyes. Sometimes the same delusion would be repeated upon my closing my eyes, sometimes it would be very different, as for instance, I could see before me hung up as it were to the cieling a piece of black velvet curiously embroidered with gold or coloured silk the ornaments being flowers seperate or grouped or in festoons. Different coloured and different patterns of Silk. all these things were in motion, the motion being invariably the same, as if drawn up gently until the whole of the piece was gone when another of another pattern followed. I always had in the left breast pocket of my dressing coat which I always wore in the house, an orange coloured Silk handkerchief, I saw myself sitting leaning back in a chair with a high back and the hankerchief rising in a spiral form from the breast pocket and disappearing and when it had disappeared another followed in the same way, and this would continue as long as I kept my eyes closed. Again I saw my wife sitting by the bed side and so perfect and so especially distinct was this vision that though I knew she was not there I was compelled to open my eyes, to see her in propria persona. This continued during the 10 days I remained in bed,

The Autobiography of Francis Place

gradually diminishing in intensity. At the expiration of 10 days I refused to remain in bed any longer, the Asthma having increased much[1]

I again took to the Shower Bath to drive away the Asthma taking the precaution which I had not previously done to put on an oiled silk cap. This practice had a bad effect on my head and made me conclude that I was doomed to bear with a deranged brain and disordered lungs. In this state of suffering I remained three months

The advice of the Doctor to refrain from reading and writing was still superfluous for full 5 months, whenever I attempted to do either, I was always, in about a quarter of an hour warned to desist and I did so lest I should have the penalty of dropping down again, to pay. I was however from the time I left my bed able to write for an hour or more by lamp light, and by lamplight only, and this power I used for the purpose of composing rough drafts for the Delhi Gazette which were copied on very thin paper by my wife and daughter Jane. I had ceased trying to read any thing and was read too for some hours at some time of each day and in the evening by my wife.

At the commencement of May 1845 I again determined to try the effect of the Shower Bath as the Asthma had increased and as the violent coughing and expectorating were producing bad effects not only on my head but were reducing my body and destroying my muscular power I was fortified against the chance of bad consequences by those I was suffering under. The effect of the Shower Bath was now very small, but the Asthma again disappeared within a fortnight.

During the summer I continued to grow better but very slowly sometimes I could read or write for an hour in the day time but I did so very seldom as I always felt, though slightly, an increase of derangement in

[1] It seems highly probable that Place suffered from a brain embolus. That is, a small clot originating from his heart or lungs had been swept into the cerebral circulation, lodging in the brain stem in the vicinity of the upper pons where movements of the eyes are coordinated and producing an imbalance in visual coordination, which apparently returned when he tired his eye muscles by prolonged reading. Peduncular hallucinations such as he described are also associated with some brain lesions at the level where the main sensory and motor tracts sweep from the brainstem to the brain proper through the cerebral peduncles. Noteworthy is the awareness of the distorted nature of both the double vision and the hallucinations, the preservation of the powers of comprehension, expression and memory, and the absence of paralysis or of sensory changes other than the visual ones. The suddenness of the attack suggests a suddenly operating cause such as an embolus, and the recovery as well as the circumscribed symptoms is indicative of a small lesion such as that produced by a tiny embolus, rather than by a more generalized process such as hardening of the arteries. The subsequent tendency for a 'warning' to occur on visual exertion indicates that there had been some degree of structural brain damage. This residual weakness, as well as the difference in the pattern of symptoms from that of migraine, shows that the area of involvement was quite different from that which had been involved in the lifelong attacks of migraine.

14.8 State of health continued, 1841–1847

my head, but no increased derangement was consequent in my writing for even an hour an a half by lamplight

The reason I have written this circumstantial account is, because as it seems to me the symptoms are peculiar, as I cannot on enquiry hear of any one who has been similarly circumstanced in respect to the visions, though I have seen several whose visual organs have been more or less deranged from apparently similar causes, and a physician in my neighbourhood has told me of an elderly gentleman, a studious man who had a similar fit to mine two years ago and has been unable either to read or write since

March 20 1846. I have had no return of the Asthma during the remarkably mild winter which has just passed away, During the last six months I have ceased to use the Shower Bath but have washed my body always once, generally twice; a day, this has kept off the Asthma without any appearance of damage to my head. I have recovered my muscular power but am short winded and limited in action thereby. I feel however that I am seriously damaged not only in my lungs but in my head which is never right well and sometime very much the contrary – three or four times since the fit I have expected to be knocked down again as I probably shall some day be, and that too as probably for the last time.

Compelled to give up reading and to be very cautious as to the time I employ in writing; my life would have become very monotinous and irksome, had I not discovered a resourse in what had at times filled up spaces and given me occupation when I was compelled to sit and hear the tales and complaints of various persons.

This occupation consisted of cutting from newspapers, notices on various subjects and especially of such as related to the working people. I had put away a great quantity of newspapers and cuttings from newspaper, these I now overhauled as I did other large quantities which were sent to me. From these I cut out whatever I thought might be useful at some future time in relation to the working classes most especially. I now arranged these papers pasted them into books and put them in form for binding whilst my wife read to me. These books have been bound and amont to many volumes[1]

I indexed these volumes at short intervals as they were composed and afterwards made fair indexes by little and little at a time until I have made up this collection to the end of the year. 1845.

And since to the end of the year 1846.

And since to the end of the year. 1847.

[1] In 181 volumes.

The Autobiography of Francis Place

NO. 9. OFFICIAL ASSIGNEE BANKRUPTCY COURT[1]

On the 22 october 1831 Mr Mill received a note from the Lord Chancellor Brougham which he gave to me –

The Note.

Thurs

My dear Mr M. ⟨Be⟩ [undecipherable word] & speak to Place whether he would not like to be one of the Official Assees[2]

I can recommd him mot conscienticy & I am sure he would be one of the vy bet & give spirit to the rest & it is 700 or 750 a year – but a good deal of work – but not overmuch

yours
H. B.

The sooner you let me know the better
J Mill Eq
East India House
Leadenhall Ln

After some conversation with Mr Mill in which the proposal of the Chancellor all circumstances considered was thought to be a somewhat handsome proceeding, and as it in no way made a compromise of any opinion I held. I consented conditionally to take the office.

As the act contains no directions or explanations of the duty of An Official Assignee. I made out an account of what appeared to me would be his duty, and on consideration began to think it not worth my acceptance[3]

[1] This document is dated 'Oct – Nov – 1831.'
[2] The 'Act to establish a Court in Bankruptcy' (1 & 2 Will. IV c. 56) empowered the Lord Chancellor to appoint as many as thirty assignees whose duty was to obtain the bankrupt's possessions and transfer them to the Bank of England. The act specified that these assignees were to be 'Merchants, Brokers, or Accountants, or Persons who are or have been engaged in Trade.'
[3] Opposite this portion of the narrative Place pasted and annotated the following Letter from Bentham:

Q.S.P. 2 Novr 1831

J. B. to F. P.
   Let not the confusion and absurdities of the Bankruptcy Court Act deter you from accepting the Office of Official Assignee.
   You will be of the greatest use. When you have read these "Observations" of mine, you and I must talk over the whole matter.

NB. The above note came from Mr Bentham with a revised proof of. "Observations on the Bankruptcy Court Bill."

14.9 Official Assignee. Lord Brougham's proposal, 1831

On saturday 13 Nov Mr Mill came again, he said he had not heard any thing on the subject since he wrote to the Chancellor on the 22 October. He said I ought to see Mr Vizard, and talk the matter over with him, that it would be necessary for me to write a letter soliciting the office and accompany it with testimonials.

I demurred to this, said I had not sought the office, and should not have sought it, that if the Chancellors recommendation was not of itself sufficient, I was not desirous of the appointment, and would not obtain it by begging. Mill argued that it was not begging nor doing any thing which the most independent man might not with the greatest propriety do, and had done. I was not however satisfied but promised to see Mr Vizard, and I went to him.

Mr Vizard is the Lord Chancellors secretary of Bankrupts and an attorney in considerable practice, known to me in consequence of business I have transacted with him, and in consequence of some interviews which became necessary in my arbitrating a matter at his request between the Chancellor when Mr Brougham and another person.

Mr Vizard talked the whole matter through with me respecting the act of parliament, and the duties of an official assignee, he asked my opinion on various matters relating to both, and we seemed to concur in all points, he said it would be necessary for me to write a letter to him, and accompany it with testimonials, which he would lay before the gentlemen who were to select and appoint the assignees. I said I had not contemplated the necessity of writing a letter, much less the procuring of testimonials, and that I did not think I should do so, but if I did the testimonials would be only those of Mr Mill and Mr Grote[1] both of whom he knew, both of whom were well know to nearly all the gentleman who were to make the selection as I myself was to some of them. That I had concluded the Lord Chancellors selection of me would be sufficient, that I should not have sought the office, was not very desirous to obtain it, and might not therefore trouble him any further on the subject.

This was on saturday. In the evening I wrote a letter to Mr Mill, and made a copy of it for Mr Grote. On sunday at noon I read the drafts of these letters and also the draft of another to Mr Joshua Evans who is one of the Commissioners of Bankrupts under the act, and I talked the matter over with him. My purpose was to ascertain the time when he and the other gentlemen appointed to make the selection were likely to meet for that purpose, and whether the Lord Chancellor had made any communication to them respecting me, as I did not much expect he had done so notwithstanding he had volunteered to do so. I told him that

[1] George Grote (1794–1871), best known for his *History of Greece*, was a philosophic radical, a friend of Mill and Bentham, an M.P. from 1831 to 1841 – and a banker.

unless the Lord Chancellor did recommend me in the terms of his note to Mill, or in equivalent terms I would not make application, and was almost determined not to make any even if he did.

Mr Evans said there were men among those appointed to make the selection who knew me well, and knew as well as he himself did that no man either was or could be better qualified than I was for the office, and that it was unlikely that any one would be found in all respects so well qualified. He said you know Brougham as well as I do, and I think his selecting you does him credit, but as yet he had made no communication on the subject.

On Monday the 15th, sent my letters to Mill and Grote by the post.

Tuesday 16 – read the letters, and the draft of a letter to Mr Warburton who said I was personally right, not to do more than I had proposed to do, and even that would be too much unless the Chancellor kept his word. But on public grounds he wished it should be done, and on public grounds he wished I should do it – ie. write to Vizard and send testimonials. That although upon the whole the Bankruptcy court was an improvement on the present system, the bill and the court were both absurdities that unless I became an official assignee, took my place at the head of them and set an example to them the business would be badly done

Read the letters to Colonel P. Thompson, in the evening, He thought as Mr Warburton did, but he very much disliked that I should apply to subordinates, as my nomination was sought for and promised by the principal, who as the act vested the appointment in him, should have made it, without making any kind of request necessary. But as it was probable a considerable amount of public good would result from my having the office he though I was not wrong in doing as much as I had done and proposed to do.

Saw Mr Bickersteth and conversed with him on the subject. He advised me by all means to accept the appointment as the offer had come spontaneously from Brougham. He said the act was a miserable sample of legislation, but that by my becoming an official assignee I should not only do the public service but become more completely a public man, be more and more known to Merchants and Lawyers, and be in the way of serving the public more effectually hereafter. That the greatest good of the bill was this, that it was another stab in the side of our abominable laws which at no very distant day must be revised, and when that day came he should have his share to perform in the business, and should then desire to have me as a coadjutor, which my holding the office of official assignee could not fail to promote.

14.9 Official Assignee. Lord Brougham's proposal, 1831

Letters referred to.

To George Grote Esqr

13 Nov. 1831.

My dear Sir

I send you a copy of a letter I have written to Mill, and also a copy of the letter I have written to Mr Vizard, which I may or may not send. When you have read the copy of the letter to Mill you will understand why I have written to you.

Yours truly.
Francis Place

To James Mill Esqr.

13 Nov. 1831

Dear Mill

I had a conversation yesterday with Mr Vizard, his notions and mine are alike in every particular respecting the duties of an Official Assignee. I have however concluded from what passed between us, that he did not expect there would be any particular recommendation of me from the Lord Chancellor, for the office. He said that I must write a a letter to him (Mr Vizard) and request the appointment, and that the letter must be accompanied by testimonials, and that he would lay them before the gentlemen who are appointed to select the Assignees. I therefore request you to write a note containing just whatever you may please to say, and to send it to me under cover sealed and addressed to Mr Vizard. I shall ask our friend Grote to do the same, and this is all, in the way of testimony I shall ask from any body. More than this I will not do, nor would I do more were the emoluments even necessary for the maintenance of my family. I never before in all my life solicited any thing as matter of favour. I do so now with great reluctance, it goes sadly against the grain, and makes me ill at ease

Yours truly
Francis Place.

Inclosed is a copy of the letter I think of sending to Mr Vizard.

To William Vizard Esqr

Charing Cross Nov 1835 [1831]

Sir

As a number of Official Assignees are to be appointed under the 'Act to establish a Court in Bankruptcy' I take the liberty to solicit the office.

I was actively employed in business on my own account upwards of

The Autobiography of Francis Place

twenty years, have been much occupied in arranging and settling the affairs of other men in business, as well privately as with their creditors, have been an assignee under a commission of bankruptcy, have many times acted as an arbitrator and umpire, occasionally in very extensive and difficult cases, have several times been and am still a trustee for creditors, and also executor and trustee for the children of persons deceased, and for others, and have many times sat as a juror in all the common law courts and at the Old Bailey. My habits of business are well known to many among whom are the two friends whose testimonies I inclose, which will I hope be considered sufficient by the gentlemen who are to appoint the official assignees.

I am Sir
Your obedient servant
Francis Place

With the letter to Mr Grote I sent what follows as a. P. S.

It is inconvenient to both of us to have conversations just at the times we might wish to have them, so I must at times trouble you to read what I should otherwise say to you.

I did wrong, so Mill seems to think in shewing Bougham's note to you, respecting his desiring me to become an official assignee. I do not concur with him, I think I did right. Brougham wrote to Mill I consented, and came to the following conclusions.

1. That Brougham would make the recommendation in the terms of his note, and say he did so on learning that I was desirous to obtain the office.

2. That his doing so was all that could be at all necessary to bring me before the gentlemen who are to appoint the official assignees.

It did not seem to me that any written testimonies were at all necessary, or that they would be required of me.

I thought that if any such testimonies were necessary that Mill would of his own mere motion have sought out opportunities to supply them without mentioning the matter to me, at least until he had supplied them.* That he would if it had found them necessary, as he told me he

* This observation respecting what Mr Mill might have done, has reference to his being employed at the East India House in 1818. As soon as I heard he had been named as a person fit for the office, I procured an introduction to Sir John Jackson M. P. Sir John was a rank tory an active and vehement opposer of all reform and reformers, a large fat, burly city of London Merchant. He was as I understood an open hearted soft headed good tempered fellow. I went to him and we soon became familiar, he came to me on his way to the house of commons, I liked him and he liked me and our intercourse became frequent. He was to be the next chairman of the Court of Directors of the East India Company, and it was said Mill's appointment would depend much on the decision of Sir John, and certain if he could be

14.9 Official Assignee. Lord Brougham's proposal, 1831

did, have procured them and sent them to Mr Vizard or to Brougham. In doing so he would have done no more than in other cases have been done by myself and others. That he would have lost no time in seeing Mr John Smith, Mr Lewis Lloyd, Mr Newman and as many more of the gentlemen who are to appoint the assignees as he is acquainted with, and most of whom know me also, that he would tell them the Chancellor thinking or rather knowing that I was such a person as he in his note to Mill says he knows I am; intended to recommend me to their notice, that he himself had known me very intimately for twenty years nearly and could also recommend me. I could not therefore contemplate beating about to procure testimonials in favour of myself. Mill I conclude has done none of these things, obvious as the doing them all appears to me, that they should be done off hand.

He wrote he says to the Lord Chancellor on the 22 october, the day he received my consent and has not heard from him since. This is I suppose all he has done. I do not know that I ought to impute much blame to him for what appears to me neglect, since he like every one else acts according to his habits. His habits induce him to be very quiet and easy respecting any interference in the concerns of others, and therefore for him to do what to me seems so very obvious and necessary might never have occurred to him as either obvious or necessary. My habits lead me to follow up such matters until all has been done that can be done, and I may therefore be somewhat too sanguine in my expectations of what other men should do.

By the time you have replied to my application to you I shall have ascertained whether or not the Chancellor has or has not recommended me. I think he has not, and if he has not I shall return your testimonial unopened and there will be an end to the business.

I know very well that *prudential* men will say I ought to collect testimonials and send them in even if no recommendation be made by the Chancellor. My answer to this is, that I never will be beholden to ordinary, vulgar thinking men for any thing. That such advisors look more to

---

induced to support him. Sir John had many doubts and some pretty strong prejudices but he was an honest man and well disposed to promote the interests of the company. I combatted his prejudices, by opposing to them the advantages which would accrue to the company from the services of Mill, and he became Mill's friend. My exertions with Sir John were not the only ones I made, I induced others to represent to him the probable advantages of having Mills services. I stood on no ceremony with any body, Mill was to be served, he deserved the best exertions in his favour of every one who knew him, and I as one who knew his trancendent merits went to work at once without consulting with any one, in a way which I knew no one would advise, no one could think likely to produce any good consequences. It was a chance well worth taking, it was the only one I had or could have of serving him effectually.

the emolument than to any thing and indeed every thing else, and not at all of the more important circumstances, which constitute ones self-satisfaction though that is of all but infinitely more importance, than money to every man who does not make his self-satisfaction rest on money. Mine to me is I know by long experience the most important of all things, mine is I hope based on the proper ground, and if it were to slip from that I should be as miserable for the future as I have hitherto been comfortable and should then probably be too much of a coward to cut my throat as I ought to do.

In conclusion here is a short account of the duties of an official assignee. Having ascertained by comparing my opinions with Mr Vizard that the duties are such as I told you I thought they should be, I can scarcly be mistaken in asserting that there are but few men of character who are competent to perform them who will not think they are much too onerous for them to undertake.

They are as follows.

On issuing a fiat, the official assignee must immediately take possession of the estate and effects of the bankrupt – his household furniture – stock in trade, of every thing indeed he can find on his premises, or in his possession or belonging to him wherever it may be, as the messenger does now, he must make out an inventory on the spot, a schedule of debts and credits and with or without the assistance of the bankrupt a balance sheet. All this if it be done correctly will be about as troublesome as disagreeable.

In all cases he must sell the bankrupt up, in many cases he must leave his wife and children destitute, in some cases he must turn them destitute into the street. This is something beyond the disagreeable. He must take upon himself the administration of the bankrupts affairs, so far as he and his creditors are concerned until in the usual way, other assignees are appointed. He must then become the accountant as well as the assignee. In the course of a year he will have at the least twenty-five bankruptcies or bankrupts estates to manage, and finally the number will be about a hundred. In every new bankruptcy he will have to go through all the steps I have mentioned, and be the accountant for them all. He must have an office, a managing clerk, under clerks, and persons to collect debts. His will be a difficult disagreeable and complicated business, it will occupy his whole time, and his undivided attention during office hours, and he will frequently be compelled to attend to business beyond office hours, as well publicly as privately. He must attend the court of commissioners, – the meetings of creditors, he will have many real difficulties to to encounter. He will have more to do in his office than any accountant now has, for he must have his business done in a way very

14.9 Official Assignee. Lord Brougham's proposal, 1831

different from that in which such business is now done, he will have many heavy responsibilities upon him which they have not. Men who have other means of procuring a comfortable subsistence will not be very desirous to take the office, which after some years have passed away will be filled by those only who cannot in any other respectable way procure the same amount of money which they may expect to realize as official assignees.

F. P.

Oh, I omitted to mention one clause in the act which must be set aside, because it cannot be complied with, in its present form. It directs that all the present commissions of bankruptcy shall be removed into the New Court and divided among the official assignees, thus each of them may perhaps have fifty in a lump, perhaps twice that number, before he will have have been able to settle down in a business-like way, with his new arrangements for his new business, he will have a waggon load of books and papers with the certainty of all manner of mischief as the consequence, of the impossibility of ever having the means of thoroughly understanding any one of these commissions in the way they have been worked.

14 Noon

Since writing the above I have learned that the Chancellor is to communicate with the chusers of assignees to day, and I am told that the applications to him personally are so numerous and of such a nature that if he were to recommend any one person he must recommend a considerable number, and that he will therefore recommend no one. I shall know all about it either this evening or tomorrow moning.

More last words. I went to Mr Vizard at Mill's suggestion that I should see him, and ask him what steps were necessary for me to take respecting testimonials, Vizard however, made this unnecessary by volunteering the information.

Thursday [Tuesday] evening 15 Novr.

Received a note from Mill, containing the draft of a letter he proposed writing as a testimonial, if I did not concur in all that he said I was to make alterations.

I returned the note and the letter with a note as follows "As I have resolved not to send in any testimonials, I return the notes."

The Autobiography of Francis Place

Wednesday. 16 Nov. 6. p.m

To Mr Grote
My dear Sir

I conclude that I have not heard from you in consequence of some exertions you are making in my behalf which are not as yet completed, so I send you this note to say that I have determined not to accept the office of official assignee under any circumstances.

Yours truly.
Francis Place

[Reply from Grote]
My dear Sir

I should have written to you yesterday, had I not anticipated, from a message sent to you through Roebuck, that I might possibly have seen you yesterday evening. I could then have given you in person my testimonial as to your competency. & it would have given me most sincere pleasure to state in most conclusive terms my persuasion that you would do credit to the office.

Your note received this morning supersedes this intention on my part. Whether you are right in declining to press your chance of success, I cannot pretend to determine. But if you should, from any new circumstances, be induced to resume the design of putting yourself forward, I shall be most happy to do all in my power to promote it.

Yours very truly
Geo Grote
Thread. St Nov. 17

N.B. Mr Roebuck's note was not delivered until after mine to Mr Grote had been put into the post.

Saturday 19 Nov.

Mr Mill came to urge upon me the propriety of writing to Mr Vizard. I told him, I had determined not to take the office, and could not therefore write to Mr Vizard.

Sunday 20 Nov

Colonel Jones came to me. He said he had had two conversations with the Lord Chancellor respecting the present state of public affairs, the Unions &c, and also respecting me, as well in respect to the Birmingham and National Political Union[1] as of the office of Official Assignee. Jones

---

[1] A society (commenced in January 1830) uniting middle and lower classes for effecting a reform in parliament. Place says this union was recommended as a model to other reform societies started in the early 1830s (Add. MS 27789, f. 146).

14.9 Official Assignee. Lord Brougham's proposal, 1831

said he wanted a memorandum of my age for the Chancellor as my being so lately turned of sixty, must not the Chancellor said be an impediment to my appointment. That my being in the office would be a great public service and he should certainly appoint me. Jones found that the chancellor had not heard of my determination not to take the office, so he, Jones, had come to see if I would not alter my determination and accept the office. I shewed him as I had done before, that he who did the business of an official assignee as it should be done, and as I would do it if I undertook to do would occupy the whole of a mans time, and his thoughts incessantly, and this was a state in which I would not place myself unless circumstances were such as to require me to exert myself in some way, in which no man ought to refuse his services, that this was not such a case and I should not become an official assignee. I then wrote and gave him a note as follows.

Dear Jones

I had sometime since for the reasons I mentioned to you determined not to be an official assignee. I told this to Mill and concluded that he made the necessary communication to the Lord Chancellor, It now appears that he did not.

I have carefully and diligently gone through every matter in detail respecting the act of parliament and the duties of an official assignee with Mr Adlard the bookseller and sometime auctioneer, he is an exceedingly able and well qualified man for the office. He has had communication with Mr Vizard and has placed some very useful papers in his hands, I therefore earnestly recommend him for the office.

Yours truly
Francis Place

In a subsequent conversation with Coln Jones he said "he had put my note into Lord Broughams hands, when he said why did not Place write to me. Oh said I. (Jones) he thinks I suppose that I have some wholesome influence with you." I therefore wrote to Lord Brougham telling him that I entertained no such notion as Jones jocosely supposed I did, but that knowing how his time was occupied, I thought he might hear the reasons why I had declined his offer from Jones without the loss of time a long letter from me would consume. I then said I would not trouble him for a note in reply.

APPENDIX

Place's list of his children[1]

	Born	Married	Ages	Died
Francis Place	3 Nov. 1771	7 Mar. 1791	19 years 4 months	
Elizabeth Chadd	28 Mar. 1774		17 – nearly	19 Oct. 1827

Children

1. Ann – born 1792. Died aged 2 years of the small pox
2. Elizabeth – April 1794. Died in Chile – Mrs. Adams
3. Annie – 27 Jan 1796 – ....Mrs Miers
4. Francis – 22 June 1798
5. Jane – died an infant
6. Henry – d°............d°
7. Mary – 6 Jany. 1804
8. Frederick Wm. – 14 Oct. 1805
9. Jane – 29 Oct. 1807
10. Alfred – died an infant
11. John – 1 Jany. 1811
12. Thomas – 4 Augst. 1812. Died at Calcutta 16 Sep. 1847. Widow & 5 Children
13. Caroline – 29 July 1814. Died 1830
14. William } Twins 6 Feb. 1817 { died – 1829
    Henry   { died an infant

[1] This list formed f. 20 of Place's manuscript (Add. MS 35142), falling before the newspaper cutting on self-reliance noted on p. 5n1 above.

INDEX

Adams, W. Davenport, *A Dictionary of the Drama*, 258 n1, 268
Adams, William, currier, father of Place's son-in-law, 16
Adlard, John, bookseller, 297
Allison, Robert, tailor, employer of P, xix, xxxiv, 94, 111, 110, 123, 124, 127, 128
Allison, Mrs, xxxiv, 125, 128
amusements
　bullock-hunting, 68–70
　cock and hen clubs, 77, 78 n*
　cutter clubs, 38, 76, 81
　fishing, 279–80
　Guy Fawkes sport, 65–8
　'nailing people,' 64–5
　palming, 77
　two-penny hops, 95
　see also tea-gardens, fairs
Anti-Corn Law League, *see* Corn Laws
Annual Register, 34 n1, 186 n2
apprentices, 17, 19 & n1, 38, 71, 72 & n1, 73–8, 83–4, 95, 98, 119
　parish apprentices, 19 & n1, 73 & n2, 74
Aristotles Masterpiece, 45 & n2
army recruiting, *see* crimping
Arnott, Dr Neil, P's physician, 283, 284, 285
Ashley, John, shoemaker, secretary of London Corresponding Society, 139, 142 n1, 143, 151, 153, 154 & n1, 155–7, 158, 236, 237, 238
Ashley, Mrs, 155–6, 157
Ashurst, Mr Justice, sentences publisher of *Age of Reason*, 168
Atkins, Mrs, wife of Richard Wild, 202–3, 210 & n*

Bain, Alexander, *James Mill*, 251 n2
Baldwin, Henry, printer, fishing companion of P's father, 279
bankruptcy, 91, 210 n*, 248, 288–97
　see also debtors
Barnes, Mrs, tailor's widow, employer of P, 136, 142, 150
Barrow, Richard, surgeon, arrested at public meeting of LCS, 1796, 155
baths, at No 16 Charing Cross, 213, 214, 225
Baxter, John, one of the 'twelve apostles' arrested for treason, 1794, 129 n2

Bayley, Mr, leather-stainer and dresser, frequenter of Simon P's pub, 88
Bayley, Mr Justice, gives opinion that *Age of Reason* is seditious, 160
Beaufort Buildings, meeting-place of General Committee of LCS, 140 & n2
Beck, Anthony, treasurer of LCS, 139, 142 n2
beer, method of storing in P's father's pub, 38–9
Bell, Andrew, educator, 15 & n1
Bennet, Grey, occasional visitor to P, 70 n1, 249
Bentham, Jeremy, xii, xv, xxii, xxvii, 5, 6, 8–9, 246, 250 & n2, 251 & n2, 288 & n3
　P's devotion to, xii, 250 n2
Benthamism, xiv n2, xviii
Besant, Sir Walter, *London in the Eighteenth Century*, 24 n1,
Bible, 15 n1, 40, 41, 44–5, 47
　see also religion
Bickersteth, Henry, attorney, friend of P, 253, 290
Binns, Benjamin, plumber, arrested at public meeting of LCS, 1796, 155, 177, 178
Binns, John, plumber, member of LCS, xxxiv, 142 n1, 143, 149, 150 & n2, 151 n1, 153, 154 n1, 177 & n2, 250 n3
　Recollections of the Life of, 140 nn 1 & 2, 177 n2
Birkbeck, George, xv, 246
Birmingham, reform activities at, x, 149–50, 154 n1, 250 n3
Blackstone, William, 18 & n*, 35 n2, 109
Bloomfield, Sir Benjamin, approves P's gun lock, 233
Bone, John, secretary of LCS, 142 n1, 151 n3, 159 n2, 181 n1, 198
Bonney, John Augustus, one of the 'twelve apostles,' arrested for treason, 1794, 129 n2
books and reading, P's observations on, 15, 17, 30, 40, 41, 46, 47, 54, 109, 117, 119, 120, 121, 126–7, 131, 143–4, 159 n2, 175–6, 196 n1, 198, 222–3, 240, 264–5
　see also Paine
Bosville, Col. William, wealthy reformer, visits P as he works, 187 & n2

299

Index

Bouvier's *Law Dictionary*, 164 n1
Bow St officers, 176
boxing, 20 & n3, 50, 74 n1
breeches-making, 71, 74, 78, 80, 82, 94–5, 101, 110, 111, 112, 116, 125, 126, 202, 215, 225
Bristow, John, breeches-maker, gives P an occasional job, 111, 113, 114 & n*
British Museum, xvii, xxvii, xxxiii
Brougham, Henry, suggests P for position as official assignee under Bankruptcy Act, xxviii, 240, 288–93, 295, 296–7
Broughton, Jack, boxer, 20 & n3
Bull Dog, satirical magazine, attacks P, 245
Burdett, Sir Francis, xi, xii, xv, xviii, 182 n2, 221 & n1, 245 n1, 247
Burke, Edmund, 35–6, 130
Burn, Richard, *The Justice of the Peace and Parish Officer*, 35 n3
Bury, William, shopkeeper, frequenter of Simon P's pub, 88

Campbell, Thomas, praises P in letter in *The Times*, 240, 244
Cestre, Charles, *John Thelwall*, 140 n2
Chadd, family of P's first wife, 96, 102–3, 104, 105
Charing Cross, No 16, *see* streets
Charrington, Jack, only fellow-apprentice of P who 'made good,' 106 n1
Chatham, Lord, fails to keep appointment with P, 235
Chatterley, Louisa Simeon, second wife of P, xxviii, 258–9, 264, 267, 268–71, 273, 274, 278, 283, 284, 285, 286
her mother, Mrs Simeon, 259, 277
her son, 259, 268, 271, 274
childbirth, P's arrangement for, 126, 184
Christmas, William, banker's clerk, involved with Mrs Chatterley, 269–70
class-consciousness, *see* social distinctions
Clowes, Mr, printer, occupies house which was once a brothel, 228
Collins, Henry, 'The London Corresponding Society,' 130 n1
Colquhoun, Patrick, *A Treatise on the Police of the Metropolis*, 36 n1
combinations, 114, 116, 119, 125
Combination Laws, xii–xiii, xiv, xxvii, 112 n1, 248
see also strike of leather breeches-makers, 1793
Congreve, Sir William, approves P's gun lock, 233 & n1

Copenhagen Fields, site of open meeting of LCS, 149
Corn Laws, xiv, 280–3
Cornwallis, Earl, employed Simon P on his estate, 20
The Correspondence of the London Corresponding Society, 140 n1
crimping, 35 & n1, 36
crimping houses, 34–5, 214, 228 & n*
Croft, Robert, tailor, employer of Richard Wild, 175, 205, 208
Crossfield, Thomas, heads LCS in its last days, 151 n3
Cumberland, Duke of, 245 n1
Cuthbertson, John, mathematical-instrument maker, in his shop P learns to turn and file, 53–4

debtors, 24 n1, 30–2, 85 n1, 86 & n1, 210 n*, 221, 226, 239
see also lock-up houses
Despard, Col. Edward, educated reformer, visits P as he works, 142 n1, 178, 181 n1, 186 n2, 187 n1, 188 n1
dress, 16, 28 n1, 51, 62–3, 78, 80, 110, 125, 192, 193, 201, 217, 279
and respectability, xxi–xxii
Drewry, Capt., admires P's gun lock, 232, 233
drinking, drunkenness, xxiv, 28, 29 n1, 38, 54, 72, 76 n3, 77, 93, 95, 106, 117, 131 n2, 135
Duke, Mr, tailor, frequenter of Simon P's pub, 87, 88
Dundas, Henry, 144, 176

East India Company, 292 n*
Ecclesiastical Court, P's father loses case in, 20, 85 & n2
education, *see* schools
Egg, D., gun-maker whose dispute with partner P arbitrates, 230–1
Ellis, James, journeyman breeches-maker, proscribed, with P, by masters after strike of 1793, 115
Erskine, Thomas, xxiii, xxxiii, 132 n2, 139, 160–8, 169–72, 194 n2
European Magazine, xv, xxxv n2, 246
Evans, Joshua, commissioner of bankrupts, 289–90
Evans, Thomas, bracemaker, forms revolutionary society with O'Quigley [O'Coigley] and Binns, 142 n1, 151 n3, 177, 178 & n1, 181
excursion places visited by P, 28–9

300

Index

fairs, ix, xxvii, 94
Greenwich, xxvi
Fenn, Mr, bookseller, 89
Fenton, Richard, gun-maker, friend of P in LCS, 175, 188, 189
Fenwick, John, member of LCS, 142 n1
Fergusson, Robert Cutler, arrested at public meeting of LCS, 1796, 154
Fielding, Sir John, 35
Flaxman, Mr, from whose employees P learned to model clay, 54
Fletcher, Jack, head of press-gang lodged in Simon P's pub, 37
food, kinds of eaten by P, 39–40, 102, 108–9, 124, 229
Ford, Sir Richard, undersecretary of state, 134, 182–3, 186 n1
France, Joe, master leather breeches-maker to whom P apprenticed, xvi, xix–xx, xxi, xxxiii, 71–2, 73–4, 78–9, 80, 82
'Francis Place of Westminster, Esq.,' *European Magazine*, xxxv
Franklin, Benjamin, 5
Frasers Magazine, xv, 246
French Revolution, 15
Frend, William, educated reformer who visits P as he works, 182 & n2, 183, 187 & n1
Friends of the Liberty of the Press, Society of, 160–1
Friends of the People, 129, 139, 140, 152

Galloway, Alexander, machinist, arrested at public meeting of LCS, 1796, and at meeting of LCS General Committee, 1798, 142 n* & n1, 155 & n1, 156 n1, 181 & n1, 182 n2, 186 n2, 237
Galton, F. W. (ed.), *Select Documents Illustrating the History of Trade Unionism: 1 The Tailoring Trade*, 112 n1
gambling, 20, 22, 23, 24, 49–50, 88
gaming, *see* lottery, state
Genest, John, *Some Account of the English Stage . . .*, 258 n1
George III, alleged attacks upon, 1795, 145–7
George, M. Dorothy, *London Life in the Eighteenth Century*, 19 n1, 36 n2, 72 n1, 73 n2
Gibbon, Edward, 8 n*
Gloucester, Duke of, 233
Godwin, William, xvii
Inquiry Concerning Political Justice, influences P's notions about shop-keeping, 136–7, 143, 217–18

Gordon Riots, 34 & n1, 228–9
Grenville, Lord, 141, 144, 145
Grey, Earl, 139
Grose, Francis, *A Classical Dictionary of the Vulgar Tongue*, 48 n1
Grote, George, xii & n1, xxx, 289–90, 291, 292–5, 296
Grote, Harriet, xx, xxii n1, xxviii–xxix, xxx, 163 n1, 210, 215 n2, 220, 247 n1, 250 n2
Guildhall, The (London), 98 n1
gun-lock improvement, P's, xxviii, xxxiv, 230–6
Gustard, William, woollen draper, principal creditor of P and Wild, 207, 208

habeas corpus, suspension of, 1794, 139 & n1, 140, 145, 168
Hadden, Col., surveyor-general to ordnance, approves P's gun lock, 233, 234, 235
Hammond, J. L. and Barbara, *The Town Labourer*, xiii, 112 n1
Hanway, Jonas, *The Defects of the Police*, 24 n1
Hardisty, George, mercer, refuses credit to P & Wild, 192
Hardy, Thomas, founder and secretary of LCS, xvii, xxii n1, xxiii n6, xxxiv, 129–30, 132 & n2, 139 & n1, 142 nn* & 1, 152, 182 & nn 1 & 2, 194 n2, 198, 199, 236
Memoir of Thomas Hardy, xxxv, 130 n1, 182 n1
Harrison, Samuel, xxx, 18 n1, 28 n2, 36 n1, 57 n1
Harrison, Thomas, watch-face painter, LCS member with whom P studied French, 142 n1, 175, 186
Hasseldon, LCS member seized in raid of 1798, 181 & n1
Hayward, clerk to Stewart Kyd, 167
Hayward, Richard, attorney, LCS member with whom P studied French, xxxiii n3, 58, 175, 193, 272
Hill, Henry, P's neighbour at Brompton Square, 284
Hitchins, LCS member, taught French badly, 175
Hobhouse, John Cam, xii, xv, 163 n1, 247 & n1, 249, 268
Hodgson, Richard, hatter, arrested at public meeting of LCS, 1796, and at meeting of LCS General Committee, 1798, 129 n2, 142 n1, 154, 155 n1, 181 & n1, 184, 186 n2, 236, 237, 238

301

Index

Holcroft, Thomas, 5, 129 & n2, 152 & n2, 187 n1, 275 & n2
Holyoake, George Jacob, *Sixty Years of an Agitator's Life*, 250 n2, 251 n2
Hone, William, *Everyday Book*, 65, 68 & n1, 76 n3
Howell's *State Trials*, 150 n2, 160, 162 n†, 163 n*, 167 n1, 169, 194 n2
Hume, Joseph, xii, xiii, xv, 247 & n1, 248, 249, 268
Hummerston, pastry cook at whose shop P met his wife, 96, 100
Hunt, Henry, *Memoirs*, 245 n1
Hutchins, wharfinger, agrees to hire P as overseer of scavengers, 119
Hyde, trading justice, 36

illness, 20, 22, 23, 52, 55, 96, 121, 228 n*, 279
   P's, xiv, 28, 275–8, 280, 283–7
   P's first wife's, 251–4
   P's second wife's, 274
   see also childbirth; Place, Simon, illnesses
Inderwick, F. A., *The King's Peace*, 85 n2

Jackson, Mrs, aunt of P's first wife, 103, 105
Jackson, Sir John, M.P., 292 n*
Jaeger, Muriel, *Before Victoria*, 160 n1
Jews, P's attitude toward, xxiv
Jones, John Gale, surgeon, sent by LCS on speaking tours, 149–50, 151 n1, 153, 154 n1, 182 n2, 197, 221 n1
   Sketch of a Political Tour through Rochester, Maidstone, Gravesend, &c, 149 n2
Jones, Col. Leslie Grove, urges P to become official assignee, 296–7
journeymen, xiii, 22, 73 & nn1 & 2, 74–5, 76 & n4, 81, 94–5, 100–2, 105–6, 107, 108, 110, 111–15, 116, 118, 119, 123, 125–6, 128, 129, 136–7, 138, 142, 149 n1, 150, 174, 199, 211, 215, 220–1, 240, 263
   see also apprentices, masters
Joyce, Jeremiah, one of 'twelve apostles' arrested for treason, 1794, 129 n2
justices of peace, 35–6, 37
   see also trading justices

Kenyon, Lord, judge at *Age of Reason* trial, 166, 168–9, 171
King, kept public house at Shepperton, 279–80

King, John [Jew King], dishonest high-living radical, 174, 236–9
   his son George, 238, 239
King, Martin Luther, xiv n1
Kingsbury, William, foreman of P's shop, 16 n*, 220
Knight, Mrs, cared for Mrs P at her death, 254
Kyd, Stewart, one of 'twelve apostles' arrested for treason, 1794, 129 n2
   defence attorney in *Age of Reason* trial, xxiii, 162 & n1, 165, 166, 167, 171

Lambert, Mrs, mistress of John Ashley, 155, 156, 157
Lambeth Church, P married in, 103, 104
Lancaster, Joseph, educator, 15 & n1
Lancastrian Associations, xii, 245 & n1
Lawrence, William, surgeon, operated on P's first wife, xxiii, 251
Lee, bookseller, seceded from LCS, 159 n2
Lemaitre, Paul Thomas, seized in raid on General Committee of LCS, 142 n1, 155 n1, 181 & n1, 182 n2, 186 n2
Light, attorney, offers to loan P money, 204, 205, 206, 207
lightermen, 53, 83–4, 106
Lingham, Thomas, tailor, hires P, 94, 101, 104, 105, 106, 108, 110, 111, 119
lock-up houses, 24–5, 26–7, 31–2, 34
   Elephant and Castle, 86
London Corresponding Society, x, xi, xiv, xvii, xxviii, xxxiii n6, xxxiv, 129–32, 138–42, 144–5, 147, 148–55, 159 & n2, 163 n1, 164 n1, 175, 176–7, 180–2, 194–200, 236
   aim of, 129, 194
   books read by members, 159 n2, 196 n1
   General Committee, 140–1
   General Committee arrested, 1798, 176, 180–1
   good effects of, 196, 198–9, 200
   organization of, 131 & n1, 148 n1, 152
   origin, 130
   radicalism of, 196–7
   religion, attitude toward, 159 n2, 197 n2, 198
   size of, 140 & n1, 144 n1
   weekly meetings, 131
lottery, state, 88, 97–8, 203
Lymans, engraver, P's landlord, 117–18

McDonald, breeches-maker, foreman to Mrs Barnes, prejudices her against P, 136, 150

Index

magistrates, 150, 154, 155
  see also justices, trading justices, Richard Ford
Mallet, French bankers, 227
Malthus, Thomas, xvii
Manchester, P's reform activities in, xiv, 280, 282–3
Manners, Sir William, xxxiv, 129 n1
manners and morals, xviii, xxv, xxvii, xxx, 14 & n*, 15–16, 20, 28 & n2, 36 & n*, 51, 57, 61, 62, 70 n1, 74–7, 81–2, 88–9, 91, 229–30
Margarot, Maurice, LCS member, 142 n*
Marshalsea Court, 24 & n*, 30–2
  see also prisons
Martyr, lottery office keeper, advanced Wild money to buy business from P, 203, 210
masters, xiii, 19, 22, 78–9, 81, 112, 113, 114, 115, 116, 117, 125–6, 157, 225
  see also apprentices, journeymen
Mendoza, Daniel, boxer, 20 n3
Miers, family of P's son-in-law, xxvii, xxxiii, 253, 255, 262, 265
  see also Place's children, Annie
Mill, James, ix, xii, xv, xxii, xxvii, xxix, 5, 6–7, 246, 247 n1, 250 n1, 251 & n2, 252, 253, 264, 278, 288–93, 295, 296, 297
Mill, John Stuart, xii, 251 n2
Moira, Lord, master-general of ordnance, approves P's gun lock, 233, 234, 235 & n1
Moore, Matthew, one of 'twelve apostles' arrested for treason, 1794, 129 n2
Moritz, Charles P., 16 & n†
Morning Chronicle, 154 n3, 155, 167 n1, 171, 172, 181 n1
Morris, manager of Haymarket theatre, 273

navy recruitment, *see* pressing
Noble, gun-maker, instructed to make P's gun lock, 233–4
Norfolk, Duke of, xxxii, 85–6
Northumberland, Duke of, xviii, 213

Old Bailey, 97, 132 & n2, 134 n*, 152, 292
  see also prisons
O'Quigley [O'Coigley], James, Irish priest executed for treason, 177 & n2, 178
Oxberry, William, *Dramatic Biography*, 258 n1, 269, 270 n2

Pain, James, chair-carver, marries P's elder sister, 92, 93, 94, 104, 107, 115

Paine, Thomas, 126, 159, 197 n1
  Age of Reason, 126, 159, 160 n1
  prosecution for publishing *Age of Reason*, 159–72
Parke, Thomas, Sr & Jr, hold freehold and house at No 16 Charing Cross, 214, 222, 223, 225
Parkes, Joseph, xii, xxvii
Parliamentary Report . . . on Drunkenness, 1834, 81 n2
Parliamentary Report . . . on Education, 1835, 43 n1, 58, 74 n1, 81 n2, 112 n1, 222 n1
Paull, James, 235
Percy, Lord, M.P. for Westminster, xviii
Perry, James, of the *Morning Chronicle*, 171, 172
Piercy, brother-in-law to P's employer Pike, 94, 95, 96, 97
Pike, John, breeches-maker, gives P a steady job, 94, 95, 96, 97
  his sister, P's mistress, 95, 96
Pitt, William, 141, 144, 145, 154
Place [Ann?], P's mother, *née* Gray, 18, 21, 22, 23, 24, 28, 29, 40, 59, 61, 74, 78, 84, 92–3, 97–100, 105–6, 108–9, 110, 115, 121, 122, 124, 129, 132, 133–5, 150, 157, 275
  appearance, 21
  family background, 18–19, 21
  becomes washerwoman, 98–9
Place, P's elder sister, 34, 40, 74, 92–3, 115, 122
Place, Ann, P's younger sister, 40, 92, 93, 110, 121–2, 132, 134
  marries Stimson, 121
  husband arrested for robbery, 132–3
  marries Roidhouse, 135
  dies, 135
Place, Ann, P's daughter, *see* P's children
Place, Annie, P's daughter, *see* P's children
Place, Caroline, P's daughter, *see* P's children
Place, Elizabeth Chadd, P's first wife, xxviii, 12, 96, 99–100, 101, 102–5, 106, 108, 109, 110, 111, 115, 117, 118, 119, 120, 122, 123, 124, 125, 126, 134, 135, 138, 142, 150 n3, 157–8, 174, 184, 187 n1, 193, 202, 203, 204–5, 218, 224, 227, 269, 298
  ancestry, 105
  appearance, 96, 99, 104, 117
  birth of first child, 111
  birth of first son, 184

Index

Place, Elizabeth Chadd (*cont.*)
  illness and death, 251–4, 256, 257, 263, 277
  temper, 255–6, 261–2, 263
  upset by Wild's treachery, 205
Place, Elizabeth, P's daughter, *see* P's children
Place, Francis
  appearance, 94, 123–4
  apprenticeship, ix, xix–xx, xxxii–xxxiii, 71, 72, 73–81, 82
  attacks upon, 245–6
  birth, 23
  Brompton Square, moves to, 273
  business methods, 12, 86–7, 106–7, 137–8, 153, 173–4, 191–3, 201–2, 215–16, 218–21, 266
  childhood, 28–30
  command of others, x, xi, xvi, xix, xx, 6, 141, 244–5
  education, learning, 29–30, 40–7, 56, 240–4; learns French, 175–6; taught by W. Frend, 187
  egotism, 6, 7, 13–14, 246
  father, attitude toward, xx–xxi, 11, 20, 62, 99
  health, xxviii, xxix, xxxiii, 28, 142 n*, 275–8, 280, 283–7
  journeyman, xxii, 93, 94, 95, 96, 99, 101, 102, 105, 106, 107, 110–15, 118, 119, 128, 129, 136–7, 142–3, 150, 225, 263
  London Corresponding Society: joins, 129; president of General Committee, 141–2; resigns, 154
  master, 157, 277
  money-making, 12, 47–50, 66–7, 93–4, 95, 101, 105–6, 110–11, 119, 126, 150–1, 173–4, 190, 192, 193, 209, 217–21, 226, 270–4
  opens shop at No 16 Charing Cross, 212, 215–16
  opens shop with R. Wild, 189–93, 201
  partnership with Wild dissolved, 204–9
  publicity, attitude toward, xv–xvi, xvii, xxvi, xxxi, 221–2
  radicalism of, xiv n1, xx–xxi, xxvi, 144, 196–7
  reading, 109, 119, 120, 143, 175–6, 217–18, 242; *see also* books
  reform activities, x–xiv, xv–xvii, xx–xxi, xxiv, xxv, 139, 141–2, 247 & n1, 249, 274 & n3
  religion, attitude toward, xxiii, xxxi–xxxii, xxxv, 11, 13, 45–6, 121, 126, 197 n2
  respectability, importance of, xxi–xxii, xxvi
  retirement, x, 120–1
  romanticism of, xxii–xxiii
  strike of leather breeches-makers (1793), directs, ix, x, xiii, 112–15
  subscription for state prisoners (1798), starts, 181–6
  tailoring, attitude toward, 216–17
  temper, xv, 61, 102, 115, 117, 256, 261
  wealth, loss of, xxviii, xxix, 270–4
  wife: first, Elizabeth Chadd: meets, 96; marries, 104; reaction to death of, 254, 256–8, 262–5, 277
  wife: second, Louisa Simeon Chatterley: decides to marry, 258–60, 264, 267; marries, 267, 268, 270, 277; separates from, 268
  working class, attitude toward, xii, xv, xviii, 127–8
  writings, xvii–xix, xxvi, xxvii–xxxvii, 267–8; autobiography, xxvii–xxxvii; censored, xxxi–xxxiii; *Delhi Gazette*, 284–5, 286; *Illustrations and Proofs of the Principle of Population*, xvii, 245; *Improvement of the Working People: Drunkenness – Education*, xxii n2, xxiv n2, 123 n*; style, xxxiii–xxxvi
Place, Francis, Junior, P's son, *see* P's children
Place, Fred, P's son, *see* P's children
Place, George, P's brother, 25, 34, 40, 42, 43, 59, 60, 61, 83–5, 98, 99, 110, 115, 119, 121, 122, 193, 275
  apprenticed, 84
Place, Hannah, P's sister, 21
Place, Jane, P's daughter, *see* P's children
Place, John, P's son, *see* P's children
Place, Mary, P's daughter, *see* P's children
Place, Simon, P's father, xxviii, xxxii, xxxiii, 17–18, 19–20, 21, 22–9, 32, 34, 35, 37–40, 43, 50, 53, 59, 60–2, 78, 80, 82 n1, 83, 85–7, 92, 96, 97–8, 99, 100, 110, 121, 275, 279–80
  ancestry, 17
  appearance, 20
  beats sons, 50, 59–61
  operates lock-up house, 24
  becomes publican, 32, 34
  Ecclesiastical Court, action taken against him in, 85
  ruined again, 86
  takes Rules of Fleet, 86

304

Index

loses all in state lottery, 97–8
illnesses, 20, 22, 23, 97, 121
death, 121
Place, Tom, P's son, *see* P's children
Place, William, P's son, *see* P's children
Place's children, 12, 157, 158, 174–5, 202, 226–7, 240, 251, 253, 254, 256, 257, 258, 259, 260, 261–2, 263, 265, 266, 268, 269, 271, 272, 274
  Ann, 111, 115
  Annie, 150, 251, 253, 255, 258, 260, 262, 264, 265, 268
  Caroline, 257 & n1, 264, 268
  Elizabeth, 126
  Francis, Jr, xxxi–xxxiii, 76 n1, 184 n1, 227 & n1, 261, 256 n2, 257 & n1, 261, 265, 267, 268–9, 273
  Fred, 253, 261
  Jane, 255, 257 & n1, 261, 264, 265, 268
  John, 253, 257 & n1, 264, 271
  Mary, xxix, 254, 255, 257 & n1, 261, 265, 268
  Tom, 257 & n1, 260, 264, 271
  William, 257 & n1, 263, 268
police, 14, 65 n*, 74 n1
Pollard, Edward W., surgeon, P's neighbour at Brompton Square, 284
Portland, Duke of, 186 n2
Powell, attorney to James Paull, 235
Powell, James, LCS member, coadjutor in revolutionary society, 142 n1, 178, 179–80, 182
pressing, 34–5, 36, 37
Price, long-time employee of P, 211
Pringle, Patrick, *Hue and Cry*, 36 n1
prisons
  Cold Bath Fields, 168, 172, 181, 186 n2
  Fleet, 34, 86, 156
  King's Bench, 34, 80
  Marshalsea Court, 24 n1, 31–3
  Newgate, 34, 132 n1, 134, 135, 181, 185
  Old Bailey, 134 n*
  Savoy, 35
Proclamation Society, 160, 161–2, 165, 166, 167 & n1
prostitution, xxv, 71, 75 & n*, 77–8, 88, 203, 213, 228 & n†, 229
public houses, *see* taverns
Pure Soft Spring Water Company, 1834–5, P and, 274

Quarterly Review, 9–10

Rag-Fair breeches, 74, 78, 80, 113–14
reason and rationality, xvi, xx, xxiv, xxvi, xxxvi, 257, 258, 276, 282

The Reasoner, xxiii–xxiv
reform of Parliament, xii, 282, 283 n*
  see also London Corresponding Society
Reid, William Hamilton, *The Rise and Dissolution of the Infidel Societies*, 159 n2
religion, 8 n*, 56, 93, 106, 159 n2, 160, 162, 197–8
  see also Place, Francis, religion, attitude toward
Report of Committee of Secrecy, 1799, 178 & n2, 179 n1, 198
respect, respectability, xviii, xix, xx, xxi–xxii, 21, 26, 72–3, 75, 87, 88–9, 92, 99, 102, 106, 121, 128, 157, 193, 205, 220, 223, 230, 232, 240, 266
revolution planned by United Englishmen, 178
Ricardo, David, 242
Richards, Richard, trimming-seller, offered to loan P money, 209, 211
Richmond, Duke of, 194 & n2
Richter, John, one of the 'twelve apostles' arrested for treason, 1794, 129 n2, 178 n2
Ridge, George, banker, told to set payment for P's gun lock, 235
Ridley, John, bootmaker, loaned P a house, 147, 210
Robinson, glazier, frequenter of Simon P's pub, 87
Roebuck, John Arthur, 296
Roidhouse, compositor-printer, marries P's sister, 121, 135
Romilly, Sir Samuel, 250–1
rotation office, 36 & n2
Rousseau, 9, 176

sailors, 17, 220, 239
  see also pressing
St Clement's Church, P's description of neighbourhood of, 88, 98 n1, 103
St George's Fields, 23, 80 & n*, 81 n2, 104
St Martin's Workhouse, 210 n*
Savage, leather-seller, offered to loan P money, 209, 211
Scholefield, son of a Birmingham M.P., 282
schools & education, 15 & n1, 17, 40–7, 54, 56–7, 72, 81, 90, 100, 226–7, 255
  see also books; Place, Francis, education
schoolmasters, described by P
  Atkinson, 227
  Bird, 42
  Bowis, xxxii, 43–7, 61, 109, 117
  Jones, 40

Index

Scotland Yard, 213, 229
Seawell, customer offers to loan P money, 207
Seldon, silk-mercer, frequenter of Simon P's pub, 88
Select Committee on Education, xxv, xxx
Sellis, Joseph, inquest on, 245 n1
sex
  books about, 45
  lack of chastity in girls, xxxii, 57, 73, 81-2
  P's attitude toward, xxv, 61
  see also songs
Seymour, steward of Duke of Norfolk, 86
Shepperton, P taken on angling trips to, xxviii, 28, 279-80
Simpkin, Thomas, keeper of Crown & Anchor pub, 92
Skillem, tailor, frequenter of Simon P's pub, 87
Skinner, tobacconist at Ship & Anchor Court, 26
Slack, Jack, boxer, 20 & n3
Smith, Adam, 119, 242
Smyth's *The Sailor's Word Book*, 34 n2
Snow, accountant, coadjutor with P in a quarrel between Tatham & Egg, 230 & n*
social distinctions & equality, 10-11, 127-8, 216-17, 221-3, 244, 246-8, 249-51
Society for Constitutional Information, 130, 152, 194-5
soldiers, 213, 229
  see also crimping
songs, prevalence of obscene, xxv-xxvi, xxxii, xxxiii & n3, 36, 57-9, 63 n1, 66, 77, 78 & n*, 229
Spa Fields, called Pipe Fields, 59
special jurors, 162-3, 165
Spectator, xxiii
spunging-house, *see* lock-up house
Stephenson (Stevenson), Joseph, sells P underlease on No 16 Charing Cross, 214, 223, 224, 225
Stiles (Styles), pastry-cook, first employer of Elizabeth Chadd Place, 96, 100
Stimson, Mat, butcher, marries P's younger sister, 121, 132-5
streets, lanes, addresses
  Angel Court, 214
  Arundel Street, 17, 32, 34, 39, 40, 92, 99
  Back of St Clement's Church, 104, 107-8

Bell Yard, 27, 29-30, 72-3
Brompton Square, 267, 268, 270, 271, 273
Brydges Street, 23, 210, 211
Butcher Row, 107
Charing Cross, xxviii, 227-30; No 16, P's shop and home, ix, x, xxxii, 212-13, 214-15, 223-4, 248 n1, 267, 272, 273; No 29, P's first shop, 192, 193
Charlotte Street, 80
Covent Garden, 47, 114
Craven Street, 210 n*
Curtis's halfpenny hatch, 80
Drury Lane, 17, 48
Earls Court, ix, 268
Edgware Road, 105
Fisher Street, 129, 143
Fleet Lane, 30, 86, 134
Foxley Terrace, 268
Gough Street, 42
Great Surrey Street, 80
Holborn, High Holborn, 151, 173, 174, 186, 187
Johnson's Court, 214 n2, 228 & n†
King's Cross Road, 28 n2
Kings Head Court, 42
Lambeth Marsh, 80 & n*
Litchfield Street, 36
Little Shire Lane, 111
Lower Marsh, 80
Maiden Lane, 47
Monmouth Street, 63 & n*
New Street, 131
New Castle Street, 48
Palace Yard, 226
Petticoat Lane, 19
Piccadilly Street, 111
Pickett Street, 25, 108
Russell Court, 23, 210
St Martin's Lane, 203
Ship and Anchor Court, 19, 25-6, 39, 279
Sloane Street, 203
Stanhope Street, 48
Star Court, 108
Strand, 25, 34, 42, 48
Trinity Place, 213 n*
Vinegar Yard, 23
Water Street, 47
Westminster Bridge Road, 80
Wilderness Lane, 99, 105
Windmill Street, 23
Windsor Court, 42
Wine Office Court, 30, 34, 40, 42
Wych Street, 107, 111, 124, 176, 225
York Street, 210

Index

strike of leather breeches-makers, 1793, 112–15, 116, 125
Stuckey, Thomas, arrested at public meeting of LCS, 1796, 154
Sturge, Joseph, Birmingham reformer, 281–3
Sunday schools, 15
Sutton, frequenter of Simon P's pub, 46

Tapster, Stephen, waiter who leases part of No 16 Charing Cross, 214 & n1, 224–5
Tatham, Henry, gun-maker, P arbitrates his dispute with Egg, 230
taverns, public houses
   Angel Inn, 124
   Cock (Clapham Common), 29
   Cock (Fleet Street), 27
   Crown and Anchor, xviii, 85, 92, 118
   King's Arms, 34, 37–40
   Kings Head (Shepperton), 279
   Queen of Bohemia, 176
   Rummer, 228 & n‡
   Ship (Charing Cross), 224
   Ship and Anchor, 25
   Three Herrings, 27
   Watermans Arms, 37, 86
Taylor, carpenter, in whose shop P learns to saw, 54
Taylor, Richard, foreman of Allison's tailoring shop, 129 n1
tea-gardens, xxvi, 28–9, 70 n1, 81 n2, 158
   Bagniggi Wells, 28 & n2
   Copenhagen House, 158
   White Conduit House, 158
theatres, 273
   Covent Garden, 258 n1, 264 n1, 270, 271
   Drury Lane, ix, 23, 271
   Haymarket, 271, 273
   Minors, 273
   Olympic, 176
Thelwall, John, LCS member, arrested for treason in 1794, 129 n2, 132, 140 & n2, 152
thieves, pickpockets, 72, 76–7, 79, 121–2, 132–5
Thomas, publican, ousts Simon P from his public house, 86, 87
Thomas, Thomas, butcher, P's next door neighbor at Charing Cross, 224, 228 n‡
Thomas, W. E. S., 'Francis Place and Working Class History,' xxxiii
Thompson, E. P., *The Making of the English Working Class*, xiii & n1, 130 n1
Thompson, Col. Perronet, consulted by P about Bankruptcy Bill, 290
Thorpe, rents baths at No 16 Charing Cross, 213
Tijou, friend of P, 58
The Times, xv, xxx, 240, 270
Tooke, John Horne, 129, 132, 152
Tories, xi, xviii, 248
trading justices, 85–6
transport, means of, 22, 27–8, 84, 279, 282, 283
Treason and Sedition Bills, 141–2, 144–5, 148–9, 154
'Twelve Apostles,' arrested for treason, 1794, 129 n2, 152, 162 n1, 178 n2

unions, *see* combinations
United Englishmen, 177–80
United Irishmen, 177 & n1

Vice Suppression Society, *see* Proclamation Society
Viggears, foreman of P's shop, 202, 210–11, 215, 220
Villiers, Charles Pelham, reformer, M.P., 282 & n1
Vizard, William, attorney, Brougham's secretary of bankrupts, 289, 291–2, 293, 294–5, 296, 297

Wallas, Graham, xxvii, xxxi & n4
   Life of Francis Place, xxxi, xxxiii, 268, 274 n3
Warburton, Henry, consulted by P about Bankruptcy Bill, 290
Ward, Ben, cook, engaged to P's sister, 92
Wardle, Col. Gwyllym Lloyd, 245 n1
Wardle, Thomas, arrested for treason, 1794, 129 n2
Webb, Sidney and Beatrice, *The History of Trade Unionism*, 112 n1
Webbe (Webb, Wibbie), John, musician, LCS member, loans P books, 154 n3, 176, 181 n1
Weld, breeches-maker, gives P an occasional job, 111
Westminster, Committee of, 195
Westminster Election, 1807, xi, xv, xviii, 221 & n1, 235
Whigs, xi, xviii, xxxv, 235, 248, 249
White, Joseph, solicitor to the Treasury, 150 & n1
Wild, Gregory, brother of P's partner, 188, 193, 207, 210 n*, 224
Wild, Richard, tailor, P's partner, x, 142 n1, 175, 176, 188–93

307

Index

Williams, law student, LCS member, loans P books, 176
Williams, Thomas, bookbinder, convicted for selling *Age of Reason*, 159–60, 166–7, 168, 169–72
Willis, publican, customer of P, 118
Wilson, John [Christopher North], 222 n*
Wood, carpenter, frequenter of Simon P's pub, 87

Woodward, John, lighterman, takes on P's brother as apprentice, 84
Woolams, hair dresser, frequenter of Simon P's pub, 87
working class, *see* apprentices, journeymen
Wroth, Warwick, *The London Pleasure Gardens of the Eighteenth Century*, 28 n2
Wyvill, Christopher, 194 & n3

Printed in Great Britain
by Amazon.co.uk, Ltd.,
Marston Gate.